'I did not think I could learn anything new about Stalin but I was wrong. A stunning performance' Dr Henry Kissinger

'Sebag Montefiore paints a detailed and fascinating picture of the complex interactions and intrigues that characterized Kremlin life under Stalin ... [he] has done a valuable service in drawing our attention to a hitherto little-studied aspect of Stalinism. As his *Stalin* demonstrates, the personal relationships of those who ran the Kremlin provided an essential dynamic for the development of the Stalinist system' Amy Knight, *TLS*

'This fascinating account of the dictator's reign ... Montefiore provides a riveting portrait of the man and his ruling circle ... this book gives us an unprecedented glimpse into his intimate life, the inner workings of his government and the relations between the members of his junta, many of whom have remained shadowy figures until now ... The result is a much finer and nuanced understanding of the Bolshevik phenomenon than we have had before. Using his sources with great skill, Montefiore has succeeded in placing Stalin and the Bolsheviks in the context of their time' Marc Lambert, *Scotsman*

'This magisterial new biography of Stalin ... Sebag Montefiore makes some interesting new assertions about Stalin's psychology ... well-written; he evidently has a superb grasp of Russian, and can operate well in that still-difficult country'
Lesley Chamberlain, *Independent*

'Montefiore drives his story forward with breathless enthusiasm ... in a work of great importance. Scholars will read it for the valuable new evidence it assembles. Others will enjoy it as a fascinating page-turner and an everyday saga of extraordinary Kremlin folk' Rodric Braithwaite, *Financial Times*

'Gripping and timely ... [Montefiore] ... had the bright idea of examining the letters, telegrams and diaries of [Stalin's] intimate associates. As a result, this is a book based on extraordinary primary research ... one of the few recent books on Stalinism that will be read in years to come. The devil is in the detail'
Robert Service, *Guardian*

'His spectacular new work ... This is an impressive and compelling work' Philip Mansel, *Spectator*

'An extraordinary book ... he has managed to persuade a whole generation of little old ladies and elderly men – the wives, granddaughters, servants, nieces and nephews of Stalin's henchmen – to give him a series of extraordinary interviews and, in some cases, lend him their hand-written memoirs ... For anyone fascinated by the nature of evil – and by the effects of absolute power on human relationships – this book will provide new insights on every page'
Anne Applebaum, *Evening Standard*

'Montefiore has travelled extensively throughout the former USSR, interviewing survivors of this extraordinary era and several descendants of those closest to the Boss and gaining access to unpublished documents and photographs ... The result is a dizzying kaleidoscope of new and well-known materials, all of which combine to give fresh insights into the bizarre world of Stalin's rule' Patrick O'Meara, *Irish Independent*

'Utilising an immense amount of original research ... offering a composite picture of the Stalin years in breathtaking detail ... Montefiore ... reveals a man who was, in so many ways, frighteningly human ... Montefiore has succeeded brilliantly in showing that Stalin and his courtiers were human beings who laughed, loved and cried while they murdered, tortured and raped' Gerard DeGroot, *Scotland on Sunday*

'A more intimate, less conventional history of ... Stalin ... a truly fascinating body of research. The result is a vivid picture of life in this murderous court' Charlotte Hobson, *Daily Telegraph*

'A graphic and highly readable account ... Montefiore has marshalled existing material, uncovered long-buried testimonies, even managed to interview three generations of Kremlin survivors ... Sex and the Kremlin are not usually mentioned in the same sentence and Montefiore's revelations are quite arresting'
Harold Shukman, *Times Higher Educational Supplement*

'Montefiore's master work charts in compelling detail the story of Georgia's two most infamous sons, the all-powerful dictator and Beria'   Andrew Cook, *The Times*

'No summary can do justice to the wealth of this book, which leaves little to be desired . . . Nevertheless, this work should be read by anyone interested in Stalin's life and times, or in the workings of a highly developed tyranny'   Clive Foss, *History Today*

'Marvellous'   Allan Massie, *Sunday Times*

BOOK OF THE YEAR 2003

'I loved the totalitarian high baroque sleaze of Montefiore's *Stalin: The Court of the Red Tsar*'
Simon Schama, *Guardian* Books of the Year

'Montefiore's *Stalin*, I should imagine, will be the standard work on this twentieth-century monster for years to come'
Jeremy Paxman, *Sunday Telegraph*

'Enormously readable and even grimly amusing . . . the details of the cruelty and depravity . . . are incredible'
Miriam Gross, *Sunday Telegraph*

'Packed with details about a man who was brilliant, often charming, sometimes kind, but also terrorised his own people . . . The story of a monster'   Charles Guthrie, *Sunday Telegraph*

'Montefiore's *Stalin* showed us the century's worst dictator wasn't merely a paranoid narcissist but also anxious, uncertain, even charming . . . Now we can see him as a human being too'
John Simpson, *Daily Telegraph*

'One of the two outstanding books of the year, *Stalin* by Simon Sebag Montefiore . . . was the most civilised and elegant chronicle of brutality and ruthlessness I have ever read, its prose cool and clear but never indifferent'   Ruth Rendell, *Daily Telegraph*

'Outstanding . . . Unforgettable'   Antony Beevor, *Daily Telegraph*

Simon Sebag Montefiore was born in 1965 and read history at Gonville & Caius College, Cambridge University. *Catherine the Great & Potemkin* was shortlisted for the Samuel Johnson, Duff Cooper, and Marsh Biography Prizes. *Young Stalin* won the Bruno Kreisky Prize for Political Literature and is the winner of the 2007 Costa Biography Award and the *Los Angeles Times* Prize for Best Biography. *Young Stalin* has also been shortlisted for the James Tait Black Memorial Prize for Best Biography. *Stalin: The Court of the Red Tsar* won the History Book of the Year Prize at the 2004 British Book Awards. Montefiore's books are world bestsellers, published in 34 languages. He has recently completed a novel, *Sashenka*. His next history book is *Jerusalem: the Biography*, a fresh history of the Middle East. A Fellow of the Royal Society of Literature, he lives in London with his wife, the novelist Santa Montefiore, and their two children. For more information, see: simonsebagmontefiore.com.

By the author

Young Stalin
Stalin: The Court of the Red Tsar
Catherine the Great & Potemkin

STALIN
1878–1939

SIMON SEBAG MONTEFIORE

PHOENIX

A PHOENIX PAPERBACK

This edition produced for The Book People Ltd,
Hall Wood Avenue, Haydock, St Helens WA11 9UL

First published in Great Britain in 2003
by Weidenfeld & Nicolson
Paperback edition published in 2004
by Phoenix,
an imprint of Orion Books Ltd,
Orion House, 5 Upper St Martin's Lane,
London WC2H 9EA

An Hachette UK company

A CIP catalogue record for this book
is available from the British Library.

ISBN 978-1-4072-2146-5

Typeset by Selwood Systems, Midsomer Norton

Printed and bound in Great Britain by
Clays Ltd, St Ives plc

The Orion Publishing Group's policy is to use papers that
are natural, renewable and recyclable products and
made from wood grown in sustainable forests. The logging
and manufacturing processes are expected to conform to
the environmental regulations of the country of origin.

www.orionbooks.co.uk

To Lily Bathsheba

Contents

Part Four: Slaughter: Yezhov the Poison Dwarf, 1937–1938

Part Five: Slaughter: Beria Arrives, 1938–1939

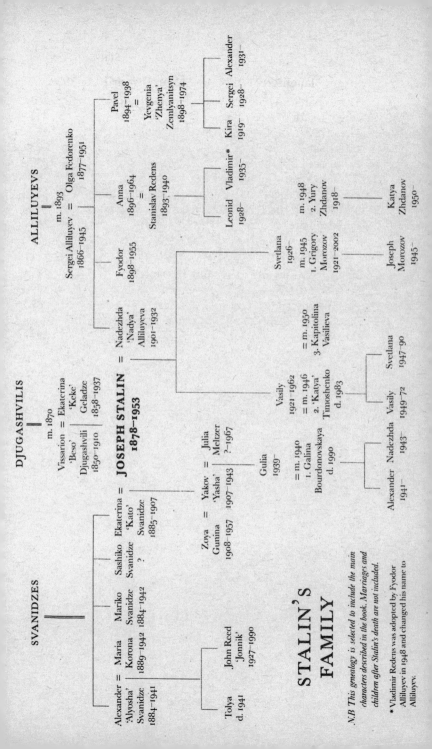

STALIN'S FAMILY

SVANIDZES

DJUGASHVILIS

m. 1870

Vissarion 'Beso' Djugashvili 1850–1910 = Ekaterina 'Keke' Geladze 1858–1937

ALLILUYEVS

m. 1893

Sergei Alliluyev 1866–1945 = Olga Fedorenko 1877–1951

Maria Korona 1889–1942

Mariko Svanidze 1884–1942

Sashiko Svanidze ?

Ekaterina 'Kato' Svanidze 1885–1907 = **JOSEPH STALIN 1878–1953**

Nadezhda 'Nadya' Alliluyeva 1901–1932

Fyodor 1898–1955

Anna 1896–1964 = Stanislav Redens 1893–1940

Pavel 1894–1938 = Yevgenia 'Zhenya' Zemlyanitsyn 1898–1974

Alexander 'Alyosha' Svanidze 1884–1941

Zoya Gunina 1908–1957 = Yakov 'Yasha' 1907–1943 = Julia Meltzer ?–1967

Vasily 1921–1962 = m. 1940 1. Galina Bourdonovskaya d. 1990 = m. 1946 2. 'Katya' Timoshenko d. 1983 = m. 1950 3. Kapitolina Vasilieva

Svetlana 1926– = m. 1945 1. Grigory Morozov 1921–2002 = m. 1948 2. Yury Zhdanov 1918–

Leonid 1928–

Vladimir* 1935–

Kira 1919–

Sergei 1928–

Alexander 1931–

John Reed 'Jonik' 1927–1990

Tolya d. 1941

Gulia 1939–

Alexander 1941–

Nadezhda 1943–

Vasily 1949–72

Svetlana 1947–'90

Joseph Morozov 1945–

Katya Zhdanov 1950–

N.B This genealogy is selected to include the main characters described in the book. Marriages and children after Stalin's death are not included.

* Vladimir Redens was adopted by Fyodor Alliluyev in 1948 and changed his name to Alliluyev.

The Soviet Union under Stalin 1929–1953

Territory won in Finnish War 1940

Territories added 1939/1940 after Molotov–Ribbentrop Pact

German and Czech territory annexed by USSR in 1945

Extent of the German invasion January – July 1942

SWEDEN

FINLAND

Baltic Sea

ESTONIA

LATVIA

LITHUANIA

BELORUSSIA

POLAND

CZECHOSLOVAKIA

HUNGARY

YUGOSLAVIA

RUMANIA

BULGARIA

GREECE

Mediterranean Sea

TURKEY

Leningrad

• Minsk

• Smolensk

• Moscow

SOVIET
UNION

• Gorky (Nizhny-Novgorod)

• Kuibyshev
(Samara)

• Kiev

Kursk

Kharkov

UKRAINE

Rostov-on-Don

• Stalingrad (Tsaritsyn)

Kerch

• Yalta

Black Sea

GEORGIA
Tbilisi •

ARMENIA

AZERBAIJAN

Baku •

Caspian
Sea

IRAN

Teheran

Selected cities named after Stalin's comrades:

Molotov (Perm)   Kuibyshev (Samara)
Zhdanov (Mariupol)   Vorashilovsk (Stavropol)
Kalinin (Tver)   Stalingrad (Tsaritsyn)
Voroshilov (Lugansk)   Stalino (Yuzhovka)
Ordzhonikidze (Vladikafkaz)   Stalinabad (Dushanbe)
Kirov (Viatka)   Kirovabad (Elizavetpol)
Gorky (Nizhny-Novgorod)

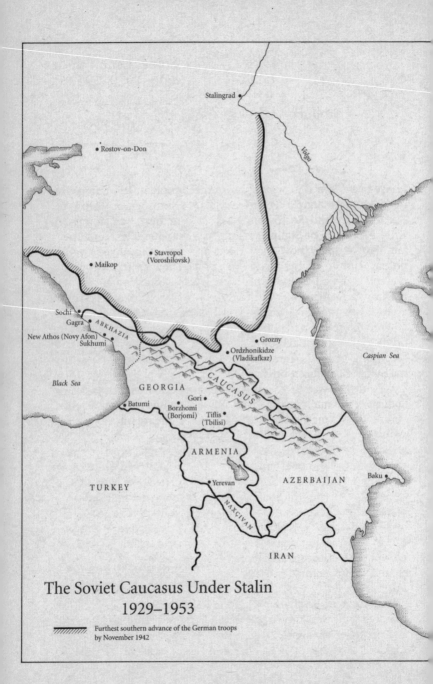

Stalingrad •

• Rostov-on-Don

Volga

• Stavropol
(Voroshilovsk)

• Maikop

Sochi •
Gagra •
New Athos (Novy Afon) •
Sukhumi •

ABKHAZIA

• Grozny

• Ordzhonikidze
(Vladikafkaz)

Caspian Sea

Black Sea

GEORGIA

_C A U C A S U S_

Batumi •

Gori •
Borzhomi
(Borjomi)
Tiflis •
(Tbilisi)

ARMENIA

AZERBAIJAN

Baku •

TURKEY

• Yerevan

NAXÇIVAN

IRAN

The Soviet Caucasus Under Stalin
1929–1953

Furthest southern advance of the German troops
by November 1942

Introduction and Acknowledgements

I have been helped generously by many people in this enterprise from Moscow and St Petersburg to Sukhumi, from Tbilisi to Buenos Aires and Rostov-on-Don. My aim here was simply to write a portrait of Stalin, his top twenty potentates, and their families, to show how they ruled and how they lived in the unique culture of his years of supreme power. This does not pretend to be a history of his foreign and domestic policies, his military campaigns, his youth or the struggle with Trotsky. This is a chronicle of his court from his acclamation as 'the leader' in 1929 to his death. It is a biography of his courtiers, a study of high politics and informal power and customs. In a way, this is a biography of Stalin himself through his relationships with his magnates: he is never off-stage.

My mission was to go beyond the traditional explanations of Stalin as 'enigma', 'madman' or 'Satanic genius', and that of his comrades as 'men without biographies', dreary moustachioed sycophants in black-and-white photographs. Deploying the arsenal of new archives and unpublished memoirs, my own interviews, and well-known materials, I hope Stalin becomes a more understandable and intimate character, if no less repellent. I believe the placing of Stalin and his oligarchs in their idiosyncratic Bolshevik context as members of a military-religious 'order of sword-bearers' explains much of the inexplicable. Stalin was utterly unique but many of his views and features, such as dependence on death as a political tool, and his paranoia, were shared by his comrades. He was a man of his time, so were his magnates.

Molotov and Beria are probably the most famous of them but many are not well known in the West. Yezhov and Zhdanov gave their names to epochs yet remain shadowy. Some, such as Mekhlis, have hardly been covered even by academics. Mikoyan was admired by many; Kaganovich widely despised. They may have presented a grey mask to the outside world but many were flamboyant, dynamic and larger-than-life. The new access to their correspondence and even their love letters will at least make them live.

In telling their stories, this is inevitably a cautionary tale: of the many mass murderers chronicled here, only Beria and Yezhov were prosecuted (and not for their true crimes). The temptation has been to blame all the crimes on one man, Stalin. There is an obsession in the West today with the cult of villainy: a macabre but inane competiton between Stalin and Hitler to find the 'world's most evil dictator' by counting their supposed victims. This is demonology not history. It has the effect of merely indicting one madman and offers us no lesson about either the danger of utopian ideas and systems, or the responsibility of individuals.

Modern Russia has not yet faced up to its past: there has been no redemption, which perhaps still casts a shadow over its development of civil society. Many modern Russians will not thank me for the intimate frankness of a history they would prefer to forget or avoid. While this book certainly does not diminish Stalin's paramount guilt, it may discourage the convenient fiction of his sole responsibility by revealing the killings of the whole leadership, as well as their own sufferings, sacrifices, vices and privileges.

I have been enormously fortunate in those who have helped me: this book was inspired by Robert Conquest, who has been the most patient, generous supporter and adviser throughout. I am superlatively grateful to Robert Service, Professor of Russian History, Oxford University, who has 'supervised' my book with generous encouragement and outstanding knowledge, and whose detailed reading and editing of the text have been invaluable. In Russia, I have been 'supervised' by the most distinguished scholar of Stalinist high politics, Oleg Khlevniuk, Senior Researcher at the State Archive of the Russian Federation (GARF) who has steered and helped me throughout. I am fortunate too that on matters of the NKVD/MGB, I have been helped by Nikita Petrov, Vice-Chairman of Moscow's Memorial Scientific Research Centre, the finest scholar of the secret police working in Russia today. On military matters, I was guided and helped, in both interpretation and archival research, by Professor Oleg Rzheshevsky and his associates. On diplomatic questions, I have treasured the knowledge, checking and charming acquaintance of Hugh Lunghi, who attended Teheran, Yalta and Potsdam, and meetings with Stalin during the later 1940s. Sir Martin Gilbert has been generous with both his knowledge and contacts in Russia. On Georgian matters, my guides have been Zackro Megrelishvili, Professor (American Studies), Tbilisi Ilia Chavchavadze State University of Language and Culture, and Gela Charkviani. On Abkhazian affairs, I must thank the top scholar in Sukhumi, Professor Slava Lakoba. I am also grateful for the guidance and ideas of the following: Geoffrey Hosking, Professor of Russian History at the University of London; Isabel de Madariaga, Professor Emeritus of Slavonic Studies at the University of London; and Alexander Kamenskii, Professor of Early and Early-Modern Russian History at Moscow's Russian State University for the Humanities. Roy Medvedev, Edvard Radzinsky, Arkady Vaksberg and Larissa Vasilieva also advised and helped me. I am most fortunate to be aided by such a towering cast and I can only humbly thank them; any wisdom is theirs; any mistakes my own.

I was most fortunate in my timing, for the opening of a chunk of the Presidential Archive in the Russian State Archive of Social and Political History (RGASPI) in 1999 meant that I was able to use a large amount of new, fascinating papers and photographs, containing the letters of Stalin, his entourage and their families, which made this book possible. In addition, I was able to access new military material in the Russian State War Archives (RGVA) and the Central Archives of the Ministry of Defence of the Russian Federation (TSAMO RF) in Podolsk. Oleg Khlevniuk was my original sponsor in both RGASPI and GARF. My greatest thanks go to Larisa A. Rogovaya, Head of Section at RGASPI, the expert on Stalin's papers and the pre-eminent interpreter of his handwriting, who helped me every step of the way. Thanks also to Dr Ludmilla Gatagova, Researcher in the Institute of Russian History. But above all, I owe thanks to the uniquely talented scholar of the History Department of the Russian State Humanities University, Galina Babkova, who helped me as much here as she did on *Potemkin*.

I have been lucky to gain access to many witnesses of this time and often to their family papers, including their fathers' unpublished memoirs. I am enormously grateful for this to Mikhail Fridman, Ingaborga Dapkunaite and Vladimir Grigoriev, Deputy Minister of Press, Television and Radio of the Russian Federation, proprietor of Vagrius publishing house; Galina Udenkova of

RGASPI, who shared her unique contacts with me; Olga Adamishina, who arranged several of my interviews; and Rosamond Richardson, who generously gave me access to her Alliluyev family contacts and her tapes of her interviews with Svetlana Alliluyeva. Kitty Stidworthy allowed me to use Vera Trail's unpublished reminiscence of Yezhov. My thanks to Dr Luba Vinogradova for her efficiency, charm, empathy and patience in helping with many of my interviews. Special thanks to Alan Hirst and Louise Campbell for their introductions to the Molotovs. Lieut.-Gen. Stepan Mikoyan and his daughter Askhen were charming, hospitable, helpful and generous. The following also proffered their memories and their time: Kira Alliluyeva, Vladimir Alliluyev (Redens), Natalya Andreyeva, Nikolai Baibakov, Nina Budyonny, Julia Khrushcheva, Tanya Litvinova, Igor Malenkov, Volya Malenkova, Sergo Mikoyan, Joseph Minervin (Kaganovich's grandson), Stas Namin, Vyacheslav Nikonov (Molotov's grandson), Eteri Ordzhonikidze, Martha Peshkova, Natalya Poskrebysheva, Leonid Redens, Natalya Rykova, Lieut.-Gen. Artyom Sergeev, Yury Soloviev, Oleg Troyanovsky, Yury Zhdanov, Nadezhda Vlasik. I am grateful to my researcher Galina Babkova for arranging the interviews with Tina Egnatashvili and Gulia Djugashvili. I must thank the admirable Mark Fielder of Granada Productions, with whom it was a pleasure to work on the BBC2 Stalin documentary. In St Petersburg, thanks to the Director and staff of the SM Kirov Museum.

In Tbilisi, Professor Megrelishvili arranged many interviews, recalled his memories of his stepfather Shalva Nutsibidze and introduced me to Maya Kavtaradze who shared her father's un-published memoirs with me. Gela Charkviani told me his memories of his youth and, above all, most generously gave me access to his father's unpublished memoirs. I also grateful to the following: Nadya Dekanozova, Alyosha Mirtskhulava, Eka Rapava, Nina Rukhadze. Thanks to Lika Basileia for accompany-ing me to the Likani Palace and Gori, and to Nino Gagoshidze and Irina Dmetradze for their energetic help; Nata Patiashvili for her help in translation and arranging interviews; Zurab Karumidze; Lila Aburshvili, Director of the Stalin Museum, Gori.

For my trip to Abkhazia, I must thank HM Ambassador to Georgia, Deborah Barnes Jones; Thadeus Boyle, Field Service Administrator, UNOMIG; the Abkhazian Prime Minister, Anri Djirgonia. It would not have been possible without Victoria

Ivleva-Yorke. Thanks to Saida Smir, Director of the Novy Afon dacha and staffs of Stalin's other residences at Sukhumi, Kholodnaya Rechka, Lake Ritsa, Museri and Sochi. In Buenos Aires, thanks to Eva Soldati for interviewing Leopoldo Bravo and his family.

Thanks for having me to stay during my visits to Moscow and elsewhere: Masha Slonim, who turned out to be Maxim Litvinov's granddaughter; Marc and Rachel Polonsky who live in Marshal Koniev's apartment on Granovsky where many events in the book happened; Ingaborga Dapkunaite, David Campbell, Tom Wilson in Moscow; the Hon. Olga Polizzi and Julietta Dexter in St Petersburg.

A special thank-you to two of the wisest historical minds: my father Dr Stephen Sebag-Montefiore MD who has been as brilliant in reading the psychology of Stalin as he was with Potemkin; and my mother April Sebag-Montefiore for her flawless gifts of language and psychology.

I must thank my agent Georgina Capel; Anthony Cheetham; my publisher Ion Trewin; and Lord and Lady Weidenfeld. Thanks for answering questions and helping in small or large ways to: Andy Apostolou, Anne Applebaum, Joan Bright Astley, Professor Derek Beales, Antony Beevor, Vadim Benyatov, Michael Bloch, Dr David Brandenburger, Pavel Chinsky, Winston Churchill, Bernadette Cini, Lady Dahrendorf, Dr Sarah Davies, Yelena Durden-Smith, Ellen, Lisa Fine, Sergei Degtiarev Foster, Mark Franchetti, Levan and Nino Gachechiladze, Professor J. Arch Getty, Nata Gologre, Jon Halliday, Andrea Dee Harris, Mariana Haseldine, Dr Dan Healy, Laurence Kelly, Dmitri Khankin, Maria Lobanova, V. S. Lopatin, Edward Lucas, Ambassador of the Republic of Georgia and Mrs Teimuraz Mamatsashvili, Neil McKendrick, the Master, Gonville & Caius College, Cambridge, Catherine Merridale, Princess Tatiana Metternich, Professor Richard Overy, Charles and Patty Palmer-Tomkinson, Martin Poliakoff, Alexander Prozverkin, David Pryce-Jones, Julia Tourchaninova and Ernst Goussinksi, Professor E. A. Rees, Count Fritz von der Schulenburg, Hugh Sebag-Montefiore, Lady Soames, Professor Boris Sokolov, Geia Sulkanishvili, Lord Thomas of Swynnerton, Count Nikolai Tolstoy, Prince George Vassiltchikov, Dr D. H. Watson, Adam Zamoyski. I owe much to my Russian tutor, Galina Oleksiuk. Thanks to Jane Birkett, my valiant copy editor, to John Gilkes for the maps, to Douglas Matthews for the index and mountainous thanks to Victoria Webb for the heroic job of collating the proofs.

Last but first, I must lovingly thank my wife Santa Montefiore, not only for translating materials on Leopoldo Bravo from the Spanish, but above all, for tolerating and even sometimes welcoming, for years on end, the brooding presence of Stalin in our lives.

List of Characters

Joseph Stalin born Djugashvili known as 'Soso' and 'Koba'. Secretary of Bolshevik Party 1922–1953 and Premier 1941–53. Marshal. Generalissimo

Family

Keke Djugashvili, Stalin's mother
Kato Svanidze, Stalin's first wife
Yakov Djugashvili, son of Stalin's first marriage to Kato Svanidze. Captured by Germans
Nadya Alliluyeva, Stalin's second wife
Vasily Stalin, Stalin's son by Nadya Alliluyeva, pilot, General
Svetlana Stalin now known as Alliluyeva, Stalin's daughter
Artyom Sergeev, Stalin and Nadya's adopted son
Sergei Alliluyev, Nadya's father
Olga Alliluyeva, Nadya's mother
Pavel Alliluyev, Nadya's brother, Red Army Commissar married to
Zhenya Alliluyeva, Nadya's sister-in-law, actress, mother of Kira
Alyosha Svanidze, brother of Kato, Georgian, Stalin's brother-in-law, banking official married to
Maria Svanidze, diarist, Jewish Georgian opera singer
Stanislas Redens, Nadya's brother-in-law, secret policeman, married to Anna Redens, Nadya's elder sister

Allies

Victor Abakumov, secret policeman, head of Smersh, MGB Minister
Andrei Andreyev, Politburo member, CC Secretary, married to
Dora Khazan, Nadya's best friend, Deputy Textiles Minister, mother of Natasha Andreyeva
Lavrenti Beria, 'Uncle Lara', secret policeman, NKVD boss, Politburo member in charge of nuclear bomb, married to
Nina Beria, scientist, Stalin treated her 'like a daughter', mother of
Sergo Beria, scientist, married to

Martha Peshkova Beria, granddaughter of Gorky, daughter-in-law of Beria

Semyon Budyonny, cavalryman, Marshal, one of the Tsaritsyn Group

Nikolai Bulganin, 'the Plumber', Chekist, Mayor of Moscow, Politburo member, Defence Minister, heir apparent

Candide Charkviani, Georgian Party chief and Stalin's confidant

Semyon Ignatiev, MGB Minister, master of the Doctors' Plot

Lazar Kaganovich, 'Iron Lazar' and 'the Locomotive', Jewish Old Bolshevik, Stalin's deputy early 1930s, Railways chief, Politburo member

Mikhail Kalinin, 'Papa', the 'Village Elder', Soviet President, peasant/worker

Nikita Khrushchev, Moscow, then Ukrainian First Secretary, Politburo member

Sergei Kirov, Leningrad chief, CC Secretary, Politburo member and Stalin's close friend

Valerian Kuibyshev, economic chief and poet, Politburo member

Alexei (A. A.) Kuznetsov, Zhdanov's deputy in Leningrad; post-WW2, CC Secretary and curator of MGB, Stalin's heir apparent as Secretary

Nestor Lakoba, Abkhazian boss

Georgi Malenkov, nicknamed 'Melanie' or 'Malanya', CC Secretary, allied to Beria

Lev Mekhlis, 'the Gloomy Demon' and 'Shark', Jewish, Stalin's secretary, then *Pravda* editor, political chief of Red Army

Akaki Mgeladze, Abkhazian, then Georgian boss; Stalin called him 'Wolf'

Anastas Mikoyan, Armenian Old Bolshevik, Politburo member, Trade and Supply Minister

Vyacheslav Molotov, known as 'Iron-Arse', and 'our Vecha', Politburo member, Premier, Foreign Minister, married to

Polina Molotova née Karpovskaya, known as Comrade Zhemchuzhina, 'the Pearl', Jewish, Fishery Commissar, perfume boss

Grigory Ordzhonikidze, known as Comrade Sergo and as 'Stalin's Arse', Politburo member, Heavy Industry chief

Karl Pauker, ex-barber of Budapest Opera, Stalin's bodyguard and head of Security

Alexander Poskrebyshev, ex-medical orderly, Stalin's *chef de cabinet*, married to

Bronka Metalikova Poskrebysheva, doctor, Jewish

Mikhail Riumin, 'Little Misha', 'the Midget', MGB Deputy Minister and manager of the Doctors' Plot

Nikolai Vlasik, Stalin's bodyguard and head of Guards Directorate

Klim Voroshilov, First Marshal, Politburo member, Defence Commissar, veteran of Tsaritsyn married to

Ekaterina Voroshilova, diarist

Nikolai Voznesensky, Leningrad economist, Politburo member, Deputy Premier, Stalin's anointed heir as Premier

Genrikh Yagoda, NKVD chief, Jewish, in love with Timosha Gorky

Abel Yenukidze, 'Uncle Abel', Secretary of Central Executive Committee, Georgian, bon viveur, Nadya's godfather

Nikolai Yezhov, 'Blackberry' or 'Kolya', NKVD boss, married to

Yevgenia Yezhova, editor, socialite, Jewess

Andrei Zhdanov, 'the Pianist', Politburo member, Leningrad boss, CC Secretary, Naval chief, Stalin's friend and heir apparent, father of

Yury Zhdanov, CC Science Dept chief, married Svetlana Stalin

Generals

Grigory Kulik, Marshal, Artillery chief, womaniser and bungler, veteran of Tsaritsyn

Boris Shaposhnikov, Marshal, Chief of Staff, Stalin's favourite staff officer

Semyon Timoshenko, Marshal, victor of Finland, Defence Commissar, veteran of Tsaritsyn; his daughter married Vasily Stalin

Alexander Vasilevsky, Marshal, Chief of Staff, priest's son

Georgi Zhukov, Marshal, Deputy Commander-in-Chief, Stalin's best general

Enemies and Former Allies

Nikolai Bukharin, 'darling of the Party', 'Bukharchik', theorist, Politburo member, Stalin's co-ruler 1925–9, friend of Nadya, Rightist. Chief defendant in last show trial

Lev Kamenev, Leftist Politburo member, defeated Trotsky with Stalin, with whom ruled 1924–5, Jewish. Defendant in first show trial

Alexei Rykov, 'Rykvodka', Rightist Politburo member, Premier and co-ruler with Stalin and Bukharin 1925–8. Defendant in last show trial

Leon Trotsky, genius of the Revolution, Jewish, War Commissar and creator of Red Army, 'operetta commander' in Stalin's words

Grigory Zinoviev, Leftist Politburo member, Leningrad boss, Jewish. Triumvirate with Stalin and Kamenev 1924–5. Defendant in first show trial

'Engineers of the Human Soul'

Anna Akhmatova, poet, 'harlot-nun,' said Zhdanov

Isaac Babel, author of *Red Cavalry* and friend of Eisenstein, Mandelstam

Demian Bedny, 'the proletarian poet', boon companion of Stalin

Mikhail Bulgakov, novelist and playwright, Stalin saw his *Days of the Turbins* fifteen times

Ilya Ehrenburg, Jewish writer and European literary figure

Sergei Eisenstein, Russia's greatest film director

Maxim Gorky, Russia's most famous novelist, close to Stalin

Ivan Kozlovsky, Stalin's court tenor

Osip Mandelstam, poet: 'Isolate but preserve,' said Stalin

Boris Pasternak, poet, 'cloud dweller', said Stalin

Mikhail Sholokhov, novelist of Cossacks and collectivization

Konstantin Simonov, poet and editor, friend of Vasily Stalin, favourite of Stalin

Prologue
The Holiday Dinner: 8 November 1932

At around 7 p.m. on 8 November 1932, Nadya Alliluyeva Stalin, aged thirty-one, the oval-faced and brown-eyed wife of the Bolshevik General Secretary, was dressing for the raucous annual party to celebrate the fifteenth anniversary of the Revolution. Puritanical, earnest but fragile, Nadya prided herself on her 'Bolshevik modesty', wearing the dullest and most shapeless dresses, draped in plain shawls, with square-necked blouses and no make-up. But tonight, she was making a special effort. In the Stalins' gloomy apartment in the two-storey seventeenth-century Poteshny Palace, she twirled for her sister, Anna, in a long, unusually fashionable black dress with red roses embroidered around it, imported from Berlin. For once, she had indulged in a 'stylish hairdo' instead of her usual severe bun. She playfully placed a scarlet tea rose in her black hair.

The party, attended by all the Bolshevik magnates, such as Premier Molotov and his slim, clever and flirtatious wife, Polina, Nadya's best friend, was held annually by the Defence Commissar, Voroshilov: he lived in the long, thin Horse Guards building just five steps across a little lane from the Poteshny. In the tiny, intimate world of the Bolshevik élite, those simple, cheerful soirées usually ended with the potentates and their women dancing Cossack jigs and singing Georgian laments. But that night, the party did not end as usual.

Simultaneously, a few hundred yards to the east, closer to Lenin's Mausoleum and Red Square, in his office on the second floor of the triangular eighteenth-century Yellow Palace, Joseph Stalin, the General Secretary of the Bolshevik Party and the *Vozhd* – the leader – of the Soviet Union, now fifty-three, twenty-two years Nadya's senior, and the father of her two children, was meeting his favoured secret policeman. Genrikh

Yagoda, Deputy Chairman of the GPU,* a ferret-faced Jewish jeweller's son from Nizhny Novgorod with a 'Hitlerish moustache' and a taste for orchids, German pornography and literary friendships, informed Stalin of new plots against him in the Party and more turbulence in the countryside.

Stalin, assisted by Molotov, forty-two, and his economics chief, Valerian Kuibyshev, forty-five, who looked like a mad poet, with wild hair, an enthusiasm for drink, women and, appropriately, writing poetry, ordered the arrest of those who opposed them. The stress of those months was stifling as Stalin feared losing the Ukraine itself which, in parts, had descended into a dystopia of starvation and disorder. When Yagoda left at 7.05 p.m., the others stayed talking about their war to 'break the back' of the peasantry, whatever the cost to the millions starving in history's greatest man-made famine. They were determined to use the grain to finance their gargantuan push to make Russia a modern industrial power. But that night, the tragedy would be closer to home: Stalin was to face a personal crisis that was the most wounding and mysterious of his career. He would replay it over and over again for the rest of his days.

At 8.05 p.m., Stalin, accompanied by the others, ambled down the steps towards the party, through the snowy alleyways and squares of that red-walled medieval fortress, dressed in his Party tunic, baggy old trousers, soft leather boots, old army greatcoat and his wolf *shapka* with earmuffs. His left arm was slightly shorter than the other but much less noticeable than it became in old age – and he was usually smoking a cigarette or puffing on his pipe. The head and the thick, low hair, still black but with specks of the first grey, radiated the graceful strength of the mountain-men of the Caucasus; his almost Oriental, feline eyes were 'honey-coloured' but flashed a lupine yellow in anger. Children found his moustache prickly and his smell of tobacco acrid but, as Molotov and his female admirers recalled, Stalin was still attractive to women with whom he flirted shyly and clumsily.

---

* The Soviet secret police was first called the Extraordinary Commission for Combating Counterrevolution and Sabotage, known as the Cheka. In 1922, it became the State Political Administration (GPU) then the United GPU: OGPU. In 1934, it was subsumed into the People's Commissariat of Internal Affairs (NKVD). However, secret policemen were still known as 'Chekists' and the secret police itself as 'the Organs'. In 1941 and 1943, State Security was separated into its own Commissariat, the NKGB. From 1954 to 1991, it became a Committee of State Security, the KGB.

This small, sturdy figure, five feet, six inches tall, who walked ponderously yet briskly with a rough pigeon-toed gait (which was studiously aped by Bolshoi actors when they were playing Tsars), chatting softly to Molotov in his heavy Georgian accent, was only protected by one or two guards. The magnates strolled around Moscow with hardly any security. Even the suspicious Stalin, who was already hated in the countryside, walked home from his Old Square office with just one bodyguard. Molotov and Stalin were walking home one night in a snowstorm 'with no bodyguards' through the Manege Square when they were approached by a beggar. Stalin gave him ten roubles and the disappointed tramp shouted: 'You damned bourgeois!'

'Who can understand our people?' mused Stalin. Despite assassinations of Soviet officials (including an attempt on Lenin in 1918), things were remarkably relaxed until the June 1927 assassination of the Soviet Ambassador to Poland, when there was a slight tightening of security. In 1930, the Politburo passed a decree 'to ban Comrade Stalin from walking around town on foot'. Yet he continued his strolling for a few more years. This was a golden age which, in just a few hours, was to end in death, if not murder.

Stalin was already famous for his Sphinxian inscrutability, and phlegmatic modesty, represented by the pipe he ostentatiously puffed like a peasant elder. Far from being the colourless bureaucratic mediocrity disdained by Trotsky, the real Stalin was an energetic and vainglorious melodramatist who was exceptional in every way.

Beneath the eerie calm of these unfathomable waters were deadly whirlpools of ambition, anger and unhappiness. Capable both of moving with controlled gradualism and of reckless gambles, he seemed enclosed inside a cold suit of steely armour but his antennae were intensely sensitive and his fiery Georgian temper was so uncontrollable that he had almost ruined his career by unleashing it against Lenin's wife. He was a mercurial neurotic with the tense, seething temperament of a highly strung actor who revels in his own drama – what his ultimate successor, Nikita Khrushchev, called a *litsedei*, a man of many faces. Lazar Kaganovich, one of his closest comrades for over thirty years who was also on his way to the dinner, left the best description of this 'unique character': he was a 'different man at different times ... I knew no less than five or six Stalins.'

However, the opening of his archives, and many newly available sources, illuminate him more than ever before: it is no longer enough to describe him as an 'enigma'. We now know how he talked (constantly about himself, often with revealing honesty), how he wrote notes and letters, what he ate, sang and read. Placed in the context of the fissiparous Bolshevik leadership, a unique environment, he becomes a real person. The man inside was a super-intelligent and gifted politician for whom his own historic role was paramount, a nervy intellectual who manically read history and literature, a fidgety hypochondriac suffering from chronic tonsillitis, psoriasis, rheumatic aches from his deformed arm and the iciness of his Siberian exile. Garrulous, sociable and a fine singer, this lonely and unhappy man ruined every love relationship and friendship in his life by sacrificing happiness to political necessity and cannibalistic paranoia. Damaged by his childhood and abnormally cold in temperament, he tried to be a loving father and husband yet poisoned every emotional well, this nostalgic lover of roses and mimosas who believed the solution to every human problem was death, and who was obsessed with executions. This atheist owed everything to priests and saw the world in terms of sin and repentance, yet he was a 'convinced Marxist fanatic from his youth'. His fanaticism was 'semi-Islamic', his Messianic egotism boundless. He assumed the imperial mission of the Russians yet remained very much a Georgian, bringing the vendettas of his forefathers northwards to Muscovy.

Most public men share the Caesarian habit of detaching themselves to admire their own figures on the world stage, but Stalin's detachment was a degree greater. His adopted son Artyom Sergeev remembers Stalin shouting at his son Vasily for exploiting his father's name. 'But I'm a Stalin too,' said Vasily.

'No, you're not,' replied Stalin. 'You're not Stalin and I'm not Stalin. Stalin is Soviet power. Stalin is what he is in the newspapers and the portraits, not you, no not even me!'

He was a self-creation. A man who invents his name, birthday, nationality, education and his entire past, in order to change history and play the role of leader, is likely to end up in a mental institution, unless he embraces, by will, luck and skill, the movement and the moment that can overturn the natural order of things. Stalin was such a man. The movement was the Bolshevik Party; his moment, the decay of the Russian monarchy.

After Stalin's death, it was fashionable to regard him as an aberration but this was to rewrite history as crudely as Stalin did himself. Stalin's success was not an accident. No one alive was more suited to the conspiratorial intrigues, theoretical runes, murderous dogmatism and inhuman sternness of Lenin's Party. It is hard to find a better synthesis between a man and a movement than the ideal marriage between Stalin and Bolshevism: he was a mirror of its virtues and faults.

* * *

Nadya was excited because she was dressing up. Only the day before at the Revolution Day parade, her headaches had been agonizing but today she was cheerful. Just as the real Stalin was different from his historical persona, so was the real Nadezhda Alliluyeva. 'She was very beautiful but you can't see it in photographs,' recalls Artyom Sergeev. She was not conventionally pretty. When she smiled, her eyes radiated honesty and sincerity but she was also po-faced, aloof and troubled by mental and physical illnesses. Her coldness was periodically shattered by attacks of hysteria and depression. She was chronically jealous. Unlike Stalin, who had a hangman's wit, no one recalls Nadya's sense of humour. She was a Bolshevik, quite capable of acting as Stalin's snitch, denouncing enemies to him. So was this the marriage of an ogre and a lamb, a metaphor for Stalin's treatment of Russia itself? Only in so much as it was a Bolshevik marriage in every sense, typical of the peculiar culture that spawned it. Yet in another way, this is simply the commonplace tragedy of a callous workaholic who could not have been a worse partner for his self-centred and unbalanced wife.

Stalin's life appeared to be a perfect fusion of Bolshevik politics and family. Despite the brutal war on the peasants and the increasing pressure on the leaders, this time was a happy idyll, a life of country weekends at peaceful dachas, cheerful dinners in the Kremlin, and languid warm holidays on the Black Sea that Stalin's children would remember as the happiest of their lives. Stalin's letters reveal a difficult but loving marriage:

'Hello, Tatka ... I miss you so much Tatochka – I'm as lonely as a horned owl,' Stalin wrote to Nadya, using his affectionate nickname for her, on 21 June 1930. 'I'm not going out of town on business. I'm just finishing up my work and then I'm going out of town to the children tomorrow ... So goodbye, don't be too long, come home sooner! My kisses! Your Joseph.' Nadya was away taking treatment for her headaches in Carlsbad, Germany. Stalin missed her and was keeping an eye on the children, like any other husband. On another occasion, she finished her letter:

'I ask you so much to look after yourself! I am kissing you passionately just as you kissed me when we were saying goodbye! Your Nadya.'

It was never an easy relationship. They were both passionate and thin-skinned: their rows were always dramatic. In 1926, she took the children to Leningrad, saying she was leaving him. But he begged her to return and she did. One feels these sorts of rows were frequent but there were intervals of a kind of happiness, though cosiness was too much to hope for in such a Bolshevik household. Stalin was often aggressive and insulting but it was probably his detachment that made him hardest to live with. Nadya was proud and severe but always ailing. If his comrades like Molotov and Kaganovich thought her on the verge of 'madness', her own family admit that she was 'sometimes crazed and oversensitive, all the Alliluyevs had unstable Gypsy blood.' The couple were similarly impossible. Both were selfish, cold with fiery tempers though she had none of his cruelty and duplicity. Perhaps they were too similar to be happy. All the witnesses agree that life with Stalin was 'not easy – it was a hard life.' It was 'not a perfect marriage', Polina Molotova told the Stalins' daughter Svetlana, 'but then what marriage is?'

After 1929, they were often apart since Stalin holidayed in the south during the autumn when Nadya was still studying. Yet the happy times were warm and loving: their letters fly back and forth with secret-police couriers and the notes follow each other in such quick succession that they resemble emails. Even among these ascetic Bolsheviks, there were hints of sex: the 'very passionate kisses' she recalled in her letter quoted above. They loved each other's company: as we have seen, he missed her bitterly when she was away and she missed him too. 'It's very boring without you,' she wrote. 'Come up here and it'll be nice together.'

They shared Vasily and Svetlana. 'Write anything about the children,' wrote Stalin from the Black Sea. When she was away, he reported: 'The children are good. I don't like the teacher, she's running round the place and she lets Vasya and Tolika [their adopted son, Artyom] rush around morning till night. I'm sure Vaska's studies will fail and I want them to succeed in German.' She often enclosed Svetlana's childish notes. They shared their health worries like any couple. When Stalin was taking the cure at the Matsesta Baths near Sochi, he reported to her: 'I've had two baths and I will have ten ... I think we'll be seriously better.'

'How's your health?' she inquired.

'Had an echo on my lungs and a cough,' he replied. His teeth were a perennial problem:

'Your teeth – please have them treated,' she told him. When she took a cure in Carlsbad, he asked caringly: 'Did you visit the doctors – write their opinions!' He missed her but if the treatment took longer, he understood.

Stalin did not like changing his clothes and wore summer suits into winter so she always worried about him: 'I send you a greatcoat because after the south, you might get a cold.' He sent her presents too: 'I'm sending you some lemons,' he wrote proudly. 'You'll like them.' This keen gardener was to enjoy growing lemons until his death.

They gossiped about the friends and comrades they saw: 'I heard Gorky [the famous novelist] came to Sochi,' she wrote. 'Maybe he's visiting you – what a pity without me. He's so charming to listen to ...' And of course, as a Bolshevik hand-maiden living in that minuscule wider family of magnates and their wives, she was almost as obsessed about politics as he was, passing on what Molotov or Voroshilov told her. She sent him books and he thanked her but grumbled when one was missing. She teased him about his appearances in White émigré literature.

The austerely modest Nadya was not afraid of giving orders herself. She scolded her husband's saturnine *chef de cabinet* Poskrebyshev while on holiday, complaining that 'we didn't receive any new foreign literature. But they say there are some new ones. Maybe you will talk to Yagoda [Deputy GPU boss] ... Last time we received such uninteresting books ...' When she returned from the vacation, she sent Stalin the photographs: 'Only the good ones – doesn't Molotov look funny?' He later teased the absurdly stolid Molotov in front of Churchill and Roosevelt. He sent her back his own holiday photographs.

However by the late twenties, Nadya was professionally discontented. She wanted to be a serious Bolshevik career woman in her own right. In the early twenties, she had done typing for her husband, then Lenin and then for Sergo Ordzhonikidze, another energetic and passionate Georgian dynamo now responsible for Heavy Industry. Then she moved to the

International Agrarian Institute in the Department of Agitation and Propaganda where, lost in the archives, we find the daily work of Stalin's wife in all its Bolshevik dreariness: her boss asks his ordinary assistant, who signs herself 'N. Alliluyeva', to arrange the publication of a shockingly tedious article entitled 'We Must Study the Youth Movement in the Village'.

'I have absolutely nothing to do with anyone in Moscow,' she grumbled. 'It's strange though I feel closer to non-Party people – women of course. The reason is they're more easy going ... There are a terrible lot of new prejudices. If you don't work, you're just a *baba*!'* She was right. The new Bolshevik women such as Polina Molotova were politicians in their own right. These feminists scorned housewives and typists like Nadya. But Stalin did not want such a wife for himself: his Nadya would be what he called a *'baba'*. In 1929, Nadya decided to become a powerful Party woman in her own right and did not go on holiday with her husband but remained in Moscow for her examinations to enter the Industrial Academy to study synthetic fibres, hence her loving correspondence with Stalin. Education was one of the great Bolshevik achievements and there were millions like her. Stalin really wanted a *baba* but he supported her enterprise: ironically, his instincts may have been right because it became clear that she was really not strong enough to be a student, mother and Stalin's wife simultaneously. He often signed off:

'How are the exams? Kiss my Tatka!' Molotov's wife became a People's Commissar – and there was every reason for Nadya to hope she would do the same.

* * *

Across the Kremlin, the magnates and their wives converged on Voroshilov's apartment, oblivious of the tragedy about to befall Stalin and Nadya. None of them had far to come. Ever since Lenin had moved the capital to Moscow in 1918, the leaders had lived in this isolated secret world, behind walls thirteen feet thick, crenellated burgundy battlements and towering fortified gates, which, more than anything, resembled a 64-acre theme park of the history of old Muscovy. 'Here Ivan the Terrible used to walk,' Stalin told visitors. He daily passed the Archangel Cathedral

---

* She certainly cared for Stalin like a good *baba*: 'Stalin has to have a chicken diet,' she wrote to President Kalinin in 1921. 'We've only been allocated 15 chickens ... Please raise the quota since it's only halfway through the month and we've only got 5 left ...'

where Ivan the Terrible lay buried, the Ivan the Great Tower, and the Yellow Palace, where he worked, had been built for Catherine the Great: by 1932, Stalin had lived fourteen years in the Kremlin, as long as he had in his parental home.

These potentates – the 'responsible workers' in Bolshevik terminology – and their staff, the 'service workers', lived in high-ceilinged, roomy apartments once occupied by Tsarist governors and major-domos, mainly in the Poteshny* or Horse Guards, existing so closely in these spired and domed courtyards that they resembled dons living in an Oxford college: Stalin was always popping into their homes and the other leaders regularly turned up at his place for a chat, almost to borrow the proverbial cup of sugar.

Most of the guests only needed to walk along the corridor to get to the second floor apartment of Kliment Voroshilov and his wife Ekaterina in the Horse Guards (nominally the Red Guards Building but no one called it that). Their home was reached through a door in the archway that contained the little cinema where Stalin and his friends often decamped after dinner. Inside it was cosy but spacious, with dark wood-panelled rooms looking out over the Kremlin walls into the city. Voroshilov, their host, aged fifty-two, was the most popular hero in the Bolshevik pantheon – a genial and swaggering cavalryman, once a lathe turner, with an elegant, almost d'Artagnanish moustache, fair hair and cherubic rosy-cheeked face. Stalin would have arrived with the priggish Molotov and the debauched Kuibyshev. Molotov's wife, the dark and formidable Polina, always finely dressed, came from her own flat in the same building. Nadya crossed the lane from the Poteshny with her sister Anna.

In 1932, there would have been no shortage of food and drink but these were the days before Stalin's dinners became imperial banquets. The food – Russian *hors d'oeuvres*, soup, various dishes of salted fish and maybe some lamb – was cooked in the Kremlin canteen and brought hot up to the flat where it was served by a housekeeper, and washed down with vodka and Georgian wine in a parade of toasts. Faced with unparalleled disaster in the regions where ten million people were starving, conspiracy in his Party, uncertain of the loyalty of his own entourage – and with the added strain of a troubled wife, Stalin felt beleaguered and at war.

---

* The Poteshny Palace, where the Stalins lived, means 'Amusement Palace' since it once housed actors and a theatre maintained by the Tsars.

Like the others at the centre of this whirlwind, he needed to drink and unwind. Stalin sat in the middle of the table, never at the head, and Nadya sat opposite him.

* * *

During the week, the Stalin household was based in the Kremlin apartment. The Stalins had two children, Vasily, eleven, a diminutive, stubborn and nervous boy, and Svetlana, seven, a freckly red-haired girl. Then there was Yakov, now twenty-five, son of Stalin's first marriage, who had joined his father in 1921, having been brought up in Georgia, a shy, dark boy with handsome eyes. Stalin found Yakov irritatingly slow. When he was eighteen, he had fallen in love with, and married, Zoya, a priest's daughter. Stalin did not approve because he wanted Yasha to study. In a 'cry for help', Yasha shot himself but only grazed his chest. Stalin regarded this 'as blackmail'. The stern Nadya disapproved of Yasha's self-indulgence: 'she was so appalled by Yasha,' Stalin mused. But he was even less sympathetic.

'Couldn't even shoot straight,' he quipped cruelly. 'This was his military humour,' explains Svetlana. Yasha later divorced Zoya, and came home.

Stalin had high, and given his own meteoric success, unfair expectations of the sons – but he adored his daughter. In addition to these three, there was Artyom Sergeev, Stalin's beloved adopted son, who was often in their house, even though his mother was still alive.* Stalin was more indulgent than Nadya, even though he smacked Vasily 'a couple of times'. Indeed, this woman portrayed as angelic in every history was, in her way, even more self-centred than Stalin. Her own family regarded her as 'utterly self-indulgent', recalls her nephew Vladimir Redens. 'The nanny complained that Nadya was not remotely interested in the children.' Her daughter Svetlana agreed that she was much more committed to her studies. She treated the children sternly and never gave Svetlana a 'word of praise'. It is surprising that she rowed most with Stalin, not about his evil policies, but about his spoiling the children!

---

* One of the few attractive traditions of Bolshevism was the adoption of the children of fallen heroes and ordinary orphans. Stalin adopted Artyom when his father, a famous revolutionary, was killed in 1921 and his mother was ill. Similarly Mikoyan adopted the sons of Sergei Shaumian, the hero of Baku; Voroshilov adopted the son of Mikhail Frunze, the War Commissar who died suspiciously in 1925. Later both Kaganovich and Yezhov, harsh men indeed, adopted orphans.

Yet it is harsh to blame her for this. Her medical report, preserved by Stalin in his archive, and the testimonies of those who knew her, confirm that Nadya suffered from a serious mental illness, perhaps hereditary manic depression or borderline personality disorder though her daughter called it 'schizophrenia', and a disease of the skull that gave her migraines. She needed special rest cures in 1922 and 1923 as she experienced 'drowsiness and weakness'. She had had an abortion in 1926 which, her daughter revealed, had caused 'female problems'. Afterwards she had no periods for months on end. In 1927, doctors discovered her heart had a defective valve – and she suffered from exhaustion, angina and arthritis. In 1930, the angina struck again. Her tonsils had recently been taken out. The trip to Carlsbad did not cure her mysterious headaches.

She did not lack for medical care – the Bolsheviks were as obsessively hypochondriacal as they were fanatically political. Nadya was treated by the best doctors in Russia and Germany. But these were not psychiatrists: it is hard to imagine a worse environment for a fragile girl than the cruel aridity of this Kremlin pressure-cooker pervaded by the martial Bolshevism that she so worshipped – and the angry thoughtlessness of Stalin whom she so revered.

She was married to a demanding egotist incapable of giving her, or probably anyone, happiness: his relentless energy seemed to suck her dry. But she was also patently the wrong person for him. She did not soothe his stress – she added to it. He admitted he was baffled by Nadya's mental crises. He simply did not possess the emotional resources to help her. Sometimes her 'schizophrenia' was so grievous, 'she was almost deranged'. The magnates, and the Alliluyevs themselves, sympathized with Stalin. Yet, despite their turbulent marriage and their strange similarity of passion and jealousy, they loved each other after their own fashion.

After all, it was Stalin for whom Nadya was dressing up. The 'black dress with rose pattern appliqué ...' had been bought as a present for her by her brother, slim brown-eyed Pavel Alliluyev who had just returned with his usual treasure chest of gifts from Berlin, where he worked for the Red Army. With Nadya's proud Gypsy, Georgian, Russian and German blood, the rose looked striking against her jet-black hair. Stalin would be surprised because, as her nephew put it, he 'never encouraged her to dress more glamorously'.

* * *

The drinking at dinner was heavy, regulated by a *tamada* (Georgian toastmaster). This was probably one of the Georgians such as the flamboyant Grigory Ordzhonikidze, always known as Sergo, who resembled 'a Georgian prince' with his mane of long hair and leonine face. Some time during the evening, without any of the other revellers noticing, Stalin and Nadya became angry with one another. This was hardly a rare occurrence. Her evening began to crumble when, among all the toasts, dancing and flirting at table, Stalin barely noticed how she had dressed up, even though she was one of the youngest women present. This was certainly ill-mannered but not uncommon in many marriages.

They were surrounded by the other Bolshevik magnates, all hardened by years in the underground, blood-spattered by their exploits in the Civil War, and now exultant if battered by the industrial triumphs and rural struggles of the Stalin Revolution. Some, like Stalin, were in their fifties. But most were strapping, energetic fanatics in their late thirties, some of the most dynamic administrators the world has ever seen, capable of building towns and factories against all odds, but also of slaughtering their enemies and waging war on their own peasants. In their tunics and boots, they were macho, hard-drinking, powerful and famous across the Imperium, stars with blazing egos, colossal responsibilities, and Mausers in their holsters. The boisterous, booming and handsome Jewish cobbler, Lazar Kaganovich, Stalin's Deputy, had just returned from presiding over mass-executions and deportations in the North Caucasus. Then there was the swaggering Cossack commander Budyonny with his luxuriant walrus moustaches and the dazzling white teeth, and the slim, shrewd and dapper Armenian Mikoyan, all veterans of brutal expeditions to raise grain and crush the peasants. These were voluble, violent and colourful political showmen.

They were an incestuous family, a web of long friendships and enduring hatreds, shared love affairs, Siberian exiles and Civil War exploits: Mikhail Kalinin, the President, had been visiting the Alliluyevs since 1900. Nadya knew Voroshilov's wife from Tsaritsyn (later Stalingrad) and she studied at the Industrial Academy with Maria Kaganovich and Dora Khazan (wife of another magnate, Andreyev, also present), her best friends along with Polina Molotova. Finally there was the small intellectual Nikolai Bukharin, all twinkling eyes and reddish beard, a painter, poet and philosopher whom Lenin had once called the 'darling of the Party' and who had been Stalin and Nadya's closest friend. He was a charmer, the Puck of the Bolsheviks. Stalin had defeated him in 1929 but he remained friends with Nadya. Stalin himself half-loved and half-hated 'Bukharchik' in that deadly combination of admiration and envy that was habitual to him. That night, Bukharin was readmitted, at least temporarily, to the magic circle.

Irritated by Stalin's lack of attention, Nadya started dancing with her louche, sandy-haired Georgian godfather, 'Uncle Abel' Yenukidze, the official in charge of the Kremlin who was already shocking the Party with his affairs with teenage ballerinas. 'Uncle Abel's' fate would illustrate the deadly snares of hedonism when private life belonged to the Party. Perhaps Nadya was trying to make Stalin angry. Natalya Rykova, who was in the Kremlin that night with her father, the former Premier, but not at the dinner, heard the next day that Nadya's dancing infuriated Stalin. The story is certainly credible because other accounts mention her flirting with someone. Perhaps Stalin was so drunk, he did not even notice.

* * *

Stalin was busy with his own flirtation. Even though Nadya was opposite him, he flirted shamelessly with the 'beautiful' wife of Alexander Yegorov, a Red Army commander with whom he had served in the Polish War of 1920. Galya Yegorova, née Zekrovskaya, thirty-four, was a brash film actress, a 'pretty, interesting and charming' brunette well known for her affairs and risqué dresses. Among those drab Bolshevik matrons, Yegorova must have been like a peacock in a farmyard for, as she herself admitted in her later interrogation, she moved in a world of 'dazzling company, stylish clothes ... flirtatiousness, dancing and fun'. Stalin's style of flirting alternated between traditional Georgian chivalry and, when drunk, puerile boorishness. On this occasion, the latter triumphed. Stalin always entertained children by throwing biscuits, orange peel and bits of bread into plates of ice-cream or cups of tea. He flirted with the actress in the same way, lobbing breadballs at her. His courtship of Yegorova made Nadya manically jealous: she could not tolerate it.

Stalin was no womanizer: he was married to Bolshevism and emotionally committed to his own drama in the cause of Revolution. Any private emotions were bagatelles compared to the betterment of mankind through Marxism-Leninism. But even

if they were low on his list of priorities, even if he was
emotionally damaged, he was not uninterested in women – and
women were definitely interested in him, even 'enamoured'
according to Molotov. One of his entourage later said that Stalin
complained that the Alliluyev women 'would not leave him
alone' because 'they all wanted to go to bed with him'. There was
some truth in this.

Whether they were the wives of comrades, relations or servants,
women buzzed around him like amorous bees. His newly opened
archives reveal how he was bombarded with fan letters not unlike
those received by modern pop stars. 'Dear Comrade Stalin ... I saw
you in my dreams ... I have hopes of an audience ...' writes a
provincial teacher, adding hopefully like a starry-eyed groupie: 'I
enclose my photograph ...' Stalin replied playfully if negatively:

'Comrade Unfamiliar! I ask you to trust that I have no wish to
disappoint you and I'm ready to respect your letter but I have to
say I have no appointment (no time!) to satisfy your wish. I wish
you all the best. J Stalin. PS Your letter and photograph returned.'
But sometimes he must have told Poskrebyshev that he would be
happy to meet his admirers. This gels with the story of Ekaterina
Mikulina, an attractive, ambitious girl of twenty-three who wrote
a treatise, 'Socialist Competition of Working People', which she
sent to Stalin, admitting it was full of mistakes and asking for his
help. He invited her to visit him on 10 May 1929. He liked her
and it was said she stayed the night at the dacha in Nadya's
absence.* She received no benefits from this short liaison other
than the honour of his writing her preface.

Certainly, Nadya, who knew him best, suspected him of having
affairs and she had every reason to know. His bodyguard Vlasik
confirmed to his daughter that Stalin was so besieged with offers
that he could not resist everyone: 'he was a man after all,'
behaving with the seigneurial sensuality of a traditional Georgian
husband. Nadya's jealousy was sometimes manic, sometimes
indulgent: in her letters, she lovingly teased him about his female
admirers as if she was proud of being married to such a great man.
But at the theatre, she had recently ruined the evening by
throwing a tantrum when he flirted with a ballerina. Most
recently, there was the female hairdresser in the Kremlin with

* She later became director of a gramophone factory from which she was sacked
many years later for taking bribes. She lived until 1998 but never spoke about her
short friendship with Stalin.

whom Stalin was evidently conducting some sort of dalliance. If he had merely visited the barber's shop like the other leaders, this anonymous girl would not have become such an issue. Yet Molotov remembered the hairdresser fifty years later.

Stalin had had his share of affairs within the Party. His relationships were as short as his spells in exile. Most of the girlfriends were fellow revolutionaries or their wives. Molotov was impressed by Stalin's 'success' with women: when, just before the Revolution, Stalin stole a girlfriend named Marusya from Molotov, the latter put it down to his 'beautiful dark brown eyes', though luring a girlfriend away from this plodder hardly qualifies Stalin as a Casanova. Kaganovich confirmed that Stalin enjoyed affairs with several comrades including the 'plump, pretty' Ludmilla Stal.* One source mentions an earlier affair with Nadya's friend Dora Khazan. Stalin may have benefited from revolutionary sexual freedom, even in his diffident way, enjoying some success with the girls who worked on the Central Committee secretariat, but he remained a traditional Caucasian. He favoured liaisons with discreet GPU staff: the hairdresser fitted the bill.

As so often with jealousy, Nadya's manic tantrums and bouts of depression encouraged the very thing she dreaded. All of these things – her illness, disappointment about her dress, politics, jealousy and Stalin's oafishness – came together that night.

* * *

Stalin was unbearably rude to Nadya but historians, in their determination to show his monstrosity, have ignored how unbearably rude she was to him. This 'peppery woman', as Stalin's security chief, Pauker, described her, frequently shouted at Stalin in public which was why her own mother thought her a 'fool'. The cavalryman Budyonny, who was at the dinner, remembered how she was 'always nagging and humiliating' Stalin. 'I don't know how he puts up with it,' Budyonny confided in his wife. By now her depression had become so bad that she confided in a friend that she was sick of 'everything, even the children'.

The lack of interest of a mother in her own children is a flashing danger signal if ever there was one, but there was no one to act on

---

* Another of his sweethearts was a young Party activist, Tatiana Slavotinskaya. The warmth of his love-letters from exile increased in proportion to his material needs: 'Dearest darling Tatiana Alexandrovna,' he wrote in December 1913, 'I received your parcel but you really didn't need to buy new undergarments ... I don't know how to repay you, my darling sweetheart!'

it. Stalin was not the only one puzzled by her. Few of this rough-hewn circle, including Party women like Polina Molotova, understood that Nadya was probably suffering from clinical depression: 'she couldn't control herself,' said Molotov. She desperately needed sympathy. Polina Molotova admitted the *Vozhd* was 'rough' with Nadya. Their roller-coaster continued. One moment, she was leaving Stalin, the next they loved each other again.

At the dinner, some accounts claim, it was a political toast that inflamed her. Stalin toasted the destruction of the Enemies of the State and noticed Nadya had not raised her glass.

'Why aren't you drinking?' he called over truculently, aware that she and Bukharin shared a disapproval of his starvation of the peasantry. She ignored him. To get her attention, Stalin tossed orange peel and flicked cigarettes at her, but this outraged her. When she became angrier and angrier, he called over, 'Hey you! Have a drink!'

'My name isn't "hey"!' she retorted. Furiously rising from the table, she stormed out. It was probably now that Budyonny heard her shout at Stalin: 'Shut up! Shut up!'

Stalin shook his head in the ensuing silence:

'What a fool!' he muttered, boozily not understanding how upset she was. Budyonny must have been one of the many there who sympathized with Stalin.

'I wouldn't let my wife talk to me like that!' declared the Cossack bravo who may not have been the best adviser since his own first wife had committed suicide or at least died accidentally while playing with his pistol.

Someone had to follow her out. She was the leader's wife so the deputy leader's wife had to look after her. Polina Molotova pulled on her coat and followed Nadya outside. They walked round and round the Kremlin, as others were to do in times of crisis. Nadya complained to Polina,

'He grumbles all the time ... and why did he have to flirt like that?' She talked about the 'business with the hairdresser' and Yegorova at the dinner. The women decided, as women do, that he was drunk, playing the fool. But Polina, devoted to the Party, also criticized her friend, saying 'it was wrong of her to abandon Stalin at such a difficult time'. Perhaps Polina's *'Partiinost'* – Partymindedness – made Nadya feel even more isolated.

'She quietened down,' recalled Polina, 'and talked about the

Academy and her chances of starting work ... When she seemed perfectly calm', in the early hours, they said goodnight. She left Nadya at the Poteshny Palace and crossed the lane, home to the Horse Guards.

Nadya went to her room, dropping the tea rose from her hair at the door. The dining room, with a special table for Stalin's array of government telephones, was the main room there. Two halls led off it. To the right was Stalin's office and small bedroom where he slept either on a military cot or a divan, the habits of an itinerant revolutionary. Stalin's late hours and Nadya's strict attendance at the Academy meant they had separate rooms. Carolina Til, the housekeeper, the nannies and the servants were further down this corridor. The left corridor led to Nadya's tiny bedroom where the bed was draped in her favourite shawls. The windows opened on to the fragrant roses of the Alexandrovsky Gardens.

* * *

Stalin's movements in the next two hours are a mystery: did he return home? The party continued *chez* Voroshilov. But the bodyguard Vlasik told Khrushchev (who was not at the dinner) that Stalin left for a rendezvous at his Zubalovo dacha with a woman named Guseva, the wife of an officer, described by Mikoyan, who appreciated feminine aesthetics, as 'very beautiful'. Some of these country houses were just fifteen minutes' drive from the Kremlin. If he did go, it is possible he took some boon companions with him when the women went to bed. Voroshilov's wife was famously jealous of her husband. Molotov and President Kalinin, an old roué, were mentioned afterwards to Bukharin by Stalin himself. Certainly Vlasik would have gone with Stalin in the car. When Stalin did not come home, Nadya is said to have called the dacha.

'Is Stalin there?'

'Yes,' replied an 'inexperienced fool' of a security guard.

'Who's with him?'

'Gusev's wife.'

This version may explain Nadya's sudden desperation. However, a resurgence of her migraine, a wave of depression or just the sepulchral solitude of Stalin's grim apartment in the early hours, are also feasible. There are holes in the story too: Molotov, the nanny, and Stalin's granddaughter, among others, insisted that Stalin slept at home in the apartment. Stalin certainly would

not have entertained women in his Zubalovo dacha because we
know his children were there. But there were plenty of other
dachas. More importantly, no one has managed to identify this
Guseva, though there were several army officers of that name.
Moreover Mikoyan never mentioned this to his children or in his
own memoirs. Prim Molotov may have been protecting Stalin in
his conversations in old age – he lied about many other matters,
as did Khrushchev, dictating his reminiscences in his dotage. It
seems more likely that if this woman was the 'beautiful' wife of a
soldier, it was Yegorova who was actually at the party and whose
flirting caused the row in the first place.

We will never know the truth but there is no contradiction
between these accounts: Stalin probably did go drinking at a
dacha with some fellow carousers, maybe Yegorova, and he
certainly returned to the apartment in the early hours. The fates
of these magnates and their women would soon depend on their
relationship with Stalin. Many of them would die terrible deaths
within five years. Stalin never forgot the part they each played
that November night.

* * *

Nadya looked at one of the many presents that her genial brother
Pavel had brought back from Berlin along with the black
embroidered dress she was still wearing. This was a present she
had requested because, as she told her brother, 'sometimes it's so
scary and lonely in the Kremlin with just one soldier on duty'. It
was an exquisite lady's pistol in an elegant leather holster. This is
always described as a Walther but in fact it was a Mauser. It is little
known that Pavel also brought an identical pistol as a present for
Polina Molotova but pistols were not hard to come by in that
circle.

Whenever Stalin came home, he did not check his wife but
simply went to bed in his own bedroom on the other side of the
apartment.

Some say Nadya bolted the bedroom door. She began to write a
letter to Stalin, 'a terrible letter', thought her daughter Svetlana.
In the small hours, somewhere between 2 and 3 a.m. when she
had finished it, she lay on the bed.

* * *

The household rose as normal. Stalin always lay in until about
eleven. No one knew when he had come home and whether he
had encountered Nadya. It was late when Carolina Til tried

Nadya's door and perhaps forced it open. 'Shaking with fright', she found her mistress's body on the floor by the bed in a pool of blood. The pistol was beside her. She was already cold. The housekeeper rushed to get the nanny. They returned and laid the body on the bed before debating what to do. Why did they not waken Stalin? 'Little people' have a very reasonable aversion to breaking bad news to their Tsars. 'Faint with fear', they telephoned the security boss Pauker, then 'Uncle' Abel Yenukidze, Nadya's last dancing partner, the politician in charge of the Kremlin, and Polina Molotova, the last person to see her alive. Yenukidze, who lived in Horse Guards like the others, arrived first – he alone of the leaders viewed the pristine scene, a knowledge for which he would pay dearly. Molotov and Voroshilov arrived minutes later.

One can only imagine the frantic uproar in the apartment as the oblivious ruler of Russia slept off his drink down one corridor while his wife slept eternally down the other. They also called Nadya's family – her brother Pavel, who lived across the river in the new House on the Embankment, and parents, Sergei and Olga Alliluyev. Someone called the family's personal doctor who in turn summoned the well-known Professor Kushner.

Peering at her later, this disparate group of magnates, family and servants, searching for reasons for this act of despair and betrayal, found the angry letter she left behind. No one knows what it contained – or whether it was destroyed by Stalin or someone else. But Stalin's bodyguard, Vlasik, later revealed that something else was found in her bedroom: a copy of the damaging anti-Stalinist 'Platform', written by Riutin, an Old Bolshevik who was now under arrest. This might be significant or it might mean nothing. All the leaders then read opposition and émigré journals so perhaps Nadya was reading Stalin's copy. In her letters to Stalin, she reported what she had read in the White press 'about you! Are you interested?' None the less, during those days in the country at large, the mere possession of this document warranted arrest.

No one knew what to do. They gathered in the dining room, whispering: should they wake up Stalin? Who would tell the *Vozhd*? How had she died? Suddenly Stalin himself walked into the room. Someone, most likely it was Yenukidze, Stalin's old friend who judging by the archives had assumed responsibility, stepped forward and said:

'Joseph, Nadezhda Sergeevna is no longer with us. Joseph, Joseph, Nadya's dead.'

Stalin was poleaxed. This supremely political creature, with an inhuman disregard for the millions of starving women and children in his own country, displayed more humanity in the next few days than he would at any other time in his life. Olga, Nadya's mother, an elegant lady of independent spirit who had known Stalin so long and always regretted her daughter's behaviour, hurried into the dining room where a broken Stalin was still absorbing the news. Doctors had arrived and they offered the heartbroken mother some valerian drops, the valium of the thirties, but she could not drink them. Stalin staggered towards her:

'I'll drink them,' he said. He downed the whole dose. He saw the body and the letter which, wrote Svetlana, shocked and wounded him grievously.

Nadya's brother, Pavel, arrived with his dimpled sunny wife Yevgenia, known to all as Zhenya, who would herself play a secret role in Stalin's life – and suffer for it. They were shocked not only by the death of a sister but by the sight of Stalin himself.

'She's crippled me,' he said. They had never seen him so soft, so vulnerable. He wept, saying something like this lament of many years later: 'Oh Nadya, Nadya ... how we needed you, me and the children!' The rumours of murder started immediately. Had Stalin returned to the apartment and shot her in a row? Or had he insulted her again and gone to bed, leaving her to kill herself? But the tragedy raised greater questions too: until that night, the existence of the magnates was a 'wonderful life', as described by Ekaterina Voroshilova in her diary. That night, it ended for ever. 'How,' she asks, 'did our life in the Party become so complex, it was incomprehensible to the point of agony?' The 'agony' was just beginning. The suicide 'altered history,' claims the Stalins' nephew, Leonid Redens. 'It made the Terror inevitable.' Naturally Nadya's family exaggerate the significance of her death: Stalin's vindictive, paranoid and damaged character was already formed long before. The Terror itself was the result of vast political, economic and diplomatic forces – but Stalin's personality certainly shaped it. Nadya's death created one of the rare moments of doubt in a life of iron self-belief and dogmatic certainty. How did Stalin recover and what was the effect of this humiliation on him, his entourage – and Russia itself? Did vengeance for this personal fiasco play its part in the coming Terror when some of the guests that night would liquidate the others?

Stalin suddenly picked up Nadya's pistol and weighed it in his hands: 'It was a toy,' he told Molotov, adding strangely, 'It was only fired once a year!'

The man of steel 'was in a shambles, knocked sideways', exploding in 'sporadic fits of rage', blaming anyone else, even the books she was reading, before subsiding into despair. Then he declared that he resigned from power. He too was going to kill himself:

'I can't go on living like this …'

Part One
That Wonderful Time:
Stalin and Nadya, 1878–1932

1

The Georgian and the Schoolgirl

Nadya and Stalin had been married for fourteen years but it extended deeper and longer than that, so steeped was their marriage in Bolshevism. They had shared the formative experiences of the underground life, intimacy with Lenin during the Revolution, then the Civil War. Stalin had known her family for nearly thirty years and he had first met her in 1904 when she was three. He was then twenty-five and he had been a Marxist for six years.

Joseph Vissarionovich Djugashvili was not born on 21 December 1879, Stalin's official birthday. 'Soso' was actually born in a tiny shack (that still exists) to Vissarion or 'Beso' and his wife Ekaterina, 'Keke', née Geladze, over a year earlier on 6 December 1878. They lived in Gori, a small town beside the Kura River in the romantic, mountainous and defiantly unRussian province of Georgia, a small country thousands of miles from the Tsar's capital: it was closer to Baghdad than St Petersburg.* Westerners often do not realize how foreign Georgia was: an independent kingdom for millennia with its own ancient language, traditions, cuisine, literature, it was only consumed by Russia in gulps between 1801 and 1878. With its sunny climate, clannish blood feuds, songs and vineyards, it resembles Sicily more than Siberia.

Soso's father was a violent, drunken semi-itinerant cobbler who savagely beat both Soso and Keke. She in turn, as the child later recalled, 'thrashed him mercilessly'. Soso once threw a dagger at his father. Stalin reminisced how Beso and Father

* This was not lost on another peasant boy who was born only a few hundred miles from Gori: Saddam Hussein. A Kurdish leader, Mahmoud Osman, who negotiated with him, observed that Saddam's study and bedroom were filled with books on Stalin. Today, Stalin's birthplace, the hut in Gori, is embraced magnificently by a white-pillared marble temple built by Lavrenti Beria and remains the centrepiece of Stalin Boulevard, close to the Stalin Museum.

Charkviani, the local priest, indulged in drinking bouts together to the fury of his mother: 'Father, don't make my husband a drunk, it'll destroy my family.' Keke threw out Beso. Stalin was proud of her 'strong willpower'. When Beso later forcibly took Soso to work as a cobbling apprentice in Tiflis, Keke's priests helped get him back.

She took in washing for local merchants. Stalin's mother was pious and became close to the priests who protected her. But she was also earthy and spicy: she may have made the sort of compromises that are tempting for a penniless single mother, becoming the mistress of her employers. This inspired the legends that often embroider the paternity of famous men. It is possible that Stalin was the child of his godfather, an affluent innkeeper, officer and amateur wrestler named Koba Egnatashvili. Afterwards, Stalin protected Egnatashvili's two sons who remained friends until his death and reminisced in old age about Egnatashvili's wrestling prowess. None the less, one sometimes has to admit that great men are the children of their own fathers. Stalin was said to resemble Beso uncannily. Yet he himself once asserted that his father was a priest.

Stalin was born with the second and third toes of his left foot joined. He suffered a pock-marked face from an attack of smallpox and later damaged his left arm, possibly in a carriage accident. He grew up into a sallow, stocky, surly youth with speckled honey-coloured eyes and thick black hair – a *kinto*, Georgian street urchin. He was exceptionally intelligent with an ambitious mother who wanted him to be a priest, perhaps like his real father. Stalin later boasted that he learned to read at five by listening to Father Charkviani teaching the alphabet. The five-year-old then helped Charkviani's thirteen-year-old daughter with her reading.

In 1888, he entered the Gori Church School and then, triumphantly, in 1894, won a 'five rouble scholarship' to the Tiflis Seminary in the Georgian capital. As Stalin later told a confidant, 'My father found out that along with the scholarship, I also earned money (five roubles a month) as a choirboy … and once I went out and saw him standing there:

'"Young man, sir," said Beso, "you've forgotten your father … Give me at least three roubles, don't be as mean as your mother!"

'"Don't shout!" replied Soso. "If you don't leave immediately,

I'll call the watchman!"' Beso slunk away.* He apparently died of cirrhosis of the liver in 1909.

Stalin sometimes sent money to help his mother but henceforth kept his distance from Keke whose dry wit and rough discipline resembled his own. There has been too much cod-psychology about Stalin's childhood but this much is certain: raised in a poor priest-ridden household, he was damaged by violence, insecurity and suspicion but inspired by the local traditions of religious dogmatism, blood-feuding and romantic brigandry. 'Stalin did not like to speak about his parents and childhood' but it is meaningless to over-analyse his psychology. He was emotionally stunted and lacked empathy yet his antennae were supersensitive. He was abnormal but Stalin himself understood that politicians are rarely normal: History, he wrote later, is full of 'abnormal people'.

* * *

The seminary provided his only formal education. This boarding school's catechismic teaching and 'Jesuitical methods' of 'surveillance, spying, invasion of the inner life, the violation of people's feelings' repelled, but impressed, Soso so acutely that he spent the rest of his life refining their style and methods. It stimulated this autodidact's passion for reading but he became an atheist in the first year. 'I got some friends,' he said, 'and a bitter debate started between the believers and us!' He soon embraced Marxism.

In 1899, he was expelled from the seminary, joined the Russian Social Democratic Workers' Party and became a professional revolutionary, adopting the *nom de revolution*, Koba, inspired by the hero of a novel, *The Parricide*, by Alexander Kazbegi, a dashing, vindictive Caucasian outlaw. He combined the 'science' of Marxism with his soaring imagination: he wrote romantic poetry, published in Georgian, before working as a weatherman at the Tiflis Meteorological Institute, the only job he held before becoming one of the rulers of Russia in 1917.

* I am grateful to Gela Charkviani for sharing with me the unpublished but fascinating manuscript of the memoirs of his father, Candide Charkviani, First Secretary of the Georgian Party, 1938 51. In old age, Stalin spent hours telling Charkviani about his childhood. Charkviani writes that he tried to find Beso's grave in the Tiflis cemetery but could not. He found photographs meant to show Beso and asked Stalin to identify him but he stated that these did not show his father. It is therefore unlikely that the usual photograph said to show Beso is correct. On Stalin's paternity, the Egnatashvili family emphatically deny that the innkeeper was Stalin's father.

'Koba' was convinced by the universal panacea of Marxism, 'a philosophical system' that suited the obsessive totality of his character. The class struggle also matched his own melodramatic pugnacity. The paranoid secrecy of the intolerant and idiosyncratic Bolshevik culture dovetailed with Koba's own self-contained confidence and talent for intrigue. Koba plunged into the underworld of revolutionary politics that was a seething, stimulating mixture of conspiratorial intrigue, ideological nitpicking, scholarly education, factional games, love affairs with other revolutionaries, police infiltration and organizational chaos. These revolutionaries hailed from every background – Russians, Armenians, Georgians and Jews, workers, noblemen, intellectuals and daredevils – and organized strikes, printing presses, meetings and heists. United in the obsessional study of Marxist literature, there was always a division between the educated bourgeois émigrés, like Lenin himself, and the rough men of action in Russia itself. The underground life, always itinerant and dangerous, was the formative experience not only of Stalin but of all his comrades. This explains much that happens later.

In 1902, Koba won the spurs of his first arrest and Siberian exile, the first of seven such exiles from which he escaped six times. These exiles were far from Stalin's brutal concentration camps: the Tsars were inept policemen. They were almost reading holidays in distant Siberian villages with one part-time gendarme on duty, during which revolutionaries got to know (and hate) each other, corresponded with their comrades in Petersburg or Vienna, discussed abstruse questions of dialectical materialism, and had affairs with local girls. When the call of freedom or revolution became urgent, they escaped, yomping across the taiga to the nearest train. In exile, Koba's teeth, a lifelong source of pain, began to deteriorate.

Koba avidly supported Vladimir Lenin and his seminal work, *What Is To Be Done?* This domineering political genius combined the Machiavellian practicality of seizing power, with mastery of Marxist ideology. Exploiting the schism that would lead to the creation of his own Bolshevik Party, Lenin's message was that a supreme Party of professional revolutionaries could seize power for the workers and then rule in their name in a 'dictatorship of the proletariat' until this was no longer necessary because socialism had been achieved. Lenin's vision of the Party as 'the advance detachment' of the 'army of proletarians ... a fighting group of leaders' set the militarist tone of Bolshevism.

In 1904, on Koba's return to Tiflis, he met his future father-in-law Sergei Alliluyev, twelve years his senior, a skilled Russian electrical artisan married to Olga Fedorenko, a strong-willed Georgian-German-Gypsy beauty with a taste for love affairs with revolutionaries, Poles, Hungarians, even Turks. It was whispered that Olga had an affair with the young Stalin who fathered his future wife, Nadya. This is false since Nadezhda was already three when her parents first met Koba, but his affair with Olga is entirely credible and he himself may have hinted at it. Olga, who, according to her granddaughter Svetlana, had a 'weakness for southern men', saying 'Russian men are boors,' always had a 'soft spot' for Stalin. Her marriage was difficult. Family legend has Nadya's elder brother Pavel seeing his mother making up to Koba. Such short liaisons were everyday occurrences among revolutionaries.

Long before they fell in love, Stalin and Nadya were part of the Bolshevik family who passed through the Alliluyev household: Kalinin and Yenukidze among others at that dinner in 1932. There was another special link: soon afterwards Koba met the Alliluyevs in Baku, and saved Nadya from drowning in the Caspian Sea, a romantic bond if ever there was one.

* * *

Koba meanwhile married another sprig of a Bolshevik family. Ekaterina, 'Kato', a placid, darkly pretty Georgian daughter of a cultured family, was the sister of Alexander Svanidze, also a Bolshevik graduate of Tiflis seminary who joined Stalin's Kremlin entourage. Living in a hut near the Baku oilfields, Kato gave him a son, Yakov. But Koba's appearances at home were sporadic and unpredictable.

During the 1905 Revolution, in which Leon Trotsky, a Jewish journalist, bestrode the Petersburg Soviet, Koba claimed he was organizing peasant revolts in the Kartli region of Georgia. After the Tsarist backlash, he travelled to a Bolshevik conference in Tammerfors, Finland – his first meeting with his hero, Lenin, 'that mountain eagle'. The next year, Koba travelled to the Congress in Stockholm. On his return, he lived the life of a Caucasian brigand, raising Party funds in bank robberies or 'expropriations': he boasted in old age of these 'heists ... our friends grabbed 250,000 roubles in Yerevan Square!'

After visiting London for a Congress, Koba's beloved, half-ignored Kato died 'in his arms' in Tiflis of tuberculosis on 25 November 1907. Koba was heartbroken. When the little procession reached the cemetery, Koba pressed a friend's hand and said, 'This creature softened my heart of stone. She died and with her died my last warm feelings for people.' He pressed his heart: 'It's desolate here inside.' Yet he left their son Yakov to be brought up by Kato's family. After hiding in the Alliluyevs' Petersburg apartment, he was recaptured and returned to his place of banishment, Solvychegodsk. It was in this remote one-horse town in January 1910 that Koba moved into the house of a young widow named Maria Kuzakova by whom he fathered a son.*

Soon afterwards, he was involved in a love affair with a school-girl of seventeen named Pelageya Onufrieva. When she went back to school, he wrote: 'Let me kiss you now. I am not simply sending a kiss but am KISSSSSING you passionately (it's not worth kissing otherwise).' The locals in the north russified 'Iosef' to 'Osip' and his letters to Pelageya were often signed by her revealing nickname: 'Oddball Osip'.

* * *

After yet another escape, Koba returned to Petersburg in 1912, sharing digs with a ponderous Bolshevik who was to be the comrade most closely associated with him: Vyacheslav Scriabin, just twenty-two, had just followed the Bolshevik custom of assuming a macho *nom de revolution* and called himself that 'industrial name' Molotov – 'the hammer'. Koba had also assumed an 'industrial' alias: he first signed an article 'Stalin' in 1913. It was no coincidence that 'Stalin' sounds like 'Lenin'. He may have been using it earlier and not just for its metallic grit. Perhaps he borrowed the name from the 'buxom pretty' Bolshevik named Ludmilla Stal with whom he had had an affair.

This 'wonderful Georgian', as Lenin called him, was co-opted by the Party's Central Committee at the end of the Prague conference of 1912. In November, Koba Stalin travelled from Vienna to Cracow to meet Lenin with whom he stayed: the leader

* The son Konstantin Kuzakov enjoyed few privileges except that it is said that during the Purges, when he came under suspicion, he appealed to his real father who wrote 'Not to be touched' on his file – but that may be simply because he was the son of a woman who was kind to Stalin in exile. In 1995, after a successful career as a television executive, Kuzakov, in an article headed 'Son of Stalin', announced: 'I was still a child when I learned I was Stalin's son.' There was almost certainly another child from a later exile.

supervised his keen disciple in the writing of an article expressing Bolshevik policy on the sensitive nationality question, henceforth Stalin's expertise. 'Marxism and the National Question', arguing for holding together the Russian Empire, won him ideological kudos and Lenin's trust.

'Did you write all of it?' asked Lenin (according to Stalin).

'Yes ... Did I make mistakes?'

'No, on the contrary, splendid!' This was his last trip abroad until the Teheran Conference in 1943.

In February 1913, Stalin was rearrested and given a suspiciously light exile: was he an agent of the Tsar's secret police, the Okhrana? The historical sensationalism of Stalin's duplicity shows a naïve misunderstanding of underground life: the revolutionaries were riddled with Okhrana spies but many were double or triple agents.* Koba was willing to betray colleagues who opposed him – but, as the Okhrana admitted in their reports, he remained a fanatical Marxist – and that is what mattered.

Stalin's final exile began in 1913 in the distant cold north-east of Siberia, where he was nicknamed 'Pock-marked Joe' by the local peasants. Fearing more escapes, exiles were moved to Kureika, a desolate village in Turukhansk, north of the Arctic Circle where his fishing prowess convinced locals of magical powers and he took another mistress. Stalin wrote pitiful letters to Sergei and Olga Alliluyev: 'Nature in this cursed region is shamefully poor' and he begged them to send him a postcard: 'I'm crazy with longing for nature scenes if only on paper.' Yet it was also strangely a happy time, perhaps the happiest of his life for he reminisced about his exploits there until his death, particularly about the shooting expedition when he skied into the *taiga*, bagged many partridges and then almost froze to death on the way back.

The military blunders and food shortages of the Great War inexorably destroyed the monarchy which, to the surprise of the Bolsheviks, collapsed suddenly in February 1917, replaced by a Provisional Government. On 12 March, Stalin reached the capital

---

* The recent *Secret File of Stalin* by Roman Brackman claims the entire Terror was Stalin's attempt to wipe out anyone with knowledge of his duplicity. Yet there were many reasons for the Terror, though Stalin's character was a major cause. Stalin liquidated many of those who had known him in the early days yet he mysteriously preserved others. He also killed over a million victims who had no knowledge of his early life. However, Brackman also gives an excellent account of the intrigues and betrayals of underground life.

and visited the Alliluyevs: once again, Nadya, a striking brunette, sixteen, her sister Anna and brother Fyodor, questioned this returning hero about his adventures. When they accompanied him by tram towards the offices of the newspaper *Pravda*, he called out,

'Be sure to set aside a room in the new apartment for me. Don't forget.' He found Molotov editing *Pravda*, which job he immediately commandeered for himself. While Molotov had taken a radical anti-Government line, Stalin and Lev Kamenev, né Rosenfeld, one of Lenin's closest comrades, were more conciliatory. Lenin, who arrived on 4 April, overruled Stalin's vacillations. In a rare apology to Molotov, Stalin conceded,

'You were closer to Lenin ...' When Lenin needed to escape to Finland to avoid arrest, Stalin hid him *chez* Alliluyev, shaved off his beard and escorted him to safety. The sisters, Anna, who worked at Bolshevik headquarters, and Nadya waited up at night. The Georgian entertained them, mimicking politicians and reading aloud Chekhov, Pushkin or Gorky, as he would later read to his sons. On 25 October 1917, Lenin launched the Bolshevik Revolution.

* * *

Stalin may have been a 'grey blur' in those days, but he was Lenin's own blur. Trotsky admitted that contact with Lenin was mainly through Stalin because he was of less interest to the police. When Lenin formed the new Government, Stalin founded his Commissariat of Nationalities with one secretary, young Fyodor Alliluyev, and one typist – Nadya.

In 1918, the Bolsheviks struggled for survival. Faced with a galloping German advance, Lenin and Trotsky were forced to make the pragmatic Brest-Litovsk agreement, ceding much of Ukraine and the Baltics to the Kaiser. After Germany's collapse, British, French and Japanese troops intervened while White armies converged on the tottering regime, which moved its capital to Moscow to make it less vulnerable. Lenin's beleaguered Empire soon shrunk to the size of medieval Muscovy. In August, Lenin was wounded in an assassination attempt, avenged by the Bolsheviks in a wave of Terror. In September, Lenin, recovered, declared Russia 'a military camp'. His most ruthless troubleshooters were Trotsky, the War Commissar, creating and directing the Red Army from his armoured train, and Stalin, the only two leaders allowed access without appointment to Lenin's study. When Lenin formed an executive decision-making organ with just five members called the Political Bureau – or Politburo – both were members. The bespectacled Jewish intellectual was the hero of the Revolution, second only to Lenin himself, while Stalin seemed a rough provincial. But Trotsky's patronising grandeur offended the plain-spoken 'old illegals' of the regions who were more impressed with Stalin's hard-nosed practicality. Stalin identified Trotsky as the main obstacle to his rise.

The city of Tsaritsyn played a decisive role in Stalin's career – and his marriage. In 1918, the key strategic city on the Lower Volga, the gateway to the grain (and oil) of the North Caucasus and the southerly key to Moscow, looked as if it was likely to fall to the Whites. Lenin despatched Stalin to Tsaritsyn as Director-General of Food Supplies in south Russia. But the latter soon managed to get his status raised to Commissar with sweeping military powers.

In an armoured train, with 400 Red Guards, Fyodor Alliluyev and his teenage typist Nadya, Stalin steamed into Tsaritsyn on 6 April to find the city beset with ineptitude and betrayal. Stalin showed he meant business by shooting any suspected counter-revolutionaries: 'a ruthless purge of the rear,' wrote Voroshilov, 'administered by an iron hand.' Lenin ordered him to be ever more 'merciless' and 'ruthless'. Stalin replied:

'Be assured our hand will not tremble.' It was here that Stalin grasped the convenience of death as the simplest and most effective political tool but he was hardly alone in this: during the Civil War, the Bolsheviks, clad in leather boots, coats and holsters, embraced a cult of the glamour of violence, a macho brutality that Stalin made his own. It was here too that Stalin met and befriended Voroshilov and Budyonny, both at that dinner on 8 November 1932, who formed the nucleus of his military and political support. When the military situation deteriorated in July, Stalin effectively took control of the army: 'I must have military powers.' This was the sort of leadership the Revolution required to survive but it was a challenge to Trotsky who had created his Red Army with the help of so-called 'military experts', ex-Tsarist officers. Stalin distrusted these useful renegades and shot them whenever possible.

He resided in the plush lounge carriage that had once belonged to a Gypsy torch singer who decorated it in light blue silk. Here Nadya and Stalin probably became lovers. She was seventeen, he was thirty-nine. It must have been a thrilling, terrifying adventure for a schoolgirl. When they arrived, Stalin used the train as his headquarters: it was from here that he ordered the constant shootings by the Cheka. This was a time when women accompanied their husbands to war: Nadya was not alone. Voroshilov and Budyonny's wives were in Tsaritsyn too.

Stalin and these swashbucklers formed a 'military opposition' against Trotsky whom he revealingly called an 'operetta commander, a chatterbox, ha-ha-ha!' When he arrested a group of Trotsky's 'specialists' and imprisoned them on a barge on the Volga, Trotsky angrily objected. The barge sank with all apparently aboard. 'Death solves all problems,' Stalin is meant to have said. 'No man, no problem.' It was the Bolshevik way.*

Lenin recalled Stalin. It did not matter that he had probably made things worse, wasted the expertise of Tsarist officers and backed a crew of sabre-waving daredevils. Stalin had been ruthless – the merciless application of pressure was what Lenin wanted. But the *kinto* had glimpsed the glory of the Generalissimo. More than that, the enmity with Trotsky and the alliance with the 'Tsaritysn Group' of cavalrymen were seminal: perhaps he admired Voroshilov and Budyonny's macho devil-may-care courage, a quality he lacked. His loathing for Trotsky became one of the moving passions of his life. He married Nadya on his return, moving into a modest Kremlin flat (shared with the whole Alliluyev family) and, later, a fine dacha named Zubalovo.

In May 1920, Stalin was appointed Political Commissar to the South-Western Front after the Poles had captured Kiev. The Politburo ordered the conquest of Poland to spread the Revolution westwards. The commander of the Western Front pushing on Warsaw was a brilliant young man named Mikhail Tukhachevsky. When Stalin was ordered to transfer his cavalry to Tukhachevsky, he refused until it was already too late. The vendettas reverberating from this fiasco ended in slaughter seventeen years later.

---

* Stalin later seemed to confirm the story of the sinking barge in a fascinating letter to Voroshilov: 'The summer after the assassination attempt on Lenin we ... made a list of officers whom we gathered in the Manege ... to shoot en masse ... So the Tsaritsyn barge was the result not of the struggle against military specialists but momentum from the centre ...' Five future Second World War marshals fought at Tsaritsyn: in ascending competence   Kulik, Voroshilov, Budyonny, Timoshenko and Zhukov (though the latter fought there in 1919 after Stalin's departure).

In 1921, Nadya showed her Bolshevik austerity by walking to hospital where she gave birth to a son, Vasily, followed five years later by a daughter, Svetlana. Nadya meanwhile worked as a typist in Lenin's office where she was to prove very useful in the coming intrigues.

* * *

The 'vanguard' of Bolsheviks, many young and now blooded by the brutality of that struggle, found themselves a tiny, isolated and embattled minority nervously ruling a vast ruined Empire, itself besieged in a hostile world. Contemptuous of the workers and peasants, Lenin was none the less surprised to discover that neither of these classes supported them. Lenin thus proposed a single organ to rule and oversee the creation of socialism: the Party. It was this embarrassing gap between reality and aspiration that made the Party's quasi-religious fidelity to ideological purity so important, its military discipline so obligatory.

In this peculiar dilemma, they improvised a peculiar system and sought solace in a uniquely peculiar view of the world. The Party's sovereign organ was the Central Committee (CC), the top seventy or so officials, who were elected annually by Party Congresses which, later, were held ever less frequently. The CC elected the small Politburo, a super-War Cabinet that decided policy, and a Secretariat of about three Secretaries to run the Party. They directed the conventional government of a radically centralized, vertical one-Party State: Mikhail Kalinin, born in 1875, the only real peasant in the leadership known as the 'All-Union peasant elder', became Head of State in 1919.* Lenin ran the country as Premier, the Chairman of the Council of People's Commissars, a cabinet of ministers which executed the Politburo's orders. There was a sort of democracy within the Politburo but after the desperate crises of the Civil War, Lenin banned factions. The Party frantically recruited millions of new members but were they trustworthy? Gradually, an authoritarian bureaucratic dictatorship

* Stalin was never the titular Head of State of the Soviet Union, nor was Lenin. Kalinin's title was the Chairman of the Central Executive Committee, technically the highest legislative body, but he was colloquially the 'President'. After the 1936 Constitution, his title was Chairman of the Presidium of the Supreme Soviet. Only with the Brezhnev Constitution did the Secretary-General of the Party add the Presidency to his titles. The Bolsheviks created a whole new jargon of acronyms in their effort to create a new sort of government. People's Commissars (*Narodny Komissar*) were known as *Narkoms*. The Council (Soviet) of Commissars was known as *Sovnarkom*.

took the place of the honest debates of earlier days but in 1921, Lenin, that superlative improviser, restored a degree of capitalism, a compromise called the New Economic Policy (NEP), to save the regime.

In 1922, Lenin and Kamenev engineered the appointment of Stalin as General Secretary – or *Gensec* – of the CC to run the Party. Stalin's Secretariat was the engine-room of the new state, giving him sweeping powers which he demonstrated in the 'Georgian Affair' when he and Sergo annexed Georgia, which had seceded from the Empire, and then imposed their will on the independent-minded Georgian Party. Lenin was disgusted but his stroke in December 1922 prevented him moving against Stalin. The Politburo, taking control of the health of the Party's greatest asset, banned him from working more than ten minutes a day. When Lenin tried to do more, Stalin insulted Lenin's wife Krupskaya, a tantrum that could have ended his career.*

Lenin alone could see that Stalin was emerging as his most likely successor so he secretly dictated a damning Testament demanding his dismissal. Lenin was felled by a fatal stroke on 21 January 1924. Against the wishes of Lenin and his family, Stalin orchestrated the effective deification of the leader and his embalming like an Orthodox saint in a Mausoleum on Red Square. Stalin commandeered the sacred orthodoxy of his late hero to build up his own power.

An outsider in 1924 would have expected Trotsky to succeed Lenin, but in the Bolshevik oligarchy, this glittery fame counted against the insouciant War Commissar. The hatred between Stalin and Trotsky was not only based on personality and style but also on policy. Stalin had already used the massive patronage of the Secretariat to promote his allies, Molotov, Voroshilov and Sergo; he also supplied an encouraging and realistic alternative to Trotsky's insistence on European revolution: 'Socialism in One Country'. The other members of the Politburo, led by Grigory

---

*Stalin's row with Lenin's wife, Krupskaya, outraged Lenin's bourgeois sentiments. But Stalin thought it was entirely consistent with Party culture: 'Why should I stand on my hindlegs for her? To sleep with Lenin does not mean you understand Marxism-Leninism. Just because she used the same toilet as Lenin ...' This led to some classic Stalin jokes, in which he warned Krupskaya that if she did not obey, the Central Committee would appoint someone else as Lenin's wife. That is a very Bolshevik concept. His disrespect for Krupskaya was probably not helped by her complaints about Lenin's flirtations with his assistants, including Yelena Stasova, the one whom Stalin threatened to promote to 'wife'.

Zinoviev, and Kamenev, Lenin's closest associates, were also terrified of Trotsky, who had united all against himself. So when Lenin's Testament was unveiled in 1924, Kamenev proposed to let Stalin remain as Secretary, little realizing that there would be no other real opportunity to remove him for thirty years. Trotsky, the Revolution's preening panjandrum, was defeated with surprising ease and speed. Having dismissed Trotsky from his powerbase as War Commissar, Zinoviev and Kamenev discovered too late that their co-triumvir Stalin was the real threat.

By 1926, Stalin had defeated them too, helped by his Rightist allies, Nikolai Bukharin and Alexei Rykov, who had succeeded Lenin as Premier. Stalin and Bukharin supported the NEP. But many of the regional hardliners feared that compromise undermined Bolshevism itself, putting off the reckoning day with the hostile peasantry. In 1927, a grain crisis brought this to a head, unleashed the Bolshevik taste for extreme solutions to their problems, and set the country on a repressive martial footing that would last until Stalin's death.

In January 1928, Stalin himself travelled to Siberia to investigate the drop in grain deliveries. Replaying his glorious role as Civil War commissar, Stalin ordered the forcible gathering of grain and blamed the shortage on the so-called kulaks, who were hoarding their harvest in the hope of higher prices. Kulak usually meant a peasant who employed a couple of labourers or owned a pair of cows. 'I gave a good shaking to the Party Organs,' Stalin said later but he soon discovered that 'the Rightists didn't like harsh measures ... they thought it the beginning of civil war in the villages.' On his return, Premier Rykov threatened Stalin:

'Criminal charges should be filed against you!' However the rough young commissars, the 'committee men' at the heart of the Party, supported Stalin's violent requisitioning of grain. Every winter, they headed into the hinterlands to squeeze the grain out of the kulaks who were identified as the main enemies of the revolution. However, they realized the NEP had failed. They had to find a radical, military solution to the food crisis.

Stalin was a natural radical and now he shamelessly stole the clothes of the Leftists he had just defeated. He and his allies were already talking of a final new Revolution, the 'Great Turn' leftwards to solve the problem of the peasantry and economic backwardness. These Bolsheviks hated the obstinate old world of the peasants: they had to be herded into collective farms, their grain forcibly collected and sold abroad to fund a manic gallop to create an instant industrial powerhouse that could produce tanks and planes. Private trade of food was stopped. Kulaks were ordered to deliver their grain and prosecuted as speculators if they did not. Gradually, the villagers themselves were forced into collectives. Anyone who resisted was a kulak enemy.

Similarly, in industry, the Bolsheviks unleashed their hatred of technical experts, or 'bourgeois specialists' – actually just middle-class engineers. While they trained their own new Red élite, they intimidated those who said Stalin's industrial plans were impossible with a series of faked trials that started at the Shakhty coalmine. Nothing was impossible. The resulting rural nightmare was like a war without battles but with death on a monumental scale. Yet the warlords of this struggle, Stalin's magnates and their wives, still lived in the Kremlin like a surprisingly cosy family.

2
The Kremlin Family

'Oh what a wonderful time it was,' wrote Voroshilov's wife in her diary. 'What simple, nice, friendly relationships.' The intimate collegiate life of the leaders up until the mid-thirties could not have been further from the cliché of Stalin's dreary, terrifying world. In the Kremlin, they were always in and out of each other's houses. Parents and children saw each other constantly. The Kremlin was a village of unparalleled intimacy. Bred by decades of fondness (and of course resentments), friendships deepened or frayed, enmities seethed. Stalin often dropped in on his neighbours the Kaganoviches for a chess game. Natasha Andreyeva remembers Stalin frequently putting his head round their door looking for her parents: 'Is Andrei here or Dora Moisevna?' Sometimes he wanted to go to the cinema but her parents were late, so she went with Stalin herself. When Mikoyan needed something, he would simply cross the courtyard and knock on Stalin's door, where he would be invited in for dinner. If he was not at home, they pushed a note under the door. 'Your leaving's most unfortunate,' wrote Voroshilov. 'I called on your apartment and no one answered.'

When Stalin was on holiday, this merry band continually dropped in on Nadya to send her husband messages and catch up on the latest political gossip: 'Yesterday Mikoyan called in and asked after your health and said he'll visit you in Sochi,' Nadya wrote to Stalin in September 1929. 'Today Voroshilov is back from Nalchik and he called me ...' Voroshilov in turn gave her news of Sergo. A few days later, Sergo visited her with Voroshilov. Next she talked to Kaganovich who sent his regards to Stalin. Some families were more private than others: while the Mikoyans were highly sociable, the Molotovs, on the same floor as them, were more reserved and blocked up the door between their apartments. If Stalin was the undoubted headmaster of this chatty, bickering school, then Molotov was its prissy prefect.

* * *

The only man to shake hands with Lenin, Hitler, Himmler, Göring, Roosevelt and Churchill, Molotov was Stalin's closest ally. Nicknamed 'Stone-Arse' for his indefatigable work rate, Molotov liked to correct people ponderously and tell them that Lenin himself had actually given him the soubriquet 'Iron-Arse'. Small, stocky with a bulging forehead, chilling hazel eyes blinking behind round spectacles, and a stammer when angry (or talking to Stalin), Molotov, thirty-nine, looked like a bourgeois student, which he had indeed been. Even among a Politburo of believers, he was a stickler for Bolshevik theory and severity: the Robespierre of Stalin's court. Yet he also possessed an instinct for the possible in power politics: 'I am a man of the Nineteenth Century,' said Molotov.

Born in Kukarla, a provincial backwater near Perm (soon renamed Molotov), Vyacheslav Scriabin was the son of a boozy salesman, a poor nobleman but no relation to the composer. He had played the violin for merchants in his home town and unusually, for Stalin's men, had a glancing secondary education though he became a revolutionary at sixteen. Molotov regarded himself as a journalist – he first met Stalin when they both worked on *Pravda*. He was cruel and vengeful, actually recommending death for those, even women, who crossed him, harsh to his subordinates, with whom he constantly lost his temper, and so disciplined that he would declare to his office that he would take 'a thirteen-minute nap', then wake up on the thirteenth minute. Unlike many of the Politburo's energetic showmen, Molotov was an uninspired 'plodder'.

A candidate Politburo member since 1921, 'our Vecha' had been Party Secretary before Stalin but Lenin denounced Molotov for the 'most shameful bureaucratism, and the most stupid'. When Trotsky attacked him, he revealed the intellectual inferiority complex he shared with Stalin and Voroshilov: 'We can't all be geniuses, Comrade Trotsky,' he replied. The chips on the shoulders of these home-grown Bolsheviks were mountainous.

Now Second Secretary after Stalin himself, Molotov admired Koba but did not worship him. He often disagreed with, and criticized, Stalin right up until the end. He could outdrink anyone in the leadership – no mean feat among so many alcoholics. He seemed to enjoy Stalin's teasing, even when he called him the Jewish 'Molotstein'.

His saving grace was his devotion to Polina Karpovskaya, his Jewish wife, known by her *nom de guerre* Zhemchuzhina, 'the Pearl'. Never beautiful but bold and intelligent, Polina dominated Molotov, worshipped Stalin and became a leader in her own right. Both devoted Bolsheviks, they had fallen in love at a women's conference in 1921. Molotov thought her 'clever, beautiful and above all a great Bolshevik'.

She was the consolation for the discipline, stress and severity of his crusade, yet Molotov was no automaton. His love letters show how he idolized her like a schoolboy in love. 'Polinka, darling, my love! I shan't hide that sometimes I'm overcome with impatience and desire for your closeness and caresses. I kiss you, my beloved, desired ... Your loving Vecha. I'm tied to you body and soul ... my honey.' Sometimes the letters were wildly passionate: 'I wait to kiss you impatiently and kiss you everywhere, adored, sweetie, my love.' She was his 'bright love, my heart and happiness, my pleasure honey, Polinka'.

Molotov's spoiled daughter, Svetlana, and the other Politburo children played in the courtyard but 'we didn't want to live in the Kremlin. We were constantly told by our parents not to be noisy. "You're not in the street now," they'd say. "You're in the Kremlin." It was like a jail and we had to show passes and get passes for our friends to visit us,' remembers Natasha, the daughter of Andreyev and Dora Khazan. The children constantly bumped into Stalin: 'When I was ten with long plaits playing hop, skip and jump with Rudolf Menzhinsky [son of the OGPU chief], I was suddenly lifted up by strong hands and I wriggled round and saw Stalin's face with its brown eyes and very intense, strict expression. "So who are you?" he asked. I said "Andreyeva." "Well, go on jumping then!" Afterwards, Stalin frequently chatted to her, particularly since the Kremlin's earliest cinema was reached by a staircase near their front door.

Often Stalin's dinner was simply a continuation of his meetings with workaholic comrades: soup was placed on the sideboard, guests could help themselves and they frequently worked until 3 a.m., recalls Stalin's adopted son Artyom. 'I saw Molotov, Mikoyan and Kaganovich all the time.' Stalin and Nadya often dined with the other Kremlin couples. 'Dinners were simple,' wrote Mikoyan in his memoirs. 'Two courses, a few starters, sometimes some herring ... Soup for first course then meat or fish and fruit for dessert – it was like anywhere else then.' There was a bottle of white wine and little drinking. No one sat at table for more than half an hour. One evening, Stalin who took a serious interest in political image, emulated Peter the Great's barbering exploits:

'Get rid of that beard!' he ordered Kaganovich, asking Nadya, 'Can I have some scissors? I'll do it myself.'* Kaganovich did it there and then. Such was the entertainment at Stalin and Nadya's for dinner.

The wives were influential. Stalin listened to Nadya: she had met a big-eared rotund young hobbledehoy, a fitter on the mines of the Donets, Khrushchev, at the Academy where he was energetically crushing the opposition. She recommended him to Stalin who launched his career. Stalin regularly had the young official to dinner with Nadya. Stalin always liked Khrushchev, partly because of Nadya's recommendation. This was, remembered Khrushchev, 'how I survived ... my lottery ticket'. He simply could not believe that here was Stalin, the demigod he worshipped, 'laughing and joking' with him so modestly.

Nadya was fearless about approaching Stalin about injustices: when an official, probably a Rightist, was sacked from his job, she pleaded for his career and told Stalin that 'these methods should not be used with such workers ... it's so sad ... He looked as if he'd been killed. I know you really hate me interfering but I think you should interfere in this case which everyone knows is unfair.' Stalin unexpectedly agreed to help and she was thrilled: 'I'm so glad you trust me ... it's a shame not to correct a mistake.' Stalin did not take such interference kindly from anyone else but he seemed to be able to take it from his young wife.

Polina Molotova was so ambitious that, when she decided her boss as Commissar for Light Industry was not up to the job, she asked Stalin during dinner if she could create a Soviet perfume industry. Stalin called in Mikoyan and placed her TeZhe perfume trust under him. She became the Tsarina of Soviet fragrance. Mikoyan admired her as 'capable, clever, and vigorous' but 'haughty'.

* * *

* Of course Kaganovich kept the moustache which remained fashionable. Even facial hair was then based on the leader cult: if a client wanted a goatee with beard and moustache, he would ask his barber for a 'Kalinin' after the Politburo member. When Stalin ordered another leader, Bulganin, to chop off his beard, he compromised by keeping a 'Kalinin' goatee.

Except for the snobbish Molotovs, these potentates still lived simply in the palaces of the Kremlin, inspired by their devout revolutionary mission with its obligatory 'Bolshevik modesty'. Corruption and extravagance were not yet widespread: indeed, the Politburo wives could barely afford to dress their children and the new archives show that Stalin himself sometimes ran out of money.

Nadya Stalin and Dora Khazan, the ascendant Andreyev's wife, daily caught the tram to the Academy. Nadya is always held up as a paragon of modesty for using her maiden name but Dora did the same: it was the style of the times. Sergo banned his daughter taking his limousine to school: 'too bourgeois!' The Molotovs on the other hand were already notoriously unproletarian: Natalya Rykova heard her father complain that the Molotovs never invited their bodyguards to eat at table with them.

At Stalin's, Nadya was in charge: Svetlana says that her mother managed the household on 'a modest budget'. They prided themselves on their Bolshevik austerity. Nadya regularly exhausted her housekeeping money: 'Please send me 50 roubles because I only get my money on 15 October and I've got none.'

'Tatka, I forgot to send the money,' replied Stalin. 'But I've now sent it (120 roubles) with colleagues leaving today ... Kiss you, Joseph.' Then he checked she had received it. She replied:

'I got the letter with the money. Thanks! Glad you're coming back! Write when you're arriving so I can meet you!'

On 3 January 1928, Stalin wrote to Khalatov, the chief of GIZ (the State Publishing House): 'I'm in great need of money. Would you send me 200 roubles!'* Stalin cultivated his puritanism out of both conviction and taste: when he found new furniture in his apartment, he reacted viciously:

'It seems someone from housekeeping or the GPU bought some furniture ... contrary to my order that old furniture is fine,' he wrote. 'Discover and punish the guilty! I ask you to remove the furniture and put it in storage!'

The Mikoyans had so many children – five boys plus some adopted children and, in the summer, the extended Armenian

---

* Stalin followed the same principle with his clothes: he refused to replace his meagre wardrobe of two or three much-darned tunics, old trousers and his favourite greatcoat and cap from the Civil War. He was not alone in this sartorial asceticism but he was aware that, like Frederick the Great whom he had studied, his deliberately modest old clothes only accentuated his natural authority.

family arrived for three months – that they were short of money even though Mikoyan himself was one of the top half-dozen men in Russia. So Ashken Mikoyan secretly borrowed money from the other Politburo wives who had fewer children. Mikoyan would have been furious if he had known about it, according to his sons. When Polina Molotova saw the shabby Mikoyan children, she reprimanded their mother, who retorted:

'I have five boys and I haven't got the money.'

'But,' snapped Polina, 'you're the wife of a Politburo member!'

3
The Charmer

This small group of idealistic, ruthless magnates, mainly in their thirties, were the engine of a vast and awesome Revolution: they would build socialism immediately and abolish capitalism. Their industrial programme, the Five-Year Plan, would make Russia a great power never again to be humiliated by the West, their war on the countryside would forever exterminate the internal enemy, the kulaks, and return to the values of 1917. It was Lenin who said, 'Merciless mass terror against the kulaks ... Death to them!' Thousands of young people shared their idealism. The Plan demanded a 110 per cent rise in productivity which Stalin, Kuibyshev and Sergo insisted was possible because everything was possible. 'To lower the tempo means to lag behind,' explained Stalin in 1931. 'And laggards are beaten! But we don't want to be beaten ... The history of old Russia consisted ... in her being beaten ... for her backwardness.'

The Bolsheviks could storm any fortress. Any doubt was treason. Death was the price of progress. Surrounded by enemies as they had been in the Civil War, they felt they were only just managing to keep control over the country. Hence they cultivated *tverdost*, hardness, the Bolshevik virtue.* Stalin was praised for it: 'Yes he vigorously chops off what is rotten ... If he didn't, he wouldn't be ... a Communist fighter.' Stalin wrote to Molotov about 'inspecting and checking by punching people in the face' and openly told officials he would 'smash their bones'.

---

* Yet their self-conscious brutality coexisted with a rigid code of Party manners: Bolsheviks were meant to behave to one another like bourgeois gentlemen. Divorces were 'frowned upon more severely than in the Catholic Church'. When Kaganovich wrote on the death sentence of an innocent general that he was a 'slut', he just put 's...'. Molotov edited Lenin's use of the word 'shitty', replacing it with '......' and talked prissily about using a 'name not used in Party circles'. When Kaganovich criticized the crude poetry of Demian Bedny, he told Stalin, 'Being a people's proletarian poet in no way means sinking to the level of the negative qualities of our masses.'

Bukharin resisted 'Stalin's Revolution' but he and Rykov were no match for either Stalin's patronage and charm, nor the Bolshevik taste for recklessly violent solutions. In 1929, Trotsky travelled into exile, with a look of stunned hauteur on his face, to become Stalin's mocking critic abroad, and his ultimate symbol of treason and heresy at home. Bukharin was voted off the Politburo. Stalin was the leader of the oligarchs but he was far from a dictator.

In November 1929, while Nadya studied for her exams at the Industrial Academy, Stalin returned refreshed from his holidays and immediately intensified the war on the peasantry, demanding 'an offensive against the kulaks ... to get ready for action and to deal the kulak class such a blow that it will no longer rise to its feet'. But the peasants refused to sow their crops, declaring war on the regime.

On 21 December 1929, at the exhilarating height of this colossal and terrible enterprise, the young magnates and their wives, weary but febrile from their remarkable achievements in building new cities and factories, blooded by the excitement of brutal expeditions against the obstinate peasants, arrived at Stalin's Zubalovo dacha to celebrate his official fiftieth birthday, the night our story really begins. That day, the magnates each wrote an article in *Pravda* hailing him as the *Vozhd*, the leader, Lenin's rightful heir.

* * *

Days after the birthday party, the magnates realized they had to escalate their war on the countryside and literally 'liquidate the kulaks as a class'. They unleashed a secret police war in which organized brutality, vicious pillage and fanatical ideology vied with one another to destroy the lives of millions. Stalin's circle was to be fatally tested by the rigours of collectivization because they were judged by their performance in this ultimate crisis. The poison of these months tainted Stalin's friendships, even his marriage, beginning the process that would culminate in the torture chambers of 1937.

Stalin spent half his letters to his men losing his temper, and the other half, apologizing for it. He treated everything personally: when Molotov had returned from a grain expedition to the Ukraine, Stalin told him, 'I could cover you with kisses in gratitude for your action down there' – hardly the dour Stalin of legend.

In January 1930, Molotov planned the destruction of the kulaks, who were divided into three categories: 'First category: ... to be immediately eliminated'; the second to be imprisoned in camps; the third, 150,000 households, to be deported. Molotov oversaw the death squads, the railway carriages, the concentration camps like a military commander. Between five and seven million people ultimately fitted into the three categories. There was no way to select a kulak: Stalin himself agonized,* scribbling in his notes: 'What does *kulak* mean?'

During 1930–31, about 1.68 million people were deported to the east and north. Within months, Stalin and Molotov's plan had led to 2,200 rebellions involving more than 800,000 people. Kaganovich and Mikoyan led expeditions into the countryside with brigades of OGPU troopers and armoured trains like warlords. The magnates' handwritten letters to Stalin ring with the fraternal thrill of their war for human betterment against unarmed peasants: 'Taking all measures about food and grain,' Mikoyan reported to Stalin, citing the need to dismiss 'wreckers': 'We face big resistance ... We need to destroy the resistance.' In Kaganovich's photograph album, we find him heading out into Siberia with his armed posse of leather-jacketed ruffians, interrogating peasants, poking around in their haystacks, finding the grain, deporting the culprits and moving on again, exhausted, falling asleep between stops. 'Molotov works really hard and is very tired,' Mikoyan told Stalin. 'The mass of work is so vast it needs horsepower ...'

Sergo and Kaganovich possessed the necessary 'horsepower': when the leaders decided on something, it could be done instantly, on a massive scale and regardless of waste in terms of human lives and resources. 'When we Bolsheviks want to get something done,' Beria, a rising Georgian secret policeman, said later, 'we close our eyes to everything else.' This pitiless fraternity lived in a sleepless frenzy of excitement and activity, driven by adrenalin and conviction. Regarding themselves like God on the

---

* His revealing thoughts on the kulaks on his scraps of paper include: 'kulaks – deserters' then, even more suggestively: 'villages and slaves'. One peasant revealed how kulaks were selected: 'Just between the three of us, the poor peasants of the village get together in a meeting and decide: "So and so had six horses ..." They notify the GPU and there you are: So-and-so gets five years.' Only novelists and poets are really capable of catching the brutish alienation of the villages: Andrei Platonov's novel *The Foundation Pit* is the finest of these.

first day, they were creating a new world in a red-hot frenzy: the big beasts of the Politburo personified the qualities of the Stalinist Commissar, 'Partymindedness, morality, exactingness, attentiveness, good health, knowing their business well' but above all, as Stalin put it, they required, 'bull nerves'.

'I took part in this myself,' wrote a young activist, Lev Kopelev, 'scouring the countryside, searching for hidden grain ... I emptied out the old folks' storage chests, stopping my ears to the children's crying and the women's wails ... I was convinced I was accomplishing the great and necessary transformation of the countryside.'

The peasants believed they could force the Government to stop by destroying their own livestock: the despair that could lead a peasant to kill his own animals, the equivalent in our world of burning down our own house, gives a hint of the scale of desperation: 26.6 million head of cattle were slaughtered, 15.3 million horses. On 16 January 1930, the government decreed that kulak property could be confiscated if they destroyed livestock. If the peasants thought the Bolsheviks would be obliged to feed them, they were mistaken. As the crisis worsened, even Stalin's staunchest lieutenants struggled to squeeze the grain out of the peasantry, especially in the Ukraine and North Caucasus. Stalin berated them but even though they were often twenty years younger, they replied with tantrums and threats of resignation. Stalin was constantly pouring unction on troubled waters. Andrei Andreyev, thirty-five, the boss of the North Caucasus, was close to Stalin (his wife Dora was Nadya's best friend). None the less, he said Stalin's demands were impossible: he needed at least five years. First Molotov tried to encourage him:

'Dear Andreievich, I got your letter on grain supplies, I see it's very hard for you. I see also that the kulaks are using new methods of struggle against us. But I hope we'll break their backs ... I send you greetings and best wishes ... PS: Hurrying off to Crimea for the holidays.' Then Stalin, overwrought, lost his temper with Andreyev who sulked until Stalin apologized:

'Comrade Andreyev, I don't think you do nothing in the field of grain supply. But the grain supplies from the North Caucasus are cutting us like a knife and we need measures to strengthen the process. Please remember, every new million poods is very valuable for us. Please remember, we have very little time. So to work? With Communist greetings, Stalin.' But Andreyev was still upset so Stalin scribbled him another letter, this time calling him by a pet name and appealing to his Bolshevik honour:

'Hello Andryusha, I'm late. Don't be angry. About strategy ... I take my words back. I'd like to stress again that close people must be trusted and honourable until the end. I speak about our top people. Without this our Party will utterly fail. I shake your hand, J. Stalin.' He often had to take back his own words.

* * *

The foundation of Stalin's power in the Party was not fear: it was charm. Stalin possessed the dominant will among his magnates, but they also found his policies generally congenial. He was older than them all except President Kalinin, but the magnates used the informal 'you' with him. Voroshilov, Molotov and Sergo called him 'Koba'. They were sometimes even cheeky: Mikoyan, who called him Soso, signed one letter: 'If you're not lazy, write to me!' In 1930, all these magnates, especially the charismatic and fiery Sergo Ordzhonikidze, were allies, not protégés, all capable of independent action. There were close friendships that presented potential alliances against Stalin: Sergo and Kaganovich, the two toughest bosses, were best friends. Voroshilov, Mikoyan and Molotov frequently disagreed with Stalin. His dilemma was that he was the leader of a Party with no *Führerprinzip* but the ruler of a country accustomed to Tsarist autocracy.

Stalin was not the dreary bureaucrat that Trotsky wanted him to be. It was certainly true that he was a gifted organizer. He 'never improvised' but 'took every decision, weighing it carefully'. He was capable of working extraordinarily long hours – sixteen a day. But the new archives confirm that his real genius was something different – and surprising: 'he could charm people'. He was what is now known as a 'people person'. While incapable of true empathy on one hand, he was a master of friendships on the other. He constantly lost his temper, but when he set his mind to charming a man, he was irresistible.

Stalin's face was 'expressive and mobile', his feline movements 'supple and graceful', he buzzed with sensitive energy. Everyone who saw him 'was anxious to see him again' because 'he created a sense that there was now a bond that linked them forever'. Artyom said he made 'we children feel like adults and feel important'. Visitors were impressed with his quiet modesty, the puffing on the pipe, the calmness. When the future Marshal Zhukov first met him, he could not sleep afterwards: 'The appearance of JV Stalin, his quiet voice, the concreteness and depth of his judgements, the attention with which he heard the report made a great impression on me.' Sudoplatov, a Chekist, thought 'it was hard to imagine such a man could deceive you, his reactions were so natural, without the slightest sense of him posing' but he also noticed 'a certain harshness ... which he did not ... conceal'.

In the eyes of these rough Bolsheviks from the regions, his flat quiet public speaking was an asset, a great improvement on Trotsky's oratorical wizardry. Stalin's lack of smoothness, his anti-oratory, inspired trust. His very faults, the chip on the shoulder, the brutality and fits of irrational temper, were the Party's faults. 'He was not trusted but he was the man the Party trusted,' admitted Bukharin. 'He's like the symbol of the Party, the lower strata trust him.' But above all, reflected the future secret police chief, Beria, he was 'supremely intelligent', a political 'genius'. However rude or charming he was, 'he dominated his entourage with his intelligence'.

He did not just socialize with the magnates: he patronized junior officials too, constantly searching for tougher, more loyal, and more tireless lieutenants. He was always accessible: 'I'm ready to help you and receive you,' he often replied to requests. Officials got through directly to Stalin. Those lower down called him, behind his back, the *Khozyain* which is usually translated as 'Boss', but it means much more: the 'Master'. Nicholas II had called himself '*Khozyain* of the Russian lands'. When Stalin heard someone use the word, he was 'noticeably irritated' by its feudal mystique: 'That sounds like a rich landowner in Central Asia. Fool!'

His magnates saw him as their patron but he saw himself as much more. 'I know you're diabolically busy,' Molotov wrote to him on his birthday. 'But I shake your fifty-year-old hand ... I must say in my personal work I'm obliged to you ...' They were all obliged to him. But Stalin saw his own role embroidered with both Arthurian chivalry and Christian sanctity: 'You need have no doubt, comrades, I am prepared to devote to the cause of the working class ... all my strength, all my ability, and if need be, all my blood, drop by drop,' he wrote to thank the Party for acclaiming him as leader. 'Your congratulations, I place to the credit of the great Party ... which bore me and reared me in its own image and likeness.' Here was how he saw himself.

None the less, this self-anointed Messianic hero worked hard to envelop his protégés in an irresistible embrace of folksy intimacy that convinced them there was no one he trusted more. Stalin was mercurial but far from a humourless drone: he was convivial and entertaining, if exhaustingly intense. 'He was such fun,' says Artyom. According to the Yugoslav Communist Milovan Djilas, his 'rough ... self-assured humour' was 'roguish' and 'impish' but 'not entirely without finesse and depth' though it was never far from the gallows. His dry wit was acute but hardly Wildean. Once when Kozlovsky, the court tenor, was performing at the Kremlin, the Politburo started demanding some particular song.

'Why put pressure on Comrade Kozlovsky?' intervened Stalin calmly. 'Let him sing what he wants.' He paused. 'And I think he wants to sing Lensky's aria from *Onegin*.' Everyone laughed and Kozlovsky obediently sang the aria.*

When Stalin appointed Isakov Naval Commissar, the admiral replied that it was too arduous because he only had one leg. Since the Navy had been 'commanded by people without heads, one leg's no handicap', quipped Stalin. He was particularly keen on mocking the pretensions of the ruling caste: when a list of tedious worthies recommended for medals landed on his desk, he wrote across it:

'Shitters get the Order of Lenin!' He enjoyed practical jokes. During the Italian invasion of Ethiopia, he ordered his bodyguards to get 'Ras Kasa on the phone at once!' When a young guard returned 'half-dead with worry', to explain that he could not get this Abyssinian mountain chieftain on the line, Stalin laughed:

'And you're in security!' He was capable of pungent repartee. Zinoviev accused him of ingratitude: 'Gratitude's a dog's disease,' he snapped back.

Stalin 'knew everything about his closest comrades – EVERYTHING!' stresses the daughter of one of them, Natasha Andreyeva. He watched his protégés, educated them, brought them to Moscow and took immense trouble with them: he

---

* At the Bolshoi, Kozlovsky suddenly lost his voice during Rigoletto. The singer peered helplessly up towards Stalin's Box A, pointing at his throat. Quick as a flash, Stalin silently pointed at the left side of his tunic near the pocket where medals are pinned and painted a medal. Kozlovsky's voice returned. He got the medal.

promoted Mikoyan, but told Bukharin and Molotov that he thought the Armenian 'still a duckling in politics ... If he grows up, he'll improve.' The Politburo was filled with fiery egomaniacs such as Sergo Ordzhonikidze: Stalin was adept at coaxing, charming, manipulating and bullying them into doing his bidding. When he summoned two of his ablest men, Sergo and Mikoyan, from the Caucasus, they argued with him and each other but his patience in soothing (and baiting) them was endless.

Stalin personally oversaw their living arrangements. In 1913, when he stayed in Vienna with the Troyanovsky family, he gave the daughter of the house a bag of sweets every day. Then he asked the child's mother: to whom would the child run if they both called? When they tried it, she ran to Stalin hoping for some more sweets. This idealistic cynic used the same incentives with the Politburo. When Sergo moved to Moscow, Stalin lent him his apartment. When Sergo loved the apartment, Stalin simply gave it to him. When young, provincial Beria visited Moscow for the Seventeenth Congress, Stalin himself put his ten-year-old son to bed at Zubalovo. When he popped into the flats of the Politburo, Maya Kaganovich remembered him insisting they light their fire. 'No detail was too small.' Every gift suited the recipient: he gave his Cossack ally Budyonny swords with inscribed blades. He personally distributed the cars and latest gadgets.* There is a list in the archives in Stalin's handwriting assigning each car to every leader: their wives and daughters wrote thank-you letters to him.

Then there was money: these magnates were often short of money because wages were paid on the basis of the 'Party Maximum', which meant that a 'responsible worker' could not earn more than a highly-paid worker. Even before Stalin abolished this in 1934, there were ways round it. Food hampers from the Kremlin canteen and special rations from the GORT (government) stores were delivered to each leader. But they also

* Kirov, his Leningrad boss, lived in a huge apartment containing a dazzling array of the latest equipment. First there was a huge new American fridge – a General Electric – of which only ten were imported into the USSR. American gramophones were specially prized: there was a 'radiola' on which Kirov could listen to the Mariinsky Ballet in his apartment; there was a 'petiphone', a wind-up gramophone without a speaker, and one with a speaker, plus a lamp radio. When the first television reached Moscow just before the war, the Mikoyans received the alien object that reflected the picture in a glass that stuck out at forty-five degrees. As for Budyonny, Stalin wrote: 'I gave you the sword but it's not a very beautiful one so I decided to send you a better one inscribed – it's on its way!'

received *pakets*, secret gifts of money, like a banker's bonus or cash in a brown envelope, and coupons for holidays. The sums were nominally decided by President Kalinin, and the Secretary of the Central Executive Committee, the major-domo of all the goodies, Yenukidze, but Stalin took great interest in these *pakets*. In the archives, Stalin underlined the amounts in a list headed 'Money Gifts from Funds of Presidium for group of responsible workers and members of their families'. 'Interesting numbers!' he wrote on it. When he noticed that his staff were short of money, he secretly intervened to help them, procuring publishing royalties for his chief secretary, Tovstukha. He wrote to the publishing chief that if Tovstukha denied he was skint, 'he's lying. He's desperately short of money.' It used to be regarded as ironic to call the Soviet élite an 'aristocracy' but they were much more like a feudal service nobility whose privileges were totally dependent on their loyalty.

Just when these potentates needed to be harsher than ever, some were becoming soft and decadent, particularly those with access to the luxuries like Yenukidze and the secret policeman Yagoda. Furthermore, the regional bosses built up their own entourages and became so powerful that Stalin called them 'Grand Dukes'. But there was no Party 'prince' as beneficent as he himself, the patron of patrons.

The party was not just a mass of self-promoting groups – it was almost a family business. Whole clans were members of the leadership: Kaganovich was the youngest of five brothers, three of whom were high Bolsheviks. Stalin's in-laws were all senior officials. Sergo's brothers were both top Bolsheviks in the Caucasus where family units were the norm. A tangle of inter-marriage* complicated the power relationships and would have fatal results: when one leader fell, everyone linked to him disappeared with him into the abyss like mountaineers tied together with one safety rope.

The backs of the peasants, in Stalin and Molotov's chilling phrase, were indeed being broken but the scale of the struggle shook even their most ruthless supporters. In mid-February 1930, Sergo and Kalinin travelled to inspect the countryside and returned to call a halt. Sergo, who as head of the Party Control

---

* For example, Kamenev's wife was Trotsky's sister; Yagoda was married into the Sverdlov family; Poskrebyshev, Stalin's secretary, was married to the sister of Trotsky's daughter-in-law. Two top Stalinists, Shcherbakov and Zhdanov, were brothers-in-law. Later the children of the Politburo would intermarry.

Commission, had orchestrated the campaign against the Rightists, now ordered the Ukraine to stop 'socializing' livestock.

Stalin had lost control. The masterful tactician bowed before the magnates and agreed to retreat – with resentful prudence. On 2 March, he wrote his famous article 'Dizzy with Success', in which he claimed success and blamed local officials for his own mistakes, which relieved the pressure* in the villages.

Stalin had regarded his allies as his 'tightest circle' of 'friends', a brotherhood 'formed historically in the struggle against ... the opportunism' of Trotsky and Bukharin. But he now sensed the Politburo was riddled with doubt and disloyalty as the 'Stalin Revolution' turned the countryside into a dystopian nightmare. Even in stormy times, Politburo meetings, at midday on Thursday round the two parallel tables in the map-covered Sovnarkom Room in the Yellow Palace, could be surprisingly light-hearted. Stalin never chaired the Politburo, leaving that to the Premier, Rykov. He was careful never to speak first, according to Mikoyan, so that no one was tied by his opinion before they had stated their own.

There was much scribbling across the table at these meetings. Bukharin, before he lost his place, drew caricatures of all the leaders, often in ludicrous poses with rampant erections or in Tsarist uniforms. They were always teasing Voroshilov for his vanity and stupidity even though this hero of the Civil War was one of Stalin's closest allies. 'Hi friend!' Stalin addressed him fondly. 'Pity you're not in Moscow. When are you coming?'

'Vain as a woman', no one liked uniforms more than Voroshilov. This proletarian boulevardier who sported white flannels at his sumptuous dacha, and full whites for tennis, was a jolly Epicurean, 'amiable and fun-loving, fond of music, parties and literature,' enjoying the company of actors and writers. Stalin heard that he was wearing his wife's scarf because of a midsummer cold: 'Of course, he loves himself so much that he takes great care of himself. Ha! He even does exercises!' laughed Stalin. 'Notoriously stupid', Voroshilov rarely saw a stick without getting the wrong end of it.

A locksmith from Lugansk (renamed Voroshilov), he had, like many of Stalin's leaders, barely completed two years at school. A Party member since 1903, Klim had shared a room with Stalin in Stockholm in 1906 but they had become friends at Tsaritsyn.

* In Sholokhov's novel, *Virgin Soil Upturned*, the Cossacks call off their revolt when they read it. But they also withdraw from the collective farm.

Henceforth Stalin backed this 'Commander-in-Chief from the lathe' all the way to become Defence Commissar in 1925. Out of his depth, Voroshilov loathed more sophisticated military minds with the inferiority complex that was one of the moving passions of Stalin's circle. Ever since he had delivered mail on horseback to the miners of Lugansk, his mind was more at home with the equine than the mechanized.

Usually described as a snivelling coward before his master, he had flirted with the oppositions and was perfectly capable of losing his temper with Stalin whom he always treated like an old buddy. He was only slightly younger than Koba and continued to call a spade a spade even after the Terror. Fair-haired, pink-cheeked, warm eyes twinkling, he was sweet-natured: the courage of this *beau sabreur* was peerless. Yet beneath his cherubic affability, there was something mean about the lips that revealed a petulant temper, vindictive cruelty, and a taste for violent solutions.* Once convinced, he was 'narrow-minded politically', pursuing his orders with rigid obedience.

His cult was second only to Stalin's: even in the West, the novelist Denis Wheatley published a panegyric entitled *The Red Eagle* – 'the amazing story of the pitboy who beat professional soldiers of three nations and is now Warlord of Russia.'

In one note passed round the table, Voroshilov wrote: 'I cannot make the speech to the brake-makers because of my headache.'

'To let off Voroshilov, I propose Rudzutak,' replied Stalin, suggesting another Politburo member.

But Voroshilov was not escaping so easily: Rudzutak refused so Kalinin suggested letting him off, providing Voroshilov did the speech after all.

'Against!' voted Voroshilov, signing himself: 'Voroshilov who has the headache and cannot speak!'

If Stalin approved of a leader's speech, he sent an enthusiastically scatological note: 'A world leader, FUCK HIS MOTHER! I've read your report – you criticized everyone – fuck their mother!' he wrote approvingly to Voroshilov who wanted more praise:

'Tell me more clearly – did I fail 100% or only 75%?' Stalin retorted in his inimitable style: 'it was a good … report. You

---

* 'You know Marapultsa,' Voroshilov wrote to Stalin in October 1930. 'He was condemned for five years … I think you agree with me that he was condemned rightly.' On another occasion, Voroshilov appealed to Stalin for a 'semi-lunatic' he had known since 1911 who was in jail. 'What do I want you to do? Almost nothing … but for you to consider for one minute the destruction of Minin and decide what to do with him …'

smacked the arses of Hoover, Chamberlain and Bukharin. Stalin.'

Serious questions were decided too: during a budget discussion, Stalin verbally nudged Voroshilov to stand up for his department: 'They're robbing you but you're silent.' When his colleagues went back to discuss something Stalin thought had already been decided, they received this across the table: 'What does this mean? Yesterday we agreed one thing about the speech but today another. Disorganization! Stalin.' Appointments were made in this way too. Their tone was often playful: Voroshilov wanted to inspect the army in Central Asia:

'Koba, can I go …? They say they're forgotten.'

'England will whine that Voroshilov has come to attack India,' replied Stalin, who wanted to avoid all foreign entanglements while he industrialized Russia.

'I'll be as quiet as a mouse,' Voroshilov persisted.

'That's worse. They'll find out and say Voroshilov came secretly with criminal intent,' scrawled Stalin. When it came to appointing Mikoyan to run Trade, Voroshilov asked,

'Koba, should we give Fishing to Mikoyan? Would he do it?' The members often bargained for appointments. Hence Voroshilov proposed to Kuibyshev, 'I was first to propose the candidature of Pyatakov in conversation with Molotov and Kaganovich, and I'll support you as your second …'

The Politburo could sit for hours, exhausting even Stalin:

'Listen,' he wrote to Voroshilov during one session, 'let's put it off until Wednesday evening. Today's no good. Already it's 4.30 and we've still got 3 big questions to get through … Stalin.' Sometimes Stalin wrote wearily: 'Military matters are so serious they must be discussed seriously but my head's not capable of serious work today.'

However, Stalin realized that the Politburo could easily unite to dismiss him. Rykov, the Rightist Premier, did not believe in his plans and now Kalinin too was wavering. Stalin knew he could be outvoted, even overthrown.* The new archives reveal how openly Kalinin argued with Stalin.

* They frequently disagreed with him, certainly on small matters such as a discussion about the Kremlin military school: 'Seems that after the objections of Comrade Kalinin and others (I know other Politburo members object too), we can forgive them because it's not an important question,' Stalin wrote to Voroshilov. Having defeated Bukharin in 1929, Stalin wanted to appoint him Education Commissar but as Voroshilov told Sergo in a letter, 'Because we were a united majority, we pushed it through (against Koba).'

"You defend the kulaks?' scribbled Stalin. He pushed it across the table to Papa Kalinin, that mild-mannered former peasant with round spectacles, goatee beard and droopy moustache.

'Not the kulaks,' Kalinin wrote back, 'but the trading peasant.'

'But did you forget about the poorest ones?' Stalin scrawled back. 'Did you ignore the Russian peasantry?'

'The middling sort are very Russian but what about non-Russians? They're the poorest,' argued Kalinin.

'Now you're the Bashkir President not the Russian one!' Stalin chided him.

'That's not an argument, that's a curse!' Stalin's curse did descend on those who opposed him during this greatest crisis. He never forgot Kalinin's betrayal. Every criticism was a battle for survival, a question of sin versus goodness, disease versus health, for this thin-skinned, neurotic egotist on his Messianic mission. During these months, he brooded on the disloyalty of those around him, for his family and his political allies were utterly interwoven. Stalin had every reason to feel paranoid. Indeed the Bolsheviks believed that paranoia, which they called 'vigilance', was an almost religious duty. Later Stalin was to talk privately about the 'holy fear' that kept even him on his toes.

His paranoia was part of a personal vicious circle that was to prove so deadly for many who knew him, yet it was understandable. His radical policies led to excessive repressions that led to the opposition he most feared. His unbalanced reactions produced a world in which he had reason to be fearful. In public he reacted to all this with a dry humour and modest tranquillity but one finds ample evidence of his hysterical reactions in private. 'You cannot silence me or keep my opinion confined inside,' Stalin wrote to Voroshilov during the struggles with the Rightists, 'yet you claim "I want to teach everyone." When will these attacks on me end? Stalin.' It extended to the family. One of his letters to Nadya went missing. Stalin was obsessed with the secrecy of his letters and travel plans. He impulsively blamed his mother-in-law but Nadya defended her: 'You unfairly accused Mama. It turns out the letter was never delivered to anyone ... She's in Tiflis.'

Nadya laughed that the students at the Academy were divided into 'Kulaks, middle-peasants and poor peasants', but she was joking about the liquidation of over a million innocent women and children. There is evidence that Nadya happily informed

Stalin about his enemies, yet that was changing. The rural struggle divided their friends: her adored Bukharin and Yenukidze confided their doubts to her. Her fellow students had 'put me down as a Rightist,' she joked to Stalin, who would have been troubled that they were getting to his wife at a time when he was entering stormy waters indeed.

* * *

On holiday in the south, Stalin learned that Riutin, an Old Bolshevik who had been in charge of Cinema, was trying to create an opposition to dismiss him. He reacted fast to Molotov on 13 September: 'with regard to Riutin, it seems it's impossible to limit ourselves to expelling him from the Party ... he will have to be expelled somewhere as far as possible from Moscow. This counter-revolutionary scum* should be completely disarmed.' Simultaneously, Stalin arranged a series of show trials and 'conspiracies' by so-called 'wreckers'. Stalin redoubled the push for collectivization and race to industrialize at red-hot speed. As the tension rose, he stoked the martial atmosphere, inventing new enemies to intimidate his real opponents in the Party and among the technical experts who said it could not be done.

Stalin frantically ordered Molotov to publish all the testimonies of the 'wreckers' immediately and then 'after a week, announce that all these scoundrels will be executed by firing squad. They should all be shot.'

Then he turned to attacking the Rightists in the Government. He ordered a campaign against currency speculation which he blamed on Rykov's Finance Commissars, those 'doubtful Communists' Pyatakov and Briukhanov. Stalin wanted blood and he ordered the cultivated OGPU boss, Menzhinsky, to arrest more wreckers. He told Molotov 'to shoot two or three dozen saboteurs infiltrated into these offices'.

Stalin made a joke of this at the Politburo. When the leaders criticized Briukhanov, Stalin scribbled to Valery Mezhlauk, reporting on behalf of Gosplan, the economic planning agency:

'For all new, existing and future sins to be hung by the balls, and if the balls are strong and don't break, to forgive him and think him correct but if they break, then to throw him into the river.' Mezhlauk was also an accomplished cartoonist and drew a picture of this particular torture, testicles and all. Doubtless

* *Nechist* means an unclean devil in peasant folklore.

everyone laughed uproariously. But Briukhanov was sacked and later destroyed.

That summer of 1930, as the Sixteenth Congress crowned Stalin as leader, Nadya was suffering from a serious internal illness – so he sent her to Carlsbad for the best medical treatment and to Berlin to see her brother Pavel and his wife Zhenya. Her medical problems were complex, mysterious and probably psychosomatic. Nadya's medical records, that Stalin preserved, reveal that at various times, she suffered 'acute abdominal pains' probably caused by her earlier abortion. Then there were the headaches as fierce as migraines that may have been symptoms of synostosis, a disease in which the cranial bones merge together, or they may simply have been caused by her earlier stress of internal war within the USSR. Even though he was frantically busy arranging the Congress and fighting enemies in the villages and the Politburo, Stalin was never more tender.

4

Famine and the Country Set:
Stalin at the Weekend

'Tatka! What was the journey like, what did you see, have you been to the doctors, what do they say about your health? Write and tell me,' he wrote on 21 June. 'We start the Congress on the 26th ... Things aren't going too badly. I miss you ... come home soon. I kiss you.' As soon as the Congress was over, he wrote: 'Tatka! I got all three letters. I couldn't reply, I was too busy. Now at last I'm free ... Don't be too long coming home. But stay longer if your health makes it necessary ... I kiss you.'

* * *

In the summer, Stalin, backed by the formidable Sergo, guided one of his faked conspiracies, the so-called 'Industrial Party' to implicate President Kalinin, and seems to have used evidence that 'Papa', a ladies' man, was wasting State funds on a ballerina. The President begged for forgiveness.

Stalin and Menzhinsky were in constant communication about other conspiracies too. Stalin worried about the loyalty of the Red Army. The OGPU forced two officers to testify against the Chief of Staff, Tukhachevsky, that gifted, dashing commander who had been Stalin's bitter enemy since the Polish War of 1920. Tukhachevsky was hated by the less sophisticated officers who complained to Voroshilov that the arrogant commander 'makes fun of us' with his 'grandiose plans'. Stalin agreed they were 'fantastical', and so over-ambitious as to be almost counter-revolutionary.

The OGPU interrogations accused Tukhachevsky of planning a coup against the Politburo. In 1930, this was perhaps too outrageous even for the Bolsheviks. Stalin, not yet dictator, probed his powerful ally, Sergo: 'Only Molotov, myself and now you are in the know ... Is it possible? What a business! Discuss it with Molotov ...' However Sergo would not go that far. There would be no arrest and trial of Tukhachevsky in 1930: the commander 'turns out to be 100% clean', Stalin wrote disingenuously to Molotov in October. 'That's very good.' It is interesting that seven years before the Great Terror, Stalin was testing the same accusations against the same victims – a dress rehearsal for 1937 – but he could not get the support. The archives reveal a fascinating sequel: once he understood the ambitious modernity of Tukhachevsky's strategies, Stalin apologized to him: 'Now the question has become clearer to me, I have to agree that my remark was too strong and my conclusions were not right at all.'

* * *

Nadya returned from Carlsbad and joined Stalin on holiday. Brooding how to bring Rykov and Kalinin to heel, Stalin did not make Nadya feel welcome. 'I did not feel you wanted me to prolong my stay, quite the contrary,' wrote Nadya. She left for Moscow where the Molotovs, ever the busybodies of the Kremlin, 'scolded' her for 'leaving you alone', as she angrily reported to Stalin. Stalin was irritated by the Molotovs, and Nadya's feeling that she was unwelcome:

'Tell Molotov, he's wrong. To reproach you, making you worry about me, can only be done by someone who doesn't know my business.' Then she heard from her godfather that Stalin was delaying his return until October. Stalin explained that he had lied to Yenukidze to confuse his enemies:

'Tatka, I started that rumour ... for reasons of secrecy. Only Tatka, Molotov and maybe Sergo know the date of my arrival.'

Close to Molotov and Sergo, Stalin no longer trusted one of his closest friends who sympathized with the Rightists: Nadya's godfather, 'Uncle Abel' Yenukidze. Nicknamed 'Tonton', this veteran conspirator, at fifty three, two years older than Stalin, had known Koba and the Alliluyevs since the turn of the century. Another ex-Tiflis Seminarist, in 1904, he had created the secret Bolshevik printing press in Batumi. He was never ambitious and was said to have turned down promotion to the Politburo, but he was everyone's friend, bearing no grudges against the defeated oppositions, always ready to help old pals. This easy-going Georgian sybarite was well-connected in the military, the Party, and the Caucasus, personifying the incestuous tangle of Bolshevism: he had had an affair with Ekaterina Voroshilova before her marriage. Yet Stalin still enjoyed Yenukidze's companionship: 'Hello Abel! What the devil keeps you in Moscow? Come to Sochi ...'

Meanwhile, Stalin turned on Premier Rykov, whose drinking

was so heavy that in Kremlin circles, vodka was called 'Rykovka'.

'What to do about Rykov (who uncontestably helped them) and Kalinin ...?' he wrote to Molotov on 2 September. 'No doubt Kalinin has sinned ... The CC must be informed to teach Kalinin never to get mixed up with such rascals again.'

Kalinin was forgiven – but the warning was clear: he never crossed Stalin again, a political husk, a craven rubber stamp for all Stalin's outrages. Yet Stalin liked Papa Kalinin and enjoyed the pretty girls at his parties in Sochi. The success of his 'handsome' charms soon reached the half-indulgent, half-jealous Nadya in Moscow.

'I heard from a young and pretty woman,' she wrote, 'that you looked handsome at Kalinin's dinner, you were remarkably jolly, made them all laugh, though they were shy in your august presence.'

On 13 September, Stalin mused to Molotov that 'our summit of state is afflicted with a terrible sickness ... It is necessary to take measures. But what? I'll talk to you when I return to Moscow ...' He posed much the same thought to other members of the Politburo. They suggested Stalin for Rykov's job:

'Dear Koba,' wrote Voroshilov, 'Mikoyan, Kaganovich, Kuibyshev and I think the best result would be the unification of the leadership of Sovnarkom and to appoint you to it as you want to take the leadership with all strength. This isn't like 1918–21 but Lenin did lead the Sovnarkom.' Kaganovich insisted it had to be Stalin. Sergo agreed. Mikoyan wrote too that in the Ukraine 'they destroyed their harvest last year – very dangerous ... Nowadays we nead strong leadership from a single leader as it was in Illich [Lenin's] time and the best decision is you to be the candidate for the Chairmanship ... Doesn't all of mankind know who's the ruler of our country?'

Yet no one had ever held the posts of both General Secretary and Premier. Furthermore, could a foreigner,* a Georgian, formally lead the country? So Kaganovich backed Stalin's nominee, Molotov.

'You should replace Rykov,' Stalin told Molotov.

On 21 October, Stalin uncovered more betrayal: Sergei Syrtsov, candidate Politburo member and one of his protégés, was

---

* Lenin himself had governed as Premier (Chairman of Sovnarkom) from 1917 to 1924. On his death, his natural successor, Kamenev, had not succeeded to the post as a Jew not a Russian. Hence Rykov got the job.

denounced for plotting against him. Denunciation was already a daily part of the Bolshevik ritual and a duty – Stalin's files are filled with such letters. Syrtsov was summoned to the Central Committee. He implicated the First Secretary of the Transcaucasus Party, Beso Lominadze, an old friend of both Stalin and Sergo. Lominadze admitted secret meetings but claimed he only disapproved of comparing Stalin to Lenin. As ever, Stalin reacted melodramatically:

'It's unimaginable vileness … They played at staging a coup, they played at being the Politburo and plumbed the lowest depths…' Then, after this eruption, Stalin asked Molotov: 'How are things going for you?'

Sergo wanted them expelled from the Party but Stalin, who understood already from his probings about Tukhachevsky, that his position was not strong enough yet, just had them expelled from the Central Committee. There is a small but important post-script to this: Sergo Ordzhonikidze protected his friend Lominadze by not revealing all his letters to the CC. Instead he went to Stalin and offered them to him personally. Stalin was shocked – why not the CC? 'Because I gave him my word,' said Sergo.

'How could you?' replied Stalin, adding later that Sergo had behaved not like a Bolshevik but 'like … a prince. I told him I did not want to be part of his secret …' Later, this would assume a terrible significance.

On 19 December, a Plenum gathered to consolidate Stalin's victories over his opponents. Plenums were the sittings of the all-powerful Central Committee, which Stalin compared to an 'Areopagus', in the huge converted hall in the Great Kremlin Palace with dark wood panelling and pews like a grim Puritan church. This was where the central magnates and regional viceroys, who ruled swathes of the country as First Secretaries of republics and cities, met like a medieval Council of Barons. These meetings most resembled the chorus of a vicious evangelical meeting with constant interjections of 'Right!' or 'Brutes!' or just laughter. This was one of the last Plenums where the old Bolshevik tradition of intellectual argument and wit still played a part. Voroshilov and Kaganovich clashed with Bukharin who was playing his role of supporting Stalin's line now that his own Rightists had been defeated:

'We're right to crush the most dangerous Rightist deviation,' said Bukharin.

'And those infected with it!' called out Voroshilov.

'If you're talking about their physical destruction, I leave it to those comrades who are ... given to bloodthirstyness.' There was laughter but the jokes were becoming sinister. It was still unthinkable for the inner circle to be touched physically, yet Kaganovich pressured Stalin to be tougher on the opposition while Voroshilov demanded 'the Procurator must be a very active organ ...'

The Plenum sacked Rykov as Premier and appointed Molotov.* Sergo joined the Politburo and took over the Supreme Economic Council, the industrial colossus that ran the entire Five-Year Plan. He was the ideal bulldozer to force through industrialization. The new promotions and aggressive push to complete the Plan in four years unleashed a welter of rows between these potentates. They defended their own commissariats and supporters. When they changed jobs they tended to change allegiances: as Chairman of the Control Commission, Sergo had backed the campaigns against saboteurs and wreckers in industry. The moment he took over Industry, he defended his specialists. Sergo started constantly rowing with Molotov, whom he 'didn't love much', over his budgets. There was no radical group: some were more extreme at different times. Stalin himself, the chief organizer of Terror, meandered his way to his revolution.

Stalin refereed the arguments that became so vicious that Kuibyshev, Sergo and Mikoyan all threatened to resign, defending their posts: 'Dear Stalin,' wrote Mikoyan coldly, 'Your two telegrams disappointed me so much that I couldn't work for two days. I can take any criticism ... except being accused of being disloyal to the CC and you ... Without your personal support, I can't work as Narkom Supply and Trade ... Better to find a new candidate but give me some other job ...' Stalin apologized to Mikoyan and he often had to apologize to the others too. Dictators do not need to apologize. Meanwhile Andreyev returned from Rostov to head the disciplinary Control Commission while Kaganovich, just thirty-seven, became Stalin's Deputy Secretary, joining the General Secretary and Premier Molotov in a ruling triumvirate.

* Stalin proudly advertised this to the novelist Maxim Gorky in Italy: 'He's a brave, clever, quite modern leader – his real name is Scriabin.' (Did Stalin, always an intellectual snob, add the 'Scriabin' to impress Gorky with Molotov's false association with the composer to whom he was not related?)

* * *

'Brash and masculine', tall and strong with black hair, long eyelashes and 'fine brown eyes', Lazar Moisevich Kaganovich was a workaholic always playing with amber worry beads or a key chain. Trained as a cobbler with minimal primary education, he looked first at a man's boots. If he was impressed with their workmanship, he sometimes forced them to take them off so he could admire them on his desk where he still kept a specially engraved tool set, presented to him by grateful workers.

The very model of a macho modern manager, Kaganovich had an explosive temper like his friend Sergo. Happiest with a hammer in his hand, he often hit his subordinates or lifted them up by their lapels – yet politically he was cautious, 'quick and clever'. He constantly clashed with plodding Molotov who regarded him as 'coarse, tough and straitlaced, very energetic, a good organizer, who floundered on ... theory' but was the leader 'most devoted to Stalin'. Despite the strong Jewish accent, Sergo believed he was their best orator: 'He really captured the audience!' A boisterous manager so tough and forceful that he was nicknamed 'The Locomotive', Kaganovich 'not only knew how to apply pressure', said Molotov, 'but he was something of a ruffian himself.' He 'could get things done,' said Khrushchev. 'If the CC put an axe in his hands, he'd chop up a storm' but destroy the 'healthy trees with the rotten ones'. Stalin called him 'Iron Lazar'.

Born in November 1893 in a hut in the remote village of Kabana in the Ukrainian-Belorussian borderlands into a poor, Orthodox Jewish family of five brothers and one sister, who all slept in one room, Lazar, the youngest, was recruited into the Party by his brother in 1911 and agitated in the Ukraine under the unlikely name of 'Kosherovich'.

Lenin singled him out as a rising leader: he was far more impressive than he seemed. Constantly reading in his huge library, educating himself with Tsarist history textbooks (and the novels of Balzac and Dickens), this 'worker-intellectual' was the brains behind the militarization of the Party state. In 1918 aged twenty-four, he ran and terrorized Nizhny Novgorod. In 1919 he demanded a tight dictatorship, urging the military discipline of 'Centralism'. In 1924, writing in clear but fanatical prose, it was he who designed the machinery of what became 'Stalinism'. After running the appointments section of the CC, 'Iron Lazar' was sent to run Central Asia then, in 1925, the Ukraine, before returning in 1928, joining the Politburo as a full member at the Sixteenth Congress in 1930.

Kaganovich and his wife Maria met romantically on a secret mission when these young Bolsheviks had to pretend to be married: they found their roles easy to play because they fell in love and got married. They were so happy together that they always held hands even sitting in Politburo limousines, bringing up their daughter and adopted son in a loving, rather Jewish household. Humorous and emotional, Lazar was an athlete who skied and rode, but he possessed the most pusillanimous instinct for self-preservation. As a Jew, Kaganovich was aware of his vulnerability and Stalin was equally sensitive in protecting his comrade from anti-Semitism.

Kaganovich was the first true Stalinist, coining the word during a dinner at Zubalovo. 'Everyone keeps talking about Lenin and Leninism but Lenin's been gone a long time ... Long live Stalinism!'

'How dare you say that?' retorted Stalin modestly. 'Lenin was a tall tower and Stalin a little finger.' But Kaganovich treated Stalin far more reverently than Sergo or Mikoyan: he was, said Molotov disdainfully, '200% Stalinist'. He so admired the *Vozhd*, he admitted, that 'when I go to Stalin, I try not to forget a thing! I so worry every time. I prepare every document in my briefcase and I fill my pockets with cribs like a schoolboy because no one knows what Stalin's going to ask.' Stalin reacted to Kaganovich's schoolboyish respect by teaching him how to spell and punctuate, even when he was so powerful: 'I've reread your letter,' Kaganovich wrote to Stalin in 1931, 'and realize that I haven't carried out your directive to master punctuation marks. I'd started but haven't quite managed it, but I can do it despite my burden of work. I'll try to have full-stops and commas in future letters.' He respected Stalin as Russia's own 'Robespierre' and refused to call him by the intimate 'thou': 'Did you ever call Lenin "thou"?'

His brutality was more important than his punctuation: he had recently crushed peasant uprisings from the North Caucasus to western Siberia. Succeeding Molotov as Moscow boss and the hero of a cult approaching Stalin's own, Iron Lazar began the vandalistic creation of a Bolshevik metropolis, enthusiastically dynamiting historic buildings.

By the summer of 1931, a serious shortage in the countryside was beginning to develop into a famine. While the Politburo softened its campaign against industrial specialists in mid-July, the rural struggle continued. The GPU and the 180,000 Party workers sent from cities used the gun, the lynch mob and the Gulag camp system to break the villages. Over two million were deported to Siberia or Kazakhstan; in 1930, there were 179,000 slaving in the Gulags; almost a million by 1935. Terror and forced labour became the essence of Politburo business. On a sheet covered in doodles, Stalin scrawled in a thick blue pencil:

1. Who can do the arrests?
2. What to do with ex-White military in our industrial factories?
3. Prisons must be emptied of prisoners. [He wanted them sentenced faster to make room for kulaks.]
4. What to do with different groups arrested?
5. To allow ... deportations: Ukraine 145,000. N. Caucasus 71,000. Lower Volga 50,000 (a lot!), Belorussia 42,000 ... West Siberia 50,000, East Siberia 30,000 ...'

On and on it goes until he totals it up to 418,000 exiles. Meanwhile he totted up the poods of grain and bread by hand on pieces of paper,* like a village shopkeeper running an empire.

* * *

'Let's get out of town,' scrawled Stalin, around this time to Voroshilov, who replied on the same note:

'Koba, can you see ... Kalmykov for five minutes?'

'I can,' answered Stalin. 'Let's head out of town and take him with us.' The war of extermination in the countryside in no way restrained the magnates' country-house existence. They had been assigned dachas soon after the Revolution where, often, the real power was brokered.

At the centre of this idyllic life was Zubalovo, near Usovo, 35 kilometres outside Moscow, where Stalin and several others had their dachas. Before the Revolution, a Baku oil nabob named Zubalov had built two walled estates, each with a mansion, one for his son, one for himself. There were four houses altogether, gabled Gothic dachas of German design. The Mikoyans shared the Big House at Zubalovo Two with a Red Army commander, a Polish

---

* Throughout his career, he would keep the crown jewels as it were, the Soviet gold reserve or the number of tanks in his reserve at the Battle of Moscow in 1941, scribbled in his personal notebook. He took a special interest in gold production, which was mostly by forced labour.

Communist and Pavel Alliluyev. Voroshilov and other commanders shared a Little House. Their wives and children constantly visited one another – the extended family of the Revolution enjoying a Chekhovian summer.

Stalin's Zubalovo One was a magical world for the children. 'It was a real life of freedom,' recalls Artyom. 'Such happiness,' thought Svetlana. The parents lived upstairs, the children downstairs. The gardens were 'sunny and abundant', wrote Svetlana. Stalin was an enthusiastic gardener though he preferred inspecting and clipping roses to real labour. Photographs show him taking his little children for strolls round the gardens. There was a library, a billiard room, a Russian bath and later a cinema. Svetlana adored this 'happy sheltered life' with its vegetable gardens, orchards and a farm where they milked cows and fed geese, chickens and guinea fowl, cats and white rabbits. 'We had huge white lilacs, dark purple lilacs, jasmine which my mother loved, and a very fragrant shrub with a lemony smell. We walked in the woods with nanny. Picked wild strawberries and blackcurrants and cherries.'

'Stalin's house,' remembers Artyom, 'was full of friends.' Nadya's parents Sergei and Olga were always there – though they now lived apart. They stayed at different ends of the house but bickered at table. While Sergei enjoyed mending anything in the house and was friendly with the servants, Olga, according to Svetlana, 'threw herself into the role of grand lady and loved her high position which my mother never did'.

Nadya played tennis with an immaculate Voroshilov, when he was sober, and Kaganovich, who played in his tunic and boots. Mikoyan, Voroshilov and Budyonny* rode horses brought from the army's cavalry. If it was winter, Kaganovich and Mikoyan skied. Molotov pulled his daughter in a sledge like a nag pulling a peasant's plough. Voroshilov and Sergo were avid hunters. Stalin

---

* The Red Army's Inspector of Cavalry, Semyon Budyonny, born on the Cossack Don, was a former sergeant in the Tsarist Dragoons, decorated during WWI with the St George Cavalryman's ribbon, the highest distinction available. He served first the Tsar, then the Revolution, and then Stalin personally for the rest of his life, distinguishing himself at Tsaritsyn in Voroshilov's Tenth Army and rising to worldwide fame as commander of the First Cavalry Army. When Babel published his *Red Cavalry* stories, telling of the cruelty, lyricism and machismo of the Cossacks and Budyonny's taciturn ruthlessness (and 'dazzling teeth'), the furious commander tried unsuccessfully to suppress them. Never rising to the Politburo, he remained one of Stalin's intimates until the war and, though always devoted to cavalry, studied hard to modernize his military knowledge.

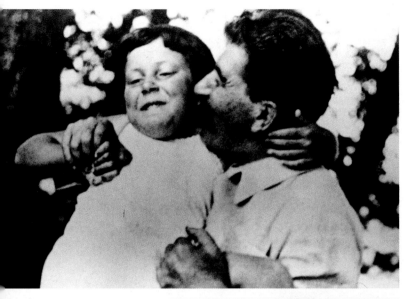

Stalin kisses his daughter Svetlana on holiday, early 1930s. He adored her: her freckles and red hair resembled his mother Keke, but her intelligence and obstinacy came from Stalin himself. He called her 'the Boss' and let her give mock orders to his henchmen. He was affectionate … until she started to grow up.

Nadya was much less affectionate, more strict and puritanical with the children: when she gave birth to their first son, she walked to hospital. She had a special relationship with the fragile and truculent Vasily – but she was primarily a Bolshevik career woman who left the upbringing of her children to nannies. Here she holds Svetlana, who longed for her love.

Top Stalin and his driver in the front with Nadya in the back of one of the Kremlin limousines: these were usually Packards, Buicks and Rolls-Royces. Nadya and Stalin lived ascetically, but he personally took great trouble to assign cars and apartments to his henchmen – and even sometimes to their children. Each family received about three cars.

Above left Stalin and Nadya enjoyed cosy, loving holidays on the Black Sea, though both had fiery tempers and there were often rows. The rulers of Soviet Russia were a tiny oligarchy who tended to holiday and dine constantly together: here are the Stalins on the right with the plodding Molotov and his clever, passionate Jewish wife, Polina. Stalin and Nadya laughed at Molotov. But the dictator never forgave Polina's friendship with Nadya.

Above right At Zubalovo, their country house near Moscow, the Stalins and the other top families enjoyed idyllic weekends. Here, Stalin comes in from the garden, carrying Svetlana.

Stalin built his power slowly, informally, and charmingly – despite the rigid façade of Party Congress, Central Committee and Politburo. The real business took place behind the scenes in the Kremlin's smoky corridors. Here in 1927, Stalin chats at a Party Congress with allies Sergo Ordzhonikidze and (right) Premier Alexei Rykov. But Rykov soon opposed Stalin's harsh policies – and paid the supreme penalty.

Stalin had been the dominant Soviet leader since the mid-Twenties – but not yet dictator. Many of his magnates were powerful in their own right. Here, at a Party Congress, Stalin holds court amongst his grandees: Sergo Ordzhonikidze (front left) and Klim Voroshilov turn to face him while the laughing Kirov (standing, to right of Stalin), along with Kaganovich and Mikoyan (far right) and Postyshev (second from left).

After her tragic death, Nadya lay in state. Stalin never recovered from her suicide and avenged himself on those whom he believed had encouraged her. 'She crippled me', he said. He sobbed when he saw her in her coffin. 'Don't cry Papa', said Vasily, who was holding his hand.

Nadya's funeral: Stalin walked for a while behind the surprisingly traditional coffin, but then drove on to the cemetery. His chief of personal security, Pauker, a Jewish former hairdresser from the Budapest Opera, arranged the orchestras that can be seen on the right.

Below Stalin leaving the Kremlin's Great Palace with two of his closest allies: Sergo Ordzhonikidze, the flamboyant, irascible and emotional scourge of his enemies, who was said to be 'the perfect Bolshevik', and to resemble a 'Georgian prince', stands in the middle. Mikhail 'Papa' Kalinin (with walking stick), the Soviet Head of State, was a genial, womanising ex-peasant. Kalinin opposed Stalin – he was lucky to survive. Sergo confronted Stalin and found himself cornered.

Above Lazar Kaganovich, a brawny and handsome Jewish cobbler, was Stalin's coarse, energetic, cruel and intelligent deputy in the 1930s. Here, during the famine that accompanied collectivisation, he personally leads an expedition into the Siberian countryside to search for grain hidden by peasants. The pace of Stalin's campaigns was punishing: Kaganovich (below, in middle) falls asleep afterwards surrounded by his officials and secret policemen.

Left The magnates were so close they were like a family: 'Uncle Abel' Yenukidze (left) was Nadya's godfather, Stalin's old friend, a senior official and a sybaritic bachelor with a taste for ballerinas. Stalin came to resent his familiarity. Voroshilov on the right, dapper, good-natured, stupid, envious and brutal, made his name in the Battle of Tsaritsyn and, in 1937, supervised the massacre of about 40,000 of his own officers.

In 1933, the first year after Nadya's death, Stalin's holiday was recorded by the secret police in a special private album given to him afterwards: it shows the surprising intimacy and informality of his life during the holiday months. H particularly enjoyed picnics. Here, he and Voroshilov (in braces) go camping (above). He adored gardening, weeding at his Sochi dacha (left) – he loved roses, but mimosas were his favourites. He wa less keen on hunting, but here sets off with (from left) Budyonny, Voroshilov and his Chekist crony Evdokimov.

Holidays were the best time to get to know Stalin: there was frantic networking amongst the grandees – even the most trivial activities were politically significant if they brought the courtiers close to the Boss. Young Lavrenti Beria, Georgian leader and vicious sadist, offered to help weed the gardens: placing an axe in his belt (above), he told Stalin that there was no tree that he would not chop down. Stalin understood.

Stalin with Lakoba and Kirov, embarking on a fishing and shooting trip on the Black Sea which was to end in a mysterious assassination attempt – did Beria arrange it? *Above* Stalin inspects the fishing catch.

Molotov, Premier during the 1930s – and the second most important leader after Stalin, who enjoyed teasing him – was dominated by his wife Polina to whom he wrote passionate love letters. Here, on holidays he plays tennis with his family; in winter, he pulled his spoilt daughter on her sledge. But this Soviet Robespierre believed in terror and never regretted signing the death warrants of the wives of his friends. Stalin nicknamed him 'Molotstein' – or more fondly 'our Vecha'.

This is how Stalin ruled his Empire: with his family and friends around him, sitting out in the sun at the Sochi dacha, reading hundreds of pages and writing his orders in a red crayon, while his henchmen fight brutal duels for his favour. Beria stands like a guard behind him, having already fallen out with his patron Lakoba (right), while Svetlana (who called Beria 'Uncle Lara') plays around them. Within five years, Lakoba and his entire family were dead.

preferred billiards. The Andreyevs were rock climbers which they regarded as a most Bolshevik pursuit. Even in 1930, Bukharin was often at Zubalovo with his wife and daughter. He brought some of his menagerie of animals – his pet foxes ran around the grounds. Nadya was close to 'Bukharchik' and they often walked together. Yenukidze was also a member of this extended family. But there was always business to be done too.

* * *

The children were used to the bodyguards and secretaries: the bodyguards were part of the family. Pauker, the head of the Guards Directorate, and Stalin's own bodyguard, Nikolai Vlasik, were always there. 'Pauker was great fun. He liked children like all Jews and did not have a high opinion of himself but Vlasik strutted around like a stuffed turkey,' says Kira Alliluyeva, Stalin's niece.

Karl Pauker, thirty-six, was the children's favourite, and important to Stalin himself. A symbol of the cosmopolitan culture of the Cheka of that time, this Jewish-Hungarian had been hairdresser at the Budapest Opera before being conscripted into the Austro-Hungarian army, captured by the Russians in 1916 and converted to Bolshevism. He was an accomplished actor, performing accents, especially Jewish ones, for Stalin. Rotund, with his belly held in by a (much-mocked) corset, bald, perfumed, with a scarlet sensuous mouth, this showman loved elaborate OGPU uniforms and pranced around on $1^1/_2$-inch-heeled boots. He sometimes returned to hairdressing, shaving Stalin like a valet, using talcum powder to fill the pock-marks. The font of delicacies, cars and new products for the Politburo, he kept the secrets of the magnates' private lives and was said to provide girls for Kalinin, Voroshilov and Stalin.

Pauker used to show off his Cadillac, a gift from Stalin, to the children. Long before Stalin officially agreed to bring back the Christmas tree in 1936, Pauker played Father Christmas, delivering presents round the Kremlin and running Christmas parties for the children. The secret policeman as Father Christmas is a symbol of this strange world.

The other figure who was never far away was Stalin's *chef de cabinet*, Alexander Poskrebyshev, thirty-nine, who scuttled round the garden at Zubalovo delivering the latest paperwork. Small, bald, reddish-haired, this bootmaker's son from the Urals had trained as a medical nurse, conducting Bolshevik meetings in his surgery. When Stalin found him working in the CC, he told him, 'You've a fearsome look. You'll terrify people.' This 'narrow-shouldered dwarf' was 'dreadfully ugly', resembling 'a monkey', but possessed 'an excellent memory and was meticulous in his work'. His Special Sector was the heart of Stalin's power machine. Poskrebyshev prepared and attended Politburos.

When Stalin exerted his patronage, helping a protégé get an apartment, it was Poskrebyshev who actually did the work: 'I ask you to HELP THEM IMMEDIATELY,' Stalin typically wrote to him. 'Inform me by letter about quick and exact carrying out of this request.' Lost in the archives until now is Stalin's correspondence with Poskrebyshev: here we find Stalin teasing his secretary: 'I'm receiving English newspapers but not German ... why? How could it be that you make a mistake? Is it bureaucratism? Greetings. J. Stalin.' Sometimes he was in the doghouse: in 1936, one finds on one of Stalin's list of things to do: '1. To forgive Poskrebyshev and his friends.'

The sad, twitchy face of this Quasimodo was a weather vane of the leader's favour. If he was friendly, you were in favour. If not, he sometimes whispered, 'You're in for it today.' The *cognoscenti* knew that the best way to get Stalin to read their letter was to address it to Alexander Nikolaievich. At work, Stalin called him Comrade but at home, he was 'Sasha' or 'the Chief'.

Poskrebyshev was part-buffoon, part-monster, but he later suffered grievously at Stalin's hands. According to his daughter Natalya, he asked if he could study medicine but Stalin made him study economics instead. But in the end, this half-trained nurse provided the only medical care Stalin received.

* * *

Stalin rose late, at about eleven, took breakfast and worked during the day on his piles of papers, which he carried around wrapped in the newspaper – he did not like briefcases. When he was sleeping, anxious parents begged children to be quiet.

The big daytime meal was an expansive 'brunch' at 3–4 p.m. with all the family and, of course, half the Politburo and their wives. When there were visitors, Stalin played the Georgian host. 'He was elaborately hospitable in that Asiatic way,' remembers Leonid Redens, his nephew. 'He was very kind to the children.' Whenever Stalin's brood needed someone to play with, there were their Alliluyev cousins, Pavel's children, Kira, Sasha and Sergei, and the younger boys of Anna Redens. Then there was the

Bolshevik family: Mikoyan's popular sons, whom Stalin nick-named the Mikoyanchiks, only had to scamper over from next door.

The children ran around together but Svetlana found there were too many boys and not enough girls to play with. Her brother Vasily bullied her and showed off by telling her sexual stories that she later admitted disturbed and upset her. 'Stalin was very loving to Svetlana but he did not really like the boys,' recalls Kira. He invented an imaginary girl named Lelka who was Svetlana's perfect alter ego. Weak Vasily was already a problem. Nadya understood this and gave him more attention. But Bolshevik parents did not raise their children: they were brought up by nannies and tutors: 'It was like an aristocratic family in Victorian times,' says Svetlana. 'So were the others, the Kaganoviches, Molotovs, Voroshilovs ... But the ladies of that top circle were all working so my mother did not dress or feed me. I don't remember any physical affection from her but she was very fond of my brother. She certainly loved me, I could tell, but she was a disciplinarian.' Once when she cut up a tablecloth, her mother spanked her hard.

Stalin kissed and squeezed Svetlana with 'overflowing Georgian affection' but she claimed later that she did not like his 'smell of tobacco and bristly moustache'. Her mother, whose love was so hard to earn, became the untouchable saint in her eyes.

* * *

The Bolsheviks, who believed it was possible to create a Leninist 'New Man', placed stern emphasis on education.* The magnates were semi-educated autodidacts who never stopped studying, so their children were expected to work hard and grew up much more cultured than their parents, speaking three languages which they had learned from special tutors. (The Stalin and Molotov children shared the same English tutor.)

The Party did not merely come *before* family, it was an *über*-family: when Lenin died, Trotsky said he was 'orphaned' and Kaganovich was already calling Stalin 'our father'. Stalin lectured

---

* Stalin's ex-secretary, now Editorial Director of *Pravda*, Lev Mekhlis, actually kept a 'Bolshevik diary' for his new born-son, Leonid, in which he confided the crazy fanatical faith in Communism for which he was creating 'this man of the future, this New Man'. On 2 January 1923, the proud father records how he has placed Lenin's portrait 'with a red ribbon' in the pram: 'The baby often looks at the portrait.' He was training the baby 'for the struggle'.

Bukharin that 'the personal element is ... not worth a brass
farthing. We're not a family circle or a coterie of close friends –
we're the political party of the working class.' They cultivated
their coldness.* 'A Bolshevik should love his work more than his
wife,' said Kirov. The Mikoyans were a close Armenian family but
Anastas was a 'stern, exacting, even severe' father who never
forgot he was a Politburo member and a Bolshevik: when he
spanked his son, he said in time with the smacks:

'It's not YOU who's Mikoyan, it's ME!' Stepan Mikoyan's mother
Ashken 'sometimes "forgot herself" and gave us a hug'. Once at a
dinner in the Kremlin, Stalin told Yenukidze, 'A true Bolshevik
shouldn't and couldn't have a family because he should give
himself wholly to the Party.' As one veteran put it: 'If you have to
choose between Party and individual, you choose the Party
because the Party has the general aim, the good of many people
but one person is just one person.'

Yet Stalin could be very indulgent to children, giving them rides
around the estate in his limousine: 'I think "Uncle Stalin" really
loved me,' muses Artyom. 'I respected him but I didn't fear him.
He managed to make one's conversation interesting. He always
made you formulate your thoughts like an adult.'

'Let's play the game of egg breaking – who can break theirs
first?' Stalin asked his nephew Leonid when boiled eggs arrived.
He entertained the children by throwing orange peel or wine
corks into the ice-cream or biscuits into their tea. 'We children
thought this was hilarious,' recalls Vladimir Redens.

It was the Caucasian tradition to let babies suck wine off the
adults' fingers and when they were older, to give them little
glasses of wine. Stalin often gave Vasily, and later Svetlana, sips of
wine, which seems harmless (though Vasily died of alcoholism)
but this infuriated the stern Nadya. They constantly argued about
it. When Nadya or her sister told him off, Stalin just chuckled:

'Don't you know it's medicinal?'

Once Artyom did something that could have become serious
because Stalin was already highly suspicious. 'When the leaders
were working in the dining room', young Artyom noticed the
soup which, as always, was on the sideboard. The boy crept

---

* Kirov, for example, had not seen his sisters for twenty years when he was
assassinated and indeed he had not even bothered to tell them who or where he was.
They only discovered when they read it in the papers that the famous Kirov was their
brother Kostrikov.

behind the backs of Stalin, Molotov and Voroshilov and naughtily sprinkled Stalin's tobacco into the broth. He then waited to see if they would eat it. 'Molotov and Voroshilov tried it and found the tobacco. Stalin asked who did it. I said it was me.'

'Have you tried it?' asked Stalin.

Artyom shook his head.

'Well, it's delicious,' replied Stalin. 'You try it and if you like it, you can go and tell Carolina Vasilevna [Til, the housekeeper] to always put tobacco in the soup. If not, you better not do it again.'

The children were aware that it was a political household. 'We looked at everything with humour and irony,' says Leonid Redens. 'When Stalin dismissed a commissar, we regarded it with amusement.' This was a joke that would not remain funny for long.

This country set knew about the unspeakable depredations in the countryside. Stanislas Redens, Stalin and Nadya's brother-in-law, was the GPU boss of the Ukraine, at the centre of the famine, a job that entailed intimate knowledge and participation: there is no doubt that his wife talked to Nadya about the Ukraine's tragedy. Soon it had poisoned not only Stalin's marriage but the Bolshevik family itself.

5

Holidays and Hell:
the Politburo at the Seaside

In late 1931, Stalin, Nadya and most of the magnates were already on holiday as the hunger turned to famine. They took their holidays very seriously. Indeed, at least ten per cent of the letters between Stalin's circle, even during the worst years of famine, concerned their holidays. (Another twenty per cent concerned their health.) Networking on holiday was the best way to get to know Stalin: more careers were made, more intrigues clinched, on those sunny verandas than on the snowy battlements of the Kremlin.*

There was a fixed ritual for taking these holidays: the question was formally put to the Politburo 'to propose to Comrade Stalin one week's holiday' but by the late twenties, the holidays had expanded from 'twenty days' to one or two months 'on the suggestion of doctors'. Once the dates were arranged, Stalin's secretary sent a memorandum to Yagoda, giving him the schedule 'so bodyguards can be arranged appropriately'.

The potentates set off in private trains, guarded by OGPU troops, southwards to the Soviet Riviera – the Politburo's southern dachas and sanatoria were spread from the Crimea in the west to the Georgian spa of Borzhomi in the east. Molotov preferred the Crimea but Stalin favoured the steamy Black Sea coastline that ran from Sochi down into the semi-tropical towns of Sukhumi and Gagra in Abkhazia. All were state-owned but it was understood that whoever supervised their building had preferential rights to use them.

The magnates moved about to visit one another, asking permission so as not to wreck anyone else's holiday, but naturally they tended to cluster around Stalin. 'Stalin would like to come to

* These long holidays were formally proposed by his colleagues so the decrees in the archives often read: 'At the proposal of Ordzhonikidze' or 'To approve the proposition of Comrades Molotov, Kaganovich, Kalinin to grant Comrade Stalin twenty days holiday.'

Mukhalatka [in the Crimea]* but does not want to disturb anyone else. Ask Yagoda to organize bodyguards ...'

There was a dark side to their holidays. The OGPU carefully planned Stalin's train journey which, during the Hunger, was accompanied by a train of provisions. If, on arrival, the staff thought there was still a shortage of food for Stalin and his guests, his assistants rapidly sent 'a telegram to Orel and Kursk' to despatch more. They eagerly reported that during the journey they had successfully cooked Stalin hot meals. 'As for the GPU,' wrote one of his assistants, 'there's lots of work, massive arrests have taken place' and they were still working on hunting down 'those who remain ... Two bands of bandits have been arrested.'

Stalin's tastes in holiday houses changed but in the thirties, Dacha No. 9 in Sochi was his favourite. Krasnaya Polyana, Red Meadow, was 'a wooden house with a veranda around the whole outside', says Artyom, who usually holidayed with 'Uncle Stalin'.† Stalin's house stood high on the hill while Molotov and Voroshilov's houses stood symbolically in the valley below. When Nadya was on holiday with her husband, they usually invited a wider family, including Yenukidze and the obese proletarian poet, Demian Bedny. It was the job of Stalin's staff, along with the secret police and the local bosses, to prepare the house before his arrival: 'The villa ... has been renovated 100%,' wrote one of his staff, 'as if ready for a great party' with every imaginable fruit.

They enjoyed holidaying in groups, like an American university fraternity house, often without their wives who were with the children in Moscow. 'Molotov and I ride horses, play tennis, skittles, boating, shooting – in a word, a perfect rest,' wrote Mikoyan to his wife, listing the others who were with them. 'It's a male Bolshevik monastery.' But at other times they took their

---

* Mukhalatka was the favourite resort of Molotov and Mikoyan, though both also holidayed in orbit around Stalin at Sochi. It remained a Soviet favourite: the resort is close to Foros where Gorbachev was arrested during the 1991 *coup d'état*. Naturally, being Bolsheviks, the leaders were always sacking the local officials at these resorts: 'Belinsky was rude ... not for the first time,' Stalin wrote to Yagoda and Molotov. 'He should be removed at once from control of Mukhalatka. Appoint someone of the Yagoda type or approved by Yagoda.' If they did not find the holiday houses to their taste, they proposed new luxuries: 'There's no good hotel on the Black Sea for tourist and foreign specialists and working leaders,' wrote Kalinin to Voroshilov. 'To hurry it up, we must give it to the GPU.'

† In the mid-thirties, Miron Merzhanov, Stalin's architect, rebuilt the house in stone. The big, dark green house is still there: there is now a museum with a dummy of Stalin at his desk and a Café Stalin, a mini-Stalin theme park in the gardens.

wives and children too: when Kuibyshev went on holiday, the shock-haired economics boss and poet travelled round the Black Sea with a 'large and jolly troupe' of pretty girls and bon viveurs.

They competed to holiday with Stalin but the most popular companion was the larger-than-life Sergo. Yenukidze often invited his fellow womanizer Kuibyshev to party with him in his Georgian village. Stalin was half jealous of these men and sounded delighted when Molotov failed to rendezvous with Sergo: 'Are you running away from Sergo?' he asked. They always asked each other who was there:

'Here in Nalchik,' wrote Stalin, 'there's me, Voroshilov and Sergo.'

'I got your note,' Stalin told Andreyev. 'Devil take me! I was in Sukhumi and we didn't meet by chance. If I'd known about your intention to visit ... I'd never have left Sochi ... How did you spend your holidays? Did you hunt as much as you wanted?' Once they had arrived at their houses, the magnates advised which place was best: 'Come to the Crimea in September,' Stalin wrote to Sergo from Sochi, adding that Borzhomi in Georgia was comfortable 'because there are no mosquitoes ... In August and half of September, I'll be in Krasnaya Polyana [Sochi]. The GPU have found a very nice dacha in the mountains but my illness prevents me going yet ... Klim [Voroshilov] is now in Sochi and we're quite often together ...'

'In the south,' says Artyom, 'the centre of planning went with him.' Stalin worked on the veranda in a wicker chair with a wicker table on which rested a huge pile of papers. Planes flew south daily bringing his letters. Poskrebyshev (often in a neighbouring cottage) scuttled in to deliver them. Stalin constantly demanded more journals to read. He used to read out letters and then tell the boys his reply. Once he got a letter from a worker complaining that there were no showers at his mine. Stalin wrote on the letter that 'If there is no resolution soon and no water, the director of the mine should be tried as an Enemy of the People.'

Stalin was besieged with questions from Molotov or Kaganovich, left in charge in Moscow. 'Shame we don't have a connection with Sochi by telephone,'* wrote Voroshilov. 'Telephone would

---

* But this has been a boon for historians: their main communication was by letter until 1935 when a safe telephone link was set up between Moscow and the south. Trotsky had paraphrased Herzen's comment on Nicholas I, 'Genghiz Khan with a telegraph', to call Stalin 'Genghiz Khan with a telephone'. Yet it is a sobering thought that for several months a year, he ruled with no telephone at all.

help us. I'd like to visit you for 2–3 days and also have a sleep. I haven't been able to sleep normally for a long time.' But Stalin relished his dominance:

'The number of Politburo inquiries doesn't affect my health,' he told Molotov. 'You can send as many inquiries as you like – I'll be happy to answer them.' They all wrote Stalin long, handwritten letters knowing, as Bukharin put it, 'Koba loves to receive letters.' Kaganovich, in charge in Moscow for the first time, took full advantage of this though the Politburo still took most of the decisions themselves, with Stalin intervening from afar if he disapproved. The vain, abrasive, emotional magnates often argued viciously in Stalin's absence: after a row with his friend Sergo, Kaganovich admitted to Stalin, 'This upset me very much.' Stalin often enjoyed such conflicts: 'Well, dear friends ... more squabbling ...' None the less, sometimes even Stalin was exasperated: 'I can't and shouldn't give decisions on every possible and imaginable question raised at Politburo. You should be able to study and produce a response ... yourselves!'

* * *

There was time for fun too: Stalin took a great interest in the gardens at the house, planting lemon bowers and orange groves, proudly weeding and setting his entourage to toil in the sun. Stalin so appreciated the gardener in Sochi, one Alferov, that he wrote to Poskrebyshev: 'it would be good to put [Alferov] in the Academy of Agriculture – he's the gardener in Sochi, a very good and honest worker ...'

His life in the south bore no resemblance to the cold solitude that one associates with Stalin. 'Joseph Vissarionovich liked expeditions into nature,' wrote Voroshilova in her diary. 'He drove by car and we settled near some small river, lit a fire and made a barbecue, singing songs and playing jokes.' The whole entourage went on these expeditions.

'We often all of us get together,' wrote one excited secretary to another. 'We fire air rifles at targets, we often go on walks and expeditions in the cars, we climb into the forest, and have barbecues where we grill kebabs, booze away and then grub's up!' Stalin and Yenukidze entertained the guests with stories of their adventures as pre-revolutionary conspirators while Demian Bedny told 'obscene stories of which he had an inexhaustible reserve'. Stalin shot partridges and went boating.

'I remember the dacha in Sochi when Klim and I were invited

over by Comrade Stalin,' wrote Voroshilova. 'I watched him
playing games such as skittles and Nadezhda Sergeevna was
playing tennis.' Stalin and the cavalryman Budyonny played
skittles with Vasily and Artyom. Budyonny was so strong that
when he threw the skittle, he broke the entire set and the shield
behind. Everyone laughed about his strength (and stupidity):

'If you're strong you don't need a brain.' They teased him for
hurting himself by doing a parachute jump. 'He thought he was
jumping off a horse!'

'Only two men were known as the first cavalrymen of the world
– Napoleon's Marshal Lannes and Semyon Budyonny,' Stalin
defended him, 'so we should listen to everything he says about
cavalry!' Years later, Voroshilova could only write: 'What a lovely
time it was!'

* * *

That September 1931, Stalin and Nadya were visited by two
Georgian potentates, one she loved, one she hated. The popular
one was Nestor Lakoba, the Old Bolshevik leader of Abkhazia
which he ruled like an independent fiefdom with unusual
gentleness. He protected some of the local princes and resisted
collectivization, claiming there were no Abkhazian kulaks. When
the Georgian Party appealed to Moscow, Stalin and Sergo
supported Lakoba. Slim and dapper, with twinkling eyes, black
hair brushed back, and a hearing aid because he was partially deaf,
this player strolled the streets and cafés of his little realm, like a
troubadour. As the maitre d' of the élite holiday resorts, he knew
everyone and was always building Stalin new homes and
arranging banquets for him – just as he is portrayed in Fasil
Iskander's Abkhazian novel, *Sandro of Chegem*. Stalin regarded him
as a true ally:

'Me Koba,' he joked, 'you Lakoba!' Lakoba was another of the
Bolshevik family, spending afternoons sitting out on the veranda
with Stalin. When Lakoba visited the dacha, bringing his feasts
and Abkhazian sing-songs, Stalin shouted: 'Vivat Abkhazia!' Artyom
says Lakoba's arrival 'was like light pouring into the house'.

Stalin allowed Lakoba to advise him on the Georgian Party,
which was particularly clannish and resistant to orders from the
centre. This was the reason for the other guest: Lavrenti (the
Georgian version of Laurence) Pavlovich Beria, Transcaucasus
GPU chief. Beria was balding, short and agile with a broad fleshy
face, swollen sensual lips and flickering 'snake eyes' behind a

glistening pince-nez. This gifted, intelligent, ruthless and tirelessly competent adventurer, whom Stalin would one day describe as 'our Himmler', brandished the exotic flattery, sexual appetites and elaborate cruelty of a Byzantine courtier in his rise to dominate first the Caucasus, then Stalin's circle, and finally the USSR itself.

Born near Sukhumi of Mingrelian parentage, probably the illegitimate son of an Abkhazian landowner and his pious Georgian mother, Beria had almost certainly served as a double agent for the anti-Communist Mussavist regime that ruled Baku during the Civil War. It was said that Stalin's ally, Sergei Kirov had saved him from the death penalty, a fate he had only escaped because there was no time to arrange the execution. Training as an architect at the Baku Polytechnic, he was attracted by the power of the Cheka, which he then joined and wherein he prospered, promoted by Sergo. Even by the standards of that ghastly organization, he stood out for his sadism. 'Beria is a man for whom it costs nothing to kill his best friend if that best friend said something bad about Beria,' said one of his henchmen. His other career as a sexual adventurer had started, he later told his daughter-in-law, on an architectural study trip to Romania when he had been seduced by an older woman – but while in prison during the Civil War, he fell in love with his cellmate's blonde, golden-eyed teenage niece, Nina Gegechkori, a member of a gentry family: one uncle became a minister in Georgia's Menshevik Government, another in the Bolshevik one. When he was twenty-two, already a senior Chekist, and she was seventeen, she asked for her uncle's release. Beria courted her and they finally eloped on his official train, hence the myth that he raped her in his carriage. On the contrary, she remained in love with her 'charmer' throughout her long life.

Beria was now thirty-two, the personification of the 1918 generation of leaders, much better educated than his elders in the first generation, such as Stalin and Kalinin, both over fifty, or the second, Mikoyan and Kaganovich, in their late thirties. Like the latter, Beria was competitive at everything and an avid sportsman – playing left-back for Georgia's football team, and practising ju-jitsu. Coldly competent, fawningly sycophantic yet gleaming with mischief, he had a genius for cultivating patrons. Sergo, then Caucasus boss, eased his rise in the GPU and, in 1926, introduced him to Stalin for the first time. Beria took over his holiday security.

'Without you,' Beria wrote to Sergo, 'I'd have no one. You're more than a brother or father to me.' Sergo steered Beria through meetings that declared him innocent of working for the enemy. In 1926, when Sergo was promoted to Moscow, Beria fell out with him and began to cultivate the most influential man in the region, Lakoba, importuning him to let him see Stalin again.

Stalin had been irritated by Beria's oleaginous blandishments on holiday. When Beria arrived at the dacha, Stalin grumbled, 'What, he came again?' and sent him away, adding, 'Tell him, here Lakoba's the master!' When Beria fell out with the Georgian bosses, who regarded him as an amoral mountebank, Lakoba backed him. Yet Beria aimed higher.

'Dear Comrade Nestor,' Beria wrote to Lakoba, 'I want very much to see Comrade Koba before his departure ... if you would remind him of it.'

But now Lakoba brought Beria to the *Vozhd*. Stalin had become infuriated by the insubordinate clans of Georgian bosses, who promoted their old friends, gossiped with their patrons in Moscow, and knew too much about his inglorious early antics. Lakoba proposed to replace these Old Bolshevik fat cats with Beria, one of the new generation devoted to Stalin. Nadya hated Beria on sight.

'How can you have that man in the house?'

'He's a good worker,' replied Stalin. 'Give me facts.'

'What facts do you need?' Nadya shrieked back. 'He's a scoundrel. I won't have him in the house.' Stalin later remembered that he sent her to the Devil:

'He's my friend, a good Chekist ... I trust him ...' Kirov and Sergo warned Stalin against Beria but he ignored their advice, something he later regretted. Now he welcomed his new protégé. None the less, 'when he came into the house', recalls Artyom, 'he brought darkness with him.' Stalin, according to Lakoba's notes, agreed to promote the Chekist but asked:

'Will Beria be okay?'

'Beria'll be fine,' replied Lakoba who would soon have reason to regret his reassurance.

After Sochi, Stalin and Nadya took the waters at Tsaltubo. Stalin wrote to Sergo from Tsaltubo to tell him about his new plan for their joint protégé. He joked that he had seen the regional bosses, calling one 'a very comical figure' and another 'now too fat'. He concluded, 'They agreed to bring Beria into the Kraikom [regional committee] of Georgia.' Sergo and the Georgian bosses were appalled at a policeman lording it over old revolutionaries. Yet Stalin happily signed off to Sergo, 'Greetings from Nadya! How's Zina?'

* * *

Taking the waters was an annual pilgrimage. In 1923, Mikoyan found Stalin suffering from rheumatism with his arm bandaged and suggested that he take the waters in the Matsesta Baths near Sochi. Mikoyan even chose the merchant's house with three bedrooms and a salon in which Stalin stayed. It was a mark of the close relationship between the two men. He often took Artyom with him 'in an old open Rolls-Royce made in 1911'. Only his personal bodyguard Vlasik accompanied them.*

Stalin seems to have been shy physically, either because of his arm or his psoriasis: among the leaders, only Kirov went to the baths with him. But he did not mind Artyom. As they soaked in the steam, Stalin told Artyom 'stories about his childhood and adventures in the Caucasus, and discussed our health'.

Stalin was obsessed with his own health and that of his comrades. They were 'responsible workers' for the people, so the preservation of their health was a matter of State. This was already a Soviet tradition: Lenin supervised his leaders' health. By the early thirties, Stalin's Politburo worked so hard and under such pressure that it was not surprising that their health, already undermined by Tsarist exile and Civil War, was seriously compromised. Their letters read like the minutes of a hypochondriacs' convention.†

'Now I'm getting healthy,' Stalin confided in Molotov. 'The waters here near Sochi are very good and work against sclerosis, neurosis, sciatica, gout and rheumatism. Shouldn't you send your wife here?' Stalin suffered the tolls of the poor diet and icy winters of his exiles: his tonsillitis flared up when he was stressed. He so liked the Matsesta specialist, Professor Valedinsky, that he often invited him to drink cognac on the veranda with his children, the

---

* The driver down south was named Nikolai Ivanovich Soloviev who was supposed to have been Nicholas II's driver. In fact Soloviev had been General Brusilov's chauffeur but had once during the First World War driven the Tsar.

† Beria was not the only future monster with whom Stalin concerned himself on this holiday. He also showed a special interest in Nikolai Yezhov, a young official who would be the secret police chief during the coming Terror: 'They say that if Yezhov extends his holidays for a month or two, it's not so bad. Yezhov himself is against this but they say he needs it. Let's prolong his holiday and let him stay in Abastuman for two more months. I'm voting "for".' Yezhov was clearly a man to watch.

novelist Maxim Gorky, and the Politburo. Later he moved Valedinsky to Moscow and the professor remained his personal physician until the war.

His dental problems might themselves have caused his aches. After his dentist Shapiro had worked heroically, at Nadya's insistence, on eight of his rotten and yellowed teeth, Stalin was grateful:

'Do you wish to ask me anything?' The dentist asked a favour. 'The dentist Shapiro who works a lot on our responsible workers asks me (now he's working on me) to place his daughter in the medical department of Moscow University,' Stalin wrote to Poskrebyshev. 'I think we must render such help to this man for the service he does daily for our comrades. So could you do this and fix it ... very quickly ... because we risk running out of time ... I'm awaiting your answer.' If he could not get the daughter into Moscow, then Poskrebyshev must try Leningrad.

Stalin liked to share his health with his friends: 'At Sochi, I arrived with pleurisy (dry),' he told Sergo. 'Now I feel well. I have taken a course of ten therapeutic baths. I've had no more complications with rheumatism.' They told theirs too.

'How's your nephritic stone?' Stalin asked Sergo who was holidaying with Kaganovich. The letters formed a hypochondriacal triangle.

'Kaganovich and I couldn't come, we're sitting on a big steamboat,' replied Sergo, telling 'Soso', 'Kaganovich's a bit ill. The cause isn't clear yet. Maybe his heart is so-so ... Doctors say the water and special baths will help him but he needs a month here ... I feel good but not yet rested ...'

Kaganovich sent a note too, from the Borzhomi Baths: 'Dear Comrade Stalin, I send you a steamy hello ... It's a pity the storm means you can't visit us.' Sergo also told Stalin about Kaganovich's health: 'Kaganovich has swollen legs. The cause isn't yet established but it's possible his heart is beating too faintly. His holiday ends on 30th August but it'll be necessary to prolong it ...' Even those in Moscow sent medical reports to Stalin on holiday: 'Rudzutak's ill and Sergo has microbes of TB and we're sending him to Germany,' Molotov reported to his leader. 'If we got more sleep, we'd make less mistakes.'

* * *

Term was starting so Nadya headed back to Moscow. Stalin returned to Sochi whence he sent her affectionate notes: 'We played bowling and skittles. Molotov has already visited us twice but as for his wife, she's gone off somewhere.' Sergo and Kalinin arrived but 'there's nothing new. Let Vasya and Svetlana write to me.'

Unlike the year before, Stalin and Nadya had got on well during the holidays, to judge by their letters. Despite Beria, her tone was confident and cheerful. Nadya wanted to report to her husband on the situation in Moscow. Far from being anti-Party, she remained as eager as ever to pass her exams and become a qualified manager: she worked hard on her textile designs with Dora Khazan.

'Moscow's better,' she wrote, 'but like a woman powdering to cover her blemishes, especially when it runs and runs in streaks.' Kaganovich's remodelling of Moscow was already shaking the city, such was his explosive energy. The destruction of the Christ the Saviour, the ugly nineteenth-century cathedral, to make way for a much more hideous Palace of the Soviets, was progressing slowly. Nadya began to report 'details' that she thought Stalin needed to know but she saw them from a very feminine aesthetic: 'The Kremlin's clean but its garage-yard's very ugly ... Prices in the shops are very high and stocks very high. Don't be angry that I'm so detailed but I'd like the people to be relieved of all these problems and it would be good for all workers ...' Then she turned back to Stalin himself: 'Please rest well ...' Yet the tensions in government could not be concealed from Nadya: indeed she was living at the heart of them, in the tiny world of the Kremlin where the other leaders visited her every day: 'Sergo called me – he was disappointed by your blaming letter. He looked very tired.'

Stalin was not angry about the 'details'. 'It's good. Moscow changes for the better.' He asked her to call Sergei Kirov, the Leningrad boss, of whom he was especially fond:

'He decided to come to you on 12th September,' she told him, asking a few days later, 'Did Kirov visit you?' Kirov soon arrived in Sochi where his house was one of those down in the valley beneath Stalin's. They played the games that perhaps reflected Stalin's spell as a weatherman:

'With Kirov, we tested the temperature in the valley where he lives and up where I live – there's a difference of two degrees.'*

---

* Later, the old dictator would preside over drinking contests in which his guests would have to drink a cup of vodka for every degree they got wrong.

Stalin was no swimmer, probably because of his bad arm though he told Artyom it was because 'mountain people don't swim'. But now he went swimming with Kirov.

'Good that Kirov visited you,' she wrote back, sweetly, to her husband who had once saved her life in the water. 'You must be careful swimming.' Later he had a special paddling pool built inside the house at Sochi, to precisely his height, so he could cool off in private.

Meanwhile the famine was gaining momentum: Voroshilov wrote to Stalin, encouraging the despatch of leaders into the regions to see what was happening.

'You're right,' Stalin agreed on 24 September 1931. 'We don't always understand the meaning of personal trips and personal acquaintance of people with affairs. We'd win a lot more often if we travelled more and got to know people. I didn't want to go on holiday but ... was very tired and my health's improving ...' He was not the only one on holiday while discussing the famine: Budyonny reported starvation but concluded, 'The building on my new country house is finished, it's very pretty ...'

'It's raining endlessly in Moscow,' Nadya informed Stalin. 'The children have already had flu. I protect myself by wrapping up warmly.' Then she teased him playfully about a defector's book about Lenin and Stalin. 'I read the White journals. There's interesting material about you. Are you curious? I asked Dvinsky [Poskrebyshev's deputy] to find it ... Sergo phoned and complained about his pneumonia ...'

There was a fearsome storm in Sochi: 'The gale howled for two days with the fury of an enraged beast,' wrote Stalin. 'Eighteen large oaks uprooted in the grounds of our *dacha* ...' He was happy to receive the children's letters. 'Kiss them from me, they're good children.'

Svetlana's note to her 'First Secretary' commanded:

'Hello *Papochka*. Come home quickly – it's an order!' Stalin obeyed. The crisis was worsening.

6

Trains Full of Corpses:
Love, Death and Hysteria

'The peasants ate dogs, horses, rotten potatoes, the bark of trees, anything they could find,' observed one witness, Fedor Belov, while, on 21 December 1931, in the midst of this crisis, Stalin celebrated his birthday at Zubalovo. 'I remember visiting that house with Kliment on birthdays and recall the hospitality of Joseph Vissarionovich. Songs, dances, yes, yes, dances. All were dancing as they could!' wrote the diarist Ekaterina Voroshilova, Jewish wife of the Defence Commissar, herself a revolutionary, once Yenukidze's mistress and now a fattening housewife. First they sang: Voroshilova recalled how they performed operatic arias, peasant romances, Georgian laments, Cossack ballads – and, surprisingly for these godless ruffians, hymns, learned in village churches and seminaries.

Sometimes they forgot the ladies and burst into bawdy songs too. Voroshilov and Stalin, both ex-choirboys, sang together: Stalin 'had a good tenor voice and he loved songs and music,' she writes. 'He had his favourite arias' – he particularly liked old Georgian melodies, arias from *Rigoletto*, and he always wanted to hear the hymn from the Orthodox liturgy, *Mnogaya leta*. He later told President Truman, 'Music's an excellent thing, it reduces the beast in men', a subject on which he was surely something of an expert. Stalin's pitch was perfect: it was a 'rare' and 'sweet' voice. Indeed, one of his lieutenants said he was good enough to have become a professional singer, a mind-boggling historical possibility.

Stalin presided over the American gramophone – he 'changed the discs and entertained the guests – he loved the funny ones'. Molotov was 'dancing the Russian way with a handkerchief' with Polina in the formal style of someone who had learned ballroom dancing. The Caucasians dominated the dancing. As Voroshilova describes it, Anastas Mikoyan danced up to Nadya Stalin. This Armenian who had studied for the priesthood like Stalin himself, was slim, circumspect, wily and industrious, with black hair, moustache and flashing eyes, a broken aquiline nose and a taste for immaculate clothes that, even when clad in his usual tunic and boots, lent him the air of a lithe dandy. Highly intelligent with the driest of wits, he had a gift for languages, understanding English and, in 1931, he taught himself German by translating *Das Kapital*.

Mikoyan was not afraid to contradict Stalin yet became the great survivor of Soviet history, still at the top in Brezhnev's time. A Bolshevik since 1915, he had managed to escape the fate of the famous Twenty-Six Commissars shot during the Civil War, and was now the overlord of trade and supply.* Svetlana, Stalin's daughter, thought him the most attractive of the magnates, 'youthful and dashing'. He was certainly the finest dancer and sharpest dresser. 'One was never bored with Mikoyan,' says Artyom. 'He's our cavalier,' declared Khrushchev. 'At least he's the best we've got!' But he warned against trusting that 'shrewd fox from the east'.

Though devoted to his modest, cosy wife Ashken, Mikoyan, perhaps trying to include Nadya in the festivities, 'for a long time scraped his feet before Nadezhda Sergeevna, asking her to dance the *lezginka* [a traditional Caucasian dance that she knew well] with him. He danced in very quick time, stretching up as if taller and thinner.' But Nadya was 'so shy and bashful' at this Armenian chivalry that she 'covered her face with her hands and, as if unable to react to this sweet and artistic dance, she slipped from his active approaches'. Perhaps she was aware of Stalin's jealousy.

Voroshilov was as light-footed a tripper on the dancefloor as he was a graceless blunderer on the political stage. He danced the *gopak* and then asked for partners for what his wife called 'his star-turn, the *polka*'. It was no wonder that the atmosphere among the magnates was so febrile. In the countryside, the regime itself seemed to be tottering.

* * *

By the summer, when Fred Beal, an American radical, visited a village near Kharkov, then capital of Ukraine, he found the inhabitants dead except one insane woman. Rats feasted on huts that had become charnel-houses.

* Mikoyan was the Vicar of Bray of Soviet politics. 'From Illich [Lenin] to Illich [Leonid Illich Brezhnev],' went the Russian saying, 'without accident or stroke!' A veteran Soviet official described Mikoyan thus: 'The rascal was able to walk through Red Square on a rainy day without an umbrella without getting wet.'

On 6 June 1932, Stalin and Molotov declared that 'no matter of deviation – regarding either amounts or deadlines set for grain deliveries – can be permitted.' On 17 June, the Ukrainian Politburo, led by Vlas Chubar and Stanislas Kosior, begged for food assistance as the regions were in 'a state of emergency'. Stalin blamed Chubar and Kosior themselves, combined with wrecking by enemies – the famine itself was merely a hostile act against the Central Committee, hence himself. 'The Ukraine,' he wrote to Kaganovich, 'has been given more than it should get.' When an official bravely reported it to the Politburo, Stalin interrupted: 'They tell us, Comrade Terekhov, that you're a good orator, but it transpires that you're a good story-teller. Fabricating such a fairy tale about famine! Thought you'd scare us but it won't work. Wouldn't it be better for you to leave the posts of ... Ukrainian CC Secretary and join the Writers' Union: you'll concoct fables, and fools will read them.' Mikoyan was visited by a Ukrainian who asked, 'Does Comrade Stalin – for that matter does anyone in the Politburo – know what is happening in Ukraine? Well if not, I'll give you some idea. A train recently pulled into Kiev loaded with corpses of people who had starved to death. It had picked up corpses all the way from Poltava ...'

The magnates knew exactly what was happening:* their letters show how they spotted terrible things from their luxury trains. Budyonny told Stalin from Sochi, where he was on holiday, 'Looking at people from the windows of the train, I see very tired people in old worn clothes, our horses are skin and bone ...' President Kalinin, Stalin's anodyne 'village elder', sneered at the 'political impostors' asking 'contributions for "starving" Ukraine. Only degraded disintegrating classes can produce such cynical elements.' Yet on 18 June 1932, Stalin admitted to Kaganovich what he called the 'glaring absurdities' of 'famine' in Ukraine.

The death toll of this 'absurd' famine, which only occurred to raise money to build pig-iron smelters and tractors, was between

* When Beal, the American, reported to the Chairman of Ukraine's Central Executive Committee (the titular President), Petrovsky, he replied: 'We know millions are dying. That is unfortunate but the glorious future of the Soviet Union will justify it.' By 1933, it is estimated that 1.1 million households, that is seven million people, lost their holdings and half of them were deported. As many as three million households were liquidated. At the start of this process in 1931, there were 13 million households collectivized out of roughly 25 million. By 1937, 18.5 million were collectivized but there were now only 19.9 million households: 5.7 million households, perhaps 15 million persons, had been deported, many of them dead.

four to five, and as high as, ten million dead, a tragedy unequalled in human history except by the Nazi and Maoist terrors. The peasants had always been the Bolshevik Enemy. Lenin himself had said: 'The peasant must do a bit of starving.' Kopelev admitted 'with the rest of my generation, I firmly believed the ends justified the means. I saw people dying from hunger.' 'They deny responsibility for what happened later,' wrote Nadezhda Mandelstam, wife of the poet, in her classic memoir, *Hope Abandoned*. 'But how can they? It was, after all, these people of the Twenties who demolished the old values and invented the formulas ... to justify the unprecedented experiment: You can't make an omelette without breaking eggs. Every new killing was excused on the grounds we were building a remarkable "new" world.' The slaughter and famine strained the Party but its members barely winced: how did they tolerate death on such a vast scale?

* * *

'A revolution without firing squads,' Lenin is meant to have said, 'is meaningless.' He spent his career praising the Terror of the French Revolution because his Bolshevism was a unique creed, 'a social system based on blood-letting'. The Bolsheviks were atheists but they were hardly secular politicians in the conventional sense: they stooped to kill from the smugness of the highest moral eminence. Bolshevism may not have been a religion, but it was close enough. Stalin told Beria the Bolsheviks were 'a sort of military-religious order'. When Dzerzhinsky, founder of the Cheka died, Stalin called him 'a devout knight of the proletariat'. Stalin's 'order of sword-bearers' resembled the Knights Templars, or even the theocracy of the Iranian Ayatollahs, more than any traditional secular movement. They would die and kill for their faith in the inevitable progress towards human betterment, making sacrifices of their own families with a fervour only seen in the religious slaughters and martyrdoms of the Middle Ages – and the Middle East.

They regarded themselves as special 'noble-blooded' people. When Stalin asked General Zhukov if the capital might fall in 1941, he said, 'Can we hold Moscow, tell me as a Bolshevik?' as an eighteenth-century Englishman might say, 'Tell me as a gentleman!'

The 'sword-bearers' had to *believe* with Messianic faith, to act with the correct ruthlessness, and to convince others they were *right* to do so. Stalin's 'quasi-Islamic' fanaticism was typical of the Bolshevik magnates: Mikoyan's son called his father 'a Bolshevik fanatic'. Most* came from devoutly religious backgrounds. They hated Judaeo-Christianity – but the orthodoxy of their parents was replaced by something even more rigid, a systematic amorality: 'This religion – or science, as it was modestly called by its adepts – invests man with a godlike authority ... In the Twenties, a good many people drew a parallel to the victory of Christianity and thought this new religion would last a thousand years,' wrote Nadezhda Mandelstam. 'All were agreed on the superiority of the new creed that promised heaven on earth instead of other worldly rewards.'

The Party justified its 'dictatorship' through purity of faith. Their Scriptures were the teachings of Marxism-Leninism, regarded as a 'scientific' truth. Since ideology was so important, every leader had to be – or seem to be – an expert on Marxism-Leninism, so that these ruffians spent their weary nights studying, to improve their esoteric credentials, dreary articles on dialectical materialism. It was so important that Molotov and Polina even discussed Marxism in their love letters: 'Polichka my darling ... reading Marxist classics is very necessary ... You must read some more of Lenin's works coming out soon and then a number of Stalin's ... I so want to see you.'

'Partymindedness' was 'an almost mystical concept', explained Kopelev. 'The indispensable prerequisites were iron discipline and faithful observance of all the rituals of Party life.' As one veteran Communist put it, a Bolshevik was not someone who believed merely in Marxism but 'someone who had absolute faith in the Party no matter what ... A person with the ability to adapt his morality and conscience in such a way that he can unreservedly accept the dogma that the Party is never wrong – even though it's wrong all the time.' Stalin did not exaggerate when he boasted: 'We Bolsheviks are people of a special cut.'

* * *

Nadya was not of 'a special cut'. The famine fed the tensions in Stalin's marriage. When little Kira Alliluyeva visited her uncle

* If anything, the Old Bolsheviks had a religious education: Stalin, Yenukidze and Mikoyan were seminarists, Voroshilov a choirboy; Kalinin attended church into his teens. Even Beria's mother spent so much time at church, she actually died there. Kaganovich's Jewish parents were *frum*: when they visited him in the Kremlin, his mother was not impressed – 'But you're all atheists!' she said.

Redens, GPU chief in Kharkov, she opened the blinds of her special train and saw, to her amazement, starving people with swollen bellies, begging to the train for food, and starving dogs running alongside. Kira told her mother, Zhenya, who fearlessly informed Stalin.

'Don't pay any attention,' he replied. 'She's a child and makes things up.'* In the last year of Stalin's marriage, we find fragments of both happiness and misery. In February 1932, it was Svetlana's birthday: she starred in a play for her parents and Politburo. The two boys Vasya and Artyom recited verses.

'Things here seem to be alright, we're all very well. The children are growing up, Vasya is ten now and Svetlana five ... She and her father are great friends ...' Nadya wrote to Stalin's mother Keke in Tiflis. It was hardly an occasion to confide great secrets but the tone is interesting. 'Altogether we have terribly little free time, Joseph and I. You've probably heard that I've gone back to school in my old age. I don't find studying difficult in itself. But it's pretty difficult trying to fit it in with my duties at home in the course of the day. Still, I'm not complaining and so far, I'm coping with it all quite successfully. ...' She was finding it hard to cope.

Stalin's own nerves were strained to the limit but he remained jealous of her: he felt old friends Yenukidze and Bukharin were undermining him with Nadya. Bukharin visited Zubalovo, strolling the gardens with her. Stalin was working but returned and crept up on them in the garden, leaping out to shout at Bukharin:

'I'll kill you!' Bukharin naïvely regarded this as an Asiatic joke. When Bukharin married a teenage beauty, Anna Larina, another child of a Bolshevik family, Stalin tipsily telephoned him during the night: 'Nikolai I congratulate you. You outspit me this time too!' Bukharin asked how. 'A good wife, a beautiful wife ... younger than my Nadya!'

At home, Stalin alternated between absentee bully and hectored husband. Nadya had in the past snitched on dissenters at the Academy: in these last months, it is hard to tell if she was denouncing Enemies or riling Stalin who ordered their arrest. There is the story of this 'peppery woman' shouting at him:

* The Alliluyevs had only recently returned from Germany and they were shocked by the changes: 'There were barriers and queues everywhere,' remembered Kira. 'Everyone was hungry and scared. My mother was ashamed to wear the dresses she brought back. Everyone made fun of European fashions.'

'You're a tormentor, that's what you are! You torment your own son, your wife, the whole Russian people.' When Stalin discussed the importance of the Party above family, Yenukidze replied: 'What about your children?' Stalin shouted, 'They're hers!' pointing at Nadya, who ran out crying.

Nadya was becoming ever more hysterical, or as Molotov put it, 'unbalanced'. Sergo's daughter Eteri, who had every reason to hate Stalin, explains, 'Stalin didn't treat her well but she like all the Alliluyevs was very unstable.' She seemed to become estranged from the children and everything else. Stalin confided in Khrushchev that he sometimes locked himself in the bathroom, while she beat on the door, shouting.

'You're an impossible man. It's impossible to live with you!' This image of Stalin as the powerless henpecked husband besieged, cowering in his own bathroom by the wild-eyed Nadya, must rank as the most incongruous vision of the Man of Steel in his entire career. Himself frantic, with his mission in jeopardy, Stalin was baffled by Nadya's mania. She told a friend that 'everything bored her – she was sick of everything'.

'What about the children?' asked the friend.

'Everything, even the children.' This gives some idea of the difficulties Stalin faced. Nadya's state of mind sounds more like a psychological illness than despair caused by political protest or even her oafish husband. 'She had attacks of melancholy,' Zhenya told Stalin, she was 'sick'. The doctors prescribed 'caffeine' to pep her up. Stalin later blamed the caffeine and he was right: caffeine would have disastrously exacerbated her despair.

* * *

Stalin became hysterical himself, feeling the vast Ukrainian steppes slipping out of his control: 'It seems that in some regions of Ukraine, Soviet power has ceased to exist,' Stalin scribbled to Kosior, Politburo member and Ukrainian boss. 'Is this true? Is the situation so bad in Ukrainian villages? What's the GPU doing? Maybe you'll check this problem and take measures.' The magnates again roamed the heartland to raise grain, more ferocious semi-military expeditions with OGPU troops and Party officials wearing pistols – Molotov headed to the Urals, the Lower Volga and Siberia. While he was there, the wheels of his car became stuck in a muddy rut and the car rolled over into a ditch. No one was hurt but Molotov claimed, 'An attempt was made on my life.'

Stalin sensed the doubts of the local bosses, making him more aware than ever that he needed a new, tougher breed of lieutenant like Beria whom he promoted to rule the Caucasus. Summoning the Georgian bosses to Moscow, Stalin turned viciously against the Old Bolshevik 'chieftains':

'I've got the impression that there's no Party organization in Transcaucasia at all,' Stalin played to the gallery. 'There's just the rule of chieftains – voting for whomsoever they drink wine with … It's a total joke … We need to promote men who work honestly … Whenever we send anyone down there, they become chieftains too!' Everyone laughed but then he turned serious: 'We'll smash all their bones if this rule of chieftains isn't liquidated …'

Sergo was away.

'Where is he?' whispered one of the officials to Mikoyan who answered:

'Why should Sergo participate in Beria's coronation? He knows him well enough.' There was open opposition to the promotion of Beria: the local chiefs had almost managed to have him removed to a provincial backwater but Stalin had saved him. Then Stalin defined the essence of Beria's career:

'He solves problems while the Buro just pushes paper!'*

'It's not going to work, Comrade Stalin. We can't work together,' replied one Georgian.

'I can't work with that charlatan!' said another.

'We'll settle this question the routine way,' Stalin angrily ended the meeting, appointing Beria Georgian First Secretary and Second Secretary of Transcaucasia over their heads. Beria had arrived.

* * *

In Ukraine, Fred Beal wandered through villages where no one was left alive and found heartbreaking messages scrawled beside the bodies: 'God bless those who enter here, may they never suffer as we have,' wrote one. Another read: 'My son. We couldn't wait. God be with you.'

Kaganovich, patrolling the Ukraine, was unmoved. He was more outraged by the sissy leaders there: 'Hello dear Valerian,' he wrote warmly to Kuibyshev, 'We're working a lot on the question of grain preparation … We had to criticize the regions a lot,

---

* Margaret Thatcher used a similar expression about her favourite minister, Lord Young: 'He brings me solutions: others bring me problems.' Every leader prizes such lieutenants.

especially Ukraine. Their mood, particularly that of Chubar, is very bad ... I reprimanded the regions.' But in the midst of this wasteland of death, Kaganovich was not going to spoil anyone's holidays: 'How are you feeling? Where are you planning to go for holidays? Don't think I'm going to call you back before finishing your holidays ...'

After a final meeting with Kaganovich and Sergo in his office on 29 May 1932, Stalin and Nadya left for Sochi. Lakoba and Beria visited them but the latter now had his access to Stalin. He ditched his patron, Lakoba, who muttered in Beria's hearing,

'What a vile person.'

We do not know how Stalin and Nadya got on during this holiday but, day by day, the pressure ratcheted up. Stalin governed a country on the edge of rebellion by correspondence, receiving the bad news in heaps of GPU reports – and the doubts of his friends.* While Kaganovich suppressed the rebellious textile workers of Ivanovo, Voroshilov was unhappy and sent Stalin a remarkable letter: 'Across the Stavropol region, I saw all the fields uncultivated. We were expecting a good harvest but didn't get it ... Across the Ukraine from my train window, the truth is it looks even less cultivated than the North Caucasus ...' Voroshilov finished his note: 'Sorry to tell you such things during your holiday but I can't be silent.'

Stalin later told Churchill this was the most difficult time of his life, harder even than Hitler's invasion: 'it was a terrible struggle' in which he had to destroy 'ten million. It was fearful. Four years it lasted. It was absolutely necessary ... It was no use arguing with them. A certain number of them had been resettled in the northern parts of the country ... Others had been slaughtered by the peasants themselves – such had been the hatred for them.'

The peasants understandably attacked Communist officials. Sitting on the terrace of the Sochi dacha in the baking heat, an angry, defensive Stalin seethed about the breakdown of discipline and betrayal in the Party. At times like this, he seemed to retreat

---

* Stalin felt the 'circle of friends', tempered by the fight with the oppositions, was falling apart under the pressure of crisis and rows between Sergo and Molotov, as he confided in Kaganovich: Comrade Kuibyshev, already an alcoholic, 'creates a bad impression. It seems he flees from work ... Still worse is the conduct of Comrade Ordzhonikidze. The latter evidently does not take into account that his conduct (with sharpness against Comrades Molotov and Kuibyshev) leads to the undermining of our leading group.' Furthermore, Stalin was dissatisfied with Kosior and Rudzutak among others in the Politburo.

into a closed melodramatic fortress surrounded by enemies. On 14 July, he put pen to paper ordering Molotov and Kaganovich in Moscow to create a draconian law to shoot hungry peasants who stole even husks of grain. They drew up the notorious decree against 'misappropriation of socialist property' with grievous punishments 'based on the text of your letter'.* On 7 August, this became law. Stalin was now in a state of nervous panic, writing to Kaganovich: 'If we don't make an effort now to improve the situation in Ukraine, we may lose Ukraine.' Stalin blamed the weakness and naïvety of his brother-in-law, Redens, Ukrainian GPU chief, and the local boss Kosior. The place 'was riddled with Polish agents, who 'are many times stronger than Redens or Kosior think'. He had Redens replaced with someone tougher.

* * *

Nadya returned early to Moscow, perhaps to study, perhaps because the tension in Sochi was unbearable. Her headaches and abdominal pains worsened. This in turn can only have added to Stalin's anxieties but his nerves were so much stronger. Her letters do not survive: perhaps he destroyed them, perhaps she did not write any, but we know she had been influenced against the campaign: 'she was easily swayed by Bukharin and Yenukidze.'

Voroshilov crossed Stalin, suggesting that his policies could have been resisted by a concerted effort of the Politburo. When a Ukrainian comrade named Korneiev shot a (possibly starving) thief and was arrested, Stalin thought he should not be punished. But Voroshilov, an unlikely moral champion, looked into the case, discovered the victim was a teenager and wrote to Stalin to support Korneiev's sentence, even if he only served a short jail term. The day he received Klim's letter, 15 August, Stalin angrily overruled Voroshilov, freed Korneiev, and promoted him.

Six days after Voroshilov's stand, on 21 August, Riutin, who earlier had been arrested for criticizing Stalin, met with some comrades to agree their 'Appeal to All Party Members', a devastating manifesto for his deposition. Within days, Riutin had been denounced to the GPU. Riutin's opposition, so soon after the Syrtsov–Lominadze affair and Voroshilov's waverings, rattled

---

* Just as the grain fuelled the industrial engine, so did the peasants themselves. The same week, Stalin and Sergo, on holiday in Sochi, ordered Kaganovich and Molotov to transfer another 20,000 slave labourers, probably kulaks, to work on their new industrial city, Magnitogorsk. The repression perhaps deliberately provided slave labour.

Stalin. On 27 August, he was back in the Kremlin meeting Kaganovich. Perhaps he also returned to join Nadya.

Whatever the ghastly situation in the country, her health alone would have been enough to undermine the morale of a strong person. She was terribly ill, suffering 'acute pains in the abdominal region' with the doctor adding on her notes: 'Return for further examination.' This was not just caused by psychosomatic tension due to the crisis but also by the aftermath of the 1926 abortion.

On 31 August, Nadya was examined again: did Stalin accompany her to the Kremlevka clinic? He had only two appointments, at 4 p.m. and 9 p.m. as if his day had been deliberately left open. The doctors noted: 'Examination to consider operation in 3–4 weeks' time.' Was this for her abdomen or her head? Yet they did not operate.

On 30 September, Riutin was arrested. It is possible that Stalin, supported by Kaganovich, demanded the death penalty for Riutin but the execution of a comrade – a fellow 'sword-bearer' – was a dangerous step, resisted by Sergo and Kirov. There is no evidence that it was ever formally discussed – Kirov did not attend Politburo sessions in late September and October. Besides, Stalin would not have proposed such a measure without first canvassing Sergo and Kirov, just as he had in the case of Tukhachevsky in 1930. He probably never proposed it specifically. On 11 October, Riutin was sentenced to ten years in the camps.

Riutin's 'Platform' touched Stalin's home. According to the bodyguard Vlasik, Nadya procured a copy of the Riutin document from her friends at the Academy and showed it to Stalin. This does not mean she joined the opposition but it sounds aggressive, though she might also have been trying to be helpful. Later it was found in her room. In the fifties, Stalin admitted that he had not paid her enough attention during those final months: 'There was so much pressure on me ... so many Enemies. We had to work day and night ...' Perhaps literary matters proved a welcome distraction.

7

Stalin the Intellectual

On 26 October 1932, a chosen élite of fifty writers were mysteriously invited to the art deco mansion of Russia's greatest living novelist, Maxim Gorky.* The tall, haggard writer with the grizzled moustache, now sixty-four, met the guests on the stairway. The dining room was filled with tables covered in smart white cloths. They waited in excited anticipation. Then Stalin arrived with Molotov, Voroshilov and Kaganovich. The Party took literature so seriously that the magnates personally edited the work of prominent writers. After some small talk, Stalin and his comrades sat down at the end table near Gorky himself. Stalin stopped smiling and started to talk about the creation of a new literature.

It was a momentous occasion: Stalin and Gorky were the two most famous men in Russia, their relationship a barometer of Soviet literature itself. Ever since the late twenties, Gorky had been so close to Stalin that he had holidayed with Stalin and Nadya. Born Maxim Peshkov in 1868, he had used his own bitter (hence his *nom de plume*, Gorky) experiences as an orphaned street Arab, who had survived 'vile abominations' living on scraps among outcasts in peasant villages, to write masterpieces that inspired the Revolution. But in 1921, disillusioned with Lenin's dictatorship, he went into exile in a villa in Sorrento, Italy. Stalin put out feelers to lure him back. Meanwhile Stalin had placed Soviet literature under RAPP (the Russian Association of Proletarian Writers), 'the literary wing of Stalin's Five-Year Plan for industry', which harassed and attacked any writers who did not depict the Great Turn with ecstatic enthusiasm. Gorky and Stalin began a complex *pas de deux* in which vanity, money and power

---

* None of the great writers, like Akhmatova, Mandelstam, Pasternak, Bulgakov or Babel, were there but Sholokhov, whom Stalin regarded as 'a great artistic talent', was present.

played their role in encouraging the writer to return. Gorky's experience of the savage backwardness of the peasantry made him support Stalin's war on the villages but he found the standard of RAPP literature to be dire. By 1930, Gorky's life was already oiled with generous gifts from the GPU.

Stalin concentrated his feline charms on Gorky.* In 1931, he returned to become Stalin's literary ornament, granted a large allowance as well as the millions he made from his books. He lived in the mansion in Moscow that had belonged to the tycoon Ryabushinsky, a large dacha outside the capital and a palatial villa in the Crimea along with numerous staff, all GPU agents. Gorky's houses became the headquarters of the intelligentsia where he helped brilliant young writers like Isaac Babel and Vasily Grossman.

The magnates embraced Gorky as their own literary celebrity while the Chekist Yagoda took over the details of running Gorky's household, spending more and more time there himself. Stalin took his children to see Gorky where they played with his grandchildren; Mikoyan brought his sons to play with Gorky's pet monkey. Voroshilov came for sing-songs. Gorky's granddaugher Martha played with Babel one day; Yagoda the next.

Stalin liked him: 'Gorky was here,' he wrote to Voroshilov in an undated note. 'We talked about things. A good, clever, friendly person. He's fond of our policy. He understands everything ... In politics he's with us against the Right.' But he was also aware of Gorky as an asset who could be bought. In 1932, Stalin ordered the celebration of Gorky's forty literary years. His home town, Nizhni Novgorod, was renamed after him. So was Moscow's main street, Tverskaya. When Stalin named the Moscow Art Theatre after the writer, the literary bureaucrat Ivan Gronsky retorted:

'But Comrade Stalin, the Moscow Art Theatre is really more associated with Chekhov.'

'That doesn't matter. Gorky's a vain man. We must bind him with cables to the Party,' replied Stalin. It worked: during the kulak liquidation, Gorky unleashed his hatred of the backward

---

* 'During the Congress I was busy with work,' he wrote to Gorky during 1930 in a friendly, confiding tone. 'Now things are different and I can write. It's not of course good, but now we have the opportunity to smooth out the fault. "No fault, no repentance, no repentance, no salvation." They say you're writing a play about the wreckers and you want new material. I'm gathering material and will send it to you ... When are you coming to the USSR?' He treated Gorky almost as a member of the Soviet Government, consulting him on Molotov's promotion. If he was late in his replies, Stalin apologized for his 'swinish' behaviour.

peasants in *Pravda*: 'If the enemy does not surrender, he must be exterminated.' He toured concentration camps and admired their re-educational value. He supported slave labour projects such as the Belomor Canal which he visited with Yagoda, whom he congratulated: 'You rough fellows do not realize what great work you're doing!'

Yagoda, the dominant secret policeman, followed in Stalin's wake. 'The first generation of young Chekists ... was distinguished by its sophisticated tastes and weakness for literature,' wrote Nadezhda Mandelstam. 'The Chekists were the avant-garde of the New People.' The *grand seigneur* of this avant-garde was Yagoda, thirty-nine, who now fell in love with Gorky's daughter-in-law, Timosha; she was 'young, very beautiful, merry, simple, delightful' and married to Max Peshkov.

Son of a jeweller, trained as a statistician and learning pharmacy as a chemist's assistant, Genrikh Yagoda (his real first name was Enoch), who had joined the Party in 1907, was also from Nizhny Novgorod, which gave him his calling card. 'Superior to' the creatures that followed him, according to Anna Larina, Yagoda became 'a corrupt ... careerist' but he was never Stalin's man. He had been closer to the Rightists but swapped sides in 1929. His great achievement, supported by Stalin, was the creation by slave labour of the vast economic empire of the Gulags. Yagoda himself was devious, short and balding, always in full uniform, with a taste for French wines and sex toys: another green-fingered killer, he boasted that his huge dacha bloomed with '2000 orchids and roses', while spending almost four million roubles decorating his residences.* He frequented Gorky's houses, courting Timosha with bouquets of his orchids. Gorky was appointed head of the Writers' Union and advised Stalin to scrap the RAPP, which was abolished in April 1932, causing both delight and confusion among the intelligentsia who eagerly hoped for some improvement. Then came this invitation.

---

* Voroshilov, another Bolshevik *seigneur*, regularly sent Yagoda gifts: 'I received the horse,' Yagoda thanked Voroshilov in one note. 'It's not just a horse but a full-blooded thoroughbred. Warmest thanks. GY.' But Yagoda was also married to revolutionary royalty: Ida, his wife, was the niece of Sverdlov, the organizing genius and first Head of State. By coincidence, Gorky had adopted Ida's uncle. Yagoda's brother-in-law was Leopold Averbakh, a proletarian writer, who had been Chairman of RAPP, who helped lure Gorky back to Moscow and who formed one of his circle when he arrived.

Playing ominously with a pearl-handled penknife and now suddenly 'stern', with a 'taste of iron' in his voice, Stalin proposed: 'The artist ought to show life truthfully. And if he shows our life truthfully he cannot fail to show it moving to socialism. This is, and will be, Socialist Realism.' In other words, the writers had to describe what life should be, a panegyric to the Utopian future, not what life was. Then there was a touch of farce, as usual provided unconsciously by Voroshilov:

'You produce the goods that we need,' said Stalin. 'Even more than machines, tanks, aeroplanes, we need human souls.' But Voroshilov, ever the simpleton, took this literally and interrupted Stalin to object that tanks were also 'very important'.

The writers, Stalin declared, were 'engineers of human souls', a striking phrase of boldness and crudity – and he jabbed a finger at those sitting closest to him.

'Me? Why me?' retorted the nearest writer. 'I'm not arguing.'

'What's the good of just not arguing?' interrupted Voroshilov again. 'You have to get on with it.' By now, some of the writers were drunk on Gorky's wine and the heady aroma of power. Stalin filled their glasses. Alexander Fadeev, the drunken novelist and most notorious of literary bureaucrats, asked Stalin's favourite Cossack novelist, Mikhail Sholokhov, to sing. The writers clinked glasses with Stalin.

'Let's drink to the health of Comrade Stalin,' called out the poet Lugovskoi. The novelist Nikoforov jumped up and said:

'I'm fed up with this! We've drunk Stalin's health one million one hundred and forty-seven thousand times. He's probably fed up with it himself ...' There was silence. But Stalin shook Nikoforov's hand:

'Thank you, Nikoforov, thank you. I am fed up with it.'

* * *

None the less Stalin never tired of dealing with writers. When Mandelstam mused that poetry was more respected in Russia, where 'people are killed for it', than anywhere else, he was right. Literature mattered greatly to Stalin. He may have demanded 'engineers of the human soul' but he was himself far from the oafish philistine which his manners would suggest. He not only admired and appreciated great literature, he discerned the difference between hackery and genius. Ever since the seminary in the 1890s, he had read voraciously, claiming a rate of five hundred pages daily: in exile, when a fellow prisoner died, Stalin purloined his library and refused to share it with his outraged comrades. His hunger for literary knowledge was almost as driving as his Marxist faith and megalomania: one might say these were the ruling passions of his life. He did not possess literary talents himself but in terms of his reading alone, he was an intellectual, despite being the son of a cobbler and a washerwoman. Indeed, it would be no exaggeration to say that Stalin was the best-read ruler of Russia from Catherine the Great up to Vladimir Putin, even including Lenin who was no mean intellectual himself and had enjoyed the benefits of a nobleman's education.

'He worked very hard to improve himself,' said Molotov. His library consisted of 20,000 well-used volumes. 'If you want to know the people around you,' Stalin said, 'find out what they read.' Svetlana found books there from the *Life of Jesus* to the novels of Galsworthy,* Wilde, Maupassant and later Steinbeck and Hemingway. His granddaughter later noticed him reading Gogol, Chekhov, Hugo, Thackeray and Balzac. In old age, he was still discovering Goethe. He 'worshipped Zola'.

The Bolsheviks, who believed in the perfectibility of the New Man, were avid autodidacts, Stalin being the most accomplished and diligent of all. He read seriously, making notes, learning quotations, like an omnipotent student, leaving his revealing marginalia in books varying from Anatole France to Vipper's *History of Ancient Greece*. He had 'a very good knowledge of antiquity and mythology', recalled Molotov. He could quote from the Bible, Chekhov and *Good Soldier Svejk*, as well as Napoleon, Bismarck and Talleyrand. His knowledge of Georgian literature was such that he debated arcane poetry with Shalva Nutsibidze the philosopher, who said, long after Stalin was no longer a god, that his editorial comments were outstanding. He read literature aloud to his circle – usually Saltykov-Shchedrin or a new edition of the medieval Georgian epic poem by Rustaveli, *The Knight in the Panther Skin*. He adored *The Last of the Mohicans*, amazing a young translator whom he greeted in *faux*-Red Indian: 'Big chief greets paleface!'

His deeply conservative tastes remained nineteenth century

---

* *The Forsyte Saga* by Galsworthy and Fenimore Cooper's *Last of the Mohicans* were probably the most popular foreign works for the entire Politburo who all seemed to be reading what they analysed as a damning indictment of a capitalist family, and of British imperialist repression in the Americas.

even during the Modernist blossoming of the twenties: he was always much happier with Pushkin and Tchaikovsky than with Akhmatova and Shostakovich. He respected intellectuals, his tone changing completely when dealing with a famous professor. 'I'm very sorry that I'm unable to satisfy your request now, illustrious Nikolai Yakovlevich,' he wrote to the linguistics professor, Marr. 'After the conference, I'll be able to give us 40–50 minutes if you'll agree ...'

Stalin could certainly appreciate genius but, as with love and family, his belief in Marxist progress was brutally paramount. He admired that 'great psychologist' Dostoevsky but banned him because he was 'bad for young people'. He enjoyed the satires of the Leningrad satirist Mikhail Zoschenko so much, even though they mocked Soviet bureaucrats, he used to read extracts to his two boys, Vasily and Artyom, and would laugh at the end: 'Here is where Comrade Zoschenko remembered the GPU and changed the ending!' – a joke typical of his brutal cynicism crossed with dry gallows humour. He recognized that Mandelstam, Pasternak and Bulgakov were geniuses, but their work was suppressed. Yet he could tolerate whimsical maestros: Bulgakov and Pasternak were never arrested. But woe betide anyone, genius or hack, who insulted the person or policy of Stalin – for the two were synonymous.

His comments are most fascinating when he was dealing with a master like Bulgakov whose Civil War play, *Days of the Turbins*, based on his novel *The White Guard*, was Stalin's favourite: he saw it fifteen times. When Bulgakov's play *Flight* was attacked as 'anti-Soviet and Rightist', Stalin wrote to the theatre director: 'It's not good calling literature Right and Left. These are Party words. In literature, use class, anti-Soviet, revolutionary or anti-revolutionary but not Right or Left ... If Bulgakov would add to the eight dreams, one or two where he would discover the international social content of the Civil War, the spectator would understand that the honest "Serafima" and the professor were thrown away from Russia, not by the caprice of Bolsheviks, but because they lived on the necks of the people. It's easy to criticize *Days of the Turbins* – it's easy to reject but it's hardest to write good plays. The final impression of the play is good for Bolshevism.' When Bulgakov was not allowed to work, he appealed to Stalin who telephoned him to say, 'We'll try to do something for you.'

Stalin's gift, apart from his catechismic rhythms of question and answer, was the ability to reduce complex problems to lucid simplicity, a talent that is invaluable in a politician. He could draft, usually in his own hand, a diplomatic telegram, speech or article straight off in the clearest, yet often subtle prose (as he showed during the war) – but he was also capable of clumsy crudity, though partly this reflected his self-conscious proletarian machismo.*

Stalin was not just supreme censor; he relished his role as imperial editor-in-chief, endlessly tinkering with other men's prose, loving nothing more than scribbling the expression that covers the pages of his library – that mirthless chuckle:

'Ha-ha-ha!'

* * *

Stalin's sneering did not help Nadya whose depression, stoked by caffeine and Stalin's own stress, worsened. Yet there were also moments of touching tenderness: Nadya took an unaccustomed drink which made her sick. Stalin put her to bed and she looked up at him and said pathetically:

'So you love me a little after all.' Years later, Stalin recounted this to his daughter.

At Zubalovo for the weekend, Nadya, who never gave Svetlana a word of praise, warned her to refuse if Stalin offered her wine:

'Don't take the alcohol!' If Nadya was taking Stalin's small indulgence of his children as a grave sin, one can only imagine how desperately she felt about his brusqueness, never mind the tragedy of the peasants. During those last days, Nadya visited her brother Pavel and his wife Zhenya, who had just returned from Berlin, in their apartment in the House on the Embankment: 'She said hello to me in the coldest way,' their daughter Kira noticed but then Nadya was a stern woman. Nadya spent some evenings working on designs with Dora Khazan, whispering in the bedroom of the latter's daughter, Natalya Andreyeva.

So we are left with a troubling picture of a husband and wife who alternated between loving kindness and vicious explosions

---

* Boris Pilniak, Russia's most respected novelist until Gorky's return, who had fallen into disfavour, wrote nervously to Stalin to ask if he could go abroad: 'Esteemed Comrade Pilniak,' replied the leader (sarcastically since he hated Pilniak for his short story 'Tale of the Unextinguished Moon', implying Stalin had arranged the medical murder of Defence Commissar Frunze in 1925), 'Inquiries show the bodies of control are not opposed to your going abroad. They doubted it but now cease to doubt. So … your going abroad is decided. Good luck. Stalin.' Pilniak was executed on 21 April 1938.

of rage, parents who treated the children differently. Both were given to humiliating one another in public yet Nadya still seemed to have loved 'my man' as she called him. It was a tense time but there was one difference between this highly-strung, thin-skinned couple. Stalin was crushingly strong, as Nadya told his mother: 'I can say that I marvel at his strength and his energy. Only a really healthy man could stand the amount of work he gets through.' She on the other hand was weak. If one was to break, it was she. His stunted emotional involvement allowed him to weather the hardest blows.

Kaganovich again headed out of his Moscow fiefdom to crush dissent in the Kuban, ordering mass reprisals against the Cossacks and deporting fifteen villages to Siberia. Kaganovich called this 'the resistance of the last remnants of the dying classes leading to a concrete form of the class struggle'. The classes were dying all right. Kopelev saw 'women and children with distended bellies, turning blue, still breathing but with vacant lifeless eyes. And corpses – corpses in ragged sheepskin coats and cheap felt boots; corpses in peasant huts, in the melting snow of old Vologda, under the bridges of Kharkov.' 'Iron Lazar' arranged an array of executions of grain hoarders and was back in time for the fatal holiday dinner for the anniversary of the Revolution.

On 7 November, the potentates took the salute from atop Lenin's newly completed grey marble Mausoleum. They gathered early in Stalin's apartment in their greatcoats and hats for it was below freezing. Nadya was already taking her place in the parade as a delegate of the Academy. The housekeeper and nannies made sure Vasily and Artyom were dressed and ready; Svetlana was still at the dacha.

Just before 8 a.m., the leaders walked chatting out of the Poteshny Palace across the central square, past the Yellow Palace towards the steps that led up to the Mausoleum. It was bitterly cold up there; the parade lasted four hours.* Voroshilov and Budyonny waited on horseback at different Kremlin gates. As the Spassky Tower, Moscow's equivalent of Big Ben, tolled, they

---

* There were chairs hidden there for those of weak disposition to take a rest and, even better, there was a room behind with a bar for those who needed Dutch courage. The first Bolshevik Head of State, Yakov Sverdlov, died in 1919 after a freezing parade; the Politburo member Alexander Shcherbakov died after attending the 1945 victory parade; the Czech President Klement Gottwald died after enduring the icy hours of Stalin's funeral on the Mausoleum.

trotted out to meet in the middle in front of the Mausoleum, then dismounted to join the leadership.

Many people saw Nadya that day. She did not seem either depressed or unhappy with Stalin. She marched past, raising her oval face towards the leaders. Afterwards she met up with Vasily and Artyom on the tribune to the right of the Mausoleum, and bumped into Khrushchev, whom she had introduced to Stalin. She looked up at her husband in his greatcoat but, like any wife, she worried that Stalin's coat was open:

'My man didn't take his scarf. He'll catch cold and get sick,' she said – but suddenly she was struck with one of her agonizing headaches. 'She started moaning, "Oh my headache!"' remembers Artyom. After the parade, the boys requested the housekeeper to ask Nadya if they could spend the holiday at Zubalovo. It was easier to persuade the housekeeper than tackle the severe mother.

'Let them go to the dacha,' Nadya replied, adding cheerfully, 'I'll soon graduate from the Academy and then there'll be a real holiday for everyone!' She winced. 'Oh! My headache!' Stalin, Voroshilov and others were carousing in the little room behind the Mausoleum where there was always a buffet.

Next morning the boys were driven off to Zubalovo. Stalin worked as usual in his office, meeting Molotov, Kuibyshev and CC Secretary, Pavel Postyshev. Yagoda showed the transcripts of another anti-Stalin meeting of the Old Bolsheviks, Smirnov and Eismont, one of whom had asked, 'Don't tell me there's nobody in this whole country capable of removing him.' They ordered their arrest, then they walked over to the Voroshilovs' for dinner. Nadya too was on her way there. She looked her best.

Some time in the early hours, Nadya took the Mauser pistol that her brother Pavel had given her and lay on the bed in her room. Suicide was a Bolshevik death: she had attended the funeral of Adolf Yoffe, the Trotskyite who protested against Stalin's defeat of the oppositions by shooting himself in 1929. In 1930, the Modernist poet, Mayakovsky, also made that supreme protest. She raised the pistol to her breast and pulled the trigger once. No one heard the voice of that tiny feminine weapon; Kremlin walls are thick. Her body rolled off the bed on to the floor.

Part Two

The Jolly Fellows:
Stalin and Kirov, 1932–1934

8

The Funeral

Nadya died instantly. Hours later, Stalin stood in the dining room absorbing the news. He asked his sister-in-law Zhenya Alliluyeva 'what was missing in him'. The family were shocked when he threatened suicide, something they 'had never heard before'. He grieved in his room for days: Zhenya and Pavel decided to stay with him to make sure he did not harm himself. He could not understand why it had happened, raging what did it mean? Why had such a terrible stab in the back been dealt to him of all people? 'He was too intelligent not to know that people always commit suicide in order to punish someone ...' wrote his daughter Svetlana, so he kept asking whether it was true he had been inconsiderate, hadn't he loved her? 'I was a bad husband,' he confessed to Molotov, 'I had no time to take her to the cinema.' He told Vlasik, 'She's completely overturned my life!' He stared sadly at Pavel, growling, 'That was a hell of a nice present you gave her! A pistol!'

Around 1 p.m., Professor Kushner and a colleague examined the body of Nadezhda Stalin in her little bedroom. 'The position of the body,' the professor scrawled on a piece of squared paper ripped from one of the children's exercise books, 'was that her head is on the pillow turned to the right side. Near the pillow on the bed is a little gun.' The housekeeper must have replaced the gun on the bed. 'The face is absolutely tranquil, the eyes semi-closed, semi-open. On the right part of face and neck, there are blue and red marks and blood ...' There were bruises on her face: did Stalin really have something to hide? Had he returned to the apartment, quarrelled with her, hit her and then shot her? Given his murderous pedigree, one more death is not impossible. Yet the bruise could have been caused by falling off the bed. No one with any knowledge of that night has ever suggested that Stalin killed her. But he was certainly aware that his enemies would whisper that he had.

'There is a five-millimetre hole over the heart – an open hole,' noted the professor. 'Conclusion — death was immediate from an open wound to the heart.' This scrap of paper, which one can now see in the State Archive, was not to be seen again for six decades.

Molotov, Kaganovich and Sergo came and went, deciding what to do: as usual in such moments, the Bolshevik instinct was to lie and cover up, even though in this case, if they had been more open, they might have avoided the most damaging slanders. It was clear enough that Nadya had committed suicide but Molotov, Kaganovich and her godfather Yenukidze got Stalin's agreement that this self-destruction could not be announced publicly. It would be taken as a political protest. They would announce she had died of appendicitis. The doctors, a profession whose Hippocratic oath was to be as much undermined by the Bolsheviks as by the Nazis, signed the lie. Servants were informed that Stalin had been at his dacha with Molotov and Kalinin – but unsurprisingly, they gossiped dangerously.

Yenukidze drafted the announcement of her death and then wrote a letter of condolence, to be published next day in *Pravda*, signed by all the leaders' wives and then the leaders themselves, starting with Nadya's four greatest friends – Ekaterina Voroshilova, Polina Molotova, Dora Khazan and Maria Kaganovich: 'Our close friend, a person with a wonderful soul ... young, vigorous and devoted to the Bolshevik Party and the Revolution.' Even this death was seen by these singular dogmatists in terms of Bolshevism.

Since Stalin was barely functioning, Yenukidze and the magnates debated how to arrange this unique funeral. The Bolshevik funeral ritual combined elements of Tsarist funeral tradition with its own idiosyncratic culture. The deceased were beautified by the finest morticians, usually the professors in charge of Lenin's cadaver, then lay in state, snowy faces often heavily rouged, among the surreal *mise-en-scène* of lush tropical palms, bouquets, red banners, all unnaturally illuminated with arc lights. The Politburo bore the open coffin to, and from, the Hall of Columns where they also stood guard like knights of old. The rigorous eminence was then cremated and a plangent, military funeral was held, with the Politburo again bearing an elaborate catafalque enclosing the urn of ashes which they placed in the Kremlin Wall. But Stalin himself must have demanded an old-fashioned funeral.

Yenukidze presided over the Funeral Commission with Dora Khazan, Andreyev's wife, and Pauker, the Chekist who was so close to Stalin. They met first thing next morning and decided on the procession, the place of burial, the guard of honour. Pauker, the theatrical expert – ex-coiffeur of the Budapest Opera – was in charge of the orchestras: there were to be two, a military one and a theatrical one of fifty instruments.

Stalin could not speak himself. He asked Kaganovich, the Politburo's best speaker, to give the oration. Even that energetic bulldozer of a man, fresh from shooting droves of innocent Kuban Cossacks, was daunted by the burden of giving such a speech in front of Stalin himself, but as with so many other macabre chores, 'Stalin asked and I did it.'

The death of Nadya from appendicitis was broken to the children out at Zubalovo: Artyom was distraught but Vasily never recovered. Svetlana, six, did not grasp this finality. Voroshilov, who was so kind in all matters outside politics, visited her but could not talk for weeping. The older children were driven to Moscow. Svetlana remained in the country until the funeral.

When the body was removed from the apartment, some time on the morning of the 10th, a little girl in the Horse Guards, opposite Stalin's Poteshny Palace, sat glued to the window of her apartment. Natalya Andreyeva, daughter of Andreyev and Dora Khazan who was managing the funeral with Yenukidze, watched as a group of men carried down the coffin. Stalin walked beside it, wearing no gloves in the freezing cold, clutching at the side of the coffin with tears running down his cheeks. The body must have been taken to the Kremlevka to cover up the bruises.

The schoolboys, Vasily Stalin and Artyom, arrived at Stalin's flat where Pavel, Zhenya and Nadya's sister Anna, took turns watching over the widower who remained in his room and would not come out for dinner. The gloomy apartment was pervaded by whispers: Artyom's mother arrived and foolishly told her son the spellbinding truth about the suicide. Artyom rashly asked the housekeeper about it. Both he and his mother were reprimanded. 'The things I saw in that house!' recalls Artyom.

During the night, the body was delivered ·to the ·Hall of Columns close to Red Square and the Kremlin. It was to be the scene of some of the great trials and lying-in-states of Stalin's rule. At eight the next morning, Yagoda joined the Funeral Commission.

The three smaller children were taken to the hall where Nadezhda Alliluyeva Stalin lay in an open casket, her round face surrounded by bouquets, her bruises exquisitely powdered and rouged away by Moscow's macabre maestros. 'She was very beautiful in her coffin, very young, her face clear and lovely,' recalls her niece Kira Alliluyeva. Zina Ordzhonikidze, the plump half-Yakut wife of the irrepressible Sergo, took Svetlana's hand and led her up to the coffin. She cried and they rushed her out. Yenukidze comforted her, despatching her back to Zubalovo. She only learned of the suicide a decade later, incongruously from the *Illustrated London News*.

Stalin arrived accompanied by the Politburo who stood guard around the catafalque, a duty to which they were to grow accustomed in the deadly years ahead. Stalin was weeping. Vasily left Artyom and ran forward towards Stalin and 'hung on to his father, saying, "Papa don't cry!"' To a chorus of sobs from Nadya's family and the hardmen of the Politburo and Cheka, the *Vozhd* approached the coffin with Vasily holding on to him. Stalin looked down at this woman who had loved, hated, punished and rejected him. 'I'd never seen Stalin cry before,' said Molotov, 'but as he stood there beside the coffin, the tears ran down his cheeks.'

'She left me like an enemy,' Stalin said bitterly but then Molotov heard him say: 'I didn't save you.' They were about to nail down the coffin when Stalin suddenly stopped them. To everyone's surprise, he leaned down, lifted Nadya's head and began to kiss her ardently. This provoked more weeping.

The coffin was carried out into Red Square where it was laid on a black funeral carriage with four little onion domes on each corner holding an intricate canopy, a cortège that seemed to belong in Tsarist times. There was an honour guard marching around it and the streets were lined with soldiers. Six grooms in black led six horses and ahead, a military brass band played the funeral march. Bukharin, who was close to Nadya but had tainted her politically, offered his condolences to Stalin. The widower insisted strangely that he had gone to the dacha after the banquet; he was not in the apartment. The death was nothing to do with him. So Stalin propagated an alibi.

The procession set off through the streets, the public held far back by police. Here was the first of many funerals in which the cause of death was concealed from most of the mourners. Stalin walked between Molotov and the shrewd, hawk-eyed Armenian

Mikoyan, themselves flanked by Kaganovich and Voroshilov. Pauker, resplendent in his uniform, belly buttressed by his invisible corset, kept pace to the side. Vasily and Artyom walked behind them along with the family, the cream of the Bolshevik movement and delegates from Nadya's Academy. Her mother Olga blamed Nadya:

'How could you do this?' she addressed her absent daughter. 'How could you leave the children?' Most of the family and leaders agreed, and sympathized with Stalin.

'Nadya was wrong,' declared the forthright Polina. 'She left him at such a difficult time.'

Artyom and Vasily fell behind the band and lost sight of Stalin. It has variously been claimed that Stalin either did not go to the funeral or that he walked all the way to the Novodevichy Cemetery. Neither is true. Yagoda insisted that it was not safe for Stalin to walk the whole route. When the procession reached Manege Square, Stalin, along with the deceased's mother, were driven to the cemetery.

At Novodevichy, Stalin stood on one side of the grave and the two boys, Vasily and Artyom, watched him from the other. Bukharin spoke, then Yenukidze announced the main speaker: 'It was so difficult,' Kaganovich remembered, 'with Stalin there.' The Iron Commissar, more used to tub-thumping broadsides, delivered his oration in that special Bolshevik language:

'Comrades, we are at the funeral of one of our best members of our Party. She grew up in the family of a Bolshevik worker ... organically connected with our Party ... she was the devoted friend of those who ruled ... fighting the great struggle. She distinguished herself by the best features of a Bolshevik – firmness, toughness in the struggle ...' Then he turned to the leader: 'We're close friends and comrades of Comrade Stalin. We understand the weight of Comrade Stalin's loss ... We understand we must share the burdens of Comrade Stalin's loss.'

Stalin picked up a handful of soil and threw it on to the coffin. Artyom and Vasily were asked to do the same. Artyom asked why it was necessary. 'So she can have some earth from your hand,' he was told. Later Stalin chose the monument that rested over her grave, with a rose to remember the one she wore in her hair and proudly emblazoned with the sacred words: 'Member of the Bolshevik Party.' For the rest of his life, Stalin ruminated on her death. 'Oh Nadya, Nadya, what did you do?' he mused in his old age, excusing himself: 'There was always so much pressure on me.' The suicide of a spouse usually affects the surviving partner, often leaving the bitter taste of guilt, betrayal and, above all, desertion. Nadya's abandonment of Stalin wounded and humiliated him, breaking one more of his meagre ties to human sympathy, redoubling his brutality, jealousy, coldness and self-pity. But the political challenges of 1932, particularly what Stalin regarded as betrayals by some of his comrades, also played their part. 'After 1932,' Kaganovich observed, 'Stalin changed.'

* * *

The family watched over Stalin, letting themselves into the apartment in case he needed anything. One night, Zhenya Alliluyeva visited him but there was no sound. Then she heard an ugly screeching and found the *Vozhd* lying on a sofa in the half-light, spitting on the wall. She knew he had been there a very long time because the wall was dripping with glistening trails of spit.

'What on earth are you doing, Joseph?' she asked him. 'You can't stay like that.' He said nothing, staring at the saliva rolling down the wall.

At the time, Maria Svanidze, the wife of Alyosha, his former brother-in-law, who now began to keep a remarkable diary,* thought Nadya's death had made him 'less of a marble hero'. In his despair, he repeated two questions:

'Never mind the children, they forgot her in a few days, but how could she do this to me?' Sometimes he saw it the other way round, asking Budyonny: 'I understand how she could do this to me, but what about the children?' Always the conversation ended thus: 'She broke my life. She crippled me.' This was a humiliating personal failure that undermined his confidence. Stalin, wrote Svetlana, 'wanted to resign but the Politburo said, "No, no, you have to stay!"'

He swiftly recovered the Messianic confidence in his mission: the war against the peasants and his enemies within the Party. His mind strayed on to the newly arrested Eismont, Smirnov and Riutin whose 'Platform' had been found in his wife's room. He was drinking a lot, suffering insomnia. A month after her death, on 17 December, he scrawled a strange note to Voroshilov:

---

* Maria 'Marusya' Svanidze was to become a vital figure in Stalin's entourage: her handwritten diary, which is one of the most revealing documents of the thirties, was preserved by Stalin in his own archive.

'The cases of Eismont, Smirnov and Riutin are full of alcohol. We see an opposition steeped in vodka. Eismont, Rykov. Hunting wild animals. Tomsky, repeat Tomsky. Roaring wild animals that growl. Smirnov and other Moscow rumours. Like a desert. I feel terrible, not sleeping much.' This letter shows how disturbed Stalin was after Nadya's death. It reeks of drink and despair.

He did not soften towards the peasants. On 28 December, Postyshev sent Stalin a note about placing GPU guards on grain elevators because so much bread was being stolen by starving people. Then he added, 'There've been strong elements of sabotage of bread supplies in the collective Machine Tractor Stations ... Let me send 2–300 kulaks from Dneipropetrovsk to the North by order of the GPU.'

'Right! *Pravilno!*' agreed Stalin enthusiastically in his blue pencil.

Nadya hung over Stalin until his own death. Whenever he met anyone who knew Nadya well, he talked about her. Two years later, when he met Bukharin at the theatre, he missed a whole act, talking about Nadya, how he could not live without her. He often discussed her with Budyonny.* The family met every 8th of November to remember her but he hated these anniversaries, remaining in the south – yet he always kept photographs of her, larger and larger ones, round his houses. He claimed he gave up dancing when Nadya died.

Thousands of letters of condolence poured into Stalin's *apparat* so the few he chose to keep are interesting: 'She was fragile as a flower,' read one. Perhaps he preserved it because it finished about him: 'Remember, we need you so take care of yourself.' Then he kept a poem sent to him, dedicated to her, that again appealed to his vision of self:

Night ocean, Wild storm ...
A haunted silhouette on the bridge of the ship.
It's the captain. Who is he?
A man of blood and flesh.
Or is he iron and steel?

When students wanted to name their institute after her, he did not agree but simply sent the request to Nadya's sister, Anna:

* Budyonny had lost his first wife in a possible suicide, perhaps when she discovered his relationship with his future second wife, the singer Olga. Ironically the other Soviet leader whose wife had committed suicide was the brilliant commander most hated by Stalin – Mikhail Tukhachevsky.

'After reading this note, leave it on my desk!' The pain of the subject was still fresh sixteen years later when a sculptor wrote to say that he wanted to give Stalin a bust of Nadya. Stalin wrote laconically to Poskrebyshev, his *chef de cabinet:* 'Tell him that you received the letter and you're returning it. Stalin.'

There was no time for mourning. The Party was at war.

* * *

At 4 p.m. on 12 November, the day after the funeral, Stalin arrived at his office to meet Kaganovich, Voroshilov, Molotov and Sergo. Alongside them was Stalin's closest friend, Sergei Mironich Kirov, First Secretary of Leningrad and Politburo member. 'After Nadya's tragic death', Maria Svanidze noticed that 'Kirov was the closest person who managed to approach Joseph intimately and simply, to give him that missing warmth and cosiness.' Stalin turned to Kirov who, he said, 'cared for me like a child'.

Always singing operatic arias loudly, brimming with good cheer and boyish enthusiasm, Kirov was one of those uncomplicated men who win friends easily. Small, handsome with deep-set brown, slightly Tartar eyes, pock-marked, brown-haired and high-cheekboned, women and men seemed to like him equally. Married without children, he was said to be a womanizer with a special eye on the ballerinas of the Mariinsky Ballet which he controlled in Leningrad.* Certainly he followed ballet and opera closely, listening to it in his own apartment by a special link. A workaholic like his comrades, Kirov liked the outdoors, camping and hunting, with his boon companion Sergo. Like Andreyev, Kirov was an avid mountaineer, an appropriate hobby for a Bolshevik. He was at ease in his own skin. It was perhaps this that made him so attractive to Stalin whose friendships resembled crushes – and, like crushes, they could turn swiftly into bitter envy. Now he wanted to be with Kirov all the time: Kirov was in and out of his office five times during the days after Nadya's funeral.

Born Sergei Kostrikov in 1886, the son of a feckless clerk who left him an orphan, in Urzhum, five hundred miles north-east of Moscow, Kirov was sent by charity to the Kazan Industrial School where he excelled. But the 1905 Revolution interfered with his plans for university and he joined the Social Democrat Party, becoming a professional revolutionary. In between exiles, he

---

* It was therefore entirely appropriate that the Mariinsky should be renamed the Kirov after his death.

married the daughter of a Jewish watchmaker but like all good Bolsheviks, his personal life 'was subordinated to the revolutionary cause', according to his wife. During the doldrums before the war, Kirov had worked as a journalist in the bourgeois press, which was strictly banned by the Party, and this was a black mark on his Bolshevik pedigree. Nineteen seventeen found him setting up power in the Terek in the North Caucasus. During the Civil War, Kirov was one of the swashbuckling commissars in the North Caucasus beside Sergo and Mikoyan. In Astrakhan he enforced Bolshevik power in March 1919 with liberal blood-letting: over four thousand were killed. When a *bourgeois* was caught hiding his own furniture, Kirov ordered him shot. He and Sergo, whose lives and deaths were parallel, engineered the seizure of Georgia in 1921, remaining in Baku afterwards, both brutal Bolsheviks of the Civil War generation. He had probably met Stalin in 1917 but got to know his patron on holiday in 1925:

'Dear Koba, I'm in Kislovodsk … I'm getting better. In a week, I'll come to you … Greetings to everyone. Say hello to Nadya,' he wrote. Kirov was a family favourite. Stalin inscribed a copy of his book *On Lenin and Leninism*: 'To SM Kirov, my friend and beloved brother.' In 1926, Stalin removed Zinoviev from his Leningrad power base and promoted Kirov to take over Peter the Great's capital, now the second largest Party in the State. He joined the Politburo in 1930.

When Kirov asked if he could fly south to join him for the 1931 holidays, Stalin replied: 'I have no right and would not advise anyone to authorize flights. I most humbly request you to come by train.' Artyom, often on these holidays, recalls, 'Stalin was so fond of Kirov, he'd personally meet Kirov's train in Sochi.' Stalin always had 'a lovely time with Kirov', even swimming and visiting the *banya*. Sometimes when Kirov swam, 'Stalin went to the beach and sat waiting for Kirov', says Artyom.

After Nadya's death, Stalin's friendship with 'my Kirich' became more insistent. Stalin often called him in Leningrad at any time of the night: the *vertushka* phone can still be seen by Kirov's bed in his apartment. When he came to Moscow, Kirov preferred to stay with Sergo who was so fond of his boon companion that his widow remembered how he once faked a car crash to ensure that Kirov missed his train.* Yet Stalin and Kirov were 'like a pair of

---

* Faked car crashes, often with fatal effects, were to become a bizarre feature of Stalin's rule.

equal brothers, teasing one another, telling dirty stories, laughing', says Artyom. 'Big friends, brothers and they needed one another.'

This did not mean that Stalin completely trusted Kirov. In the autumn of 1929, Stalin orchestrated *Pravda*'s criticism of Kirov. However fond he was of Kirov, Stalin could also be cross with him. In June 1928, one of his articles seemed to have been edited when it appeared in *Leningradskaya Pravda*, provoking a letter that revealed Stalin's thin-skinned paranoia on even small matters: 'I understand ... the technical reasons ... Yet I've heard no other such examples of articles by Politburo members ... It seems strange that the 40–50 words reduced are the brightest about how the peasantry are a capitalist class ... I await your explanation.'

Kirov did not regard Stalin as a saint: during the 1929 birthday celebrations that raised Stalin to *Vozhd*, the Leningraders dared to mention Lenin's views on Stalin's rudeness. Kirov knew Stalin's unusual mentality well: when a student sent him some questions on ideology, he forwarded them to Kirov with this note: 'Kirov! You must read the letter of student Fedotov ... an absolutely politically illiterate young man. Maybe you will telephone him and talk to him, probably he is a corrupted drunken "Party member". We must not introduce the GPU I think. By the way, the student is a very good trickster with an anti-Soviet face which he conceals artistically beneath a simple face that says "Help me understand. Maybe you understand all – I don't." Greetings! Stalin.' No doubt Kirov's intimacy with Sergo, Kuibyshev and Mikoyan worried Stalin. The challenges of 1932 – the Riutin Platform, Kirov's possible resistance to Riutin's execution, the famine, the suicide of Nadezhda – had shown Stalin needed firmer loyalty.

After Nadya's death, Kirov was almost part of the family: Stalin insisted he stay with him, not Sergo. Kirov stayed at Stalin's apartment so often he knew where the sheets and pillows were and he would bed down on the sofa. The children loved Kirov and sometimes when he was there, Svetlana would put on a doll show for him. Her favourite game was her own mock government. Her father was 'First Secretary'. This Stalinette wrote orders like: 'To my First Secretary, I order you to allow me to go with you to the theatre.' She signed it 'The Mistress or Boss (*khozyaika*) Setanka.' She hung the notes in the dining room above the telephone table. Stalin replied: 'I obey.' Kaganovich, Molotov and Sergo were Setanka's Second Secretaries, but 'she has a special friendship with

Kirov', noticed Maria Svanidze, 'because Joseph is so good and close with him'.

Stalin returned to the ascetic Bedouin life of the underground Bolshevik, with the tension and variety of the revolutionary on the run, except that now his restless progress more resembled the train of a Mongol Khan. Though a creature of routine, he needed perpetual movement: there were beds in his houses but there were also big, hard divans in every room. 'I never sleep on a bed,' he told a visitor. 'Always a divan' and on whichever one he happened to be reading. 'Which historical person had the same Spartan habit?' he asked, answering with that autodidactic omniscience: 'Nicholas I.' Nadya's death naturally changed the way Stalin and his children lived.

9

The Omnipotent Widower and his
Loving Family: Sergo the Bolshevik Prince

Stalin could not bear to go on living in the Poteshny Palace apartment and the Zubalovo mansion because Nadya's homes were too painful for him. Bukharin offered to swap apartments. Stalin accepted this comradely offer and moved into Bukharin's apartment on the first floor of the triangular Yellow Palace, the old Senate,* roughly beneath his office. Since his office stood where the two wings of the Senate met at an angle, it was known to the *cognoscenti* as the 'Little Corner'. Its polished floors, with their red and green carpets running down the centre, its wooden panelling up to shoulder height, its dreary drapes, were kept as clean and silent as a hospital. His secretary, Poskrebyshev, sat at the front of the anteroom, his desk immaculate, controlling access. Stalin's office itself was long, airy and rectangular, heavy with drapes, and lined with ornate Russian stoves against which he would lean to ease the aching in his limbs. A huge desk stood at the far right corner while a long green baize table, with straight-backed chairs in white covers, stood to the left beneath portraits of Marx and Lenin.

Downstairs, his 'formal', gloomy apartment with the 'vaulted ceilings' was to be his Moscow residence until his death. 'It was not like a home,' wrote Svetlana. It had once been a corridor. He expected the children to be there every evening when he returned for supper to review and sign their homework, like every parent.

* President Putin still rules from this building, the seat of power in Russia since Lenin. Putin's Chief of Staff works in Stalin's old office. Until 1930, Stalin kept his main office on the fifth floor of the grey granite edifice of the Central Committee building on Old Square, up the hill from the Kremlin, where he had been well served by his successive secretaries, Lev Mekhlis, who went on to greater things, and Tovstukha who died prematurely. It was here that Stalin planned his campaigns against Trotsky, Zinoviev and Bukharin. In 1930, Poskrebyshev and the Special Sector, the fulcrum of Stalin's dictatorship, moved into the Yellow Palace (also known as the Sovnarkom or Council of Ministers building) where the Politburo met, Stalin worked – and now lived.

Until the war, he maintained this dutiful routine – some of his parental reports to the children's teachers survive in the archive.

The children adored Zubalovo – it was their real home so Stalin decided not to uproot them but to build his own 'wonderful, airy modern one-storey' dacha at Kuntsevo, nine kilometres from the Kremlin. This now became his main residence, until he died there twenty years later, developing over the years into a large but austere two-storey mansion, painted a grim camouflage green, with a complex of guardhouses, guest villas, greenhouses, a Russian bath and a special cottage for his library, all surrounded by pinewoods, two concentric fences, innumerable checkpoints and at least a hundred guards.* Here he indulged his natural craving for privacy, the external expression of his emotional detachment: no guards or servants stayed in the house; unless friends came for the night, he henceforth closed himself in, quite alone. Stalin drove out to Kuntsevo after dinner – it was so close it was often called 'Nearby' by his circle because he also sometimes stayed at his other home, 'Faraway', at Semyonovskoe. The idyllic life went on at Zubalovo, Svetlana's 'paradise like an enchanted island'.

Stalin did not become a haunted hermit after Nadya's death. It was true he spent ever more time with his all-male magnates, almost like the segregated court of a seventeenth-century Tsar. But the all-powerful widower also found himself in the loving but overwhelming embrace of a newly reconstructed family. Pavel and Zhenya Alliluyev, recently returned from Berlin, became his constant companions. Nadya's sister Anna and her husband Stanislas Redens had returned from Kharkov for his new appointment as Moscow GPU boss. Redens, a handsome burly Pole with a quiff, always sporting his Chekist uniform, had been the secretary of the founder of the secret police, Dzerzhinsky. He and Anna fell in love during Stalin and Dzerzhinsky's expedition to investigate the fall of Perm in 1919. Redens had a reputation among austere Old Bolsheviks of 'putting on airs' and being a drinker because of an unfortunate incident. Until 1931, he had

* Kuntsevo was, like most of his other residences, built by Merzhanov: Stalin constantly ordered renovations and, after the war, the second floor. After his death, the contents were packed up but under Brezhnev, these were reassembled by Stalin's reunited staff. It remains today closed up under the aegis of the FSB security organ, but exactly as it was when Stalin lived, even down to his shaving brushes and gramophone.

been Georgian GPU boss. However, his deputy, Beria had, according to the family, outwitted Redens in a prank more worthy of a hearty stag night than a secret police intrigue – but it worked none the less. Beria got Redens drunk and sent him home naked. Family legends rarely tell the whole story: Stalin's letters reveal that Redens and local bosses tried to have Beria removed to the Lower Volga but someone, probably Stalin, intervened. Beria never forgave him. But it was Redens, not Beria, who left.

Stalin liked his cheerful brother-in-law but doubted his competence as a Chekist, removing him from the Ukraine. Anna, a loving mother to their two sons, was a good-natured but imprudent woman who, her own children admit, talked too much. Stalin called her 'a chatterbox'.

A third couple made up this sextet of loving relatives. Alyosha Svanidze, also just back from abroad, was the brother of Stalin's first wife, Kato, who died in 1907. 'Handsome, blonde, with blue eyes and an aquiline nose', he was a Georgian dandy, speaking French and German, who held high positions in the State Bank. Stalin loved him – 'they were like brothers,' wrote Mikoyan. His wife, Maria, was a Jewish Georgian soprano 'with a tiny upturned nose, peaches and cream complexion and big blue eyes', who was the *prima donna* in the full-time opera of her own life.* Svetlana said this glossy couple were brash, always bearing presents from abroad. That avid diarist, Maria, like all the ladies of Stalin's court, seemed somewhat in love with their *Vozhd*. There was constant, bitchy competition for his favour among these ladies who were so busy feeling superior to, and undermining, the others that they often missed dangerous signs of Stalin's seething moods.

Meanwhile, Yakov, now twenty-seven, was qualifying as an electrical engineer though Stalin had wanted him to be a soldier. Yasha 'resembled his father in voice and looks' but irritated him. Sometimes Stalin managed to show brisk affection: he sent him one of his books, *The Conquest of Nature*, inscribing it: 'Yasha read this book at once. J. Stalin.'

As Svetlana grew up into a freckly redhead, Stalin said she precisely resembled his mother, always the highest praise from him – but really, she was like him: intelligent, stubborn and determined. 'I was his pet. After mother's death, he tried to be

---

* They saddled their son with the absurd Bolshevik name Johnreed in honour of the author of *Ten Days That Shook the World*.

closer. He was very affectionate – he just wanted to see how I was doing. I do appreciate now that he was a very loving father ...' Maria Svanidze recorded how Svetlana buzzed around her father. 'He kissed her, admired her, fed her from his plate, selecting the best slices for her.' Svetlana, at seven, often declared: 'Providing daddy loves me, I don't care if the whole world hates me! If daddy told me, "fly to the moon," I'd do it!' Yet she found his affection stifling – 'always that tobacco smell, puffing clouds of smoke with moustache and he was hugging and kissing me.' Svetlana was really raised by her beloved nanny, the sturdy Alexandra Bychkova, and the stalwart housekeeper, Carolina Til.

A month after Nadya's death, Artyom remembers that she was still asking when her mother would be back from abroad. Svetlana was terrified of the dark, which she believed was connected to death. She admitted that she could not love Vasily who was either bullying her, spoiling her fun, or telling her disturbing sexual details that she believed damaged her view of sex.

Vasily, now twelve, was the most damaged: 'he suffered a terrible shock,' wrote Svetlana, 'ruining him completely.' He became a truculent, name-dropping, violent lout who swore in front of women, expected to be treated as a princeling and yet was tragically inept and unhappy. He ran riot at Zubalovo. No one told Stalin of his outrageous antics. Yet Artyom says Vasily was really 'kind, gentle, sweet, uninterested in material things; he could be a bully, but also defended smaller boys.' But he was terrified of Stalin whom he respected like 'Christ for the Christians'. In the absence of his disappointed father, Vasily grew up in the sad emotionally undernourished realm of bodyguards, rough and sycophantic secret policemen instead of loving but firm nannies. Pauker supervised this Soviet Fauntleroy. The Commandant of Zubalovo, Efimov, reported on him to Vlasik who then informed 'the Boss'.

Stalin trusted his devoted bodyguard, a brawny, hard-living but uncouth peasant, Nikolai Vlasik, thirty-seven, who had joined the Cheka in 1919 and guarded the Politburo, and then exclusively the *Vozhd*, since 1927. He became a powerful *vizier* at Stalin's side but remained the closest thing to Vasily's father-figure: Vasily introduced his girlfriends to Vlasik for his approval.

When his behaviour at school became impossible, it was Pauker who wrote to Vlasik that his 'removal to another school is absolutely necessary'. Vasily craved Stalin's approval: 'Hello father!' he wrote in a typical letter in which he talks in a childish version of Bolshevik jargon. 'I'm studying at the new school, it's very good and I think I'm going to become a good Red Vaska! Father, write to me how you are and how is your holiday. Svetlana is well and studies at school too. Greetings from our working collective. Red Vaska.' But he also wrote letters to the secret policemen:

'Hello Comrade Pauker. I'm fine. I don't fight with Tom [Artyom]. I catch a lot [of fish] and very well. If you're not busy, come and see us. Comrade Pauker, I ask you to send me a bottle of ink for my pen.' So Pauker, who was so close to Stalin that he shaved him, sent the ink to the child. When it arrived, Vasily thanked 'Comrade Pauker', claimed he had not reduced another boy to tears, and denounced Vlasik for accusing him of it. Already his life among schoolboys and secret policemen was leading the spoilt child to denounce others, a habit that could prove deadly for his victims in later life. The princely tone is unmistakable: 'Comrade Efimov has informed you that I asked you to send me a shotgun but I have not received it. Maybe you forgot so please send it. Vasya.'

Stalin was baffled by Vasily's insubordination and suggested greater discipline. On 12 September 1933, Carolina Til went on holiday, so Stalin, who was in the south, wrote the following instructions to Efimov at Zubalovo: 'Nanny will stay at the Moscow home. Make sure that Vasya doesn't behave outrageously. Don't give him free playtime and be strict. If Vasya won't obey Nanny and is offensive, keep him "in blinders",' wrote Stalin, adding: 'Take Vasya away from Anna Sergeevna [Redens, Nadya's sister] – she spoils him by harmful and dangerous concessions.' While the father was on holiday, he sent his son a letter and some peaches. 'Red Vaska' thanked him. Yet all was not well with Vasily. The pistol that had killed Nadya remained around Stalin's house. Vasily showed it to Artyom and gave him the leather holster as a keepsake.

It was only years later that Stalin understood how damaged the children had been by his absence and the care of bodyguards – what he called 'the deepest secret in his heart':

'Children growing up without their mother can be raised perfectly by nannies but they can't replace the mother ...'

* * *

In January 1933, Stalin delivered a swaggering Bolshevik rodomontade to the Plenum: the Five-Year Plan had been a remarkable success. The Party had provided a tractor industry, electric power, coal, steel and oil production. Cities had been built where none stood before. The Dnieper River dam and power station and the Turk-Sib railway had all been completed (built by Yagoda's growing slave labour force). Any difficulties were the fault of the enemy opposition. Yet this was Hungry Thirty-Three when millions more starved, hundred of thousands were deported.

In July 1933, Kirov joined Stalin, Voroshilov, OGPU Deputy Chairman Yagoda and Berman, boss of Gulag, the labour camp system, on the ship *Anokhin* to celebrate the opening of a gargantuan project of socialist labour: the Baltic–White Sea Canal or, in Bolshevik acronym, the Belomor,* a 227-kilometre canal begun in December 1931 and completed by the Pharaonic slavery of 170,000 prisoners, of whom around 25,000 died in a year and a half. Voroshilov later praised Kirov and Yagoda for their contributions to this crime.

By the summer, the magnates were exhausted after five years of Herculean labour in driving the triumphant Five-Year Plan, defeating the opposition and most of all, crushing the peasantry. After bearing such strain, they needed to relax if they were not going to crack – but even if the crisis of Hungry Thirty-Three had been weathered due to the massive repression, this was no time to rest. Sergo, who as People's Commissar for Heavy Industry, directed the Five-Year Plan, suffered heart and circulatory complaints – Stalin himself supervised his treatments. Kirov was also breaking under the pressure, suffering from 'irregular heartbeat ... severe irritability and very poor sleep'. The doctors ordered him to rest. Kirov's friend Kuibyshev, Gosplan boss, who had the impossible task of making the planning figures work, was drinking and chasing women: Stalin complained to Molotov, later muttering that he had become 'a debauchee'.

On 17 August, Stalin and Voroshilov set off in their special train.† We know from an unpublished note that the *Vozhd* was

---

* Belomor cigarettes now became one of the most popular brands, smoked by Stalin himself when his favourite Herzogovina Flor were not to hand. The Belomor Canal was one of the triumphs that were celebrated by writers and film-makers: Gorky, the novelist who had become a shameful apologist for the worst excesses of Bolshevism, edited a book, *The Canal Named for Stalin*, that amazingly praised the humanitarian aspects of Belomor.

† We are especially well-informed on this holiday because not only do we have Stalin's correspondence with Kaganovich, in charge in Moscow, but the GPU took photographs which they mounted in a special album for Stalin, and Lakoba, the host in Abkhazia, also kept notes: therefore we have both sound and vision.

already paranoid about his movements, fed up with his sister-in-law Anna Redens and keen for Klim to be more discreet:

'Yesterday, around my sister-in-law (a chatterbox) and near the doctors (they gossip), I did not want to say my exact departure. Now I'm informing you that I've decided to go tomorrow ... It's not good to talk widely. We're both tasty tidbits and we should not inform everyone by our openness. So if you agree, we go tomorrow at two. So I'll order Yusis [Stalin's Lithuanian bodyguard who shared duties with Vlasik] to ask immediately the chief of the railway station and order him to add one wagon, without information as to who it is for. Until tomorrow at two ...' It was to be a most eventful holiday: there was even an assassination attempt.

* * *

At Krasnaya Polyana, Sochi, he found Lakoba, the Abkhazian chief, waiting on the veranda along with President Kalinin and Poskrebyshev. When Stalin and Lakoba strolled in the gardens, Beria, now effective viceroy of the Caucasus, joined them. Lakoba and Beria, already enemies, had come separately. After breakfast on the verandas, the *Vozhd*, followed by this swelling entourage, which was soon joined by Yan Rudzutak, a Latvian Old Bolshevik who headed the Control Commission but was increasingly distrusted by Stalin, toured his gardens.

'Stop being idle,' said the green-fingered Stalin. 'The wild bushes here need to be weeded.' The leaders and the guards set to work, collecting wood and cutting brambles while Stalin in his white tunic with baggy white trousers tucked into boots, supervised, puffing on his pipe. Taking a fork, he even did some weeding himself. Beria worked with a rake while one of the leaders from Moscow hacked away with an axe. Beria seized the axe and, chopping away to impress Stalin, joked, with rather obvious *double entendre*:

'I'm just demonstrating to the master of the garden, Joseph Vissarionovich, that I can chop down any tree.' No leader was too big for Beria to fell. He would soon get the chance to wield his little axe.

Stalin sat down on his wicker chair and Beria sat behind him like a medieval courtier with the axe in his belt. Svetlana, who now called Beria 'Uncle Lara', was brought down to join them. When Stalin did some work on his papers, Lakoba listened to music on headphones while Beria called over to Svetlana, sat her on his knee and was photographed in a famous picture with his pince-nez glistening in the sun and his hands on the child, while the leader worked patiently in the background.

Voroshilov and Budyonny, who had also turned up, took Stalin, in the front seat of an open Packard, to inspect their horses bred by the army stud. They went on a cruise and then they went hunting, Stalin cheerfully carrying his rifle over his shoulder, with his hat on the back of his head, as his Chekist guard wiped the sweat off his forehead. After a day's hunting, they pitched tents for an *al fresco* picnic and barbecue. Later, Stalin went fishing. The informality of the whole trip is obvious: it was one of the last times he lived like this.

* * *

Meanwhile Stalin was outraged when, in his absence, Sergo managed to manipulate the Politburo against him. Kaganovich remained in charge as more and more leaders went on their holidays. He wrote to Stalin virtually every day, ending always with the same request: 'Please inform us of your opinion.' The magnates were constantly fighting one another for resources: the tougher the struggle for collectivization, the faster the tempo of industrialization, the more accidents and mistakes made in the factories, the greater the struggle within the Politburo for control over their own fiefdoms. 'Iron-Arse' Molotov, the Premier, rowed with Ordzhonikidze, the quick-tempered Heavy Industry Commissar, and Kaganovich who fought with Kirov who clashed with Voroshilov and so on. But suddenly, the Politburo united against Stalin's own wishes.

In the summer of 1933, Molotov received a report that a factory in Zaporozhe was producing defective combine harvester parts due to sabotage. Molotov, who agreed with Stalin that since their system was perfect and their ideology scientifically correct, all industrial mistakes must be the result of sabotage by wreckers, ordered Procurator-General Akulov to arrest the guilty. The local leaders appealed to Sergo. When the case came before the Supreme Court, the government case was represented by the Deputy Procurator, an ex-Menshevik lawyer, Andrei Vyshinsky, who would be one of Stalin's most notorious officials in the coming Terror. But with Stalin on holiday, Sergo passionately defended his industrial officials and persuaded the Politburo, including Molotov and Kaganovich, to condemn Vyshinsky's summing-up.

On 29 August, Stalin discovered Sergo's mischief and fired off a telegram of Pharisaical rage: 'I consider the position adopted by the Politburo incorrect and dangerous ... I find it lamentable that Kaganovich and Molotov were not capable of resisting bureaucratic pressure from the People's Commissariat of Heavy Industry.' Two days later, Kaganovich, Andreyev, Kuibyshev and Mikoyan officially annulled their resolution. Stalin brooded about the danger of Sergo's ability to use his undoubted prestige and force of personality to sway his potentates, letting off steam to Molotov:

'I consider Sergo's actions the behaviour of a hooligan. How can you have let him have his way?' Stalin was flabbergasted that Molotov and Kaganovich could have fallen for it. 'What's the matter? Did Kaganovich pull a fast one? ... And he's not the only one.' He fired off reprimands: 'I've written to Kaganovich to express to him my astonishment that he found himself, in this case, in the camp of reactionary elements.'

Two weeks later, on 12 September, he was still ranting to Molotov that Sergo was showing anti-Party tendencies in defending 'reactionary elements of the Party against the Central Committee'. He punished Molotov by calling him back from his holiday in the Crimea – 'neither I nor Voroshilov like the fact that you're vacationing for six weeks instead of two weeks' – and then felt guilty about it: 'I am a little uncomfortable with being the reason for your early return,' he apologized but then showed his continuing anger with Kaganovich and Kuibyshev: 'It's obvious it would be rash to leave the centre's work to Kaganovich alone (Kuibyshev may start drinking).' Molotov miserably returned to Moscow.

Stalin easily defeated Sergo but the vehemence of his attack on the 'hooligan' shows how seriously he took the strongest leader after himself. Moody and excitable, yet the very personification of the tough Stalinist administrator, Sergo Ordzhonikidze was born in 1886, the son of Georgian nobility. Orphaned when he was ten, he was barely educated but trained incongruously as a nurse.* He had already joined the Party at seventeen and was arrested at least

---

* After WW2, Stalin reminisced about how, in exile, 'I, as a peasant, was given 8 roubles monthly. Ordzhonikidze as a nobleman got 12 roubles so deported noblemen cost the Treasury 50% more than peasants.' The other trained male nurse in the leadership was Poskrebyshev.

four times before joining Lenin in Paris in 1911, one of the few Stalinists to experience emigration (briefly). A member of the Central Committee since 1912 (like Stalin), he was personally responsible in 1921 for brutally annexing and Bolshevizing Georgia and Azerbaijan where he was known as 'Stalin's Arse'. Lenin attacked him for slapping a comrade and for indulging in drunken orgies with hussies but also defended him for his aggressive shouting by joking, 'He does shout … but he's deaf in one ear.'

In the Civil War, Sergo had been a dashing, leonine hero, at home on horseback (he was accused of riding a white horse through conquered Tiflis), so 'young and strong', it 'seemed as if he had been born in his long military coat and boots'. He was explosively temperamental. In the early twenties, he actually punched Molotov in a row over Zinoviev's book, *Leninism*, an incident that demonstrates how seriously they took matters of ideology: Kirov had separated them. Sergo's daughter, Eteri, recalls that this volcanic Georgian often got so heated that he slapped his comrades but the eruption soon passed – 'he would give his life for one he loved and shoot the one he hated,' said his wife Zina.

Promoted to run the Control Commission in 1926, Sergo was Stalin's most aggressive ally in the fight against the oppositions until he was placed in charge of Heavy Industry. He did not understand the subtleties of economics but he employed experts who did, driving them by charm and force. 'You terrorize comrades at work,' complained one of his subordinates who were constantly appealing against his tempers. 'Sergo really slapped them!' wrote Stalin approvingly to Voroshilov in 1928. 'The opposition were scared!'

Sergo, who had flirted with, then betrayed Bukharin, was a forceful supporter of Stalin's Great Turn – 'he accepted the policy heart and soul', said Kaganovich. Beloved by friends from Kaganovich to Bukharin and Kirov, Sergo was 'the perfect Bolshevik', thought Maria Svanidze, and 'chivalrous' too, according to Khrushchev. 'His kind eyes, grey hair and big moustache,' wrote Beria's son, 'gave him the look of an old Georgian prince.' Owing his career to Stalin, he remained the last big beast of the Politburo, sceptical about Stalin's cult, with his own clientele in industry and the Caucasus whom he was capable of defending. He was certainly never afraid to disagree with

Stalin* whom he treated like a prickly elder brother: sometimes he even gave him quasi-orders.

In September 1933, Sergo was holidaying in Kislovodsk, his favourite resort, whence he was soon in brisk correspondence with Stalin who resented this big-hearted 'prince'. Sergo was, Stalin complained, 'vain to the point of folly.'

* * *

'Here on vacation,' Stalin wrote, 'I do not sit in one place but move from one location to another …' After a month, Stalin moved southwards to his newly-built house at Museri. Set atop a hill in a semi-tropical park, it was an ugly grey two-storey residence with his beloved wood-panelling, expansive verandas, large dining room and a beautiful view down to a harbour where Lakoba had constructed a special jetty. It was surrounded by walks along serpentine paths that led to a round summerhouse, where Stalin worked, and down steps to the sea. Often Lakoba and Stalin strolled down to a nearby village where the locals laid on *al fresco* Abkhazian feasts.

On 23 September, Lakoba arranged a boating and shooting trip: Stalin and Vlasik motored along the coast from the specially-built jetty on a motor yacht, *Red Star*, with their guns on their knees. Suddenly there was a burst of machine-gun fire from the coast.

---

* Stalin treated Sergo like an uncontrollable younger brother: 'You were trouble-making this week,' Stalin wrote typically to him, 'and you were successful. Should I congratulate you or not?' On another occasion: 'Tomorrow, the meeting on bank reform. Are you prepared? You must be.' When Stalin scolded him, he added, 'Don't dress me down for being rude … Actually, tell me off as much as you like.' He usually signed himself 'Koba'. Sergo's notes almost always disagree with some decision of Stalin's: 'Dear Soso,' he carped in one note, 'is the new Russia being built by Americans?' He was quite capable of giving Stalin instructions too: 'Soso, they want to put Kaganovich on civil aviation … Write to Molotov and Kaganovich and tell them not to!'

10

Spoiled Victory: Kirov, the Plot
and the Seventeenth Congress

Vlasik threw himself on to Stalin on the deck of the *Red Star*, requesting permission to return fire. Firing shots landwards, the boat turned to the open sea. Stalin initially thought it had just been Georgians firing a greeting but he changed his mind. He received a letter from the border guards admitting they had fired, mistaking it for a foreign vessel. Beria investigated personally, displaying his ruthlessness to get results which impressed Stalin, but he aroused suspicions that he had contrived the attack to undermine Lakoba, who was responsible for security inside Abkhazia. The guards were despatched to Siberia. Vlasik and Beria became closer to Stalin.

Back on dry land, the entourage progressed into Gagra, where the GPU had found a new dacha in the hills which Lakoba had started to rebuild. This became a favourite residence, Kholodnaya Rechka, Coldstream, a Stalinist eyrie built on a cliff with views of dazzling natural beauty.* Returning to Sochi, Svetlana stayed with Stalin but when she went back to school, he found himself 'like a lonely owl' and craved Yenukidze's company. 'What keeps you in Moscow?' he wrote to Abel. 'Come to Sochi, swim in the sea and let your heart rest. Tell Kalinin from me that he commits a crime if he doesn't send you on holiday immediately ... You could live with me at the *dacha* ... I've visited the new *dacha* at Gagra today ... Voroshilov and his wife are enchanted with it ... Your Koba.'

* * *

* The Gagra house is one of the most beautiful of Stalin's residences but also the least accessible. The children later got their own houses. A snake path of steps twists down to the sea. Yet it is invisible from the land. Like most of these houses, it is still under the control of the Abkhazian presidential security, hidden, eerie but perfectly preserved. Museri adjoins the same secret CC resort, Pitsunda, where Khrushchev had a house as First Secretary and where, in the eighties, Mikhail Gorbachev and Raisa his wife were criticized for building a multi-million-pound holiday house in the last Soviet years. All remain empty yet guarded in the steamy Abkhazian heat.

After this long holiday, the 'lonely owl' returned to Moscow on 4 November to plan the coming Congress of Victors which was to crown him for the triumphs of the last four years. Moscow felt as if it was waking up and stretching after a long nightmare. The famine was over. The harvest had improved. The starving millions were buried and forgotten in villages that had disappeared for ever off the map.

There was much to celebrate as the delegates started to arrive for the Seventeenth Congress in late January. It must have been an exciting and proud time for the 1,966 voting delegates to be visiting Moscow from every corner of the sprawling workers' paradise. The Congress was the highest Party organ, which theoretically elected the Central Committee to govern in its place until it met again, usually four years later. But by 1934, this was a pantomine of triumphalism, supervised by Stalin and Kaganovich, minutely choreographed by Poskrebyshev.

None the less, a Congress was not all business: the Great Kremlin Palace was suddenly filled with outlandish costumes as bearded Cossacks, silk-clad Kazakhs and Georgians paraded into the great hall. Here the viceroys of Siberia, the Ukraine, or Transcaucasia, renewed their contacts with allies in the centre while the younger delegates found patrons.* Lenin's generation, who regarded Stalin as their leader but not their God, still dominated but the *Vozhd* took special care of his younger protégés.

He invited Beria, his blonde wife Nina and their son to the Kremlin to watch a movie with the Politburo. Sergo Beria,† aged ten, and Svetlana Stalin, who would become friends, watched the cartoon, *Three Little Pigs*, with Stalin before they set off for Zubalovo where the Berias joined the magnates in feasting and singing Georgian songs. When Sergo Beria was cold, Stalin hugged him and let him snuggle into his coat lined with wolf fur before tucking him into bed. It must have been thrilling for Beria,

* These provincials wanted to meet their heroes and a great amount of time was spent posing for the photographers in the hall where they gathered in eager groups, beaming, in their boots, tunics and caps, around Stalin, Kalinin, Voroshilov, Kaganovich and Budyonny. At the Fifteenth Congress in 1927, Stalin was just one of the leaders who posed with his fans. At the Seventeenth, Stalin is always at the centre. The album is mutilated by the huge number of figures either crossed out or cut out as they were arrested and executed during the following four years: out of 1,966 delegates, 1,108 would be arrested. Few survived.

† Named, of course, after Beria's former patron, Ordzhonikidze, a friendship that had disintegrated into mutual hatred.

the ambitious provincial entering the inner portals of power.

'STALIN!' gasped *Pravda* when he attended the Bolshoi. 'The appearance of the ardently loved *Vozhd*, whose name is linked inseparably with all the victories scored by the proletariat, by the Soviet Union, was greeted with tumultuous ovations' and 'no end of cries of "Hurrah!" and "Long Live our Stalin!"'

However, some regional bosses had been shaken by Stalin's brutal mismanagement. A cabal seems to have met secretly in friends' apartments to discuss his removal. Each had their own reasons: in the Caucasus, Orakhelashvili was insulted by the promotion of the upstart Beria. Kosior's cries for help in feeding the Ukraine had been scorned. Some of these meetings supposedly took place in Sergo's flat in the Horse Guards where Orakhelashvili was staying. But who was to replace Stalin? Kirov, popular, vigorous and Russian, was their candidate. In the Bolshevik culture with its obsession with ideological purity, the former Kadet and bourgeois journalist with no ideological credentials, who owed his career to Stalin, was an unlikely candidate. Molotov, as loyal to Stalin as ever, sneered that Kirov was never a serious candidate.

When he was approached in Sergo's apartment, Kirov had to consider fast what to do: he informed them that he had no interest in replacing Stalin but that he would be able to see that their complaints were heard. Kirov was still ill, recovering from flu, and his reaction shows that he lacked the backbone for this poisoned chalice. His immediate instinct was to tell Stalin, which he did, probably in his new apartment where he denounced the plot, repeated the complaints, and denied any interest in becoming leader himself.

'Thank you,' Stalin is supposed to have replied, 'I won't forget what I owe you.' Stalin was surely disturbed that these Old Bolsheviks considered 'my Kirich' his successor. Mikoyan, Kirov's friend, stated that Stalin reacted with 'hostility and vengefulness towards the whole Congress and of course towards Kirov himself'. Kirov felt threatened but showed nothing publicly. Stalin concealed his anxiety.

In the Congress hall, Kirov ostentatiously sat, joking, with his delegation, not up on the Presidium, the sort of demagoguery that outraged Stalin, who kept asking what they were laughing about. His victory had been spoiled. Yet this constant struggling against traitors also suited his character and his ideology. No political leader was so programmed for this perpetual fight against enemies as Stalin, who regarded himself as history's lone knight riding out, with weary resignation, on another noble mission, the Bolshevik version of the mysterious cowboy arriving in a corrupt frontier town.

There was no hint of any of this in the public triumph: 'Our country has become a country of mighty industry, a country of collectivization, a country of victorious socialism,' declared Molotov, opening the Congress on 26 January. Stalin enjoyed the satisfaction of watching his enemies, from Zinoviev to Rykov, old and new, praise him extravagantly: 'The glorious field marshal of the proletarian forces, the best of the best – Comrade Stalin,' declared Bukharin, now editor of *Izvestiya*. But when Postyshev, another Old Bolshevik hardman newly promoted to run the Ukraine, called Kirov, Congress gave him a standing ovation. Kirov rose to the occasion, mentioning Stalin ('the great strategist of liberation of the working people of our country and the whole world') twenty-nine times, ending excitedly:

'Our successes are really tremendous. Damn it all … you just want to live and live – really, just look what's going on. It's a fact!' Stalin joined the 'thunderous applause'.

The last duty of a Congress was to elect the Central Committee. Usually this was a formality. The delegates were given the ballot, a list of names prepared by the Secretariat (Stalin and Kaganovich) who were proposed from the floor: Kirov had to propose Beria. The voters crossed out names they opposed and voted for the names left unmarked. As the Congress ended on 8 February, the delegates received their ballots but when the vote-counting commission started work, they received a shock. These events are still mysterious, but it seems that Kirov received one or two negatives while Kaganovich and Molotov polled over 100 each. Stalin got between 123 and 292 negatives. They were automatically elected but here was another blow to Stalin's self-esteem, confirming that he rode alone among 'two-faced double-dealers'.

When Kaganovich, managing the Congress, was informed by the voting commission, he ran to Stalin to ask what to do. Stalin almost certainly ordered him to destroy most of the negative votes (though naturally Kaganovich denied this, even in old age). Certainly 166 votes are still missing. On the 10th, the 71 CC members were announced: Stalin received 1,056 votes and Kirov 1,055 out of 1,059. The new generation, personified by Beria and

Khrushchev, became members while Budyonny and Poskrebyshev were elected candidates. The Plenum of this new body met straight afterwards to do the real business.

Stalin devised a plan to deal with Kirov's dangerous eminence, proposing his recall from Leningrad to become one of the four Secretaries, thereby cleverly satisfying those who wanted him promoted to the Secretariat: on paper, a big promotion; in reality, this would bring him under Stalin's observation, cutting him off from his Leningrad clientele. In Stalin's entourage, a promotion to the centre was a mixed blessing. Kirov was neither the first nor the last to protest vigorously – but, in Stalin's eyes, a refusal meant placing personal power above Party loyalty, a mortal sin. Kirov's request to stay in Leningrad for another two years was supported by Sergo and Kuibyshev. Stalin petulantly stalked out in a huff.

Sergo and Kuibyshev advised Kirov to compromise with Stalin: Kirov became the third Secretary but remained temporarily in Leningrad. Since he would have little time for Moscow, Stalin reached out to another newly elected CC member who would become the closest to Stalin of all the leaders: Andrei Zhdanov, boss of Gorky (Nizhny Novgorod), moved to Moscow as the fourth Secretary.

Kirov staggered back to Leningrad, suffering from flu, congestion in his right lung and palpitations. In March, Sergo wrote to him: 'Listen my friend, you must rest. Really and truly, nothing is going to happen there without you there for 10–15 days ... Our fellow countryman [their codename for Stalin] considers you a healthy man ... none the less, you must take a short rest!' Kirov sensed that Stalin would not forgive him for the plot. Yet Stalin was even more suffocatingly friendly, insisting that they constantly meet in Moscow. It was Sergo, not Stalin, with whom Kirov really needed to discuss his apprehensions. 'I want awfully to have a chat with you on very many questions but you can't say everything in a letter so it is better to wait until our meeting.' They certainly discussed politics in private, careful to reveal nothing on paper.

There were hints of Kirov's scepticism about Stalin's cult: on 15 July 1933, Kirov wrote formally to 'Comrade Stalin' (not the usual Koba) that portraits of Stalin's photograph had been printed in Leningrad on rather 'thin paper'. Unfortunately they could not do any better. One can imagine Kirov and Sergo mocking Stalin's vanity.

In private,* Kirov imitated Stalin's accent to his Leningraders.

When Kirov visited Stalin in Moscow, they were boon companions but Artyom remembers a competitive edge to their jokes. Once at a family dinner, they made mock toasts:

'A toast to Stalin, the great leader of all peoples and all times. I'm a busy man but I've probably forgotten some of the other great things you've done too!' Kirov, who often 'monopolized conversations so as to be the centre of attention', toasted Stalin, mocking the cult. Kirov could speak to Stalin in a way unthinkable to Beria or Khrushchev.

'A toast to our beloved leader of the Leningrad Party and possibly the Baku proletariat too, yet he promises me he can't read all the papers – and what else are you beloved leader of?' replied Stalin. Even the tipsy banter between Stalin and Kirov was pregnant with ill-concealed anger and resentment, yet no one in the family circle noticed that they were anything but the most loving of friends. However the 'vegetarian years', as the poetess Akhmatova called them, were about to end: 'the meat-eating years' were coming.

On 30 June, Adolf Hitler, newly elected Chancellor of Germany, slaughtered his enemies within his Nazi Party, in the Night of the Long Knives – an exploit that fascinated Stalin.

'Did you hear what happened in Germany?' he asked Mikoyan. 'Some fellow that Hitler! Splendid! That's a deed of some skill!' Mikoyan was surprised that Stalin admired the German Fascist but the Bolsheviks were hardly strangers to slaughter themselves.

---

* Amongst his possessions in his apartment, preserved in Leningrad, is one of his cigarette boxes emblazoned with a unprepossessing portrait of Stalin with a very long nose. The box is opened by pressing the nose.

11

Assassination of the Favourite

That summer, their own repression seemed to be easing. In May, the Chairman of the OGPU, Menzhinsky, a shadowy scholar who was permanently ill and spent most of his time in seclusion studying Persian manuscripts in any of the twelve languages of which he was master, died. The press announced that the hated OGPU had perished with him, swallowed by a new People's Commissariat of Internal Affairs – the NKVD. This aroused hopes that the dawning jazz age really did herald a new freedom in Russia – but the new Commissar was Yagoda who had been running the OGPU for some time.

The illusion of this thaw was confirmed when Yagoda came to Stalin and recited a poem by Osip Mandelstam, who, with his friend, the beautiful Leningrad poetess Anna Akhmatova, wrote verses with a searing emotional clarity which still shines through that twilight of humanity like beams of heart-rending honesty. Naturally they found it hard to conform with Soviet mediocrity.

Yagoda paid Mandelstam the back-handed compliment of learning the verse by heart, sixteen lines of poetry that damned and mocked Stalin as a bewhiskered 'Kremlin crag-dweller' and 'peasant-slayer' whose 'fat fingers' were 'as oily as maggots'. The poet Demian Bedny had complained to Mandelstam that Stalin left greasy fingermarks on the books he constantly borrowed. His fellow leaders were a 'rabble of thin-necked bosses', a line he wrote after noticing Molotov's neck sticking out from his collar and the smallness of his head. Stalin was outraged – but understood Mandelstam's value. Hence that heartless order to Yagoda that sounds as if it concerned a priceless vase: 'Preserve but isolate.'

On the night of 16–17 May, Mandelstam was arrested and sentenced to three years' exile. Meanwhile the poet's friends rushed to appeal to his patrons among the Bolshevik magnates.

His wife Nadezhda and fellow poet Boris Pasternak appealed to Bukharin at *Izvestiya*, while Akhmatova was received by Yenukidze. Bukharin wrote to Stalin that Mandelstam was a 'first class poet ... but not quite normal ... PS: Boris Pasternak is utterly flabbergasted by Mandelstam's arrest and nobody else knows anything.' Perhaps most tellingly, he reminded Stalin that 'Poets are always right, history is on their side ...'

'Who authorized Mandelstam's arrest?' muttered Stalin. 'Disgraceful.' In July, knowing that news of his interest would spread like ripples on a pond before the coming Writers' Congress, Stalin telephoned Pasternak. His calls to writers already had their ritual. Poskrebyshev called first to warn the recipient that Comrade Stalin wished to speak to him: he must stand by. When the call arrived, Pasternak took it in his communal apartment and told Stalin he could not hear well since there were children yelling in the corridor.

'Mandelstam's case is being reviewed. Everything will be all right,' Stalin said, before adding, 'If I was a poet and my poet-friend found himself in trouble, I would do anything to help him.' Pasternak characteristically tried to define his concept of friendship which Stalin interrupted: 'But he's a genius, isn't he?'

'But that's not the point.'

'What is the point then?' Pasternak, who was fascinated by Stalin, said he wanted to come for a talk. 'About what?' asked Stalin.

'About life and death,' said Pasternak. The baffled Stalin rang off. However, the most significant conversation took place afterwards, when Pasternak tried to persuade Poskrebyshev to put him through again. Poskrebyshev refused. Pasternak asked if he could repeat what had been said. The answer was a big yes.

Stalin prided himself on understanding brilliance: 'he's doubtless a great talent,' he wrote about another writer. 'He's very capricious but that's the character of gifted people. Let him write what he wants, and when!'

Pasternak's whimsy may have saved his life for, later, when his arrest was proposed, Stalin supposedly replied:

'Leave that cloud-dweller in peace.'

* * *

Stalin's intervention is famous but there was nothing new about it: as Nicholas I was for Pushkin, so Stalin was for all his writers. Stalin pretended he considered himself just a casual observer:

'Comrades who know the arts will help you – I am just a dilettante' but he was both gourmet and gourmand. His papers reveal his omnipotent critiques of writers, who wrote to him in droves.

Stalin's ultimate pet writer was 'the Proletarian Poet', Demian Bedny, a Falstaffian rhymester, with good-natured eyes gazing out of a head 'like a huge copper cauldron', whose works appeared regularly in *Pravda* and who holidayed with Stalin, rendering an endless repertoire of obscene anecdotes. Rewarded with a Kremlin apartment, he was a member of the literary Politburo. But Bedny began to irritate Stalin: he bombarded him with complaints, and his egregious poems, in a long and farcical correspondence, while engaging in drunken escapades inside the Kremlin: 'Ha-ha-ha! Chaffinch!' Stalin exclaimed on one such letter. Worse, Bedny stubbornly resisted Stalin's criticisms: 'What about the present in Russia?' Stalin scribbled to him. 'Bedny leaves in the mistakes!'

'I agree,' added Molotov. 'Must not be published without improvements.' Stalin was tired of his drunken poet and expelled him from the Kremlin:

'There must be no more scandals inside the Kremlin walls,' he wrote in September 1932. Bedny was hurt but Stalin reassured him: 'You must not see leaving the Kremlin as being sacked from the Party. Thousands of respected comrades live outside the Kremlin and so does Gorky!' Vladimir Kirshon was one of Gorky's circle and another recipient of GPU funds who liked to send Stalin everything he wrote. When he was in favour, he could do no wrong:

'Publish immediately,' Stalin scrawled on Kirshon's latest article when returning it to *Pravda*'s editor. When Kirshon sent in his new play, Stalin read it in six days and wrote back:

'Comrade Kirshon, your play's not bad. It must be put on in the theatre at once.' But Kirshon was being rewarded for his political loyalty: he was one of the hacks who viciously destroyed Bulgakov's career. However, after the creation of Socialist Realism, Kirshon wrote to Stalin and Kaganovich to ask if he was out of favour:

'Why are you putting the question of trust?' Stalin replied by hand. 'I ask you to believe the Central Committee is absolutely happy with your work and trusts you.' The writers also turned to Stalin to sort out their feuds: Panferov wrote to Stalin to complain that Gorky was mocking his work. Stalin's comment? 'Vain. File in my archive. Stalin.'

When he did not like a writer, he did not mince words: 'Klim,' he wrote to Voroshilov about an article, 'My impression: a first-rate chatterer who thinks he's the Messiah. Yeah! Yeah! Stalin.'*
When the American novelist Upton Sinclair wrote to Stalin asking him to release an arrested movie-maker, Stalin commented: 'Green steam!' Stalin's favourite theatre was the Moscow Arts so he was gentler with its famous director, Stanislavsky, blaming his opinion on his colleagues. 'I didn't highly praise the play "Suicide" (by N. Erdman) ... My nearest comrades think it empty and even harmful ...'

His 'nearest comrades', much less literary than he, became unlikely literary tyrants too: Stalin, Molotov and Kaganovich (an uneducated cobbler) decided artistic matters. Molotov turned on Bedny, for example, with an absurd mixture of personal threat and literary criticism. Bedny, a gossip, even dared to play Stalin off against Molotov who lectured him gravely:

'I read Stalin's letter to you. I agree absolutely. It cannot be said better than by him ...' Molotov warned him about rumours of disagreements between the leaders – 'You did your bit too, Comrade Bedny. I didn't expect such things. It's not good for a proletarian poet ...' Molotov even gave poetical advice: 'It's very pessimistic ... you need to give a window through which the sun can shine (heroism of socialism).'

Stalin often informed Gorky and other writers that he was correcting their articles with Kaganovich, a vision that must have horrified them. At the theatres, Stalin evolved a pantomime of giving his judgement on a new play which was followed to the letter by Kaganovich and Molotov. In the Politburo's *loge* and the room behind it, the *avant-loge*, where they ate between acts, Stalin commented on the actors, plays, even the décor of the foyer. Every comment became the subject of rumours, myths and decisions that affected careers.

Stalin attended a new play on Peter the Great by Alexei Tolstoy, another newly returned émigré writer who, besides Gorky, was the richest author of the Imperium. Count Tolstoy, an illegitimate and renegade nobleman, had returned to Russia in 1923 where he was hailed as the 'Worker-Peasant-Count'. This literary gymnast

---

* When Stalin read Andrei Platonov's satire on the 'Higher Command' of collectivization, *For Future Use*, he supposedly wrote 'Bastard!' on the manuscript and told Fadeev, 'Give him a belt "for future use."' Platonov was never arrested but died, in great deprivation, of TB.

specialized in understanding Stalin, boasting, 'You really do have to be an acrobat.' His *On the Rack* was attacked by Bolshevik writers. Stalin left shortly before the end, accompanied to his car by the crestfallen director. Sensing Imperial disapproval, the play was attacked viciously inside the theatre until the director returned triumphantly to announce: 'Comrade Stalin, in speaking with me, passed the following judgement: "A splendid play. Only it's a pity Peter was not depicted heroically enough."' Stalin received Tolstoy and gave him 'the right historical approach' for his next project, a novel *Peter the Great*.

This pantomime was repeated exactly when Kaganovich rejected a new production by the avant-garde theatrical director Meyerhold and was pursued to his car by the disappointed artist. Yet he protected the Yiddish actor, Solomon Mikhoels. Like eighteenth-century *grands seigneurs*, the magnates patronized their own theatres, their own poets, singers and writers, and defended their protégés* whom they 'received' at their dachas and visited at home. 'Everyone goes to see someone,' wrote Nadezhda Mandelstam in her memoirs that provide a peerless moral guide to this era. 'There's no other way.' But when the Party turned against their protégés, the leaders abandoned them swiftly.

The artists were fascinated by Stalin: Pasternak longed to meet him. 'Can I meet you?' wrote the poet Gidosh eagerly. Meyerhold appealed to Stalin for a meeting which he said would 'lift my depression as an artist' and signed it 'Loving you.'

'Stalin not here now,' wrote Poskrebyshev.

* * *

On 30 July, a month after Hitler's Night of the Long Knives, Stalin headed down to the Sochi dacha where he was meeting his old favourite, Kirov, who had no wish to be there, and his new one, Andrei Zhdanov, who must have been honoured to be invited. There were four of them because Zhdanov brought along his son, Yury, Stalin's future son-in-law, a young man whom the *Vozhd* was

---

* There was one other returned émigré whom Stalin personally favoured. Ilya Ehrenburg, a Jewish Bohemian, friends with Picasso and Malraux, complained of persecution by the Party. His old schoolfriend Bukharin appealed for him. Stalin scrawled on the letter: 'To Comrade Kaganovich, pay attention to the attached document – don't let the Communists drive Ehrenburg mad. J. Stalin.' Molotov and Bukharin helped Mandelstam. Voroshilov aided his own stable as well as his 'court painter' Gerasimov. Kirov protected the Mariinsky Ballet, Yenukidze the Bolshoi. Yagoda patronized his own writers and architects, often meeting them at Gorky's mansion. Poskrebyshev received the tenor Kozlovsky at home.

to regard as an ideal Soviet man. They had gathered to write the new history of Russia.

Already ill and exhausted, Kirov was the sort of man who wanted to go camping and hunting with friends like Sergo. There was nothing relaxing about a holiday with Stalin. Indeed, escaping from holidays with Stalin was to become a common experience for all his guests. Kirov tried to get out of it but Stalin insisted. Kirov, realizing that 'Stalin was conducting a struggle of wills', could not refuse. 'I'm not in a happy mood,' he told his wife. 'I'm bored here ... At no time can I have a quiet vacation. To hell with it.' This was hardly the attitude Stalin needed or expected from 'my Kirich' but had he read such letters, they would have confirmed his already ambiguous feelings for Kirov.

The three leaders and the boy 'sat at a table on the balcony in gorgeous weather on the enclosed veranda' of the huge Sochi house with its courtyard and its small indoor pool for Stalin. Servants brought hors d'oeuvres and drinks. 'The four of us came and went,' says Yury Zhdanov. 'Sometimes we went into the study indoors, sometimes we went down the garden to the wooden summerhouse.' The atmosphere was relaxing and free and easy. In the breaks, Kirov took Yury picking blackberries which they brought back for Stalin and Zhdanov. Every evening Kirov returned to his dacha and the Zhdanovs to theirs. Sometimes the lonely Stalin went home with them. 'There were no bodyguards, no accompanying vehicles, no NKVD cars,' says Yury Zhdanov. 'There was just me in the front, next to the driver and my father and Stalin in the back.' They set off at dusk and when they turned on the lights, they saw two girls hitchhiking by the roadside.

'Stop!' said Stalin. He opened the door and let the girls get into the middle seats of the seven-seater Packard. The girls recognized Stalin:

'That's Stalin!' Yury heard one whisper. They dropped the girls off in Sochi. 'That was the atmosphere of the time.' It was about to change.

However informal it might have been, Zhdanov, like Beria, was one of the few magnates who could have brought his son to attend a meeting with Stalin even though the teenager had known him since he was five. 'Only Zhdanov received from Stalin the same kind of treatment that Kirov enjoyed,' explained

Molotov. 'After Kirov, Stalin loved Zhdanov best. He valued him above everyone else.'

Attractive, brown-eyed, broad-chested and athletic, though asthmatic, Zhdanov was always hearty and smiling, with a ready supply of jokes. Like Kirov, a sunny companion, he loved to sing and play the piano. Zhdanov already knew Stalin well. Born at the Black Sea port of Mariupol in 1896, Andrei Alexandrovich Zhdanov, a hereditary nobleman (like Lenin and Molotov), was the scion of Chekhovian intellectuals. Son of a Master of Religious Studies at the Moscow Religious Academy, who worked like Lenin's father as an inspector of public schools (his thesis was 'Socrates as Pedagogue'), and a mother who had graduated from the Moscow Musical Conservatoire and was herself the daughter of a rector of a religious academy, Zhdanov was the sole representative in top Party circles of the nineteenth-century educated middle-class. His mother, a gifted pianist, taught Zhdanov to play well too.

Zhdanov studied at a church school (like Stalin), dreamed of being an agriculturalist, then at twenty attended the Junior Officers' Training College in Tiflis. This 'acquainted him with Georgian culture and songs'. He grew up with three sisters who became Bolsheviks: two of them never married and became revolutionary maiden aunts who lived in his house, dominating Zhdanov and greatly irritating Stalin. Joining the Party in 1915, Zhdanov won his spurs in the Civil War as a commissar, like so many others. By 1922, he ran Tver, then Nizhny Novgorod, whence he was called to greater things.

Strait-laced and rigid in Party matters, his papers reveal a man of meticulous diligence who could not approach a subject without becoming an encyclopaedic expert on it. Despite never completing higher education though he attended Agricultural College, Zhdanov was another workaholic obessesive, who voraciously studied music, history and literature. Stalin 'respected Zhdanov', says Artyom, 'as his fellow intellectual', whom he constantly telephoned to ask:

'Andrei, have you read this new book?' The two were always pulling out Chekhov or Saltykov-Shchedrin to read aloud. Jealous rivals mocked his pretensions: Beria nicknamed him 'The Pianist'. Zhdanov and Stalin shared religious education, Georgian songs, a love of history and classical Russian culture, autodictactic and ideological obsessions, and their sense of humour – except that

Zhdanov was a prig.* He was personally devoted to Stalin whom he called 'Joseph Vissarionovich' but never Koba. 'Comrade Stalin and I have decided ...' was his favourite pompous way to begin a meeting.

On the veranda or in the summerhouse, they discussed history, epoch by epoch, on a table spread with revolutionary and Tsarist history textbooks. Zhdanov took notes. The supreme pedagogue could not stop showing off his knowledge.† Their mission was to create the new history that became the Stalinist orthodoxy. Stalin adored studying history, having such happy memories of his history teacher at the Seminary that he took the trouble in September 1931 to write to Beria:

'Nikolai Dmitrievich Makhatadze, aged 73, finds himself in Metechi Prison ... I have known him since the Seminary and I do not think he can present a danger to Soviet power. I ask you to free the old man and let me know the result.' He had been a history addict ever since. In 1931, Stalin decisively intervened in academia to create the historical precursor of 'Socialist Realism' in fiction: henceforth, history was not what the archives said but what the Party decreed on a holiday like this. 'You speak about history,' Stalin told his magnates. 'But one must sometimes correct history.' Stalin's historical library was read and annotated thoroughly: he paid special attention to the Napoleonic Wars, ancient Greece, nineteenth-century relations between Germany, Britain and Russia, and all Persian Shahs and Russian Tsars. A born student, he always mugged up on the history of that day's issue.

While Zhdanov was in his element in the discussions in Sochi, Kirov was out of his depth. It is said that Kirov tried to escape by saying,

'Joseph Vissarionovich, what kind of a historian am I?'

'Never mind. Sit down,' replied Stalin, 'and listen.' Kirov got so sunburnt he could not even play *gorodki*: 'However strange, for

---

* His wife Zinaida was even prissier: she once told Svetlana Stalin that the urbane novelist Ehrenburg 'loves Paris because there are naked women there'. It was Zinaida who was tactless enough to tell Svetlana her mother was mentally 'sick'.

† Yury Zhdanov, the boy at table with Stalin, Kirov and his father, is the main source for this account and now lives in Rostov-on-Don where he generously agreed to be interviewed for this book. The holiday became famous because of Kirov's fate soon afterwards: it forms a set piece in Anatoly Rybakov's novel *Children of the Arbat*. Yury Zhdanov remembers Stalin asking him: 'What was the genius of Catherine the Great?' He answered his own question. 'Her greatness lay in her choice of Prince Potemkin and other such talented lovers and officials to govern the State.'

most of the day, we are busy. This isn't what I expected for recreation. Well, to the devil with it,' he wrote to a friend in Leningrad. 'I'll just take to my heels as soon as possible.' Yet Yury Zhdanov recalled 'happy warmth' between Stalin and Kirov who swapped earthy jokes which Zhdanov received in prim silence. Yury still remembers Stalin's Jesus joke: they were working in the summerhouse, which stood under a big oak tree, when Stalin glanced at his closest friends:

'Look at you here with me,' he said, pointing at the tree. 'That's the Mamre tree.' Zhdanov knew from his Bible that the Mamre tree was where Jesus assembled his Apostles.*

There may have been a more sinister development that worried Kirov: some time when he was out of town, Moscow tried to remove his trusted NKVD boss in Leningrad, Medved, a close family friend, and replace him with a thuggish ex-criminal, Evdokimov, one of Stalin's rougher drinking pals on southern holidays. Stalin was trying to loosen Kirov's local patronage, and perhaps even control his security. Kirov refused to accept Evdokimov.

As Kirov headed back to Leningrad, Stalin despatched Zhdanov to Moscow to supervise the first Writers' Congress. This was Zhdanov's first test, which he passed with flying colours, managing, with Kaganovich's help, to cope with Gorky's demands and Bukharin's hysteria. Zhdanov reported every detail to Stalin in twenty-page letters in a fastidious hand that showed their close relationship and the younger man's new eminence. (There seems to have been an unspoken competition among his men to write the longest letters: if so, Zhdanov was the winner.) Like a schoolboy to his tutor, Zhdanov boasted of his good work: 'The opinion of all the writers – ours and foreigners – was good. All the sceptics who predicted failure now have to admit the colossal success. All the writers saw and understood the Party's attitude.' He admitted, 'the Congress cost me a lot in terms of my nerves but I think I did it well.' Stalin appreciated his openness about his weaknesses. Once the Congress was over, Zhdanov even had to apologize to Stalin that 'I didn't write to you. Congress took so much time ...' but he also apologized for writing 'such a long letter – I can't do it any other way'.

---

* When the writer Mikhail Sholokhov criticized the praise for the leader, Stalin replied with a sly smile, 'What can I do? The people need a god.'

By now the other leaders had gone off on holiday: 'Molotov, Kaganovich, Chubar and Mikoyan left today. Kuibyshev, Andreyev and me stayed.' Zhdanov, not even a Politburo candidate, and new in the Secretariat, was left in charge of the country, signing decrees himself. Here was another sign that the Politburo's importance was shrinking: proximity to Stalin was the source of real power.* Soviet Russia was enjoying its last months of oligarchy and approaching the first of dictatorship.

Zhdanov, one of the more fragile of Stalin's workhorses, was exhausted: 'I ask for one month's holiday in Sochi ... I feel very tired,' he wrote to Stalin. Of course he would work on their beloved history: 'During the holiday, I'd like to look through the textbooks on history ... I've already looked through the second level textbooks – not good. A big greeting to you, dear Comrade Stalin!'

What was Stalin's mood in this calm before the storm? He was frustrated by the NKVD's blunders and the 'whining' of Party bigwigs. On 11 September, Stalin complained to Zhdanov and Kuibyshev about misguided secret-police coercion: 'Find out all the mistakes of the deduction methods of the workers of the GPU ... Free persecuted persons who are innocent if they are innocent and ... purge the OGPU' of people with specific 'deduction methods' and punish them all – 'whoever they may be' [in Stalin's words: 'without looking at their faces']. A few days later, a sailor defected to Poland.

Stalin immediately ordered Zhdanov and Yagoda to enforce the punishment of the sailor's family: 'Inform me at once that 1. members of sailor's family were arrested and 2. if not, then who is guilty for the mistake [of not having done so] in our Organs and has the culprit been punished for this betrayal of the Motherland?' The tension was rising too in his relationship with Kirov.

* * *

On 1 September, Stalin despatched the Politburo around the countryside to check the harvest: Kirov was sent to Kazakhstan where there was a strange incident which might have been an

* After the Seventeenth Congress, formal Politburo meetings became gradually less frequent. Often a Politburo sitting was really just Stalin chatting with a couple of comrades: Poskrebyshev's minutes are simply marked 'Comrades Stalin, Molotov, Kaganovich – for' and the others were sometimes telephoned by Poskrebyshev who marked their votes and signed his 'P' underneath. By the end of the year, there was one meeting in September, none in October and one in November.

assassination attempt or meant to resemble one. The circumstances are murky but when he returned to Leningrad, four more Chekists were added to his NKVD guard, bringing it to about nine men who worked in shifts at different locations. This made Kirov one of the most guarded of all the Soviet leaders and he did not like it, sensing it was another attempt to separate him from his trusted local Chekists, particularly his bodyguard Borisov, middle-aged and overweight but loyal. After their tour, Sergo and Voroshilov joined Stalin on holiday while Zhdanov inspected Stalingrad, whence he managed another thirteen-page letter, showing his toughness by demanding, 'Some workers must be sent to trial here.' He signed off heartily: 'A hundred times: Devil curse the details!'

When Stalin returned to Moscow on 31 October, he again longed to see Kirov who was arguing against Stalin's plan to end bread rationing on which he depended to feed Leningrad's huge population. Kuibyshev was Kirov's ally: 'I need your support,' he wrote from Leningrad. On 3 November, Maria Svanidze recorded Stalin arriving in his apartment with Kaganovich while the 'absurd fat' Zhdanov ran along behind him. He rang a reluctant Kirov and invited him to Moscow 'to defend the interests of Leningrad'. Stalin gave the phone to Kaganovich who 'talked Kirov into coming down'. Maria said that Stalin really just wanted to 'go to the steambath and joke around with him'.

A few days later, Kirov drove out with Stalin and his son Vasily to Zubalovo to watch a puppet show put on by Svetlana, and then played billiards. Khrushchev, attending the Politburo as a rising star, witnessed 'an exchange of sharp words' between Stalin and Kirov. Khrushchev was shocked that the *Vozhd* behaved 'disrespectfully to another Party member'. Svanidze noticed Stalin was 'in a bad mood'. Kirov anxiously returned to Leningrad: he longed to discuss the rising tension with his friend: 'I haven't seen Sergo in such a long time.'

On 7 November, there was another sign of the apparent thaw. At the diplomatic reception in the Andreevsky Hall, presided over by Stalin, Kalinin and Voroshilov, the traditional Red Army oompah band packed up and were replaced, to the amazement of all, by Antonin Ziegler and his Jazz Revue. The wild swing music seemed completely out of place and no one knew whether they should dance or not. Then the light-footed Voroshilov, who was taking dancing lessons in cabaret jazz, started to foxtrot strenuously with his wife Ekaterina Davidovna.

On 25 November, Kirov rushed back to Moscow for the Plenum, hoping to consult with Ordzhonikidze. Sergo did not make it to the Plenum. Earlier that month, visiting Baku with Beria, he was suddenly taken ill after dinner. Beria took Sergo back to Tiflis by train. After the 7 November parade, Sergo fell ill again with intestinal bleeding, then suffered a serious heart attack. The Politburo sent three specialists down to examine him but they were confounded by his mysterious symptoms. Sergo was none the less determined to return for the Plenum but Stalin formally ordered him to 'strictly fulfil doctor's instructions and not return to Moscow before 26 November. Don't take your illness lightly. Regards. Stalin.'

When Beria was involved, it was indeed foolish to take one's illnesses lightly: Stalin perhaps did not want Sergo and Kirov to meet at the Plenum. Beria, who had offered to use his axe for Stalin, was already aware of the leader's disillusionment with Sergo. He was to prove adept with poisons. Indeed, the NKVD already boasted a secret department of medical poisoners under Dr Grigory Maironovsky but Beria needed little help in such matters. He truly brought the venom of the Borgias to the court of the Bolsheviks. But Stalin himself brooded about poison; reflecting on venomous intrigues at the eighteenth-century Persian court, which he was studying, he had earlier scribbled on his pad during a Politburo meeting: 'Poison, poison, Nadir Khan.'

After the Plenum, on the 28th, Stalin personally escorted Kirov to the Red Arrow train, embracing him in his compartment. Kirov was back at work in Leningrad the next day. On 1 December, he started work at home, preparing a speech, then, wearing his worker's peaked cap and raincoat, he set off from his apartment on foot to his office. He entered the grand neoclassical Smolny Institute by the public entrance. At 4.30 p.m. Kirov, followed by his bodyguard Borisov, walked up to his third-floor office. Old Borisov fell behind, either from unfitness or being strangely delayed by some Chekists from Moscow who appeared at the door.

Kirov turned right out of the stairwell and passed a dark-haired young man named Leonid Nikolaev, who pressed himself against the wall to let Kirov pass – and then trailed along behind him. Nikolaev pulled out a Nagan revolver and shot Kirov from three feet away in the back of the neck. The bullet passed through his cap. Nikolaev turned the pistol on himself and squeezed the trigger but an electrician working nearby somehow knocked him down and the second bullet hit the ceiling. Borisov the guard staggered up breathlessly, gun drawn impotently. Kirov fell face down, head turned to the right, his cap's peak resting on the floor, and still gripping his briefcase – a Bolshevik workaholic to the last.

Several minutes of chaos followed in which witnesses and police ran in every direction, seeing the same events differently and giving conflicting evidence: even the gun was variously seen on the floor and in the assassin's hand. There seems to be a special sort of miasma in the air at terrible events and this one was no different. What matters is that Kirov lay lifeless on the floor near the unconscious Nikolaev. Kirov's friend Rosliakov knelt beside him, lifting his head and whispering: 'Kirov, Mironich.' They lifted Kirov, with Rosliakov holding his lolling head, on to a conference table, with the blood seeping from his neck leaving a trail of heroic Bolshevik sacrament down the corridor. They loosened his belt and opened his collar. Medved, the Leningrad NKVD boss, arrived but was stopped at the door by Moscow Chekists.

Three doctors arrived, including a Georgian, Dzhanelidze. All declared Kirov dead but they still kept on giving him artificial respiration until almost 5.45 p.m. Doctors in totalitarian states are terrified of eminent dead patients – and with good reason. As the doctors surrendered, those present realized that someone would have to tell Stalin. Everyone remembered where they were when Kirov was assassinated: the Soviet JFK.

Part Three

On the Brink, 1934–1936

Part Two

12

'I'm Orphaned':
the Connoisseur of Funerals

Poskrebyshev answered Stalin's telephone in his office. Kirov's deputy, Chudov, broke the terrible news from Leningrad. Poskrebyshev tried Stalin's phone line but he could not get an answer, sending a secretary to find him. The *Vozhd*, according to his journal, was meeting with Molotov, Kaganovich, Voroshilov and Zhdanov, but hurriedly called Leningrad, insisting on interrogating the Georgian doctor in his native language. Then he rang back to ask what the assassin was wearing. A cap? Were there foreign items on him? Yagoda, who had already called to demand whether any foreign objects had been found on the assassin, arrived at Stalin's office at 5.50 p.m.

Mikoyan, Sergo and Bukharin arrived quickly. Mikoyan specifically remembered that 'Stalin announced that Kirov had been assassinated and on the spot, without any investigation, he said the supporters of Zinoviev [the former leader of Leningrad and the Left opposition to Stalin] had started a terror against the Party.' Sergo and Mikoyan, who were so close to Kirov, were particularly appalled since Sergo had missed seeing his friend for the last time. Kaganovich noticed that Stalin 'was shocked at first'.

Stalin, now showing no emotion, ordered Yenukidze as Secretary of the Central Executive Committee to sign an emergency law that decreed the trial of accused terrorists within ten days and immediate execution without appeal after judgement. Stalin must have drafted it himself. This 1st December Law – or rather the two directives of that night – was the equivalent of Hitler's Enabling Act because it laid the foundation for a random terror without even the pretence of a rule of law. Within three years, two million people had been sentenced to death or labour camps in its name. Mikoyan said there was no discussion and no objections. As easily as slipping the safety catch on their Mausers, the Politburo clicked into the military emergency mentality of the Civil War.

If there was any opposition, it came from Yenukidze, that

unusually benign figure among these amoral toughs, but it was he who ultimately signed it. The newspapers declared the laws were passed by a meeting of the Presidium of the Central Executive Committee – which probably meant Stalin bullying Yenukidze in a smoky room after the meeting. It is also a mystery why the craven Kalinin, the President who was present, did not sign it. His signature had appeared by the time it was announced in the newspapers. Anyway the Politburo did not officially vote until a few days later.

Stalin immediately decided that he would personally lead a delegation to Leningrad to investigate the murder. Sergo wanted to go but Stalin ordered him to remain behind because of his weak heart. Sergo had indeed collapsed with grief and may have suffered another heart attack. His daughter remembered that 'this was the only time he wept openly'. His wife, Zina, travelled to Leningrad to comfort Kirov's widow.

Kaganovich also wanted to go but Stalin told him that someone had to run the country. He took Molotov, Voroshilov and Zhdanov with him along with Yagoda and Andrei Vyshinsky, the Deputy Procurator, who had crossed Sergo earlier that year. Naturally they were accompanied by a trainload of secret policemen and Stalin's own myrmidons, Pauker and Vlasik. In retrospect, the most significant man Stalin chose to accompany him was Nikolai Yezhov, head of the CC's Personnel Department. Yezhov was one of those special young men, like Zhdanov, on whom Stalin was coming to depend.

The local leaders gathered, shell-shocked, at the station. Stalin played his role, that of a Lancelot heartbroken and angry at the death of a beloved knight, with self-conscious and preplanned Thespianism. When he dismounted from the train, Stalin strode up to Medved, the Leningrad NKVD chief, and slapped his face with his gloved hand.

Stalin immediately headed across town to the hospital to inspect the body, then set up a headquarters in Kirov's office where he began his own strange investigation, ignoring any evidence that did not point to a terrorist plot by Zinoviev and the Left opposition. Poor Medved, the cheerful Chekist slapped by Stalin, was interrogated first and criticized for not preventing the murder. Then the 'small and shabby' murderer himself, Nikolaev, was dragged in. Nikolaev was one of those tragic, simple victims of history, like the Dutchman who lit the Reichstag fire with which this case shares many resemblances. This frail dwarf of thirty had been expelled from, and reinstated in, the Party but had written to Kirov and Stalin complaining of his plight. He was apparently in a daze and did not even recognize Stalin until they showed him a photograph. Falling to his knees before the jackbooted leader, he sobbed,

'What have I done, what have I done?' Khrushchev, who was not in the room, claimed that Nikolaev kneeled and said he had done it on assignment from the Party. A source close to Voroshilov has Nikolaev stammering, 'But you yourself told me ...' Some accounts claim that he was punched and kicked by the Chekists present.

'Take him away!' ordered Stalin.

The well-informed NKVD defector, Orlov, wrote that Nikolaev pointed at Zaporozhets, Leningrad's deputy NKVD boss, and said, 'Why are you asking me? Ask him.'

Zaporozhets had been imposed on Kirov and Leningrad in 1932, Stalin and Yagoda's man in Kirov's fiefdom. The reason to ask Zaporozhets was that Nikolaev had already been detained in October loitering with suspicious intent outside Kirov's house, carrying a revolver, but had been freed without even being searched. Another time, the bodyguards had prevented him taking a shot. But four years later, when Yagoda was tried, he confessed, in testimony filled with both lies and truths, to having ordered Zaporozhets 'not to place any obstacles in the way of the terrorist act against Kirov'.

Then the assassin's wife, Milda Draul, was brought in. The NKVD spread the story that Nikolaev's shot was a *crime passionnel* following her affair with Kirov. Draul was a plain-looking woman. Kirov liked elfin ballerinas but his wife was not pretty either: it is impossible to divine the impenetrable mystery of sexual taste but those who knew both believed they were an unlikely couple. Draul claimed she knew nothing. Stalin strode out into the anteroom and ordered that Nikolaev be brought round with medical attention.

'To me it's already clear that a well-organized counter-revolutionary terrorist organization is active in Leningrad ... A painstaking investigation must be made.' There was no real attempt to analyse the murder forensically. Stalin certainly did not wish to find out whether the NKVD had encouraged Nikolaev to kill Kirov.

Later, it is said that Stalin visited the 'prick' in his cell and spent an hour with him alone, offering him his life in return for testifying against Zinoviev at a trial. Afterwards Nikolaev wondered if he would be double-crossed.

The murkiness now thickens into a deliberately blind fog. There was a delay. Kirov's bodyguard, Borisov, was brought over to be interrogated by Stalin. He alone could reveal whether he was delayed at the Smolny entrance and what he knew of the NKVD's machinations. Borisov rode in the back of an NKVD Black Crow. As the driver headed towards the Smolny, the front-seat passenger reached over and seized the wheel so that the Black Crow swerved and grazed its side against a building. Somehow in this dubious car crash, Borisov was killed. The 'shaken' Pauker arrived in the anteroom to announce the crash. Such ham-handed 'car crashes' were soon to become an occupational hazard for eminent Bolsheviks. Certainly anyone who wanted to cover up a plot might have wished Borisov dead. When Stalin was informed of this reekingly suspicious death, he denounced the local Cheka: 'They couldn't even do that properly.'

The mystery will never now be conclusively solved. Did Stalin order Kirov's assassination? There is no evidence that he did, yet the whiff of his complicity still hangs in the air. Khrushchev, who arrived in Leningrad on a separate train as a Moscow delegate, claimed years later that Stalin ordered the murder. Mikoyan, a more trustworthy witness in many ways than Khrushchev and with less to prove, came to believe that Stalin was somehow involved in the death.

Stalin certainly no longer trusted Kirov whose murder served as a pretext to destroy the Old Bolshevik cliques. His drafting of the 1st December Law minutes after the death seems to stink as much as his decision to blame the murder on Zinoviev. Stalin had indeed tried to replace Kirov's friend Medved and he knew the suspicious Zaporozhets who, shortly before the murder, had gone on leave without Moscow's permission, perhaps to absent himself from the scene. Nikolaev was a pathetic bundle of suspicious circumstances. Then there were the strange events of the day of the murder: why was Borisov delayed at the door and why were there already Moscow NKVD officers in the Smolny so soon after the assassination? Borisov's death is highly suspect. And Stalin, often so cautious, was also capable of such a reckless gamble, particularly after admiring Hitler's reaction to the Reichstag fire and his purge.

Yet much of this appears less sinister on closer analysis. The lax security around Kirov proves nothing, since even Stalin often only had one or two guards. The gun is less suspicious when one realizes that all Party members carried them. Stalin's deteriorating relationship with Kirov was typical of the friction within his entourage. Stalin's swift reaction to the murder, and his surreal investigation, did not mean that he arranged it. When, on 27 June 1927, Voikov, Soviet Ambassador to Poland, was assassinated, Stalin had reacted with the same speed and uninterest in the real culprits. In that case, he told Molotov that he 'sensed the hand of Britain' and immediately ordered the shooting of scores of so-called 'monarchists'. The Bolsheviks always regarded justice as a political tool. The local NKVD, desperate to conceal their incompetence, may well have arranged Borisov's murder. So much can be explained by the habitual clumsiness of totalitarian panic.

However, it is surely naïve to expect written evidence of the crime of the century. We know that, in other murders, Stalin gave verbal orders in the name of the *Instantsiya*, an almost magical euphemism for the Highest Authority, with which we will become very familiar.* The direct involvement of Yagoda seems unlikely because he was not particularly close to Stalin but there were many Chekists, from Agranov to Zaporozhets, who were both personally trusted and amoral enough to do anything the Party asked of them. It is unlikely to have been a Henrician 'Rid me of this turbulent priest' because Stalin had to micromanage everything. So he may have read Nikolaev's letter to him and exploited his loser's resentment against Kirov.

Stalin's friendship with Kirov was one-sided and flimsy but there is no doubt that 'Stalin simply loved him,' according to 'Iron Lazar', who added that 'he treated everyone politically'. His friendships, like teenage infatuations, meandered between love, admiration and venomous jealousy. He was an extreme example of Gore Vidal's epigram that 'Every time a friend succeeds, a little bit of me dies.' He had adored Bukharin whose widow explains that Stalin could love and hate the same person 'because love and hate born of envy ... fought with each other in the same breast'. Perhaps Kirov's betrayal of his sincere friendship provoked a rage

---

* *Instantsiya* derives from the nineteenth-century German usage of *aller instanzen*, meaning to appeal to the highest court.

like a woman scorned, followed by terrible guilt after the murder. But even with his 'friends', Stalin cultivated his privacy and detachment: he wanted to be supremely elusive.

Stalin was always a more loyal friend to those he knew much less well. When a schoolboy of sixteen wrote to him, Stalin sent him a present of ten roubles and the boy wrote a thank-you letter. He was always indulging in bursts of sentimentality for the friends of his youth: 'I'm sending you 2,000 roubles,' he wrote to Peter Kapanadze, his friend from the Seminary who became a priest, then a teacher, in December 1933. 'I haven't got more now ... Your needs are a special occasion for me so I send my [book] royalties to you. You'll [also] be given 3,000 roubles as a loan ... Live long and be happy' and he signed the letter with his father's name, 'Beso.'

One strange unpublished letter illustrates this distant warmth: during 1930, Stalin received a request from the head of a collective farm in distant Siberia as to whether to admit a Tsarist policeman who claimed to have known Stalin. This old gendarme had actually been Stalin's guard in exile. But Stalin wrote a long, handwritten recommendation: 'During my exile in Kureika 1914–16, Mikhail Merzlikov was my guard/police constable. At that time he had one order – to guard me ... It's clear that I could not be in 'friendly' relations with Merzlikov. Yet I must testify that while not being friendly, our relations were not as hostile as they usually were between exile and guard. It must be explained why, it seems to me, Merzlikov carried out his duties without the usual police zeal, did not spy on me or persecute me, overlooked my often going away and often scolded police officers for barring his "orders" ... It's my duty to testify to all this. It was so in 1914–16 when Merzlikov was my guard, differing from other policemen for the better. I don't know what he did under Kolchak and Soviet power, I don't know how he is now.'

There, in a man who killed his best friends, was true friendship. Whether or not he killed Kirov, Stalin certainly exploited the murder to destroy not only his opponents but the less radical among his own allies.

* * *

Kirov lay in state in an open casket, wearing a dark tunic and surrounded by the red banners, inscribed wreaths and tropical palms of the Bolshevik funeral amidst the Potemkinian neoclassical grandeur of the Taurida Palace.* At 9.30 p.m. on 3 December, Stalin and the Politburo formed the honour guard, another part of Bolshevik necro-ritual. Voroshilov and Zhdanov appeared upset but Molotov was stony. 'Astonishingly calm and impenetrable was the face of JV Stalin,' noted Khrushchev, 'giving the impression that he was lost in thought, his eyes glazing over Kirov's bullet-struck corpse.' Before departing, Stalin appointed Zhdanov as Leningrad boss while remaining a CC Secretary. Yezhov also stayed behind to oversee the investigation.

At ten, Stalin and the others bore Kirov's coffin to a gun-carriage. The body travelled slowly through the streets to the station where it was loaded on to the train that was to take Stalin back to Moscow. Draped in garlands, this death train shunted into the darkness after midnight, leaving behind Kirov's brain where it was to be studied for signs of revolutionary brilliance in the Leningrad Institute.†

Even before the train arrived in Moscow, Agranov, the Chekist running the investigation, interrogated the assassin: 'Stubborn as a mule,' he reported to Stalin.

'Nourish Nikolaev well, buy him a chicken,' replied Stalin, who so enjoyed chicken himself. 'Nourish him so he will be strong, then he'll tell us who was leading him. And if he doesn't talk, we'll give it to him and he'll tell … everything.'

At Moscow's October Station, the casket was again transferred to a gun carriage and deposited in the Hall of Columns for the funeral next day. Soon afterwards, Stalin briefed the Politburo on his unconvincing investigation. Mikoyan, who had loved Kirov, was so upset that he asked how Nikolaev had twice escaped arrest with a pistol and how Borisov had been killed.

'How could it happen?' Stalin agreed indignantly. 'Someone should answer for this, shouldn't they?' exclaimed Mikoyan,

* The Taurida Palace had been the scene of Prince Potemkin's extravagant ball for Catherine the Great in 1791 but it was also the home of the Duma, the Parliament gingerly granted by Nicholas II after the 1905 Revolution. In 1918, the palace housed the Constituent Assembly that Lenin ordered shut down by drunken Red Guards. It was thus both the birthplace and graveyard of Russia's first two democracies before 1991.

† This brain study was part of the rationalist-scientific ritual of the death of great Bolsheviks. Lenin's brain had been extracted and was now studied at the Institute of the Brain. When Gorky died, his brain was delivered there too. This was surely a scientific Marxist distortion of the tradition in the Romantic age for the hearts of great men, whether Mirabeau or Potemkin, to be buried separately. But the age of the heart was over.

focusing on the strange behaviour of the NKVD. 'Isn't the OGPU Chairman [Yagoda] responsible for Politburo security? He should be called to account.' But Stalin protected Yagoda, concentrating on his real targets, the Old Bolsheviks like Zinoviev. Afterwards, Sergo, Kuibyshev and Mikoyan were deeply suspicious: Mikoyan discussed Stalin's 'unclear behaviour' with Sergo, probably on their walks around the Kremlin, the traditional place for such forbidden chats. Both were 'surprised and amazed and could not understand it'. Sergo lost his voice with grief. Kuibyshev is said to have proposed a CC investigation to check the one being carried out by the NKVD. It is surely doubtful that Mikoyan, who still fervently admired Stalin and served him loyally until his death, believed at that time that his leader was responsible. These Bolsheviks were accustomed to self-delude and double-think their way out of such nagging doubts.

That night, Pavel Alliluyev replayed his role after Nadya's death by staying with Stalin at Kuntsevo. Leaning on his hand, Stalin murmured that after Kirov's death, 'I am absolutely an orphan.' He said it so touchingly that Pavel hugged him. There is no reason to doubt the sincerity of his anguish that someone had done this to Kirov – or that they had needed to do it.

At 10 a.m. on the 5th, with Gorky Street closed and tight security under the command of Pauker (as at Nadya's funeral), Stalin's entourage gathered in the Hall of Columns. The funeral was an extravaganza of Bolshevik sentimental kitsch – with burning torches, scarlet velvet curtains and banners hanging all the way from the ceiling and more palm trees – and modern media frenzy, with a press pack snapping their cameras and arc lights illuminating the body as if it was a prop in a neon-lit theatre. The orchestra of the Bolshoi played the funeral marches. It was not only the Nazis who could lay on a brilliant funeral for their fallen knights; even the colours were the same: everything was red and black. Stalin had already declared Kirov his closest martyred comrade: his home town, Viatka, Leningrad's Mariinsky Ballet and hundreds of streets were renamed 'Kirov'.

The coffin rested on scarlet calico, the face 'a greenish colour' with a blue bruise on his temple where he fell. Kirov's widow sat with the sisters he had not seen or bothered to contact for thirty years. Redens, Moscow NKVD chief, escorted his pregnant wife, Anna Alliluyeva, and the Svanidzes to their places beside the Politburo wives. Silence fell. Only the click of the sentry's boots echoed in the hall. Then Maria Svanidze heard the 'footsteps of that group of tough and resolute eagles': the Politburo took up position around the head of Kirov.

The Bolshoi orchestra broke into Chopin's Funeral March. Afterwards, in the silence, there was the clicking and whirring of cine-cameras: Stalin, fingers together across his stomach, stood beside the swaggering Kaganovich, with a leather belt around the midriff of his bulging tunic. The guards began to screw on the coffin lid. But just like at Nadya's funeral, Stalin dramatically stopped them by stepping up to the catafalque. With all eyes on his 'sorrowful' face, he slowly bent down and kissed Kirov's brow. 'It was a heart-breaking sight, knowing how close they were' and the whole hall burst into audible weeping; even the men were openly sobbing.

'Goodbye dear friend, we'll avenge you,' Stalin whispered to the corpse. He was becoming something of a connoisseur of funerals.

One by one the leaders wished Kirov adieu: a pale-faced Molotov, Zhdanov, Kaganovich leaned over but did not kiss Kirov, while Mikoyan placed his hand on the rim of the coffin and leaned in. Kirov's wife collapsed and doctors had to give her valerian drops. For Stalin's family, the loss of Kirov, 'this completely charming person loved by all', was linked to the death of Nadya because they knew he had 'transferred all the pain and burden of loss' of his wife on to this dear friend.

The leaders left and the coffin was closed up and driven away to the crematorium where Pavel and Zhenya Alliluyev watched the casket disappear into the furnace. The Svanidzes and others returned to Voroshilov's apartment in the Horse Guards, scene of Nadya's last supper, for a late dinner. Molotov and the other magnates dined with Stalin at Kuntsevo.

Next morning, Stalin, in his old greatcoat and peaked cap, Voroshilov, Molotov and Kalinin carried the urn of ashes, standing in an ornate mini Classical temple the size of a coffin, piled high with flowers, across Red Square where a million workers stood in the freezing silence. Kaganovich spoke – another parallel with Nadya's funeral, before trumpets blared out a salute, heads and banners were lowered, and that 'perfect Bolshevik', Sergo, placed the urn where it still rests in the Kremlin Wall. 'I thought Kirich would bury me but it's turned out the opposite,' he told his wife afterwards.

The executions had already started: by 6 December, sixty-six

'White Guardists' arrested for planning terrorist acts even before Kirov was assassinated, were sentenced to death by the Supreme Court's Military Collegium under the presidency of Vasily Ulrikh, a bullet-headed Baltic German nobleman who became Stalin's hanging judge. Another twenty-eight were shot in Kiev. On the 8th, Nikolai Yezhov, accompanied by Agranov, returned to Moscow from Leningrad to report for three hours on their hunt for the 'terrorists'.

Despite the tragedy and the dangerous signs that even Bolsheviks were soon to be shot for Kirov's murder, the life of Stalin's circle continued normally if sombrely. After the meeting with Yezhov, Molotov, Sergo, Kaganovich and Zhdanov dined with Stalin, Svetlana and Vasily, the Svanidzes and Alliluyevs at his flat as usual on 8 December. Svetlana received presents to help her recover from the loss of her beloved 'Second Secretary', Kirov. Stalin 'had got thinner, paler with a hidden look in his eyes. He suffers so much.' Maria Svanidze and Anna Alliluyeva bustled round Stalin. Alyosha Svanidze warned Maria to keep her distance. It was good advice but she did not take it because she thought he was just jealous of a relationship that possibly included an affair in the distant past. There was not enough food so Stalin called in Carolina Til and ordered her to rustle up more dinner. Stalin hardly ate. That night, he took Alyosha Svanidze, with Svetlana and Vasily, to spend the night at Kuntsevo while the others went on to Sergo's flat.

Since Stalin had declared within a couple of hours of Kirov's death that Zinoviev and his supporters were responsible, it was no surprise that Yezhov and the NKVD arrested a 'Leningrad Centre' and a 'Moscow Centre', lists drawn up by Stalin himself. Nikolaev, interrogated to 'prove' the connection with Zinoviev, admitted a link on 6 December. Zinoviev and Kamenev, Lenin's two closest comrades and both ex-Politburo members who had saved Stalin's career in 1925, were arrested. The Politburo were shown the testimonies of the 'terrorists'. Stalin personally ordered Deputy Procurator-General Vyshinsky and Ulrikh to sentence them to death.

All the witnesses remember that, as Yury Zhdanov puts it, 'everything changed after Kirov's death'. Security was massively tightened at a time when the informality of Stalin's court with its sense of fun, its bustling ambitious women, and scampering children, seemed more important than ever to comfort the bereaved *Vozhd*. Yet the atmosphere had changed for ever: on 5 December, Rudzutak thought he saw Stalin pointing at him and accusing this proudly semi-educated Old Bolshevik of having 'studied in college so how could his father be a labourer?' Rudzutak wrote to Stalin 'I wouldn't bother you with such trifles but I hear so much gossip about me, it's sad, it's reached you.' Yan Rudzutak was an intelligent Latvian, a Politburo member and Stalin ally, an alumni of ten years in Tsarist prisons, with 'tired expressive eyes', a 'slight limp from his hard labour', and an enthusiastic nature photographer, but he clearly felt a chill from Stalin who no longer trusted him.

'You're wrong, Rudzutak,' Stalin replied, 'I was pointing at Zhdanov not you. I know well you didn't study at college. I read your letter in the presence of Molotov and Zhdanov. They confirmed you're wrong.'

Soon after the assassination, Stalin was walking through the Kremlin with a naval officer, past the security guards who were now posted at ten-yard intervals along the corridors, trained to follow every passer-by with their eyes.

'Do you notice how they are?' Stalin asked the officer. 'You're walking down the corridor and thinking, "Which one will it be?" If it's this one, he'll shoot you in the back after you've turned; if it's that one, he'll shoot you in the face.'

* * *

On 21 December, shortly before these executions, the entourage arrived at Kuntsevo to celebrate Stalin's fifty-fifth birthday. When there were not enough chairs at the table, Stalin and the men started moving the places and carrying in other tables, adding more place settings. Mikoyan and Sergo were elected *'tamada'*. Stalin was still depressed by the loss of Kirov but gradually regained his spirits. Yet when Maria Svanidze prepared a poem to read, Alyosha banned her from reading it, perhaps knowing that its sycophancy, or its obvious request for a ladies' trip to the West, would irritate Stalin.*

The dinner was *shchi*, cabbage soup, then veal. Stalin served soup for the guests, from the Molotovs, Poskrebyshev (with new

---

* Maria's poem's reveals both the devotion and cheekiness of Stalin's female courtiers: 'We wish much happiness to our Dear Leader and endless life. Let the enemies be scared off. Liquidate all Fascists ... Next year, take the world under your sway, and rule all mankind. Shame the ladies can't go West to Carlsbad. It's all the same at Sochi.'

wife) and Yenukidze to his children. 'Stalin ate his from his soup bowl, just taking his fork and taking the meat,' remembers Artyom. Beria, and his former patron, deaf Lakoba, master of Abkhazia, arrived in the middle of dinner.

Stalin toasted Sashiko Svanidze, sister of his first wife Kato and Alyosha. This infuriated Alyosha's wife, Maria Svanidze: there was a constant war among the women for Stalin's favour. Then Stalin noticed the children and 'he poured me and Vasily some wine', recalls Artyom, 'asking, "What's wrong with you two? Have some wine!"' Anna Redens and Maria Svanidze grumbled that it was not good for them, like Nadya, but Stalin laughed:

'Don't you know it's medicinal? It can cure all sorts of things!'

Now the evening took a maudlin turn: just as the family had thought of Nadya during Kirov's funeral, now this female Banquo turned up at this feast too. Toastmaster Sergo raised a glass for Kirov:

'Some bastard killed him, took him away from us!' The silence was broken by weeping. Someone drank to Dora Khazan, Andreyev's wife, who was one of Stalin's favourite women, and to her studies at the Academy. This reminded Stalin of Nadya for he stood up:

'Three times, we have talked about the Academy,' he said, 'so let us drink to Nadya!' Everyone rose with tears running down their faces. One by one, each walked silently round the table and clinked glasses with Stalin who looked agonized. Anna Redens and Maria Svanidze kissed him on the cheek. Maria thought Stalin was 'softer, kinder'. Later, Stalin played the disc jockey, putting his favourite records on the gramophone while everyone danced. Then the Caucasians sang laments with their all-powerful choirboy.

Afterwards, by way of relaxing after the sadness, Vlasik the bodyguard, who doubled as court photographer, assembled the guests for a photograph, a remarkable record of Stalin's court before the Terror: even this photograph would cause more rows among the competitive women.

Stalin sat in the middle surrounded by his worshipful women – on his right sat the pushy Sashiko Svanidze, then Maria Kaganovicha and the busty soprano Maria Svanidze, and on his left, the slim, elegant First Lady, Polina Molotova. Uniforms mixed with Party tunics: Voroshilov, always resplendent as the country's senior officer, Redens in NKVD blue, Pavel Alliluyev in his military Commissar's uniform. On the floor sat the laughing Caucasians Sergo, Mikoyan and Lakoba while Beria and Poskrebyshev just managed to squeeze in by lying almost flat. But at Stalin's feet, even more noticeable when he posed again with just the women, sat a Cheshire cat smiling at the camera as if she had got the cream: Zhenya Alliluyeva.

13

A Secret Friendship:
the Rose of Novgorod

'You dress so beautifully,' Stalin said admiringly to his sister-in-law Zhenya Alliluyeva. 'You should make designing your profession.'

'What! I can't even sew a button,' retorted the giggling Zhenya. 'All my buttons are sown on by my daughter.'

'So? You should teach Soviet women how to dress!' retorted Stalin.

After Nadya's death, Zhenya almost moved in to watch over him. In 1934, it seems, this relationship grew into something more. Statuesque and blue-eyed, with wavy blonde hair, dimples, an upturned nose and wide, beaming mouth, Zhenya, thirty-six, was a priest's daughter from Novgorod. She was not beautiful but this 'rose of the Novgorod fields' with golden skin and her quick mischievous nature, radiated health. When she was pregnant with her daughter Kira, she split some logs just before giving birth. While Dora Khazan dressed in austere shifts and Voroshilova got fatter, Zhenya was still young, fresh and completely feminine in her frilly dresses, flamboyant collars and silk scarves.

These women found Stalin all the more appealing because he was so obviously lonely after Nadya's and now Kirov's death: 'his loneliness is always on one's mind,' wrote Maria Svanidze. If power itself is the great aphrodisiac, the addition of strength, loneliness and tragedy proved to be a heady cocktail. However, Zhenya was different. She had known Stalin since marrying Nadya's brother, Pavel, around the Revolution, but they had been abroad a lot and returned from Berlin just before the suicide. Then a fresh relationship developed between Stalin the widower and this funny, blithe woman. The marriage of Pavel and Zhenya had not been easy. Unsuited to military life, Pavel was gentle but hysterical like Nadya. Zhenya grumbled about his weakness. Their marriage had almost ended in the early thirties, when Stalin ordered them to stay together. Despite having given the pistol to Nadya, Pavel often stayed with Stalin.

Stalin admired Zhenya's *joie de vivre*. She was unafraid of him: the first time she arrived at Zubalovo after her return from Berlin, she found a meal on the table and ate it all. Stalin then walked in and asked:

'Where's my onion soup?' Zhenya admitted she had eaten it. This might have provoked an explosion but Stalin merely smiled and said, 'Next time, they better make two.' She said whatever she thought – it was she, among others, who told him about the famine in 1932, yet Stalin forgave her for this. She was well read and Stalin consulted her about what he should read. She suggested an Egyptian history but joked that he 'started copying the Pharoahs'. Zhenya made him laugh uproariously with her earthy wit. Their conversation resembled his banter with rough male friends. She was an expert singer of the *chastushka*, bawdy rhymes with puns that resemble limericks. They do not translate well but Stalin's favourites were such gems as 'Simple to shit off a bridge, but one person did it and fell off' or 'Sitting in one's own shit, feels as safe as a fortress.'

Zhenya could not help tactlessly puncturing the balloons of the stiff Party women and Stalin always enjoyed playing off his courtiers. When Polina Molotova, mistress of the perfume industry, boasted to Stalin that she was wearing her latest product, Red Moscow, Stalin sniffed:

'That's why you smell so nice,' he said.

'Come on, Joseph,' interrupted Zhenya. 'She smells of Chanel No. 5!' Afterwards, Zhenya realized she had made a mistake: 'Why on earth did I say it?' This made the family enemies among the politicians at a time when politics was about to become a blood sport. None the less she alone could get away with these comments because Stalin 'respected her irreverence'.

When Stalin inaugurated the 1936 Constitution, Zhenya, who was late for everything, was late for that too. She crept in and thought no one had noticed until Stalin himself greeted her afterwards:

'How did you spot me?' she asked.

'I see everything, I can see two kilometres away,' replied Stalin whose senses were ferally acute. 'You're the only one who'd dare be late.'

Stalin needed female advice on his children. When Svetlana, maturing early, appeared in her first skirt, Stalin lectured her on 'Bolshevik modesty' but asked Zhenya:

'Can a girl wear a dress like that? I don't want her to bare her knees.'

'It's only natural,' replied Zhenya.

'And she asks for money,' said the father.

'That's all right, isn't it?'

'What's the money for?' he persisted. 'A person can live well on ten kopeks!'

'Come on, Joseph!' Zhenya teased him. 'That was before the Revolution!'

'I thought you could live on ten kopeks,' murmured Stalin.

'What are they doing? Printing special newspapers for you?' Only Zhenya could say this sort of thing to him.

Stalin and Zhenya probably became lovers at this time. Historians never know what happens behind bedroom doors, and Bolshevik conspiratorial secrecy and prudish morality make these matters especially difficult to research.* But Maria Svanidze observed their relationship and recorded it in her diary, which Stalin himself preserved: that summer, Maria spotted how Zhenya went out of her way to be alone with Stalin. The following winter, she records how Stalin arrived back in his apartment to find Maria and Zhenya. He 'teased Zhenya about getting plump again. He treated her very affectionately. *Now that I know everything I have watched them closely ...*'

'Stalin was in love with my mother,' asserts Zhenya's daughter Kira. Daughters perhaps tend to believe great men are in love with their mothers but her cousin Leonid Redens also believes it was 'more than a friendship'. There is other evidence too: later in the thirties, Beria approached Zhenya with an offer that sounds like Stalin's clumsy proposal of marriage. When she remarried after her husband's death, Stalin reacted with jealous fury.

Stalin himself was always gently courteous with Zhenya. While he barely telephoned Anna Redens or Maria Svanidze, Svetlana remembered how he often phoned her for a chat, even after their relationship was over.

Zhenya was far from the only attractive woman around Stalin. During the mid-thirties, he was still enjoying a normal social life with an entourage that included a cosmopolitan circle of young

* Even today, those that know such secrets persist in believing, in the words of Stalin's adopted son General Artyom Sergeev, now eighty, that his 'private life is secret and irrelevant to his place in history'. So far no love letters to anyone other than Nadya have emerged.

and flighty women. But for the moment, it was Zhenya who sat at Stalin's feet.

* * *

Just after the party, on 28 and 29 December the assassin Nikolaev and his fourteen co-defendants were tried by Ulrikh in Leningrad. That reptilian hanging judge called Stalin for orders.

'Finish it,' the *Vozhd* ordered laconically. Following the 1st December Law, they were shot within an hour – and their innocent families soon after. In the month of December, 6,501 people were shot. Stalin had no precise plan for the growing Terror, just the belief that the Party had to be terrorized into submission and that old enemies had to be eradicated. Opportunistic and supersensitive, Stalin meandered towards his goal. The NKVD could not link Leningrad to the 'Moscow Centre' of Zinoviev and Kamenev but it had the means to persuade its prisoners to do so. By mid-January, they had indeed encouraged a prisoner to implicate Zinoviev and Kamenev who were sentenced to ten and five years respectively. Stalin distributed a secret letter that warned that all the opposition had to be 'treated like White Guards' and 'arrested and isolated'. The flood of arrests was so huge that the camps were deluged by 'Kirov's Torrent', yet, simultaneously, Stalin orchestrated a jazz-playing 'thaw': 'Life has become merrier, comrades,' he said. 'Life has become better.'*

* * *

On 11 January, Stalin and most of the Politburo attended a gala celebration of the Soviet film industry at the Bolshoi which was a sort of 'Oscars without the jokes'. The directors were handed Orders of Lenin.

'For us,' Lenin had said, 'the most important of all the arts is cinema,' the art form of the new society. Stalin personally controlled a 'Soviet Hollywood' through the State Film Board, run by Boris Shumiatsky with whom he had been in exile. Stalin did not merely interfere in movies, he minutely supervised the directors and films down to their scripts: his archive reveals how he even helped write the songs. He talked about films with his entourage and passed every film before it was shown to the public, becoming his own supreme censor. Stalin was Joseph Goebbels combined with Alexander Korda, an unlikely pair united by love of celluloid, rolled into one.

* Here was Stalin's version of Harold Macmillan's 'You've never had it so good.'

He was an obsessional movie-buff. In 1934, he had already seen the new Cossack 'Eastern' *Chapaev* and *The Jolly Fellows* so often he knew them by heart. Directed by Grigory Alexandrov, the latter was personally supervised by Stalin. When this director finished *The Jolly Fellows*,* Shumiatsky decided to tantalize Stalin by showing only the first reel, pretending the second was unfinished. The *Vozhd* loved it:

'Show me the rest!' Shumiatsky summoned Alexandrov, nervously waiting outside:

'You're wanted at court!'

'It's a jolly film,' Stalin told Alexandrov. 'I felt I'd had a month's holiday. Take it away from the director. He might spoil it!' he quipped.

Alexandrov immediately started a series of these happy-go-lucky light musical comedies: *Circus* was followed by Stalin's all-time favourite, *Volga, Volga.* When the director came to make the last in the series, he called it *Cinderella* but Stalin wrote out a list of twelve possible titles including *Shining Path* which Alexandrov accepted. Stalin actually worked on the lyrics of the songs too: there is an intriguing note in his archive dated July 1935 in which he writes out the words for one of the songs in pencil, changing and crossing out to get the lyric to scan:

A joyful song is easy for the heart;
It doesn't bore you ever;
And all the villages small and big adore the song;
Big towns love the tune.

Beneath it, he scrawls the words: 'To spring. Spirit. Mikoyan' and then 'Thank you comrades.'

When the director Alexander Dovzhenko appealed for Stalin's help with his movie *Aerograd*, he was summoned to the Little Corner within a day and asked to read his entire script to Voroshilov and Molotov. Later Stalin suggested his next movie, adding that 'neither my words nor newspaper articles put you under any obligation. You're a free man … If you have other plans, do something else. Don't be embarrassed. I summoned you

---

* The star was his wife Liuba Orlova and the songs were by the Jewish song writer Isaac Dunaevsky. The Russians, emerging from an era of starvation and assassination, flocked to see musicals and comedies – like Americans during the Depression. The style was singing, dancing and slapstick: a pig jumps on to a banqueting table, causing much messy hilarity with trotters and snout.

so you should know this.' He advised the director to use 'Russian folk songs – wonderful songs' which he liked to play on his gramophone.

'Did you ever hear them?' asked Stalin.

No, replied the director, who had no phonograph.

'An hour after the conversation, they brought the gramophone to my house, a present from our leader, that,' concluded Dovzhenko, 'I will treasure to the end of my life.'

Meanwhile, the magnates discussed how to manage Sergei Eisenstein, thirty-six, the Lavtian-German-Jewish *avant-garde* director of *Battleship Potemkin*. He had lingered too long in Hollywood and, as Stalin informed the American novelist Upton Sinclair, 'lost the trust of his friends in the USSR'. Stalin told Kaganovich he was a 'Trotskyite if not worse'. Eisenstein was lured back and put to work on *Bezhin Meadow*, inspired by the story of Pavlik Morozov, the boy-hero who denounced his own father for kulakism. The tawdry project did not turn out as Stalin hoped. Kaganovich loudly denounced his colleagues' trust:

'We can't trust Eisenstein. He'll again waste millions and give us nothing ... because he's against Socialism. Eisenstein was saved by Vyacheslav [Molotov] and Andrei Zhdanov who were willing to give the director another chance.' But Stalin knew he was 'very talented'. As tensions rose with Germany, he commissioned Eisenstein to make a film about that vanquisher of foreign invaders, *Alexander Nevsky*, promoting his new paradigm of socialism and nationalism. Stalin was delighted with it.

When Stalin wrote a long memorandum to the director Friedrich Emmler about his film *The Great Citizen*, his third point read: 'The reference to Stalin must be excluded. Instead of Stalin, mention the Central Committee.'

* * *

Stalin's modesty was in its way as ostentatious as the excesses of his personal cult. The leaders themselves had promoted Stalin's cult that was the triumph of his inferiority complex. Mikoyan and Khrushchev blamed Kaganovich for encouraging Stalin's concealed vanity and inventing Stalinism:

'Let's replace Long Live Leninism with Long Live Stalinism!' Stalin criticized Kaganovich but he knew Stalin better and he continued to promote 'Stalinism'.

'Why do you eulogize me as if a single person decides everything!' asked Stalin. Meanwhile he personally supervised the cult that was flourishing in the newspapers: in *Pravda*, Stalin was mentioned in half the editorials between 1933 and 1939. He was always given flowers and photographed with children. Articles appeared: 'How I got acquainted with Comrade Stalin.' The planes that flew over Red Square formed the word 'Stalin' in the skies. *Pravda* declared: 'Stalin's life is our life, our beautiful present and future.' When he appeared at the Seventh Congress of Soviets, two thousand delegates screamed and cheered. A writer described the reaction as 'love, devotion, selflessness'. A female worker whispered: 'How simple he is, how modest!'

There were similar cults for the others: Kaganovich was celebrated as 'Iron Lazar' and the 'Iron Commissar' and in thousands of pictures at parades. Voroshilov was honoured in the 'Voroshilov Rations' for the army and the 'Voroshilov Marksman's Prize' and his birthday celebrations were so grandiose that Stalin gave one of his most famous speeches at them. Schoolchildren traded picture postcards of these heroes like football players, the dashing Voroshilov trading at a much higher price than the dour Molotov.

Stalin's modesty was not completely assumed: in his many battles between vainglory and humility, he simultaneously encouraged eulogy and despised it. When the Museum of the Revolution asked if they could display the original manuscripts of his works, he wrote back: 'I didn't think in your old age, you'd be such a fool. If the book is published in millions, why do you need the manuscript? I burned all the manuscripts!' When the publishers of a Georgian memoir of his childhood sent a note to Poskrebyshev asking permission, Stalin banned Zhdanov from publishing it, complaining that it was 'tactless and foolish' and demanding that the culprits 'be punished.' But this was partly to keep control of the presentation of his early life.

He was aware of the absurdities of the cult, intelligent enough to know that the worship of slaves was surely worthless. A student at a technical college was threatened with jail for throwing a paper dart that struck Stalin's portrait. The student appealed to Stalin who backed him:

'They've wronged you,' he wrote. 'I ask ... do not punish him!' Then he joked: 'The good marksman who hits the target should be praised!' Yet Stalin needed the cult and secretly fostered it. With his trusted *chef de cabinet*, he could be honest. Two notes buried in Poskrebyshev's files are especially revealing: when a collective farm asked the right to name itself after Stalin, he gave Poskrebyshev blanket authority to name anything after himself:

'I'm not opposed to their wish to "be granted the name of Stalin" or to the others ... I'm giving you the right to answer such proposals with agreement [underlined] in my name.' One admirer wrote to say, 'I've decided to change my name to Lenin's best pupil, Stalin' and asked the titan's permission.

'I'm not opposed,' replied Stalin. 'I even agree. I'd be happy because this circumstance would give me the chance to have a younger brother. (I have no brother.) Stalin.' Just after the film prize-giving, death again touched the Politburo.

14

The Dwarf Rises; Casanova Falls

On 25 January 1935, Valerian Kuibyshev, who was forty-seven, died unexpectedly of heart disease and alcoholism, just eight weeks after his friend Kirov. Since he had questioned the NKVD investigation and allied himself with Kirov and Sergo, it has been claimed that he was murdered by his doctors, an impression not necessarily confirmed by his inclusion in the list of those supposedly poisoned by Yagoda. We are now entering a phase of such devious criminality and shameless gangsterism that all deaths of prominent people are suspect. But not every death cited as 'murder' in Stalin's show trials was indeed foul play: one has to conclude there were some natural deaths in the 1930s. Kuibyshev's son Vladimir believed his father was killed but this heroic drinker had been ill for a while. The magnates lived such an unhealthy existence that it is amazing so many survived to old age.

None the less it was well-timed for Stalin who took the opportunity on 1 February* to promote two younger stars who were the very spirit of the age. As Kaganovich took over the colossal job of running the railways, he handed over Moscow to Nikita Khrushchev, the semi-literate worker who would one day succeed Stalin.

Kaganovich met Khrushchev during the February 1917 Revolution in the Ukrainian mining town of Yuzovka. Despite a flirtation with Trotskyism, Khrushchev's patrons were unbeatable: 'Kaganovich liked me very much,' he recalled. So did both Nadya ('my lottery ticket,' said Khrushchev) and Stalin himself. Resembling a cannonball more than a whirlwind, Khrushchev's bright porcine eyes, chunky physique and toothy smile with its

---

* Mikoyan and Chubar, a senior official in Ukraine, as the two senior candidate members of the Politburo, were made full members, with Zhdanov and Eikhe, boss of West Siberia, taking their place as candidates.

golden teeth, exuded primitive coarseness and Promethean energy but camouflaged his cunning. As the capital's First Secretary, he drove the transformation of 'Stalinist-Moscow'; by a huge building programme, the destruction of old churches, and the creation of the Metro, he entered the élite. Already a regular at Kuntsevo, this pitiless, ambitious believer regarded himself as Stalin's 'son'. Born in 1894, son of a peasant miner, this meteoric bumpkin became Stalin's 'pet'.

It was Kaganovich's other protégé who suddenly emerged as the coming man. Yezhov was already the overlord of the Kirov case. Now he was promoted to Kirov's place as CC Secretary, and on 31 March was officially designated to supervise the NKVD. Soon to be notorious as one of history's monsters, 'the bloody dwarf', and a ghost whom no one remembered even knowing, Yezhov was actually liked by virtually everyone he met at this time. He was a 'responsive, humane, gentle, tactful man' who tried to help with any 'unpleasant personal matter', remembered his colleagues. Women in particular liked him. His face was almost 'beautiful', recalled one lady, his grin wide, his eyes a bright clever green-blue, his hair thick and black. He was flirtatious and playful, 'modest and agreeable'. Not only was he an energetic workaholic; this 'small slender man, always dressed in a crumpled cheap suit and a blue satin shirt' charmed people, chattering away in his Leningrad accent. He was shy at first but could be fun, exuberant with a keen sense of humour. He suffered from a slight limp but he had a fine baritone, played the guitar and danced the *gopak*. However, he was skinny and tiny: in a government of small men, he was almost a pygmy, 151 centimetres tall.

Born in 1895 to a forest warden, who ran a tearoom-cum-brothel, and a maid, in a small Lithuanian town, Yezhov, like Kaganovich and Voroshilov, only passed a few years at primary school before going to work in Petersburg's Putilov Works. No intellectual, he was another obsessive autodidact, nicknamed 'Kolya the book-lover' – but he possessed the Bolshevik managerial virtues: drive, hardness, organizational talent and an excellent memory, that bureaucratic asset described by Stalin as a 'sign of high intelligence'. Too short to serve in the Tsarist Army, he mended guns, joining the Red Army in 1919: in Vitebsk, he met Kaganovich, his patron. By 1921, he was working in the Tartar Republic where he aroused hatred by showing his contempt for the local culture and fell ill, the first of many signs of his fragility. He would now have met Stalin. In June 1925, he rose to be one of the secretaries of Kirgizia. After studying at the Communist Academy, he was promoted to work at the CC, then to Deputy Agriculture Commissar. In November 1930, Stalin received him in his office. At Kaganovich's suggestion, Yezhov began to attend the Politburo. In the early thirties, he headed the CC Personnel Assignments Department and helped Kaganovich purge the Party in 1933, flourishing in a frenzy of exhausting bureaucratic dynamism. Yet already there were signs of danger and complexity.

'I don't know a more ideal worker,' observed a colleague. 'After entrusting him with a job, you can leave him without checking and be sure he would do it,' but there was one problem: 'He does not know how to stop.' This was an admirable and deadly characteristic in a Bolshevik during the Terror but it also extended to Yezhov's personal life.

His humour was oafishly puerile: he presided over competitions to see which trouserless Commissar could fart away handfuls of cigarette ash. He cavorted at orgies with prostitutes, but was also an enthusiastic bisexual, having enjoyed avid encounters with his fellow tailoring apprentices, soldiers at the front and even high Bolsheviks like Filipp Goloshchekin, who had arranged the murder of the Romanovs. His only hobby apart from partying and fornicating was collecting and making model yachts. Unstable, sexually confused and highly strung, he was too weak to compete with bulldozers like Kaganovich, not to mention Stalin himself. Yezhov suffered constant nervous illnesses, including sores and itchy skin, TB, angina, sciatica, psoriasis (a nervous condition he probably shared with Stalin) and what they called 'neurasthenia'. He often sank into gloomy depression, drank too much and had to be nurtured by Stalin, just to keep him at work.

Stalin embraced him into his circle: Yezhov had exhausted himself so Stalin insisted on more rest cures. 'Yezhov himself is against this but they say he needs it,' he wrote in September 1931. 'Let's prolong his holiday and let him sit in Abastuman for two more months.' Stalin gave nicknames to his favourites: he called Yezhov 'my blackberry' (*yezhevika*). Stalin's notes were often curt personal questions: 'To Comrade Yezhov. Give him some work,' or 'Listen and help.' Yet he instinctively understood the essence of Yezhov: there is an unpublished note from August 1935 to his lieutenant in the archive that sums up their relationship. 'When you say something,' Stalin wrote, 'you always do it!' There was the heart of their partnership. When Vera Trail, whose memoir of her encounter remains unpublished, met him at his peak, she noticed Yezhov was so perceptive of the wishes of others that he could literally 'finish one's sentences'. Yezhov was uneducated, but also sly, able, perceptive and without moral boundaries.

Yezhov did not rise alone: he was accompanied by his wife who was to become the most flamboyant and, literally, fatal flirt of Stalin's entourage. It happened that Mandelstam, the poet, witnessed their courtship. In one of those almost incredible meetings, the encounter of Russia's finest poet with its greatest killer, Mandelstam found himself staying at the same sanatorium in Sukhumi as Yezhov and his then wife Tonya in 1930. The Mandelstams were in the attic of the mansion in Dedra Park that was shaped like a giant white wedding cake.*

Yezhov had married the educated and sincerely Marxist Antonina Titova in 1919. By 1930, Tonya was sunbathing in a deckchair at the Sukhumi mansion, reading *Das Kapital* and enjoying the attentions of an Old Bolshevik while her husband rose early every morning to cut roses for a girl, also married, who was staying there too. Cutting roses, pursuing adulterous romances, singing and dancing the *gopak*, one gets an idea of the incestuous world of the Bolsheviks on holiday. But Yezhov's new mistress was no Old Bolshevik but the Soviet version of a flapper who had already introduced him to her writer friends in Moscow. Yezhov divorced Tonya that year and married her.

Slim with flashing eyes, Yevgenia Feigenberg, at twenty-six, was a seductive and lively Jewess from Gomel. This avid literary groupie was as promiscuous as her new husband: she possessed the amorous enthusiasm of Messalina but none of her guile. She had first married an official, Khayutin, then Gadun, who was posted to the Soviet Embassy in London. She went too but when he was sent home, she stayed abroad, typing in the Berlin

---

* This dacha, built by a Jewish millionaire, later known as Dom (house of) Ordzhonikidze and now notorious as 'Stalin's house', was a favourite of the leadership: the founder of the Cheka, Felix Dzerzhinsky, often stayed there. Trotsky was recuperating there at the time of Lenin's death when Stalin and Ordzhonikidze managed to ensure he missed the funeral. Stalin (and Beria) stayed here after the war: the grand billiard room was installed specially for him and he took a great interest in the lush trees and flowers planted by local Party bosses up to his death. In one of the most sinister parts of the research for this book, the author stayed almost alone in this strange but historic house, probably in Mandelstam's attic.

legation. It was there that she met her first literary star, Isaac Babel, whom she seduced with the line of so many flirtatious groupies meeting their heroes:

'You don't know me but I know you well.' These words later assumed a dreadful significance. Back in Moscow, she met 'Kolya' Yezhov. Yevgenia yearned to hold a literary salon: henceforth Babel and the jazz star Leonid Utsesov were often *chez* Yezhov. It was she who asked the Mandelstams: 'Pilniak comes to see us. Whom do you go to see?' But Yezhov was also obsessionally devoted to Stalin's work – writers did not interest him. The only magnate who was a friend of both Yezhovs was Sergo, as was his wife Zina: photographs show the two couples at their *dachas*. Sergo's daughter Eteri remembers how Yevgenia 'was much better dressed than the other Bolshevik wives'.

By 1934, Yezhov was once again so weary that he almost collapsed, covered in boils. Stalin, on holiday with Kirov and Zhdanov, despatched Yezhov to enjoy the most luxurious medical care available in *Mitteleuropa* and ordered Poskrebyshev's deputy, Dvinsky, to send the Berlin Embassy this coded note:

'I ask you to pay very close attention to Yezhov. He's seriously ill and I cannot estimate the gravity of the situation. Give him help and cherish him with care ... He is a good man and a very precious worker. I will be grateful if you will inform the Central Committee regularly* on his treatment.'

No one objected to Yezhov's rise. On the contrary, Khrushchev thought him an admirable appointment. Bukharin respected his 'good heart and clean conscience' though he noticed that he grovelled before Stalin – but that was hardly unique. 'Blackberry' worked uneasily with Yagoda to force Zinoviev, Kamenev and their unfortunate allies to confess to being responsible for the murder of Kirov and all manner of other dastardly deeds.

* * *

*As Stalin wrote his history books with his dear friends Zhdanov and Kirov, he was receiving detailed reports on the health of his 'precious' comrade. The Yezhov case is a classic illustration of the Party's obsessive control over every detail of its leaders. 'The radioactive baths of Badgastein' had improved Yezhov's health, the Embassy reported after five days. A few days later, the patient was feeling energyless after the baths, he was following a diet but he was still chain smoking – and the sores on his thighs and legs had almost disappeared. The CC voted to send him the huge sum of 1,000 roubles. Next he had pains in his appendix, but having consulted Moscow doctors, Kaganovich sent an order that he was not to undergo surgery 'unless absolutely necessary'. After another rest in an Italian sanatorium, the Yezhovs returned that autumn.

It was not long before 'Blackberry's' chainmail fist reached out to crush one of Stalin's oldest friends: Abel Yenukidze. That genial sybarite flaunted his sexual affairs with ever younger girls, including teenage ballerinas. Girls filled his office, which came to resemble a sort of Bolshevik dating agency for future and cast-off mistresses.

Stalin's circle was already abuzz with his antics: 'Being dissolute and sensual', Yenukidze left a 'stench everywhere indulging himself to procure women, breaking up families, seducing girls', wrote Maria Svanidze. 'Having all the goodies of life in his hands …. he used this for his own filthy personal purposes, buying girls and women.' What is more, Yenukidze was 'sexually abnormal', picking up younger and younger girls and finally sinking to children of nine to eleven years old. The mothers were paid off. Maria complained to Stalin who surely began to listen: Stalin had not trusted him as early as 1929.

Nadya's godfather crossed the line between family and politics in Stalin's life and this proved a dangerous fence to straddle. A generous friend to Left and Right, he may have objected to the 1st December Law but he also personified the decadence of the new nobility. Abel was not the only one: Stalin felt himself surrounded by pigs at the trough. Stalin was always alone even among his convivial entourage, convinced of his separateness and often lonely. As recently as 1933, he had begged Yenukidze to holiday with him. In Moscow, Stalin often asked Mikoyan and Alyosha Svanidze, who was like 'a brother' to him, to stay overnight. Mikoyan stayed a few times but his wife was unhappy about it: 'How could she check whether I was really at Stalin's?' Svanidze stayed more often.

The catalyst for Yenukidze's fall was Stalin's favourite subject: personal history for the Bolsheviks was what genealogy was for the medieval knights. When his book *The Secret Bolshevik Printing Presses* was published, it was eagerly sent to Stalin by his weasel-faced *Pravda* editor, Mekhlis, with a note that 'some parts are … marked'. Stalin's marginalia in his copy show his almost Blimpish irritation: 'That's false!', 'fibs' and 'balderdash!' When Yenukidze wrote an article about his activities in Baku, Stalin distributed it to the Politburo peppered with 'Ha-ha-ha!' Yenukidze made a grievous mistake in not lying about Stalin's heroic exploits. This was understandable because the outstanding part in the creation of the Baku movement had been played by himself.

'What more does he want?' Yenukidze complained. 'I am doing

everything he has asked me to do but it is not enough for him. He wants me to admit he is a genius.'

Others were not so proud. In 1934, Lakoba published a sycophantic history of Stalin's heroic role in Batumi. Not to be outdone, Beria mobilized an array of historians to falsify his *On the History of the Bolshevik Organizations in the Transcaucasus* which was published later in the year under his own name.

'To my dear, adored master,' Beria inscribed his book, 'to the Great Stalin!'

* * *

Now Nadya's death caught up with Yenukidze: a terrorist cell was 'uncovered' by Yezhov in the Kremlin, which Abel ran. Kaganovich raged, Shakespearean style, 'There was something rotten there.' The NKVD arrested 110 of Yenukidze's employees, librarians and maids, for terrorism. Stalinist plots always featured a wicked beauty: sure enough, there was a 'Countess', said to have poisoned book pages to kill Stalin. Two were sentenced to death and the rest from five to ten years in the camps. Like everything that happened around Stalin, this 'Kremlin Case' had various angles: it was partly aimed at Yenukidze, partly at clearing the Kremlin of possibly disloyal elements, but it was also somehow connected to Nadya. A maid, whose appeal to President Kalinin is in the archives, was arrested for gossiping with her friends about Nadya's suicide. Stalin had surely not forgotten that Yenukidze had 'swayed' Nadya politically, and been the first to see the body.

Yenukidze was sacked, made to publish a 'Correction of Errors', demoted to run a Caucasian sanatorium and viciously attacked by Yezhov (and Beria) at a Plenum. 'Blackberry' first raised the stakes: Zinoviev and Kamenev were not just *morally* responsible for Kirov's murder – they planned it. Then he turned to poor 'Uncle Abel' whom he accused of political blindness and criminal complacency in letting the 'counter-revolutionary Zinoviev-Kamenev and Trotskyite terrorists' feather their nests inside the Kremlin while plotting to kill Stalin. 'This nearly cost Comrade Stalin his life,' he alleged. Yenukidze was 'the most typical representative of the corrupt and self-complacent Communists, playing the "liberal" gentleman at the expense of the Party and State.' Yenukidze defended himself by blaming Yagoda:

'No one was hired for work without security clearance!'

'Not true!' retorted Yagoda.

'Yes it is! ... I – more than anyone else – can find a host of blunders. These may be indignantly characterized – as treason and duplicity.'

'Just the same,' intervened Beria, attacking Yenukidze for his generous habit of helping fallen comrades, 'why did you give out loans and assistance?'

'Just a minute ...' answered Yenukidze, citing an old friend who had been in the opposition, 'I knew his present and past better than Beria.'

'We knew his present situation as well as you do.'

'I didn't help him personally.'

'He's an active Trotskyite,' retorted Beria.

'Deported by the Soviet authorities,' intervened Stalin himself.

'You acted wrongly,' Mikoyan added.

Yenukidze admitted giving another oppositionist some money because his wife appealed to him.

'So what if she starves to death,' said Sergo, 'so what if she croaks, what does it have to do with you?'

'What are you? Some kind of child?' Voroshilov called out. The attacks on Yenukidze's lax security were also attacks on Yagoda: 'I admit my guilt,' he confessed, 'in that I did not ... seize Yenukidze by the throat ...'

On the question of how to punish Yenukidze, there was disagreement: 'I must admit,' Kaganovich said, 'that not everyone found his bearings in this matter ... but Comrade Stalin at once smelled a rat ...' The rat was finally expelled from the Central Committee and the Party (temporarily).

Days afterwards, at Kuntsevo, a grumpy Stalin suddenly smiled at Maria Svanidze:

'Are you pleased Abel's been punished?' Maria was delighted at his overdue cleansing of the suppurating wound of depravity. On May Day, Zhenya and the Svanidzes joined Stalin and Kaganovich for kebabs, onions and sauce but the *Vozhd* was tense until the women started bickering. Then they toasted Nadya: 'she crippled me,' reflected Stalin. 'After condemning Yasha for shooting himself, how could Nadya kill herself?'*

---

* Ignoring the fall of Uncle Abel, Svetlana decided she wanted to go to the dacha at Lipki, which had been Nadya's choice for a holiday home, all decorated in her style. Stalin agreed, even though 'it was hard for Joseph to be there', wrote Maria. The whole wider family, along with Mikoyan, set off in a convoy of cars. Stalin was very warm towards Mikoyan. Svetlana asked if she could stay up for dinner and Stalin let her. Vasily too was often at dinner with the adults.

15

The Tsar Rides the Metro

Amidst the Yenukidze Case, Stalin, Kaganovich and Sergo attended the birthday party of Svetlana's beloved nanny at his apartment. 'Joseph has bought a hat and wool stockings' for the nanny. He cheerfully and lovingly fed Svetlana from his own plate. Everyone was filled with excitement and optimism because the great Moscow underground, named the Kaganovich Metro, a magnificent Soviet showpiece with marble halls like palaces, had just opened. Its creator Kaganovich had brought ten tickets for Svetlana, her aunts and the bodyguards to ride the Metro. Suddenly Stalin, encouraged by Zhenya and Maria, decided he would go too.

This change of plan provoked a 'commotion' among Stalin's courtiers which is hilariously described in Maria's diary. They became so nervous at this unplanned excursion that even the Premier was telephoned; almost half the ruling Politburo was involved within minutes. All were already sitting in their limousines when Molotov scurried across the courtyard to inform Stalin that 'such a trip might be dangerous without preparation'. Kaganovich, 'the most worried of all, went pale' and suggested they go at midnight when the Metro was closed but Stalin insisted. Three limousines of magnates, ladies, children and guards sped out of the Kremlin to the station, dismounted and descended into Kaganovich's tunnels. Once they arrived on the platform, there was no train. One can only imagine Kaganovich's frantic efforts to find one fast. The public noticed Stalin and shouted compliments. Stalin became impatient. When a train finally arrived, the party climbed aboard to cheers.

They got out at Okhotny Ryad to inspect the station. Stalin was mobbed by his fans and Maria almost crushed against a pillar but the NKVD finally caught up with them. Vasily was frightened, Maria noticed, but Stalin was jovial. There was then a thoroughly Russian mix-up as Stalin decided to go home, changed his mind and got out at the Arbat where there was another near-riot before they all got back to the Kremlin. Vasily was so upset by the whole experience that he cried on his bed and had to be given valerian drops.

The trip marked another decline in relations between the leaders and the Svanidze and Alliluyev ladies, those unBolshevik actresses, all 'powder and lipstick' in Maria's words. Kaganovich was furious with the women for persuading Stalin to travel on the Metro without any warning: he hissed at them that he would have arranged the trip if only they had given him some notice. Only Sergo would have shaken his head at this ludicrous scene. Dora Khazan, working her way up the Light Industry Commissariat, thought they were 'trivial women who did nothing, frivolous time-wasters'. The family began to feel that 'we were just poor relations', said Kira Alliuyeva. 'That's how they made us feel. Even Poskrebyshev looked down on us as if we were in the way.' As for Beria, the family, with fatal misjudgement, made no bones of their dislike of him. The women interfered and gossiped in a way that Nadya never had. But in the stern Bolshevik world, and especially given Stalin's views of family, they went too far. Maria, who had sneaked to Stalin about Yenukidze's amours, boasted to her diary, 'They even say I'm stronger than the Politburo because I can overturn its decrees.'

Worse, the women pursued vendettas against each other: The photograph of the 1934 birthday party now caused another row that undermined Stalin's trust. When Sashiko Svanidze stayed with him at Kuntsevo, she found the photograph on Stalin's desk and borrowed it in order to print up some copies, the sort of pushy behaviour often found in ambitious women at imperial courts, suggesting that these ladies regularly read the papers on Stalin's desk. Maria, who loathed Sashiko's brazen climbing, discovered this, warning Stalin:

'You can't let her make a shop out of your house and start trading on your kind-heartedness.' It was a rare occasion indeed when Stalin was criticized for his big-heartedness. He became irritated, blaming his secretaries and Vlasik for losing the photographs. Eventually he said Sashiko could 'go to the devil' but his fury applied equally to all the family:

'I know she did wonderful things for me and other Old Bolsheviks ... but none the less, she always takes offence, writes letters to me at the drop of a hat, and demands my attention. I have no time to look after myself and I couldn't even look after my own wife …' Nadya was constantly on his mind at this time.

Sashiko was dropped, to Zhenya and Maria's delight, yet they themselves took liberties. The Svanidzes still acted as if Joseph was their kind-hearted paterfamilias, not the Great Stalin. When Stalin invited the Svanidzes and Alliluyevs to join him for dinner after watching the Kirov Ballet, 'we badly miscalculated the time and did not arrive until almost midnight when the ballet ended at ten. Joseph does not like to wait.' This understates the case: it is hard to imagine anyone forgetting the time and leaving an American president waiting for two hours. Here we see Stalin through the eyes of his friends before the Terror turned him into a latter-day Ivan the Terrible: we find him 'stood up' by his dinner dates for two hours, left at Kuntsevo to play billiards with the bodyguards! Stalin, his sense of historic and sacerdotal mission despoiled, must have reflected on the disrespect of these Soviet aristocrats: they were not remotely afraid of him.

When they arrived, the men went off to play billiards with the disgruntled Stalin who was distinctly unfriendly to the women. But after the wine, he shone with pride about Svetlana, recounting her charming sayings like any father. None the less they would pay for their tardiness.

* * *

Stalin had loved his unscheduled Metro ride, telling Maria how moved he was 'by the love of the people for their leader. Here nothing was prepared and fixed. As he said … the people need a Tsar, whom they can worship and for whom they can live and work.' He had always believed the 'Russian people are Tsarist'. At various times, he compared himself to Peter the Great, Alexander I and Nicholas I but this child of Georgia, a Persian satrapy for centuries, also identified with the Shahs. He named two monarchs as his 'teachers' in his own notes: one was Nadir Shah, the eighteenth-century Persian empire-builder of whom he wrote: 'Nadir Khan. Teacher'. (He was also interested in another Shah, Abbas, who beheaded a father's two sons and sent him their heads: 'Am I like the Shah?' he asked Beria.)

But he regarded Ivan the Terrible as his true *alter ego*, his 'teacher'* something he revealed constantly to comrades such as

---

* In his entourage, Stalin even called Bukharin 'Shuisky', according to Kaganovich, referring either to the Shuisky family of *boyars* who lorded it over the young Ivan, or the so-called '*Boyars*' Tsar' after Ivan's death. Either way, Stalin was identifying his own position with that of Ivan against his *boyars*.

Molotov, Zhdanov and Mikoyan, applauding his necessary murder of over-mighty *boyars*. Ivan too had lost his beloved wife, murdered by his *boyars*. This raises the question of how his grandees could have claimed to be 'tricked' by Stalin's real nature when he openly lauded a Tsar who systematically murdered his nobility.

Now, in late 1935, he also began to reproduce some of the trappings of Tsardom: in September, he restored the title Marshal of the Soviet Union (though not Field Marshal), promoting Voroshilov and Budyonny and three other heroes of the Civil War including Tukhachevsky whom he hated, and Alexander Yegorov, the new Chief of Staff, whose wife had so upset Nadya on the night of her suicide. For the NKVD, he created a rank equivalent to Marshal, promoting Yagoda to Commissar-General of State Security. Sartorial splendour suddenly mattered again: Voroshilov and Yagoda gloried in their uniforms. When Stalin sent Bukharin on a trip to Paris, he told him,

'Your suit is threadbare. You can't travel like that ... Things are different with us now; you have to be well dressed.' Such was Stalin's eye for detail that the tailor from the Commissariat of Foreign Affairs called that afternoon. More than that, the NKVD had access to the latest luxuries, money and houses. 'Permit me 60,000 gold Roubles to buy cars for our NKVD workers,' wrote Yagoda in a pink pen to Molotov on 15 June 1935. Interestingly Stalin (in blue) and Molotov (in red) signed it but reduced it to 40,000. But that was still a lot of Cadillacs. Stalin had already ordered that the Rolls-Royces in the Kremlin be concentrated in the 'special garage.'

Stalin had become a Tsar: children now chanted 'Thank you, Comrade Stalin, for our happy childhood' perhaps because he now restored Christmas trees. But unlike the bejewelled Romanovs, identified so closely with the old Russian village and peasantry, Stalin created his own special kind of Tsar, modest, austere, mysterious and urban. There was no contradiction with his Marxism.

Sometimes Stalin's loving care for his people was slightly absurd. In November 1935, for example, Mikoyan announced to the Stakhanovites in the Kremlin that Stalin was taking great interest in soap and had demanded samples, 'after which we received a special Central Committee decree on the assortment and composition of soap', he announced to cheers. Then Stalin moved from soap to lavatories. Khrushchev ran Moscow with Mayor Nikolai Bulganin, another rising star, a handsome but ruthless blond ex-Chekist with a goatee beard: Stalin nicknamed them the 'city fathers'. Now he summoned Khrushchev: 'Talk it over with Bulganin and do something ... People hunt around desperately and can't find anywhere to relieve themselves ...' But he liked to play the Little Father intervening from on high for his people. In April, a teacher in Kazakhstan named Karenkov appealed to Stalin about losing his job.

'I order you to stop the persecution of teacher Karenkov at once,' he ordered* the Kazakh bosses. It is hard to imagine either Hitler or even President Roosevelt investigating urinals, soap or that smalltown teacher.

The dim but congenial Voroshilov initiated another step deeper into the mire of Soviet depravity when he read an article about teenage hooliganism. He wrote a note to the Politburo saying that Khrushchev, Bulganin and Yagoda 'agree there is no alternative but to imprison the little vagabonds ... I don't understand why one doesn't shoot the scum.' Stalin and Molotov jumped at the chance to add another terrible weapon to their arsenal for use against political opponents, decreeing that children of twelve could now be executed.

* * *

On holiday in Sochi, Stalin was still infuriated by the antics of fallen friends and truculent children. The relentlessly convivial Yenukidze was still chattering about politics to his old pal, Sergo. Once a man had fallen, Stalin could not understand how any loyalist could remain friends with him. Stalin confided his distrust of Sergo to Kaganovich (Sergo's friend):

'Strange that Sergo ... continues to be friends with' Yenukidze. Stalin ordered that Abel, this 'weird fellow', be moved away from his resort. Fulminating against 'the Yenukidze group' as 'scum' and the Old Bolsheviks as '"old farts" in Lenin's phrase', Kaganovich moved Abel to Kharkov.

Vasily, now fourteen, worried him too: the more absolute Stalin

---

* When he received no reply, again showing the attitude of the local bosses to the centre, Poskrebyshev chased up the Kazakh First Secretary: 'We have not received confirmation of our order.' This time, the local boss replied instantly. But this only illustrates how the local bosses ignored Moscow in small matters and great, following the old Russian tradition of apparent obedience while avoiding actual execution of orders.

became, the more delinquent Vasily became. This mini-Stalin aped his Chekist handlers, denouncing teachers' wives:

'Father, I've already asked the Commandant to remove the teacher's wife but he refused ...' he wrote. The harassed Commandant of Zubalovo reported that while 'Svetlana studies well, Vasya does badly – he is lazy.' The schoolmasters called Carolina Til to ask what to do. He played truant or claimed 'Comrade Stalin' had ordered him not to work with certain teachers. When the housekeeper found money in his pocket, Vasily would not reveal where he had come by it. On 9 September 1935, Efimov reported chillingly to Stalin that Vasily had written: 'Vasya Stalin, born in March 1921, died in 1935.' Suicide was a fact in that family but also in the Bolshevik culture: as Stalin cleansed the Party, his opponents began to commit suicide, which only served to outrage him more: he called it 'spitting in the eye of the Party'. Soon afterwards, Vasily entered an artillery school, along with other leaders' children including Stepan Mikoyan; his teacher also wrote to Stalin to complain of Vasily's suicide threats:

'I've received your letter about Vasily's tricks,' wrote Stalin to V. V. Martyshin. 'I'm answering very late because I'm so busy. Vasily is a spoilt boy of average abilities, savage (a type of Scythian), not always honest, uses blackmail with weak "rules", often impudent with the weak ... He's spoilt by different patrons who remind him at every step that he's "Stalin's son". I'm happy to see you're a good teacher who treats Vasily like other children and demands he obey the school regime ... If Vasily has not ruined himself until now, it's because in our country there are teachers who give no quarter to this capricious son of a baron. My advice is: treat Vasily MORE STRICTLY and don't be afraid of this child's false blackmailing threats of "suicide". I'll support you ...'

Svetlana, on holiday with her father, remained the adored favourite: 'my little sparrow, my great joy', as Stalin wrote so warmly in his letters to her. As one reads Stalin's letters to Kaganovich (usually about persecuting Yenukidze), one can almost see her sitting near him on the veranda as he writes out his orders in his red pencils, enthroned in his wicker chair at the wicker table with piles of papers wrapped in newspaper which were brought daily by Poskrebyshev. He often mentions her. Kaganovich seemed to have replaced Kirov as Svetlana's 'Party Secretary', greeting her in his letters to Stalin and adding:

'Hail to our Boss Svetlana! I await instructions ... on postponement by 15/20 days of the school term. One of the Secretaries LM Kaganovich.' Vasily was 'Svetlana the Boss's colleague'.

Three days later, Stalin informed Kaganovich that 'Svetlana the Boss* ... demands decisions ... in order to check on her Secretaries.'

'Hail Boss Svetlana!' replied Kaganovich. 'We await her impatiently.' When she was back in Moscow, she visited Kaganovich who reported to her father: 'Today our Boss Svetlana inspected our work ...' Indeed Stalin encouraged her interest in politics:

'Your little Secretaries received your letter and we discussed its contents to our great satisfaction. Your letter enabled us to find our way in complicated international and domestic political questions. Write to us often.' Soon she was commanding him in her 'Daily Order No. 3. I order you to show me what happens in the Central Committee! Strictly confidential. Stalina, the mistress of the house.'

Then Stalin heard from Beria that his mother Keke was getting frailer. On 17 October, he headed across to Tiflis to visit her for only the third time since the Revolution.

Beria had taken over the responsibility for caring for the old lady like a courtier looking after a dowager empress. She had lived for years in comfortable rooms in the servant's quarters of the palace of the nineteenth-century Tsarist Governor, Prince Michael Vorontsov, where she was accompanied by two old ladies. All of them wore the traditional black headdress and long dress of Georgian widows. Beria and his wife Nina called on Keke frequently, recalling her spicy taste for sexual gossip:

'Why don't you take a lover?' she asked Nina. Stalin was a negligent son but still wrote his dutiful notes:

'Dear mother, please live for 10,000 years. Kisses, Soso.' He apologized, 'I know you're disappointed in me but what can I do? I'm busy and can't write often.' Mother sent sweets; Soso, money; but, as the son who had replaced her husband as the man of the family, he always played the hero, revealing his dreams of destiny and courage:

'Hello my mama, the children thank you for the sweets. I'm healthy, don't worry about me ... I'll stand up for my destiny! You need more money? I sent you 500 roubles and photos of me and

---

* *Khozyaika* means mistress, the female of *Khozyain*, boss, master, Stalin's nickname amongst the bureaucracy, though it also usually means 'housewife'.

the children. PS the children bow to you. After Nadya's death, my private life is very hard but a strong man must *always* be valiant.'

Stalin took special trouble to protect the Egnatashvili brothers, the children of the innkeeper who was the benefactor of his mother. Alexander Egnatashvili, a Chekist officer in Moscow (supposedly Stalin's food-taster, nicknamed 'the Rabbit'), kept this old link alive:

'My dear spiritual mother,' Egnatashvili wrote in April 1934, 'yesterday I visited Soso and we talked a long time ... he's put on weight ... In the last four years, I had not seen him so healthy ... He was joking a lot. Who says he's older? No one thinks he's more than 47!' But she was ailing.

'I know you're ill,' Stalin wrote to her. 'Be strong. I'm sending you my children ...' Vasily and Svetlana stayed at Beria's residences and then visited the old lady in her 'tiny room', filled with portraits of her son. Svetlana remembered how Nina Beria chatted to her in Georgian but the old lady could not speak Russian.

Now Stalin recruited his old brother-in-law Alyosha Svanidze and Lakoba to visit his mother with him while Beria briskly made the arrangements. He did not stay long. If he had looked around the rooms, he would have noticed that not only did she have photographs of Stalin but also a portrait of Beria in her bedroom. Beria had his own cult of personality in Georgia but more than that, he must have become like a son to her.

Stalin's real feelings for his mother were complicated by her taste for beating him and alleged affairs with her employers. There is a clue to this possible saint–whore complex in his library where he underlined a passage in Tolstoy's *Resurrection* about how a mother is both kind and wicked. But she also had the tendency of making tactless, if drily witty, comments. She wondered why Stalin fell out with Trotsky: they should have ruled together. Now when Stalin sat smiling beside her, he revealingly asked her:

'Why did you beat me so hard?'

'That's why you turned out so well,' she replied, before asking: 'Joseph, what exactly are you now?'

'Well, remember the Tsar? I'm something like a Tsar.'

'You'd have done better to become a priest,' she said, a comment that delighted Stalin.

The newspapers reported the visit with the queasy sentimentality of a Bolshevik version of *Hello!* magazine:

'Seventy-five-year-old Keke is kind and lively,' gushed *Pravda*. 'She seems to light up when she talks about the unforgettable moments of their meeting. "The whole world rejoices when it looks upon my son and our country. What would you expect me, his mother, to feel?" '

Stalin was irritated by this outbreak of Stalinist *Hello!*-ism. When Poskrebyshev sent him the article, Stalin wrote back: 'It's nothing to do with me.' But then he penned another Blimpish note to Molotov and Kaganovich: 'I demand we ban *petit-bourgeois* tidbits that have infliltrated our press ... to insert the interview with my mother and all this other balderdash. I ask to be freed of the incessant publicity din of these bastards!' But he was glad his mother was healthy, telling her 'Our clan is evidently very strong' and sending some presents: a headdress, a jacket and some medicine.

Back in Moscow,* Stalin decided to reopen and expand the Kirov Case that had subsided with the shooting of Nikolaev and sentencing of Zinoviev and Kamenev in early 1935. Now the two Old Bolsheviks were reinterrogated and the net of arrests was spread wider. Then a former associate of Trotsky's named Valentin Olberg was arrested by the NKVD in Gorky. His interrogation 'established' that Trotsky was also involved in the murder of Kirov. More arrests followed.

---

* In case we have forgotten that this was a state based on repression, Zhdanov and Mikoyan were inspecting the NKVD's slave labour projects in the Arctic such as the Belomor Canal: 'the Chekists here have done a great job,' Zhdanov wrote enthusiastically to Stalin. 'They allow ex-kulaks and criminal elements to work for socialism and they may become real people ...'

16

Take Your Partners; Mount Your Prisoners: the Show Trial

Oblivious of these lengthening shadows, Stalin's birthday party, attended by the magnates, Beria and the family, was 'noisy and cheerful'. Voroshilov was resplendent in his new white Marshal's uniform while his dowdy wife stared jealously at Maria Svanidze's dress from Berlin. After dinner, there were songs and dancing like old times: with Zhdanov on harmonies, they sang Abkhazian, Ukrainian, student and comic songs. Stalin decided to order a piano so Zhdanov could play. Amidst general hilarity, Postyshev, one of the Ukrainian bosses, slow-danced with Molotov – and 'this couple very much amused Joseph and all the guests'. Here was the first example of the notorious stag slow-dancing that was to become more forced after the war.

Stalin took over the gramophone and even did some Russian dancing. Mikoyan performed his leaping *lezginka*. The Svanidzes did the foxtrot and asked Stalin to join them but he said he had given up dancing since Nadya's death. They danced until four.

In the spring of 1936, the arrests of old Trotskyites spread further and those already in camps were resentenced. Those convicted of 'terror' offences were to be shot. But the real work was the creation of a new sort of political show: the first of Stalin's great trials. Yezhov was the supervisor of this case – this hopeful theoretician was even writing a book about the Zinovievites, corrected personally by Stalin. Yagoda, Commissar-General of State Security, who was sceptical about this 'nonsense', remained in charge but Yezhov constantly undermined him. This process exhausted frail Yezhov. Soon he was once again so debilitated that Kaganovich suggested, and Stalin approved, that he be sent on another special holiday for two months with a further 3,000 roubles.

The chief defendants were to be Zinoviev and Kamenev. Their old friends were arrested to help persuade them to perform. Stalin followed every detail of the interrogations. The NKVD interrogators were to devote themselves body and soul to achieving the confessions. Stalin's instructions to the NKVD were suggestive of this terrible process:

'Mount your prisoner and do not dismount until they have confessed.' The NKVD defector Alexander Orlov left the best account of how Yezhov rigged up this trial, promising the 'witnesses' their lives in return for testifying against Zinoviev and Kamenev who refused to co-operate. Stalin's office phoned hourly for news.

'You think Kamenev may not confess?' Stalin asked Mironov, one of Yagoda's Chekists.

'I don't know,' replied Mironov.

'You don't know?' said Stalin. 'Do you know how much our State weighs with all the factories, machines, the army with all the armaments and the navy?' Mironov thought he was joking but Stalin was not smiling. 'Think it over and tell me?' Stalin kept staring at him.

'Nobody can know that, Joseph Vissarionovich; it is the realm of astronomical figures.'

'Well, and can one man withstand the pressure of that astronomical weight?'

'No,' replied Mironov.

'Well then ... Don't come to report to me until you have in this briefcase the confession of Kamenev.' Even though they were not physically tortured, the regime of threats and sleeplessness demoralized Zinoviev, suffering from asthma, and Kamenev. The heating was turned up in their cells in midsummer. Yezhov threatened that Kamenev's son would be shot.

* * *

While the interrogators worked on Zinoviev and Kamenev, Maxim Gorky was dying of influenza and bronchial pneumonia. The old writer was now thoroughly disillusioned. The dangers of his Chekist companions became obvious when Gorky's son Maxim died mysteriously of influenza. Later, Yagoda would be accused, with the family doctors, of killing him. After his death, Maxim's daughter Martha remembers how Yagoda would visit the Gorky household every morning for a cup of coffee and a flirtation with her mother, on his way to the Lubianka: 'he was in love with Timosha and wanted her to return his affection,' said Alexei Tolstoy's wife.

'You still don't know me, I can do anything,' he threatened the distraught Timosha: the writer Alexander Tikhonov claimed they began an affair; her daughter denies it. When Stalin visited, Yagoda lingered, still in love with Timosha and increasingly worried about himself. After the Politburo had left, he asked Gorky's secretary: 'Did they come? They've left now? What did they talk about? ... Did they say anything about us ...?'

Stalin had asked Gorky to write his biography, but he recoiled from the task. Instead he bombarded Stalin and the Politburo with crazy proposals such as a project to commission Socialist Realist writers to 'rewrite the world's books anew'. Stalin's apologies for late replies became ever more extreme: 'I'm as lazy as a pig on things marked "correspondence",' confessed Stalin to Gorky. 'How do you feel? Healthy? How's your work? Me and my friends are fine.' The NKVD actually printed false issues of *Pravda*, especially for Gorky, to conceal the persecution of his friend, Kamenev.* Gorky himself realized that he was now under house arrest: 'I'm surrounded,' he muttered, 'trapped.'

In the first week of June, Gorky slept much of the days as his condition worsened. He was supervised by the best doctors but he was failing.

'Let them come if they can get here in time,' said Gorky. Stalin, Molotov and Voroshilov were pleased to see that he had recovered – after a camphor injection. Stalin took control of the sickroom:

'Why are there so many people here?' he asked. 'Who's that sitting beside Alexei Maximovich dressed in black? A nun, is she? All she lacks is a candle in her hands.' This was Baroness Moura Budberg, the mistress Gorky shared with H. G. Wells. 'Get them all out of here except for that woman, the one in white, who's looking after him ... Why's there such a funereal mood here? A healthy person might die in such an atmosphere.' Stalin stopped Gorky discussing literature but called for wine and they toasted him and then embraced. Day later, Stalin arrived only to be told that Gorky was too ill to see him:

'Alexei Mikhailovich, we visited you at two in the morning,' he wrote. 'Your pulse was they say 82. The doctors did not allow us to come in to you. We submitted. Hello from all of us, a big hello. Stalin.' Molotov and Voroshilov signed underneath.

Gorky started to spit blood and died on 18 June, of TB,

---

* An old trick: Kuibyshev had suggested printing false issues of *Pravda* to disinform the dying Lenin.

pneumonia and heart failure. Later it was claimed that his doctors and Yagoda had murdered him deliberately: they certainly confessed to his murder. His death was convenient before Zinoviev's trial but his medical records in the NKVD archives suggest that he died naturally.

Yagoda was skulking in the dining room at Gorky's house but Stalin had already turned against him. 'And what's that creature hanging around here for? Get rid of him.'

* * *

Finally in July, Zinoviev asked to be able to talk to Kamenev on his own. Then they demanded to speak to the Politburo: if the Party would guarantee there would be no executions, they would confess. Voroshilov was itching to get at the 'scum': when he received some of the testimonies against them, he wrote to Stalin that 'these bad people ... all typical representatives of *petit bourgeois* with the face of Trotsky ... are finished people. There's no place for them in our country and no place among the millions ready to die for the Motherland. This scum must be liquidated absolutely ... we need to be sure the NKVD starts the purge properly ...' Here, then, was one leader who genuinely seemed to approve of a terror and the liquidation of the former oppositions. On 3 July, Stalin replied to 'dear Klim, did you read the testimonies ...? How do you like the bourgeois puppies of Trotsky ...? They wanted to wipe out all the members of the Politburo ... Isn't it weird? How low people can sink? J.St.'

Yagoda accompanied these two broken men on the short drive from the Lubianka to the Kremlin, where they had both once lived. When they arrived in the room where Kamenev had chaired so many Politburo meetings, they discovered that only Stalin, Voroshilov and Yezhov were present. Where was the rest of the Politburo?

Stalin replied that he and Voroshilov were a commission of the Politburo. Given Klim's venom, it is easy to see why he was there but where was Molotov? Perhaps the punctilious Iron-Arse was worried about the etiquette of lying to Old Bolsheviks: he certainly did not object to killing people.

Kamenev begged the Politburo for a guarantee of their lives.

'A guarantee?' replied Stalin, according to Orlov's version. 'What guarantee can there be? It's simply ridiculous! Maybe you want an official treaty certified by the League of Nations? Zinoviev and Kamenev forget they're not in a market-place haggling over a stolen horse but at the Politburo of the Bolshevik Communist Party. If an assurance by the Politburo is not enough, I don't see any point in talking further.'

'Zinoviev and Kamenev behave as if they're in a position to make conditions to the Politburo,' exclaimed Voroshilov. 'If they had any common sense, they'd fall to their knees before Stalin ...'

Stalin proposed three reasons why they would not be executed – it was really a trial of Trotsky; if he had not shot them when they were opposing the Party, then why shoot them when they were helping it; and finally, 'the comrades forget that we are Bolsheviks, disciples and followers of Lenin, and we don't want to shed the blood of Old Bolsheviks, no matter how grave their past sins ...'

Zinoviev and Kamenev wearily agreed to plead guilty, provided there were no shootings and their families were protected.

'That goes without saying,' Stalin finished the meeting.

Stalin set to work on the script for the Zinoviev trial, revelling in his hyperbolic talent as a hack playwright. The new archives reveal how he even dictated the words of the new Procurator-General, Andrei Vyshinsky, who kept notes of his leader's perorations.

Stalin issued a secret circular of 29 July which announced that a terrorist leviathan named the 'United Trotskyite-Zinovievite Centre' had attempted to assassinate Stalin, Voroshilov, Kaganovich, Kirov, Sergo, Zhdanov and others. These lists of purported targets became a bizarre honour since inclusion signified proximity to Stalin. One can imagine the leaders checking the list like schoolboys rushing to the noticeboard to make sure they are in the football team. Significantly, Molotov was not on the team, which was interpreted as a sign of opposition to the Terror but it seems he was indeed temporarily out of favour because of a different disagreement with Stalin. Molotov boasted, 'I'd always supported the measures taken,' but there is one intriguing hint in the archives that Molotov was under fire from Yezhov. The NKVD had arrested the German nurse of his daughter Svetlana Molotova* and her father had grumbled to Yagoda. A Chekist denounced Molotov for 'improper

* Many of the ruling families employed Volga Germans as housekeepers and nannies: Carolina Til managed Stalin's house; another Volga German ran Molotov's and the Berias employed Ella as their nanny-housekeeper. They would all prove vulnerable to the anti-German Terror of 1937.

behaviour … Molotov behaved badly.' On 3 November, Yezhov sent Molotov the denunciation, perhaps a shot across his bows.

Yezhov was Stalin's closest associate in the days before the trial while Yagoda, now in disfavour for his resistance to it, was received only once. Stalin complained about his work: 'You work poorly. The NKVD suffers a serious disease.' Finally he called Yagoda, shouting that he would 'punch him in the nose' if he did not pull himself together. We have Stalin's notes from his 13 August meetings with Yezhov, which catch his mood. In one he considers sacking an official: 'Get him out? *Yes, get him out!* Talk with Yezhov.' Again and again: 'Ask Yezhov.'

* * *

The first of the famous show trials opened on 19 August in the October Hall upstairs in the House of Unions. The 350 spectators were mainly NKVD clerks in plain clothes, foreign journalists and diplomats. On a raised dais in the centre, the three judges, led by Ulrikh, sat on portentous throne-like chairs covered in red cloth. The real star of this theatrical show, the Procurator-General Andrei Vyshinsky, whose performance of foaming ire and articulate pedantry would make him a European figure, sat to the audience's left. The defendants, sixteen shabby husks, guarded by NKVD troopers with fixed bayonets, sat to the right. Behind them was a door that led to the suite that might be compared to the 'celebrity hospitality green room' in television studios. Here in a drawing room with sandwiches and refreshments sat Yagoda who could confer with Vyshinsky and the defendants during the trial.

Stalin was said to be lurking in a recessed gallery with darkened windows at the back where the orchestras once played for aristocratic quadrilles and whence puffs of pipe smoke were alleged to be emanating.

On the 13th, six days before the trial began, Stalin departed by train for Sochi, after a meeting with Yezhov. It is a mark of the impenetrable secrecy of the Soviet system that it has taken over sixty years for anyone to discover that Stalin was actually far away, though he followed the legal melodrama almost as closely as if he had been listening to it in his office. Eighty-seven NKVD packages of interrogations plus records of confrontations and the usual pile of newspapers, memos and telegrams arrived at the wicker table on the veranda.

Kaganovich and Yezhov checked every detail with Stalin. The protégé was now more powerful than his former patron – Yezhov signed his name ahead of Kaganovich in every telegram. While the will of the great actor-manager controlled all from afar, the two in Moscow doubled as PR-men and impresarios. On the 17th, Kaganovich and Yezhov reported to the *Khozyain* that 'we've fixed the press coverage ... in the following manner: 1. *Pravda* and *Izvestiya* to publish a page-length account of the trial daily.' On the 18th Stalin ordered the trial to proceed next day.

The accused were indicted with a fantastical array of often bungled crimes ordered by the shadowy conspiracy led by Trotsky, Zinoviev and Kamenev ('The United Trotskyite-Zinovievite Centre') that had successfully killed Kirov but repeatedly failed to kill Stalin and the others (though never bothering with Molotov). For six days, they confessed to these crimes with a docility that amazed Western spectators.

The language of these trials was as obscure as hieroglyphics and could only be understood in the Aesopian imagery of the closed Bolshevik universe of conspiracies of evil against good in which 'terrorism' simply signified 'any doubt about the policies or character of Stalin'. All his political opponents were *per se* assassins. More than two 'terrorists' was a 'conspiracy' and, putting together such killers from different factions, created a 'Unified Centre' of astonishing global, indeed Blofeldian, reach, that reveals much about Stalin's internal melodrama as well as about Bolshevik paranoia, formed by decades of underground life.

While these crushed men delivered their lines, Procurator-General Vyshinsky brilliantly combined the indignant humbug of a Victorian preacher and the diabolical curses of a witch doctor. Small with 'bright black eyes' behind horn-rimmed spectacles, thinning reddish hair, pointed nose, and dapper in 'white collar, checked tie, well-cut suit, trimmed grey moustache', a Western witness thought he resembled 'a prosperous stockbroker accustomed to lunching at Simpson's and playing golf at Sunningdale'. Born into an affluent, noble Polish family in Odessa, Vyshinsky had once occupied a cell with Stalin with whom he shared hampers from his parents, an investment that may have saved his life. But as an ex-Menshevik, he was absolutely obedient and ravenously bloodthirsty: during the thirties, his notes to Stalin constantly propose shooting of defendants, usually 'Trotskyites preparing the death of Stalin', always ending with the words: 'I recommend VMN – death by shooting.'

Vyshinsky, fifty-three, was notoriously unpleasant to his

subordinates but cringingly sycophantic to his seniors: he used the word 'Illustrious' in his letters to Molotov and even Poskrebyshev (whom he cleverly cultivated). Even his subordinates found him a 'sinister figure' who, regardless of his 'excellent education', believed in the essential rule of Stalinist management: 'I believe in keeping people on edge' but he was always on the edge himself, suffering bouts of eczema, living in fear and helping to breed it. Alert, vigorous, vain and intelligent, he impressed Westerners as much as he chilled them with his forensic mannerisms and vicious wit: it was he who later described the Romanians as 'not a nation, but a profession'. He was very proud of his notoriety: presented to Princess Margaret in London in 1947, he whispered to the diplomat introducing them, 'Please add my former title as Procurator in the famous Moscow trials.'

Every day, Yezhov and Kaganovich, who must have been listening to the trial in the 'hospitality suite', reported to Stalin on the proceedings like this: 'Zinoviev declared that he confirms the depositions of Bakaiev on the fact that the latter had made a report to Zinoviev on the preparation of a terrorist act against Kirov ...' They revelled in reporting to the actor-manager-playwright the successful 'unfolding' of this theatrical piece.

However there was severe doubt among many of the journalists, exacerbated by the NKVD's comical blunders: the court heard how Trotsky's son, Sedov, ordered the assassinations in a meeting at the Hotel Bristol in Denmark – yet it emerged that the hotel had been demolished in 1917.

'What the devil did you need the hotel for?' Stalin is said to have shouted. 'You ought to have said "railway station". The station is always there.'

This show had a wider cast than the players actually on-stage because others were carefully implicated, raising the prospect of other famous 'terrorists' appearing in later trials. The defendants took great care to implicate a couple of military commanders and then both Leftists, such as Karl Radek, and Rightists, such as Bukharin, Rykov and Tomsky. Vyshinsky announced that he was opening new cases against these celebrated names.

The members of this off-stage cast performed their roles very differently: the gifted journalist, Karl Radek, a famous international revolutionary who cut an absurd figure with his round glasses, whiskers, pipe, leather boots and coats, had been close to Stalin during the early thirties, advising him on German politics.

Writers always imagine they can write their way out of danger. Now Stalin decreed that 'although not very convincing, I suggest to delay for the moment the question of Radek's arrest and to let him publish in *Izvestiya* a signed article ...' Opportunities, even temporary indulgence towards old friends, could change Stalin's meandering progress.*

On the 22nd, the accused refused to plead for their defence. The Politburo – Kaganovich, Sergo, Voroshilov and Chubar – along with Yezhov, asked for instructions: 'It's not convenient to authorize any appeal,' Stalin retorted, at 11.10 next night giving exact instructions on the press coverage of the sentences. Revealingly, the playwright thought the verdict required a little bit of 'stylistic polishing'. Half an hour later, he wrote again, worrying that the trial would be regarded as just a '*mise-en-scène*'.

Stalin's spin-doctors engineered public outrage against the terrorists. Khrushchev, rabid supporter of the trials and shootings, arrived one evening at the Central Committee to find Kaganovich and Sergo bullying the poet Demian Bedny to produce a blood-curdling ditty for *Pravda*. Bedny recited his effort. There was an awkward pause:

'Not what we had in mind, Comrade Bedny,' said Kaganovich. Sergo lost his temper and shouted at Bedny. Khrushchev glared at him.

'I can't!' protested Bedny, but he could. His 'No Mercy' was published the next day, while *Pravda* shrieked:

'Crush the Loathsome Creatures! The Mad Dogs Must Be Shot!' In the court, Vyshinsky summed up:

'These mad dogs of capitalism tried to tear limb from limb the best of our Soviet land' – Kirov. 'I demand that these mad dogs should be shot – every one of them!' The dogs themselves now made their pathetic pleas and confessions. Even seventy years later, they are tragic to read. Kamenev finished his confession but then rose again, obviously off-message, to plead for his children whom he had no other means of addressing: 'No matter what my sentence will be, I in advance consider it just. Don't look back,' he

* Not all the off-stage cast behaved so conveniently. At 5.46 p.m. on 22 August, Stalin received the following telegram from Kaganovich, Yezhov and Ordzhonikidze: 'This morning Tomsky shot himself. He left a letter to you in which he tried to prove his innocence ... We have no doubt that Tomsky ... knowing that now it is no longer possible to hide his place in the Zinoviev-Trotskyite band had decided to dissimulate ... by suicide ...' As ever, the press release was the most important thing.

told his sons. 'Go forward ... Follow Stalin.' The judges withdrew to consider their pre-decided verdict, returning at two-thirty to sentence all to death, at which one defendant shouted:

'Long live the cause of Marx, Engels, Lenin and Stalin!'

Back in prison, the scared 'terrorists' shakily appealed for mercy, remembering Stalin's promise to spare them. As Zinoviev and Kamenev waited in their cells, Stalin, waiting in sunny Sochi, received a telegram at 8.48 p.m. from Kaganovich, Sergo, Voroshilov and Yezhov who informed him that the appeal of the defendants had been received. 'The Politburo proposed to reject the demands and execute the verdict tonight.'* Stalin did not answer, perhaps congratulating himself on his imminent revenge, perhaps having dinner, but surely aware that the murder of two of Lenin's closest comrades marked a giant step towards his next colossal gamble, an intense reign of terror against the Party itself, a slaughter that would consume even his own friends and family. Stalin waited for three long hours.

* Stalin had sent Mikoyan on a 12,000-mile tour of the American food industry. The shrewd Armenian made sure Stalin knew that he supported the verdict, writing to 'dear Lazar' Kaganovich from Chicago. 'Don't forget to write in your next letter to him that I send my warmest greetings to Our Master. How good that we have so quickly got rid of the Trotskyite gang of Zinoviev and Kamenev!' Mikoyan met Secretary of State Cordell Hull in DC, debated with Henry Ford – and inspected Maceys in New York. The trip had two effects: Mikoyan gave the Russians American hamburgers and ice-cream – and he lost his taste for wearing the Party tunic, sporting natty American-style suits for the rest of his career.

Part Four

Slaughter: Yezhov the Poison Dwarf,
1937–1938

17

The Executioner: Beria's Poison
and Bukharin's Dosage

Minutes before midnight, Stalin sent this laconic telegram: 'Okay.'1 During the first hour of 25 August, a number of limousines cruised through the gates of the Lubianka prison, containing the officials to witness the executions.

A dignified Kamenev and a feverish Zinoviev were led out of their cells and down the steps. Yezhov and Yagoda were accompanied by the ex-hairdresser, Pauker. Vyshinsky as Procurator-General was meant to attend important executions but was said to be so squeamish that he usually sent one of his chief investigators, Lev Sheinin. Mikoyan supposedly said that Voroshilov represented the Politburo.

Stalin never attended torture or execution (though he witnessed a hanging as a child and must have observed violent death in Tsaritsyn) but he respected his executioners. Execution was officially called the 'Highest Measure of Punishment', usually shortened to the terrible letters 'VMN' or the acronym *Vishka*, but Stalin called it 'black work', which he regarded as noble Party service. The master of 'black work' under Stalin presided over this sombre but brisk ritual: Blokhin, a pugnacious Chekist of forty-one with a stalwart face and black hair pushed back, was one of the most prolific executioners of the century, killing thousands personally, sometimes wearing his own leather butcher's apron to protect his uniform. Yet the name of this monster has slipped through history's fingers.* In the theatre of Stalin's court, Blokhin henceforth lurks in the background, but is rarely off-stage.

* There were many Chekists who sometimes doubled as executioners but Blokhin himself, assisted by two murderous brothers, Vasily and Ivan Zhigarev, handled important cases. V. M. Blokhin was a veteran of the Tsarist army in the First World War and a Chekist since March 1921, who had risen to head the Kommandatura Branch that was attached to the Administrative Executive Department. This meant he was in charge of the internal prison at Lubianka; among other things, he was responsible for executions. Major-General Blokhin was retired after Stalin's death and praised for his 'irreproachable service' by Beria himself. After Beria's fall, he was stripped of rank in November 1954 and died on 3 February 1955.

Zinoviev shouted that this was a 'Fascist coup' and begged the executioners:

'Please, comrade, for God's sake, call Joseph Vissarionovich! Joseph Vissarionovich promised to save our lives!' Some accounts have him actually hugging and licking the Chekist's boots. Kamenev reportedly answered:

'We deserve this because of our unworthy attitude at the trial' and told Zinoviev to be quiet and die with dignity. Zinoviev made such a noise that an NKVD lieutenant took him into a nearby cell and despatched him there and then. They were shot through the back of the head.

The bullets, with their noses crushed, were dug out of the skulls, wiped clean of blood and pearly brain matter, and handed to Yagoda, probably still warm. No wonder Vyshinsky found these events sickening. Yagoda labelled the bullets 'Zinoviev' and 'Kamenev' and treasured these macabre but sacred relics, taking them home to be kept proudly with his collection of erotica and ladies's stockings.* The bodies were cremated.

Stalin was always fascinated by the conduct of his enemies at the supreme moment, enjoying their humiliation and destruction: 'A man may be physically brave but a political coward,' he said. Weeks later, at a dinner to celebrate the founding of the Cheka, Pauker, Stalin's comedian, acted the death and pleadings of Zinoviev. To the raucous guffaws of the *Vozhd* and Yezhov, plump, corseted and shiny-pated Pauker was dragged back into the room by two friends playing the role of guards. There he performed Zinoviev's cries of 'For God's sake call Stalin' but improvised another ingredient. Pauker, a Jew himself, specialized in telling Stalin Jewish jokes in the appropriate accent with much rolling of 'R's and cringing. Now he combined the two, depicting Zinoviev raising his hands to the Heavens and weeping. 'Hear oh Israel the Lord is our God, the Lord is one',† Stalin laughed so much that Pauker repeated it. Stalin was almost sick with merriment and waved at Pauker to stop.

* * *

* When he was arrested they were found among his belongings and passed on to Yezhov who also kept them until his downfall.
† Zinoviev was unlikely to have recited the Shema prayer, the holiest in Jewish faith, since he, like all the Jews among these internationalist Bolsheviks, despised religion, but equally he would have remembered it from his childhood.

Bukharin was hill-climbing in the Pamirs when he read in the newspapers that he had been implicated in the Zinoviev trial. He frantically rushed back to Moscow. Bukharin had seemed forgiven for past sins. As the editor of *Izvestiya*, he had returned to prominence with frequent access to Stalin. In 1935, at a banquet, Stalin had even publicly toasted Bukharin: 'Let's drink to Nikolai Ivanovich Bukharin. We all love ... Bukharchik. May whoever remembers the past, lose an eye!' Whether to preserve Bukharin for his own trial (after Tomsky's suicide), because of a lingering fondness or just feline sadism, Stalin proceeded to play with beloved Bukharchik who waited anxiously in his Kremlin apartment.

On 8 September, the Central Committee summoned Bukharin to a meeting with Kaganovich, where, along with Yezhov and Vyshinsky, he was amazed to encounter his childhood friend, Grigory Sokolnikov, a venerable Old Bolshevik, who was delivered to the room by the NKVD. The 'confrontation' was one of Stalin's bizarre rituals in which, like an exorcism, Good was meant to confront and vanquish Evil. They were presumably designed to terrify the accused but also, and this may have been their main function, to convince the presiding Politburo members of the victim's guilt. Kaganovich played impartial observer while Sokolnikov declared there was a Left-Right Centre, involving Bukharin, which was planning the murder of Stalin.

'Can you have lost your reason and not be responsible for your own words?' Bukharin 'turned on the tears'. When the prisoner was led out, Kaganovich boomed: 'He's lying, the whore, from beginning to end! Go back to the newspaper, Nikolai Ivanovich, and work in peace.'

'But why is he lying, Lazar Moisevich?'

'We'll find out,' replied an unconvinced Kaganovich who still 'adored' Bukharin but told Stalin his 'role will yet be uncovered'. Stalin's antennae sensed that the time was not right: on 10 September, Vyshinsky announced that the investigation against Bukharin and Rykov had been closed due to lack of criminal culpability. Bukharin returned to work, safe again, while the investigators moved on to their next trial – but the cat did not stop caressing the mouse.

* * *

Stalin remained on holiday, directing a series of parallel tragedies in his escalating campaign to eliminate his enemies while devoting much of his energy to the Spanish Civil War. On 15 October, Soviet tanks, planes and 'advisers' started arriving in Spain to support the Republican Government against General Francisco Franco, backed by Hitler and Mussolini. Stalin treated this less as a rehearsal for World War 2 and more as a replay of his own Civil War. The internecine struggle with the Trotskyites on his own side, and the Fascists on the other, created a war fever in Moscow, stoking up the Terror. Stalin's real interest was to keep the war going as long as possible, embroiling Hitler without offending the Western powers, rather than helping the Republicans win. Furthermore, like an accomplished 'barrow boy', Stalin systematically swindled the Spanish of several hundred million dollars by rescuing their gold reserves and then tricking them into paying inflated prices for their arms.*

Gradually, instructing Voroshilov in military, Kaganovich in political, and Yezhov in security matters by telephone from Sochi, he presided over the effective NKVD takeover of the Republic itself, where he found himself in a genuine struggle with the Trotskyites. He set about the liquidation of Trotskyites along with his own men. The Soviet diplomats, journalists and soldiers serving in Spain spent as much time denouncing one another as fighting the Fascists.

After a short stay at the new little dacha built for him by Lakoba at Novy Afon (New Athos),† to the south in Abkhazia right beside Alexander III's monastery, Stalin returned to Sochi where he was joined by Zhdanov and President Kalinin. Yezhov was expanding the lists of suspects to include the whole of the old oppositions but also entire nationalities, particularly the Poles. Simultaneously he was pushing for the role of NKVD chief, attacking Yagoda for 'complacency, passivity, and bragging', in a letter that may have been sent to Stalin in a shameless job application: 'Without your intervention, things will come to no good.' Meanwhile Yagoda

* On the subject of Stalin's 'barrow boy' tendencies, he was always interested in discounts in his foreign dealings: 'How much was the purchase of the Italian warship?' he wrote to Voroshilov. 'If we buy two warships, what discount can they give us? Stalin.'

† Stalin had started to use this charmingly small house, a picturesque yellow bungalow on the hillside at Novy Afon, in 1935. There were walks up the hill to a summerhouse where Stalin held barbecues. Later he would build another house next to the first that would become one of his favourite residences in old age. Used by the President of Abkhazia, it is fully staffed. When the author visited in 2002, the manageress invited him to stay and offered to hold a banquet in his honour in Stalin's dining room.

bugged Yezhov's calls to Stalin, learning that Blackberry had been summoned to Sochi. Yagoda left immediately for Sochi but when he arrived, Pauker turned him back from the gates of Stalin's dacha.

On 25 September Stalin, backed by Zhdanov, decided to remove Yagoda and promote Yezhov:

'We consider it absolutely necessary and urgent to appoint Comrade Yezhov to the post of People's Commissar of Internal Affairs. Yagoda is not up to the task of exposing the Trotskyite-Zinovievite Bloc ... Stalin, Zhdanov.'

Sergo visited the dacha to discuss Yezhov's appointment and his own battles with the NKVD. Stalin felt he needed to win over Sergo to Yezhov's appointment, even though Blackberry and his wife were family friends of Sergo. 'This remarkably wise decision by our father suits the attitude of the Party and country,' Kaganovich wrote cheerfully to Sergo after he had sacked Yagoda and appointed him to Rykov's job as Communications Commissar.

There was relief at Yezhov's appointment: many, including Bukharin, regarded it as the end of the Terror, not the beginning, but Kaganovich knew his protégé better: he praised Yezhov's 'superb ... interrogations' to Stalin, suggesting his promotion to Commissar-General. 'Comrade Yezhov is handling things well,' Kaganovich told Sergo. 'He's dispensed with the bandits of the counter-revolutionary Trotskyites in Bolshevik style.' The dwarfish Blackberry was now the second most powerful man in the USSR.

Stalin was deeply dissatisfied with the 'sickness' inside the NKVD, which he rightly regarded as the ultimate Bolshevik old-boy network, filled with dubious Poles, Jews and Letts. He needed an outsider to get control of this self-satisfied élite and make it his own. There is evidence that during the thirties, he discussed appointing both Kaganovich and Mikoyan to run the NKVD and he had recently offered the job to Lakoba.*

Lakoba refused to move to Moscow from his paradisaical fiefdom. Loyal as he was to Stalin, Lakoba was better suited to

---

* Interestingly, none of these candidates are ethnic Russians but a Jew, an Armenian and an Abkhazian. Some historians believe there had always been a secret policy of placing Poles, Balts and Jews and other minorities to perform the unsavoury roles in the NKVD. This is credible but it is true that Stalin desperately needed NKVD officials he trusted: he was often closest to his fellow Caucasians. He had no interest in provoking Russian resentment of Georgians in high positions.

playing the magnanimious host in the resorts of Abkhazia than torturing innocents in the cellars of the Lubianka. But his refusal drew attention to the rule of Lakoba's clan in Abkhazia, known as 'Lakobistan', which he wanted to be made into a full Soviet republic, a dangerous idea in the fragile multinational USSR. There was no greater 'prince' than Lakoba. Stalin had already banned the use of Abkhazian names in Lakoba's fiefdom and foiled his plan to raise Abkhazia's constitutional status.

On 31 October, Stalin returned to Moscow where he dined with Lakoba. All seemed well. But it was not. When Lakoba returned to Abkhazia, Beria invited him to dinner in Tiflis. Lakoba refused until Beria's mother telephoned to insist. They dined on 27 December and then went to the theatre where Lakoba was overcome with nausea. Returning to his hotel, he sat by the window groaning,

'That snake Beria has killed me.' At 4.20 a.m., Lakoba died of a 'heart attack' aged forty-three. Beria saw off the coffin on its way back by train to Sukhumi. Lakoba's doctors were convinced he had been poisoned but Beria had the organs removed, later exhuming and destroying the cadaver. Lakoba's family were also killed. He was denounced as an Enemy of the People. Lakoba was the first of Stalin's circle to be killed. 'Poison, poison,' as Stalin wrote. He had given Beria *carte blanche* to settle scores in the Caucasus. In Armenia, Beria had earlier visited the First Secretary, Aghasi Khanchian, who had either killed himself or been murdered. Across the Imperium, the regions began to expose conspiracies of 'wreckers'* to justify the inefficiencies and corruption. The clock was ticking towards war with Hitler's Germany. But as tension was mounting with aggressive Japan in the Far East, and Soviet 'advisers' fought in Spain, the USSR was already at war.

* * *

Shortly before Lakoba's sinister death, Beria arrested Papulia Ordzhonikidze, Sergo's elder brother, a railway official. Beria knew that his former patron, Sergo, had warned Stalin that he was a 'scoundrel'. Sergo refused to shake hands with Beria and built a special fence between their dachas.

---

* In West Siberia, there was a regional show trial of 'wreckers' accused of trying to murder the local leader Eikhe – and of trying to assassinate Molotov during his earlier trip there. His driver testified that he planned to sacrifice himself and kill Molotov by driving over a precipice but he lost his nerve and only managed to capsize the car in a muddy rut. No doubt this cock-and-bull story consoled Molotov for being left off the list for the Zinoviev trial.

Beria's vengeance was just one of the ways in which Stalin began to turn the heat on to the emotional Sergo, the industrial *magnifico* who supported the regime's draconian policies but resisted the arrest of his own managers. The star of the next show trial was to be Sergo's Deputy Commissar, Yury Pyatakov, an ex-Trotskyite and skilled manager. The two men were fond of one another and enjoyed working together.

In July, Pyatakov's wife had been arrested for her links to Trotsky. Shortly before the Zinoviev trial, Yezhov summoned Pyatakov, read him all the affidavits implicating him in Trotskyite terrorism and informed him that he was relieved of his job as Deputy Commissar. Pyatakov offered to prove his innocence by asking to be 'personally allowed to shoot all those sentenced to death at the trial, including his former wife and to publish this in the press'. As a Bolshevik, he was willing even to execute his own wife.

'I pointed out to him the absurdity of his proposal,' Yezhov reported drily to Stalin. On 12 September, Pyatakov was arrested. Sergo, recuperating in Kislovodsk, voted for his expulsion from the Central Committee but he must have been deeply worried. A shadow of his former self, grey and exhausted, he was so ill that the Politburo restricted him to a three-day week. Now the NKVD began to arrest his specialist non-Bolshevik advisers and he appealed to Blackberry: 'Comrade Yezhov, please look into this.' He was not alone. Kaganovich and Sergo, those 'best friends', not only shared the same swaggering dynamism but both headed giant industrial commissariats. Kaganovich's railway experts were being arrested too. Meanwhile Stalin sent Sergo transcripts of Pyatakov's interrogations in which his deputy confessed to being a 'saboteur'. The destruction of 'experts' was a perennial Bolshevik sport but the arrest of Sergo's brother revealed Stalin's hand: 'This couldn't have been done without Stalin's consent. But Stalin's agreed to it without even calling me,' Sergo told Mikoyan. 'We were such close friends! And suddenly he lets them do such a thing!' He blamed Beria.

Sergo appealed to Stalin, doing all he could to save his brother. He did too much: the arrest of a man's clan was a test of loyalty. Stalin was not alone in taking a dim view of this bourgeois emotionalism: Molotov himself attacked Sergo for being 'guided only by emotions ... thinking only of himself.'

On 9 November, Sergo suffered another heart attack.

Meanwhile, the third Ordzhonikidze brother, Valiko, was sacked from his job in the Tiflis Soviet for claiming that Papulia was innocent. Sergo swallowed his pride and called Beria, who replied:

'Dear Comrade Sergo! After your call, I quickly summoned Valiko ... Today Valiko was restored to his job. Yours L. Beria.' This bears the pawprints of Stalin's cat-and-mouse game, his meandering path to open destruction, perhaps his moments of nostalgic fondness, his supersensitive testing of limits. But Stalin now regarded Sergo as an enemy: his biography had just been published for his fiftieth birthday and Stalin studied it carefully, scribbling sarcastically next to the passages that acclaimed Sergo's heroism:

'What about the CC? The Party?' Stalin and Sergo returned separately to Moscow where fifty-six of the latter's officials were in the toils of the NKVD. Sergo however remained a living restraint on Stalin, making brave little gestures towards the beleaguered Rightists. 'My dear kind warmly blessed Sergo,' encouraged Bukharin: 'Stand firm!' At the theatre, when Stalin and the Politburo filed into the front seats, Sergo spotted ex-Premier Rykov and his daughter Natalya (who tells the story), alone and ignored, twenty rows up the auditorium. Leaving Stalin, Sergo galloped up to kiss them. The Rykovs were moved to tears in gratitude.*

At the 7 November parade, Stalin, on the Mausoleum, spotted Bukharin in an ordinary seat and sent a Chekist to say, 'Comrade Stalin has invited you on to the Mausoleum.' Bukharin thought he was being arrested but then gratefully climbed the steps.

Bukharin, the enchanting but hysterical intellectual whom everyone adored, bombarded Stalin with increasingly frantic letters through which we can feel the screw tightening. When writers fear for their lives, they write and write: 'Big child!' Stalin scribbled across one letter; 'Crank!' on another. Bukharin could not stop appealing to Stalin, about whom he was having dreams:

'Everything connected with me is criticized,' he wrote on 19 October 1936. 'Even for the birthday of Sergo, they did not propose me to write an article ... Maybe I'm not honourable. To whom can I go, as a beloved person, without expecting a smash

* 'Men have gone to heaven for smaller things than that,' wrote Oscar Wilde in *De Profundis* about Robbie Ross waiting amongst the crowd at Reading Station and being the only one to step forward and raise his hat as the disgraced writer travelled to Reading Gaol. The stakes were even higher for Sergo.

in the teeth? I see your intention but I write to you as I wrote to Illich [Lenin] as a really beloved man whom I even see in dreams as I did Illich. Maybe it's strange but it's so. It's hard for me to live under suspicion and my nerves are already on edge.' Finally, on a sleepless night, he wrote a poem, an embarrassing hymn to 'Great Stalin!'

Bukharin's other old friend was Voroshilov. The two had been so close that Bukharin called him his 'honey seagull' and even wrote his speeches for him. Klim had presented him with a pistol engraved with his love and friendship. Voroshilov tried to avoid Bukharin's letters: 'Why do you hurt me so?' he asked Klim in one letter.

Now in real danger, Bukharin wrote a long plea to Klim in which he even announced that he was 'delighted the dogs [Zinoviev and Kamenev] were shot ... Forgive this confused letter: a thousand thoughts are rushing around inside my head like strong horses and I have no strong reins. I embrace you because I am clean. N Bukharin.' Voroshilov decided he had to end this ghost of a friendship so he ordered his adjutant to copy the letter to the Politburo and write: 'I enclose herewith, on Comrade Voroshilov's orders, Comrade Voroshilov's reply to Bukharin.' Voroshilov's reply was a study in amorality, cruelty, fear and cowardice:

To Comrade Bukharin, I return your letter in which you permit yourself to make vile attacks on the Party leadership. If you were hoping ... to convince me of your complete innocence, all you have convinced me of is that henceforth I should distance myself from you ... And if you do not repudiate in writing your foul epithets against the Party leadership, I shall even regard you as a scoundrel.
    K Voroshilov 3 Sept 1936.

Bukharin was heartbroken by 'your appalling letter. My letter ended with "I embrace you". Your letter ends with "scoundrel".'

Yezhov was creating the case against the so-called Leftists Radek and Pyatakov, but by December, he had also managed to procure evidence against Bukharin and Rykov. The December Plenum was a sort of arraignment of these victims and, as always with Stalin, a test of the conditions necessary to destroy them. Stalin was the dominant will, but the Terror was not the work of one man. One can hear the evangelical enthusiasm of their blood-lust that sometimes totters on the edge of tragicomedy. Kaganovich even told a Stalinist shaggy-dog story.

Yezhov proudly listed the two hundred persons arrested in the Trotskyite Centre in the Azov–Black Sea organization, another three hundred in Georgia, four hundred in Leningrad. Molotov was not the only one who had avoided assassination: Kaganovich had just escaped death in the Urals. First Yezhov dealt with the Pyatakov–Radek trial that was about to begin. When he read out Pyatakov's description of the workers as a 'herd of sheep', these frightened fanatics reacted as if at a nightmarish revivalist meeting.

'The swine!' shouted Beria. There was a 'noise of indignation in the room'. Then the record reveals:

A voice: 'The brutes!'

'That's how low this vicious Fascist agent, this degenerate Communist has sunk, God knows what else! These swine must be strangled!'

'What about Bukharin?' a voice called.

'We need to talk about them,' agreed Stalin.

'There's a scoundrel for you,' snarled Beria.

'What swine!' exclaimed another comrade. Yezhov announced that Bukharin and Rykov were indeed members of the 'back-up Centre'. They were actually terrorists yet these assassins were sitting there with them. Bukharin was now meant to confess his sins and implicate his friends. He did not.

'So you think I too aspired to power? Are you serious?' he asked Yezhov. 'After all there are many old comrades who know me well … my very soul, my inner life.'

'It's hard to know someone's soul,' sneered Beria.

'There isn't a word of truth said against me … Kamenev stated at his trial that he met me every year up to 1936. I asked Yezhov to find out when and where so I could refute this lie. They told me Kamenev was not asked … and now it's impossible to ask him.'

'They shot him,' added Rykov sadly. Few of the old leaders kicked Bukharin but Kaganovich, Molotov and Beria hunted him zealously. Then, amidst deadly allegations, Kaganovich remembered Zinoviev's dog:

'In 1934, Zinoviev invited Tomsky to his *dacha* … After drinking tea, Tomsky and Zinoviev went in Tomsky's car to pick out a dog for Zinoviev. You see what friendship, what help they went together to pick out a dog.'

'What about this dog?' said Stalin. 'Was it a hunting dog or a guard dog?'

'It was not possible to establish this,' Kaganovich went on with gleeful, if chilling humour.

'Anyway, did they fetch the dog?' persisted Stalin.

'They got it,' boomed Kaganovich. 'They were searching for a four-legged companion not unlike themselves.'

'Was it a good dog or a bad dog?' asked Stalin. 'Anybody know?' There was 'laughter in the hall'.

'It was hard to establish this at the confrontation,' replied Kaganovich.

Finally, Stalin, sensing how many of the older members were not joining in against Bukharin, summed up more in sadness than anger:

'We believed in you and we were mistaken ... We believed in you ... we moved you up the ladder and we were mistaken. Isn't it true Comrade Bukharin?' Yet Stalin ended the Plenum without a vote in support of Yezhov; just an ominous decision to consider 'the matter of Bukharin and Rykov unfinished'. The regional 'princes' realized that even such a giant could be destroyed.

Stalin, assisted by Yezhov, shaped the febrile fears of war with Poland and Germany and the very real dangers of the Spanish Civil War, the inexplicable industrial failures caused by Soviet incompetence, and the resistance of the regional 'princes', into a web of conspiracies that dovetailed with the paranoic soul and glorious, nostalgic brutality of the Russian Civil War, and personal feuds of the Bolsheviks. Stalin was particularly suspicious of the infiltration of spies across the porous border with Poland, traditional enemy of Russia's western marches that had defeated Russia (and Stalin personally) in 1920.* At the Plenum, Khrushchev was denounced as a secret 'Pole'. Chatting in the corridor to his friend Yezhov, Stalin walked over, pushing a finger into Khrushchev's shoulder:

'What's your name?'

'Comrade Stalin, it's Khrushchev.'

'No you're not Khrushchev ... So-and-so says you're not.'

'How can you believe that? My mother's still alive ... Check.' Stalin cited Yezhov who denied it. Stalin let it pass but he was checking those around him.

---

* Stalin's political and personal obsessions often found a parallel in his favourite operas: he constantly attended performances of the opera *Ivan Susanin* by Glinka but only waited until the scene when the Poles are lured into a forest by a Russian and freeze to death there. He would then leave the theatre and go home.

Stalin was finally determined to bring the regional 'princes' to heel: Ukraine was a special case, the grain store, the second republic with a strong sense of its own culture. Kosior and Chubar had demonstrated their weakness during the famine while the Second Secretary, Postyshev, behaved like a 'prince' with his own entourage. On 13 January, Stalin struck with a telegram attacking Postyshev, for lacking the 'most basic Party vigilance'. Kaganovich, already the scourge of the Ukraine which he had governed in the late twenties, descended on Kiev, where he soon managed to find a 'little person' crushed by the local 'prince'. A half-mad crone and Party busybody named Polia Nikolaenko had criticized Postyshev and his wife, also a high official. Mrs Postyshev expelled the troublesome Nikolaenko from the Party. When Kaganovich informed Stalin of this 'heroic denunciatrix', he immediately grasped her usefulness.

On 21 December, the family and magnates danced until dawn at Stalin's birthday party. But the struggles and conspiracies took their toll on the actor-manager: Stalin often suffered from chronic tonsillitis when under pressure. Professor Valedinsky, the specialist from the Matsesta Baths, whom he had brought to Moscow, joined his personal physician, the distinguished Vladimir Vinogradov, who had been a fashionable doctor before the Revolution and still lived in an apartment filled with antiques and fine pictures. The patient lay on a sofa with a high temperature for five days, surrounded by professors and Politburo. The professors visited twice a day and kept vigil at night. By New Year's Eve, he was well enough to attend the party where the whole family danced together for the last time. When the doctors visited him on New Year's Day 1937, he reminisced about his first job as a meteorologist and his fishing exploits during his Siberian exiles. But Stalin's duel with Sergo again took a toll on him as he prepared for his most reckless gamble since collectivization: the massacre of Lenin's Party.

* * *

Stalin arranged a 'confrontation' between Bukharin and Pyatakov before the Politburo. Pyatakov, the abrasive industrial manager soon to star in his own show trial, testified to Bukharin's terrorism but was now a walking testament to the methods of the NKVD. 'Living remains,' Bukharin told his wife, 'not of Pyatakov but of his shadow, a skeleton with its teeth knocked out.' He spoke with his head lowered, trying to cover his eyes with his hands. Sergo stared intensely at his former deputy and friend:

'Is your testimony voluntary?' he asked.

'My testimony is voluntary,' retorted Pyatakov.

It seems absurd that Sergo even had to ask the question but to do more would be to go against the Politburo itself where men like Voroshilov were working themselves up into paroxyms of hatred:

'Your deputy turned out to be a swine of the first class,' Klim told him. 'You must know what he told us, the pig, the son of a bitch!' When Sergo read the signed pages of Pyatakov's interrogation, he 'believed it and came to hate him' but it was not a happy time for him.

Stalin was supervising Pyatakov's coming trial of the 'Parallel Anti-Soviet Trotskyite Centre' that was really an assault on Sergo's Commissariat of Heavy Industry where ten of the seventeen defendants worked. Stalin's intimate role in the famous trials has always been known but the archives reveal how he even dictated the words of Vyshinsky's summing-up. Recovering from his tonsillitis, Stalin must have seen Vyshinsky at Kuntsevo. One can imagine Stalin pacing up and down, smoking, as the cringing Procurator scribbled in his notebook: 'These villains don't even have any sense of being citizens ... they're afraid of the nation, afraid of the people ... Their agreements with Japan and Germany are the agreements of the hare with the wolf ...' Vyshinsky noted down Stalin's words: 'While Lenin was alive, they were against Lenin.' He used exactly the same words in court on 28 January. But Stalin's thoughts in 1937 reveal the broadest reason for the imminent murder of hundreds of thousands of people for little apparent reason: 'Maybe it can be explained by the fact that you lost faith,' Stalin addressed the Old Bolsheviks. Here was the essence of the religious frenzy of the coming slaughter.

Stalin's tonsillitis flared again. He lay on the dining-room table so the professors could examine his throat. Then the Politburo joined Stalin and the doctors for dinner. There were toasts and after dinner, the doctors were amazed to see the leaders dancing. But Stalin's mind was on the brutal tasks of that terrible year. He toasted Soviet medicine, then added that there were 'Enemies among the doctors – you'll find out soon!' He was ready to begin.

18

Sergo: Death of a 'Perfect Bolshevik'

The legal melodrama opened on 23 January and immediately expanded the Terror to thousands of new potential victims. Radek, who may have been coached personally by Stalin, revelled in his black humour, joking that he was not tortured under interrogation; on the contrary, he had tortured his investigators for months by refusing to co-operate. Then he delivered what were probably Stalin's own lines: 'But there are in our country semi-Trotskyites, quarter-Trotskyites, one-eighth Trotskyites, people who helped us [Trotskyites] not knowing of the terrorist organization but sympathizing with us.' The message was clear and when it is combined with Vyshinsky's own notes, the mystery of the crazy randomness of the Terror is solved. Those without blind faith were to die.

At 7.13 p.m. on 29 January, the judges retired to confer and at 3.00 next morning, they returned. Thirteen of the defendants, including Pyatakov, were sentenced to death but Radek received ten years. Blokhin again supervised the executions. Yezhov was rewarded with the rank of Commissar-General of State Security, and a Kremlin apartment.

In Moscow, 200,000 people, bedazzled by propaganda, massed in Red Square, despite temperatures of –27°C, bearing banners that read: 'The court's verdict is the people's verdict.' Khrushchev addressed them, denouncing the 'Judas-Trotsky', a line that strongly implied that Stalin was the metaphorical Jesus. (We know from Yury Zhdanov that he jokily compared himself to Jesus.) 'By raising their hand against Comrade Stalin,' Khrushchev told the crowds, 'they raised their hand against all the best that humanity has, because Stalin is hope … Stalin is our banner. Stalin is our will, Stalin is our victory.' The country was swept by the 'emotional effervescence' of hatred, fear and blood-lust. Maria Svanidze wrote in her diary that Radek's 'human baseness … exceeded all imagination. These moral monsters deserved their end .... How could we so blindly trust this band of scoundrels?'

Today it seems impossible that virtually every factory and railway line was being sabotaged by Trotskyite terrorists within their management but Soviet industry was riddled with mistakes and cursed with accidents thanks to poor management and the breakneck speed of the Five-Year Plans. There were thousands of accidents: for example in 1934 alone, there were 62,000 accidents on the railways! How could this happen in a perfect country? Enemies among the corrupt élite explained the failures. The arrest of saboteurs and wreckers in the industrial factories and railways spread. The staffs of Sergo and Kaganovich were again hit hard.

Stalin carefully prepared for the Plenum that would formally open the Terror against the Party itself. On 31 January, the Politburo appointed the two industrial kingpins to speak about wrecking in their departments. Stalin reviewed their speeches. Sergo accepted that wreckers had to be stopped but wanted to say that now they had been arrested, it was time to return to normality. Stalin angrily scribbled on Sergo's speech: 'State with facts which branches are affected by sabotage and exactly how they are affected.' When they met, Sergo seemed to agree but he quietly despatched trusted managers to the regions to investigate whether the NKVD was fabricating the cases: a direct challenge to Stalin.

An ailing Sergo realized that the gap between them was widening. He faced a rupture with the Party to which he had devoted his life.

'I don't understand why Stalin doesn't trust me,' he confided to Mikoyan probably walking round the snowy Kremlin at night. 'I'm completely loyal to him, don't want to fight with him. Beria's schemes play a large part in this – he gives Stalin the wrong information but Stalin trusts him.' Both were baffled, according to Mikoyan, 'about what was happening to Stalin, how they could put honest men in prison and then shoot them for sabotage'.

'Stalin's started a bad business,' said Sergo. 'I was always such a close friend of Stalin's. I trusted him and he trusted me. And now I can't work with him, I'll commit suicide.' Mikoyan told him suicide never solved anything but there were now frequent suicides. On 17 February, Sergo and Stalin argued for several hours. Sergo then went to his office before returning at 3 p.m. for a Politburo meeting.

Stalin approved Yezhov's report but criticized Sergo and

Kaganovich who retired to Poskrebyshev's study, like schoolboys to rewrite their essays. At seven, they too walked, talking, around the Kremlin: 'he was ill, his nerves broken,' said Kaganovich.

Stalin deliberately turned the screw: the NKVD searched Sergo's apartment. Only Stalin could have ordered such an outrage. Besides, the Ordzhonikidzes spent weekends with the Yezhovs, but friendship was dust compared to the orders of the Party. Sergo, as angry and humiliated as intended, telephoned Stalin:

'Sergo, why are you upset?' said Stalin. 'This Organ can search my place at any moment too.' Stalin summoned Sergo who rushed out so fast, he forgot his coat. His wife Zina hurried after him with the coat and fur hat but he was already in Stalin's apartment. Zina waited outside for an hour and a half. Stalin's provocations only confirmed Sergo's impotence, for he 'sprang out of Stalin's place in a very agitated state, did not put on his coat or hat, and ran home'. He started retyping his speech, then, according to his wife, rushed back to Stalin who taunted him more with his sneering marginalia: 'Ha-ha!'

Sergo told Zina that he could not cope with Koba whom he loved. The next morning, he remained in bed, refusing breakfast. 'I feel bad,' he said. He simply asked that no one should disturb him and worked in his room. At 5.30 p.m. Zinaida heard a dull sound and rushed into the bedroom.

Sergo lay bare-chested and dead on the bed. He had shot himself in the heart, his chest powder-burned. Zina kissed his hands, chest, lips fervently and called the doctor who certified he was dead. She then telephoned Stalin who was at Kuntsevo. The guards said he was taking a walk but she shouted:

'Tell Stalin it's Zina. Tell him to come to the phone right away. I'll wait on the line.'

'Why the big hurry?' Stalin asked. Zina ordered him to come urgently:

'Sergo's done the same as Nadya!' Stalin banged down the phone at this grievous insult.

It happened that Konstantin Ordzhonikidze, one of Sergo's brothers, arrived at the apartment at this moment. At the entrance, Sergo's chauffeur told him to hurry. When he reached the front door, one of Sergo's officials said simply:

'Our Sergo's no more.' Within half an hour, Stalin, Molotov and Zhdanov (for some reason wearing a black bandage on his forehead) arrived from the countryside to join Voroshilov,

Kaganovich and Yezhov. When Mikoyan heard, he exclaimed, 'I don't believe it' and rushed over. Again the Kremlin family mourned its own but suicide left as much anger as grief.

Zinaida sat on the edge of the bed beside Sergo's body. The leaders entered the room, looked at the corpse and sat down. Voroshilov, so soft-hearted in personal matters, consoled Zina:

'Why console me,' she snapped, 'when you couldn't save him for the Party?' Stalin caught Zina's eye and nodded at her to follow him into the study. They stood facing each other. Stalin seemed crushed and pitiful, betrayed again.

'What shall we say to people now?' she asked.

'This must be reported in the press,' Stalin replied. 'We'll say he died of a heart attack.'

'No one will believe that,' snapped the widow. 'Sergo loved the truth. The truth must be printed.'

'Why won't they believe it? Everyone knew he had a bad heart and everyone will believe it,' concluded Stalin. The door to the death-room was closed but Konstantin Ordzhonikidze peeped inside and observed Kaganovich and Yezhov in consultation, sitting at the foot of the body of their mutual friend. Suddenly Beria, in Moscow for the Plenum, appeared in the dining room. Zinaida charged at him, trying to slap him, and shrieked: 'Rat!' Beria 'disappeared right afterwards'.

They carried Sergo's bulky body from the bedroom and laid him on the table. Molotov's brother, a photographer, arrived with his camera. Stalin and the magnates posed with the body.

On the 19th, the newspapers announced the death of Sergo by heart attack. A list of doctors signed the mendacious bulletin: 'At 17.30, while he was having his afternoon rest, he suddenly felt ill and a few minutes later died of paralysis of the heart.' The Plenum was delayed by Sergo's funeral, but Stalin's obstacle had been removed. The death of 'the perfect Bolshevik' shocked Maria Svanidze who described the lying-in-state in the Hall of Columns among 'garlands, music, the scent of flowers, tears, honorary escorts. Thousands upon thousands passed' the open coffin. Sergo was sanctified by a cult. Some mourned him more than others. Bukharin penned a poem: 'He cracked like lightning in foamy waves' but also wrote another pathetic letter to Stalin:

'I wanted to write to Klim and Mikoyan. And if they hurt me too? Because the slanders have done their work. I am not me. I can't even cry on the body of an old comrade ... Koba, I can't live in such a situation ... I really love you passionately ... I wish you quick and resolute victories.' The suicide remained a tight secret. Stalin and others like the Voroshilovs* believed Sergo was a self-indulgent disappointment. At the Plenum, Stalin attacked that Bolshevik nobleman for behaving like a 'prince'.

Stalin was chief bearer of the urn of ashes that was buried near Kirov in the Kremlin Wall. But his antennae sensed other doubters who might follow Sergo's line. During the funeral, he reminded Mikoyan about his escape from the shooting of Twenty-Six Commissars during the Civil War: 'You were the only one to escape' in that 'obscure and murky story. Anastas, don't force us to try to clear it up.' Mikoyan must have decided not to rock the boat but he could hardly miss the warning and gathering darkness.

'I cannot live like this any more ...' wrote Bukharin to Stalin days later. 'I am in no physical or moral condition to come to the Plenum ... I will begin a hunger strike until the accusations of betrayal, wrecking and terrorism are dropped.' But Bukharin's agony was just starting: Anna his wife accompanied him to the first sitting during a snowstorm. It is striking that the main victims of the Plenum, Bukharin and Yagoda, both lived in the Kremlin just doors away from Stalin and the Politburo while simultaneously being accused of planning their murder. The Kremlin remained a village – but one of unsurpassed malevolence.

At 6 p.m. on 23 February, this febrile, cruel Plenum opened under the pall of Sergo's death, Pyatakov's execution, the spreading arrests and the bloodthirsty public effervescence whipped up by the media. If there was any moment when Stalin emerged as dictator with power over life and death, it was now. Yezhov opened with a savage indictment of Bukharin and his hunger strike.

'I won't shoot myself,' he replied, 'because people will say I killed myself to harm the Party. But if I die, as it were, from an illness, what will you lose from it?'

'Blackmailer!' shouted several voices.

---

* Ekaterina Voroshilova wrote twenty years later in her diaries: maybe Zinaida 'was right that Ordzhonikidze was a man of great soul but on this I have my own opinion.' Sergo's daughter Eteri recalled how Stalin called a couple of times to comfort the widow and then no one called them. Only Kaganovich still visited them. Years later, Khrushchev praised Sergo at Kuntsevo. Beria was insulting about him. Stalin said nothing. But when they left, Malenkov pulled Khrushchev aside: 'Listen, why did you speak so carelessly about Sergo? He shot himself ... Didn't you know? Didn't you notice how awkward it was after you said his name?' None the less the city of Vladikavkaz, in the Caucasus, was renamed Ordzhonikidze.

'You scoundrel,' shrieked Voroshilov at his ex-friend. 'Keep your trap shut! How vile! How dare you speak like that!'

'It's very hard for me to go on living.'

'And it's easy for us?' asked Stalin. 'You really babble a lot.'

'You abused the Party's trust!' declaimed Andreyev. This venom encouraged less senior officials to prove their loyalty:

'I'm not sure there's any reason for us to go on debating this matter,' declared I. P. Zhukov (no relation of the Marshal). 'These people ... must be shot just as the [other] scoundrels were shot!' This was so rabid that the leaders hooted with laughter: in the midst of the witch hunt, it was perhaps a relief to be able to laugh. But there were more jokes. Bukharin quipped that the testimonies against him were false:

'Demand produces supply – that means that those who give testimony know the nature of the general atmosphere!' More laughter. But it was all to no avail: a commission of magnates, chaired by Mikoyan, met to decide the fate of Bukharin and Rykov but when they returned after sleepless nights, no one would shake hands with them. Even before Yezhov came in for the kill, Stalin taunted Bukharin:

'Bukharin's on hunger strike. Who is your ultimatum aimed at, Nikolai, the Central Committee?'

'You're about to throw me out of the Party.'

'Ask the Central Committee for its forgiveness!'

'I'm not Zinoviev and Kamenev and I won't lie about myself.'

'If you won't confess,' replied Mikoyan, 'you're just proving you're a Fascist hireling.'

The 'hirelings' waited at home. In Stalin and Nadya's old apartment in the Poteshny Palace, Bukharin worked frantically on a letter to a future Central Commitee and Posterity, asking his beautiful wife Anna, just twenty-three, to memorize it. 'Again and again Nikolai Ivanovich read his letter in a whisper to me and I had to repeat it after him,' she wrote. 'Then I read and reread it myself, softly repeating the phrases aloud. Ah how he gripped [me] when I made a slip!'

Just across the river, in his apartment in the House on the Embankment, Rykov would only say: 'They'll send me to prison!' His wife suffered a stroke as the attacks on her husband became more deadly. His devoted 21-year-old daughter, Natalya, helped him dress each day for the Plenum – as her mother had done.

The commission voted on their fate. Many of Stalin's devotees such as Khrushchev wanted a trial but 'without application of the death penalty'. Yezhov, Budyonny and Postyshev, himself already under fire, voted for death. Molotov and Voroshilov slavishly supported 'the suggestion of Comrade Stalin' which was enigmatic because his vote originally suggested 'exile' but then was changed by hand to 'Transfer their case to NKVD'.

Bukharin and Rykov were summoned. Both faced the anguished panic and sad regrets of last goodbyes. Rykov asked his daughter to phone Poskrebyshev to find out his fate.

'When I need him,' replied Poskrebyshev, 'I'll send a car.' At dusk, this usher of doom called: 'I'm sending the car.' Natalya helped her beloved father dress in suit, tie, waistcoat and overcoat. He said nothing as they took the lift downstairs, walking out on to the Embankment. When they looked towards the Kremlin, they saw the black limousine. Father and daughter turned to one another on the pavement. They awkwardly shook hands then they kissed formally *à la russe*, three times on the cheek. Without a word, 'my father climbed into the car that sped off towards the Kremlin'. Natalya never forgot that moment: 'And I never saw him again – except in my dreams.'

When Poskrebyshev called Bukharin, Anna 'began to say farewell', in that heart-rending moment of eternal parting, which was to be shared by millions in the coming years. Poskrebyshev called again: the Plenum was waiting but Bukharin was in no hurry. He fell to his knees before his young Anna: 'With tears in his eyes, he begged forgiveness for my ruined life. But he begged me to raise our son as a Bolshevik – "A Bolshevik without fail," he said twice.' He swore her to deliver the memorized letter to the Party: 'You're young and you'll live to see it.' He then rose from the floor, hugged her, kissed her and said, 'See you don't get angry, Anyutka. There are irritating misprints in history but the truth will triumph.'

'We understood,' Anna wrote, 'we were parting for ever.' She could only say, 'See that you don't lie about yourself, but this was much to ask.' Pulling on his leather coat, he disappeared into the alleyways around the Great Kremlin Palace.

Moments later, Boris Berman, a fat, flashy old-fashioned Chekist in 'a stylish suit' with big rings on his fingers and one elongated fingernail, arrived with the NKVD to search the apartment. Meanwhile, at the Plenum, Stalin proposed that they be 'handed over to the NKVD'.

'Does anyone wish to speak?' Andreyev asked. 'No. Are there any other proposals besides the one made by Comrade Stalin? No. Let's vote ... All those against? None. Any abstentions? Two. So the resolution carries with two abstentions – Bukharin and Rykov.' The two, who had once ruled Russia alongside Stalin, were arrested as they left the Plenum. Bukharin took that one step that was like falling a thousand miles: one minute, he was living in the Kremlin, with cars, dachas and servants. The next minute, he was passing through the gates of the Lubianka, handing over his possessions, being stripped, having his rectum checked, his clothes returned though without belt or shoelaces, and then being locked in a cell with the usual stool pigeon to provoke him. But Bukharin was not tortured.

Bukharin's Anna and Rykov's half-paralysed wife and daughter Natalya were arrested soon afterwards, serving almost two decades of slave-labour.*

This ugly meeting dealt other blows too: Yezhov attacked Yagoda. Molotov, giving Sergo's report, cited 585 wreckers in Heavy Industry; Kaganovich ranted about the 'unmasking' of Enemies on the railways.

Stalin used the 'heroic denunciatrix' of Kiev, Polia Nikolaenko, against the Ukrainian potentate, Postyshev. Stalin hailed her as a 'simple member of the Party' treated by Postyshev like 'an annoying fly ... Sometimes the simple people are much closer to the truth than certain higher examples.' Postyshev was moved to another job, not arrested. The warning was clear: no Politburo 'Prince' and his 'family group' were safe. 'We old members of the Politburo, we're soon leaving the scene,' Stalin explained ominously. 'It's the law of nature. We would like to have some teams of replacements.'

Stalin, politician and man, was brilliantly equipped for the constant intensification of struggle which he formulated into his creed of Terror: 'The further we move forward, the more success we have, the more embittered will the remnants of the destroyed

---

* Natalya Rykova survived fifteen years of slave labour on the White Sea because 'of the beauty of nature that I saw every day in the forests and the kindness of people for there were more kind people than bad people'. The author thanks Natalya Rykova, aged eighty-five, indomitable and alive today in Moscow, who generously told her story without bitterness, but with tears running down her cheeks. Anna Larina was parted from her and Bukharin's baby son. But she too survived and wrote her memoirs.

exploiter classes become, the sooner they will resort to extreme forms of struggle.'

* * *

Blackberry set about converting the NKVD into a 'secret sect' of sacred executioners. Yezhov despatched Yagoda's officers to inspect the provinces and then arrested them on the train. Three thousand Chekists were to be executed. Security chief Pauker and Stalin's brother-in-law Redens remained in their posts. Between 19 and 21 March, Yezhov summoned the surviving Chekists to the Officers' Club. There, the diminutive Commissar-General announced that Yagoda had been a German spy since 1907 (when he joined the Party) and was also a corrupt thief. Yezhov referred absurdly to his own tininess: 'I may be small in stature but my hands are strong – Stalin's hands.' The killing would be deliberately random: 'There will be some innocent victims in this fight against Fascist agents,' Yezhov told them. 'We are launching a major attack on the Enemy; let there be no resentment if we bump someone with an elbow. Better that ten innocent people should suffer than one spy get away. When you chop wood, chips fly.'

19

The Massacre of Generals, Fall
of Yagoda, and Death of a Mother

Yezhov 'discovered' that Yagoda had tried to poison him by spraying mercury on to the curtains of his office. It later emerged that Yezhov had faked this outrage. None the less, Yagoda was arrested at his Kremlin apartment, even before the Politburo had formally given the order. The power of the Politburo was officially delegated to the so-called 'Five', Stalin, Molotov, Voroshilov, Kaganovich and Yezhov, even though the latter was not a member.

The search of Yagoda's residences – he had two apartments in central Moscow and the luxurious dacha – revealed the debauchery of NKVD élite in the list of his possessions. His pornographic collection contained 3,904 photographs plus eleven early pornographic movies. His career as a womanizer was amply illustrated by the female clothing he kept in his apartment which sounds as if he was running a lingerie store not a police force, but then the NKVD bosses could never resist exploiting their power. There were 9 foreign female coats, 4 squirrel coats, 3 sealskin cloaks, another in Astrakhan wool, 31 pairs of female shoes, 91 female berets, 22 female hats, 130 pairs of foreign silk stockings, 10 female belts, 13 bags, 11 female suits, 57 blouses, 69 nighties, 31 female jackets, another 70 pairs of silk tights, 4 silk shawls – plus a collection of 165 pornographic pipes and cigarette holders, and one rubber dildo.

Finally there was the macabre fetishism of the two labelled bullets that had been extracted from the brains of Zinoviev and Kamenev. Like holy relics in a depraved distortion of the apostolic succession, Yezhov inherited them, storing them in his office.

Yagoda, accused of diamond-dealing and corruption, complaisantly implicated the next generation of victims, guided by Yezhov, who ensured that his own protégés were left out, before the testimonies were sent over to Stalin. Within three weeks of his interrogation, starting on 2 April, Yezhov was reporting that Yagoda admitted encouraging Rykov to resist the

Party in the late twenties: 'You act. I won't touch you.' Then he denounced Pauker and confessed to the sprinkling of mercury around Blackberry's office. More importantly, Yagoda implicated Abel Yenukidze for planning a coup along with Marshal Tukhachevsky, Stalin's old enemy from the Civil War. By the time of his trial, along with Bukharin and Rykov, Yagoda had confessed to the medical murders of Gorky and his son and to the assassination of Kirov.

In his private hell, he knew his family and friends faced destruction with him: the rule in Stalin's world was that when a man fell, all those connected to him, whether friends, lovers or protégés, fell with him. His brother-in-law and father-in-law were soon shot, along with his salon of writers. Yagoda's sister and parents were exiled. Yagoda's father wrote to Stalin, disowning 'our only surviving son' for his 'grave crimes'. Two sons had given their lives for Bolshevism in earlier times. Now the 78-year-old jeweller of Nizhny Novgorod was losing the third. Both Yagoda's parents died in the camps.

Yagoda seemed to undergo a Damascene conversion. 'For the first time in my life, I'll have to tell the whole truth about myself,' the world-weary Chekist sighed as if it was a relief. Vladimir Kirshon, the writer whom Stalin had advised on his plays and who was to be shot soon afterwards, was placed as the stool pigeon in his cell. Yagoda asked what the town was saying about him, musing sadly:

'I simply want to ask you about Ida [his wife] and Timosha [his mistress, Gorky's daughter-in-law], the baby, my family, and to see some familiar faces before death.' He talked about death. 'If I was sure to be allowed to live, I'd bear the burden of admitting murdering' Gorky and his son. 'But it's intolerably hard to declare it historically in front of all, especially Timosha.' Yagoda told his interrogator, 'You can put down in your report to Yezhov that I said there must be a God after all. From Stalin I deserved nothing but gratitude for my faithful service; from God, I deserved the most severe punishment for having violated his commandments thousands of times. Now look where I am and judge for yourself: is there a God or not?'

Yagoda's belladonna bore fatal fruit: the Hungarian hairdresser and favourite of Kremlin children, Pauker, forty-four, was arrested on 15 April, guilty of knowing too much and living too well: Stalin no longer trusted the old-fashioned Chekists with foreign connections.

Pauker was shot quietly on 14 August 1937 – the first courtier to die. Yenukidze was arrested too and executed on 20 December. The NKVD now belonged to Stalin, who turned to the army.

* * *

On the evening of 1 May 1937, after the May Day Parade, there was the usual party at Voroshilov's but the mood was effervescent with blood-lust and tension. Budyonny* recorded how Stalin talked openly about the imminent slaughter with his inner circle: it was time, he said, 'to finish with our enemies because they are in the army, in the staff, even in the Kremlin'. It is often claimed, that Stalin planned the Terror alone with Yezhov and Molotov: this proves that, even socially, he was open with his entire circle, from his doctors to the Politburo, that they were about to 'finish with' their enemies across the whole regime. 'We must finish with them, not looking at their faces.' Budyonny guessed that this meant Marshal Tukhachevsky and senior commanders like Jonah Yakir and Jan Garmarnik, all of whom had been standing on the Mausoleum with them earlier that day. Budyonny claimed that he hoped this was not so. Yet the archives show how Voroshilov and Budyonny had been urging Stalin to 'destroy' Enemies within the Red Army for over a year. It is most likely that Voroshilov's guests not only backed Stalin but wildly encouraged him: a year earlier, Voroshilov, for example, sent Stalin an intelligence intercept of the German Embassy's reports to Berlin on how Tukhachevsky had suddenly ceased to be a 'Francophile' and now displayed 'big respect for the German Army'.

Tukhachevsky, Stalin's Civil War foe and probably his most talented general, was bound to be his main target. That 'refined nobleman, handsome, clever and able', as Kaganovich described him, did not suffer fools gladly which was why he was hated by Voroshilov and Budyonny. The dashing womanizer was so forceful and charismatic that Stalin nicknamed him 'Napoleonchik', while Kaganovich paraphrased Bonaparte's dictum: 'Tukhachevsky hid Napoleon's baton in his rucksack.'

He was as ruthless as any Bolshevik, using poison gas on peasant rebels. In the late twenties and early thirties, this 'entrepreneur of military ideas', as a recent historian calls him,

---

* Semyon Budyonny published his conventional, cautious memoirs long after Stalin's death but his personal notes, seventy-six mainly unpublished pages preserved by his daughter, provide fascinating glimpses of the time. I am grateful to Nina Budyonny for allowing me to use them.

advocated a huge expansion of the Red Army and the creation of mechanized forces to be deployed in so-called 'deep operations': he understood the era of Panzers and air power which brought him into conflict with Stalin's cronies, still living for cavalry charges and armoured trains. Stalin tried to indict Tukhachevsky for treason in 1930 but Sergo among others resisted and helped bring him back as Deputy Defence Commissar. But there was another row with the touchy, vindictive Voroshilov in May 1936. Voroshilov became so heated with Tukhachevsky's justified criticism that he shouted 'Fuck you!' They made up but it was just at that time that the first of the Red Army generals was arrested and interrogated to implicate Tukhachevsky. More generals were mentioned in the January trial. Yagoda, Yenukidze and the benighted generals delivered more kindling for this bonfire.

On 11 May, Tukhachevsky was sacked as Deputy Commissar and demoted to the Volga District. On the 13th, Stalin put his hand on Tukhachevsky's shoulder and promised he would soon be back in Moscow. He was as good as his word, for on the 22nd, Tukhachevsky was arrested and returned to Moscow. Yezhov and Voroshilov orchestrated the arrest of virtually the whole high command.

Yezhov took personal control of the interrogations. At a meeting with Stalin, Vyshinsky curried favour by recommending the use of torture.

'See for yourself,' Stalin ordered his Blackberry, who rushed back to the Lubianka to supervise the Marshal's agonies, 'but Tukhachevsky should be forced to tell everything ... It's impossible he acted alone.' Tukhachevsky was tortured.

Amidst this drama, Stalin's mother died on 13 May 1937, aged seventy-seven. Three professors and two doctors signed her death certificate, testifying to her cardiosclerosis. Poskrebyshev approved the official announcements.* Stalin himself wrote out his note for her wreath in Georgian, which read: 'Dear and beloved mother from her son Joseph Djugashvili', using his original name perhaps to signify the distance between Soso and Stalin. Embroiled in the Tukhachevsky plot, he did not attend the funeral: Beria, his wife and son Sergo presided in his stead but later Stalin asked about it as if guilty about not being there.

---

* Her apartment contained busts of Stalin and portraits of Lenin and Stalin. She owned 505 roubles in bonds but left 42 roubles and 20 kopeks in cash and 4,533 roubles to her lady friends plus lottery tickets worth 3 roubles. In her bedroom, there were a few packs of cigarettes, and more portraits of Stalin and, tellingly, Beria.

A few days later, as Yezhov buzzed in and out of Stalin's office, a broken Marshal Tukhachevsky confessed that Yenukidze had recruited him in 1928, that he was a German agent in cahoots with Bukharin to seize power. Tukhachevsky's confession, which survives in the archives, is dappled with a brown spray that was found to be blood spattered by a body in motion.

Stalin had to convince the Politburo of the soldiers' guilt. Yakir, one of the arrested commanders, was best friends with Kaganovich who was called into the Politburo and interrogated by Stalin about this friendship. Kaganovich reminded Stalin that it was he who had insisted on promoting Yakir, at which the *Vozhd* muttered, 'Right, I remember ... The matter's closed.' Faced with the amazing confessions beaten out of the generals, Kaganovich believed 'that there was a conspiracy of officers'. Mikoyan too was friends with many arrested. Stalin read him extracts from Uborevich's confessions as a German spy:

'It's incredible,' admitted Stalin, 'but it's a fact, they admit it.' They even signed on each page to avoid 'falsification'.

'I know Uborevich very well,' said Mikoyan. 'A most honest man.' So Stalin reassured him that the military themselves would judge the generals: 'They know the case and they'll figure out what's true and what's not.'

Stalin tossed Deputy Premier Rudzutak into this broth perhaps *pour encourager les autres*, the first of the Politburo (a candidate member) to be arrested. 'He indulged too much in partying with Philistine friends,' recalled Molotov, which in Bolshevik doublespeak meant cultured friends. Becoming something of a bon viveur, 'he kept his distance from us'. Typical of Stalin's allies in the twenties, he was unreliable, even accusing Stalin of slandering him just after Kirov's assassination. 'You're wrong, Rudzutak,' Stalin had replied. He was arrested at dinner with some actors – it was said that the ladies were still wearing the rags of their ball gowns in the Lubianka weeks later. 'He was entangled ... mixed up with devil knows what kind of people, with women ...' said Molotov, and, added Kaganovich, 'young girls'. Perhaps he was shot for conviviality. Yet Molotov explained, 'I think consciously he was not a participant [in a conspiracy]', but he was guilty none the less: 'One must not act on personal impressions. After all we had materials incriminating him.' The NKVD now began to arrest many of the Old Bolsheviks, especially those obstinate Georgian 'old farts' who had crossed Stalin.

At first the leadership were actually canvassed on arrests, according to Party tradition: the signed votes in the archives capture the vile frenzy of this process. Usually the leaders just voted 'For' or 'Agreed' but sometimes in their desperation to show their bloodthirstiness, they added rabid exclamations:* 'Unconditionally yes,' wrote Budyonny on the arrests of Tukhachevsky and Rudzutak. 'It's necessary to finish off this scum.' Marshal Yegorov, whose actress wife (Stalin's flirtation at that dinner in November 1932) was already under investigation, wrote: 'All these traitors to be wiped off the face of the earth as the most hostile enemies and disgusting scum.'

On 1 June, Stalin, Voroshilov and Yezhov gathered over a hundred commanders in the Kremlin and broke the news that their high command overwhelmingly consisted of German agents. Voroshilov unveiled this 'counter-revolutionary conspiracy fascist organization', admitting he himself was close to the conspirators. He was guilty of not wanting to believe it! The next day, Stalin spoke, conjuring a miasma of mystery over the terrified meeting:

'I hope no one doubts that a military–political conspiracy existed,' he threatened, explaining that Tukhachevsky had been suborned by Trotsky, Bukharin, Rykov, Yenukidze, Yagoda and Rudzutak. As in any good spy novel, Stalin sought to *chercher la femme*, playing on Tukhachevsky and Yenukidze's womanizing. 'There's one experienced female spy in Germany, in Berlin ... Josephine Heinze ... she's a beautiful woman ... She recruited Yenukidze. She helped recruit Tukhachevsky.' Officers were actually arrested during the meeting so it was hardly surprising the survivors supported Stalin.

Voroshilov revelled in his vengeance. 'I never trusted Tukhachevsky, I never particularly trusted Uborevich ... They were scoundrels ...' he declared to the Defence Commissariat, embroidering Stalin's tale of sexual depravity. 'Comrades,' he said, 'we have not purged everyone yet. I personally don't doubt there are people who thought they were only talking, that's all. They chattered: "It would be a good thing to kill Stalin and Voroshilov"

---

* Sometimes they realized they had not been vicious enough, hence Veinberg wrote: 'Today when I voted for the expulsion of Rudzutak and Tukhachevsky from the Central Committee, I remembered that in voting for the expulsion of ... Eliava and Orakhelashvili, I accidentally forgot to add the words "and removal of their files to the NKVD" so I inform you I'm voting for the expulsion of all these traitors but also the removal of their files to the NKVD.'

Stalin's friendship was suffocating. After Nadya's death, Sergei Kirov, handsome, easy-going Leningrad boss, became Stalin's closest friend – here, he holidays with Stalin and Svetlana at Sochi. But there was tension when Kirov became dangerously popular. Did Stalin arrange his death?

Even before Kirov's assassination, Andrei Zhdanov, ebullient, burly yet frail, pretentious, self-important and ruthless, became Stalin's favourite – the only other magnate who qualified as his 'fellow intellectual'. Here, Zhdanov joins the family, probably at the Coldstream dacha (from left): Vasily, Zhdanov, Svetlana, Stalin and Yakov. *Right* On the same occasion, Stalin and Svetlana.

The Court of the Red Tsar in the mid-1930s. Stalin is surrounded by his male comrades and the circle of outspoken, bossy women who ultimately became over-familiar and paid the price. On 21 December 1934, still reeling from the assassination of Kirov, the courtiers, family and grandees gathered for Stalin's birthday at his Kuntsevo dacha and were photographed by General Vlasik. Lakoba and Beria arrived late. (Back row standing, from left): Stan Redens, Kaganovich, Molotov, Alyosha Svanidze, Anna Alliluyeva Redens; Vlas Chubar, Dora Khazan (married to Andreyev); Andrei Andreyev; Zinaida Ordzhonikidze; Pavel Alliluyev. (Middle Row): Maria Svanidze; Maria Kaganovich; Sashiko Svanidze; Stalin; Polina Molotova; Voroshilov. (Front row): unknown, possibly Shalva Eliava; Lakoba; possibly Lakoba's wife; Sergo Ordzhonikidze; Zhenya Alliluyeva; Bronislava Poskrebysheva; unknown; and at the bottom front Beria, Mikoyan and Poskrebyshev.

Stalin's women: his beaming mistress Zhenya Alliluyeva sits at his feet in her lace collar; she said what she liked to Stalin and it made her enemies. Pretty Bronislava Poskrebysheva, sits to the right of Zhenya. Bronislava's daughter claims she was also Stalin's mistress. Nonetheless she was liquidated.

Stalin micro-managed the theatre as he dominated cinema, literature and politics. The grandees ate in the avant-loge behind the box in between scenes. Here, in the former imperial box at the Bolshoi, sits (from left): Voroshilov, Kaganovich, Stalin, Sergo Ordzhonikidze, Mikoyan and their wives.

Stalin's mother Keke possessed the same sardonic and mocking wit as her son. They were not close but Stalin sent dutiful letters, leaving Beria to act as his surrogate son. Shortly before her death when he was on holiday in Georgia, Beria arranged for him to visit the ailing Keke. Former friends, now bitter rivals, Beria and Lakoba sit behind mother and son in her bedroom.

Left Like three boulevardiers in the sun, Beria, Caucasian viceroy (centre) hosts Voroshilov and Mikoyan (right) in Tiflis for the Rustaveli Festival at the height of the Terror, 1937.

Below A Jewish jeweller's son with a knowledge of poisons, and ruthless ambition, Genrikh Yagoda was the NKVD boss who had reservations about the Terror. Stalin threatened to punch him in the face. Yagoda enjoyed the good life: collecting wines, growing orchids, courting Gorky's daughter-in-law, amassing ladies underwear, and buying German pornographic films and obscene cigarette holders. Left to right: Yagoda in uniform, Kalinin, Stalin, Molotov, Vyshinsky, Beria.

Marshal Semyon Budyonny, swaggering Cossack horseman and hero of Tsaritsyn, famous for his handlebar moustaches, white teeth and equine level of intelligence, poses with Kaganovich on the left and Stalin amongst swooning females. Budyonny proved a better general than most of Stalin's cavalry cronies, but he was happiest breeding horses, which he believed were more useful than tanks.

The two most depraved monsters of Stalin's court. At the 17th Congress in 1934 when they joined the leadership (but before their rise to supreme power), Beria and Yezhov, a rising Central Committee official, hug for the camera. Yezhov was an ambitious fanatic, good-natured if prone to illness, a bisexual dwarf who was liked by everyone until he was promoted to NKVD boss in 1936 and became Stalin's frenzied killer. Beria was an unscrupulous but able and intelligent secret policeman. In 1938, he was brought to Moscow to destroy Yezhov whose execution he supervised.

Left Ascendant grandee Yezhov (hugging his adopted daughter Natasha) and his promiscuous literary wife Yevgenia, who slept with writers from Isaac Babel to Mikhail Sholokhov, entertain their powerful friend, Sergo Ordzhonikidze. Yezhov would soon help Stalin harass Sergo to his death. Yevgenia Yezhova became the 'black widow' of Stalin's circle: many of her lovers, including Babel, died because of their connections to her. She sacrificed herself to try to save their daughter Natasha. *Above right* Sergo and Yezhov

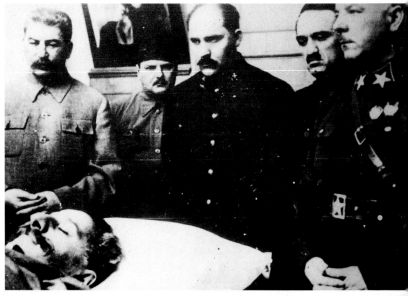

As the Terror gained pace, Sergo Ordzhonikidze clashed with Stalin. A shot rang out in Sergo's flat. His mysterious death solved a problem for Stalin who rushed to his Kremlin apartment where Sergo was lifted onto his table for this photograph. Stalin, Zhdanov (in a comical anti-headache bandage), Kaganovich, Mikoyan and Voroshilov pose with the body. Kaganovich and Mikoyan were especially close to Sergo and look particularly shocked.

In 1937, at the height of the Great Terror, two young magnates join the leadership: Yezhov, now NKVD boss in full uniform as Commissar-General of State Security (second from right) and (far right) his friend Nikita Khrushchev, newly appointed Moscow boss and later one of Stalin's successors, accompany Molotov, Kaganovich, Stalin, Mikoyan and Kalinin. Stalin trusted the ruthless bumpkin Khrushchev who described himself as the leader's 'pet'. He idolised Stalin.

Stalin regarded himself as an intellectual. He persuaded the famous novelist Gorky to return to become the regime's great writer, giving him a mansion in Moscow and two dachas outside. Gorky's house became the literary venue for the Politburo who visited regularly. There, Stalin told writers to become 'engineers of human souls'. Here, Stalin and Molotov (second from left) take tea with Gorky. When Stalin became disenchanted with Gorky, his death in 1936 proved convenient.

When she tipsily dropped a cream cake on his tunic, Poskrebyshev fell in love with a pretty, glamorous and well-connected young doctor Bronislava who became familiar with Stalin and his family. But her Jewish, Lithuanian origins, her friendship with Yezhov's wife and, worst of all, her distant connection to Trotsky led to her arrest by Beria and execution. Poskrebyshev wept when he heard her name, but remained working at Stalin's side, on good terms with Beria – and managed to remarry. Poskrebyshev with Bronislava (right) and her sister.

More powerful than many a magnate, Alexander Poskrebyshev (right) was Stalin's chef de cabinet for most of his reign. This former male nurse and master of detail ran the office and kept the secrets while at the leader's dinners, Stalin challenged him to drinking contests, nicknamed him the 'commander-in-chief' and laughed when he was dragged vomiting from the table.

Poskrebyshev ran the politics but General Nikolai Vlasik, Stalin's chief bodyguard and court photographer, ran his home life. This hard-drinking debauchee with a harem of 'concubines', also acted as Vasily Stalin's father figure. Here, just before the war, is Vlasik, on the left with Stalin's doomed son Yakov, probably at Kuntsevo.

Stalin remained close and affectionate with Svetlana but, by her early teens at the end of the 1930s, she was maturing early and this alarmed her father. When she sent him this photograph of her sporting her Young Pioneer's uniform, he sent it back scrawling, 'Your expression is not suitable for someone your age.' When she fell in love with an older man in the middle of the Second World War, Stalin was appalled and it destroyed their relationship for ever. Henceforth his fondest epithet to her was 'You little fool.'

... Our government will exterminate such people.'

'Right,' shouted his applauding audience.

'They were degenerates,' said Voroshilov. 'Filthy in their private lives!'

On 9 June, Vyshinsky interviewed the accused and reported to Stalin twice, arriving at the Little Corner at 10.45 p.m. The Politburo reviewed the officers' appeals, passing them round the table. On Yakir's plea, Stalin wrote:

'A scoundrel and a prostitute.'

'A completely precise description,' Voroshilov slavishly added. Molotov signed but Yakir's best friend, Kaganovich, almost had to dance on his grave:

'For this traitor, bastard and s—t, there is only one punishment – execution.'

On the 11th, the Supreme Court convened a special military tribunal to try the 'traitors'. The reptilian Ulrikh represented the Military Collegium but the key judges were the Marshals themselves. Budyonny was one of the most active, accusing them of 'wrecking' by urging the formation of armoured divisions.

'I feel I'm dreaming,' Tukhachevsky remarked of the accusations. There was no mention of Josephine, the gorgeous German spy. Ominously, many of the generals were accused of serving a 'second Motherland', Yakir being a Bessarabian Jew. Most of the judges were terrified: 'Tomorrow I'll be put in the same place,' one of them, Corps Commander Belov, told his friends afterwards. (He was right.) All were sentenced to death at 23.35 that day. Ulrikh rushed over to report to Stalin who, waiting with Molotov, Kaganovich and Yezhov, did not examine the sentences. He just said: 'Agreed.' Yezhov returned with Ulrikh to supervise the executions which took place within the hour early on the morning of 12 June. As ever, Stalin was sadistically curious.

'What were Tukhachevsky's last words?' Stalin asked Yezhov.

'The snake said he was dedicated to the Motherland and Comrade Stalin. He asked for clemency. But it was obvious he was not being straight, he hadn't laid down his arms.'

All the judges were later shot except Ulrikh, Budyonny and Shaposhnikov. If Budyonny had any doubts about supporting the Terror, the NKVD arrived to arrest him soon after the trial. He pulled out a pistol and threatened to kill the Chekists while he telephoned Stalin who cancelled the arrest. His wife was not so fortunate.

Voroshilov unleashed a massive purge of the army, personally demanding the arrests of three hundred officers in letters to the NKVD:* by 29 November 1938, Voroshilov boasted that 40,000 had been arrested and 100,000 new officers promoted. Three of the five marshals, fifteen of the sixteen commanders, sixty of the sixty-seven corps commanders, and all seventeen commissars were shot. Stalin earnestly encouraged the witchhunt at informal meetings with officers:

'We don't know up to now whether we can speak openly about Enemies of the People or not ...' naval commander Laukhin asked.

'To speak in public?' responded Stalin.

'No, here, internally?'

'We must – it's obligatory!' answered Stalin. The commanders discussed individual officers:

'Gorbatov is now worried,' reported Kulikov, a divisional commander in Ukraine.

'Why should he worry,' replied Stalin, 'if he is an honest man?'

'I wouldn't say he is pure. He was clearly connected,' said Kulikov.

'Is he scared?' asked Stalin.

The army had been the last force capable of stopping Stalin, reason enough for the destruction of its High Command. It is possible that the generals knew about Stalin's record as an Okhrana double agent and had considered action. The usual explanation is that German disinformation persuaded Stalin that they were plotting a coup. Hitler's spymaster, Heydrich, had concocted such evidence that was passed to Stalin by the well-meaning Czech President Beneš. But no German evidence was used at Tukhachevsky's trial – nor was it necessary. Stalin needed neither Nazi disinformation nor mysterious Okhrana files to persuade him to destroy Tukhachevsky. After all, he had played with the idea as early as 1930, three years before Hitler took power. Furthermore, Stalin and his cronies were convinced that officers were to be distrusted and physically exterminated at the slightest suspicion. He reminisced to Voroshilov, in an undated note, about the officers arrested in the summer of 1918. 'These

---

* A typically sinister note from Voroshilov to Yezhov read like this: 'N(ikolai) I(vanovich)! Nikolayev inquired whether Uritsky should be arrested. When can you take him in? You've already managed to take in Slavin and Bazenkov. It would be good if you could take in Todorovsky ... KV.' All named, except Todorovsky, were shot.

officers', he wrote, 'we wanted to shoot en masse.' Nothing had changed.

Voroshilov was assisted in this slaughter by one man who personified the tragedy that was to befall the Red Army. Stalin and Yezhov planned the publicity with the editor of *Pravda*, Lev Mekhlis, one of the most extraordinary of all his courtiers who now exploded on to the national stage, transformed from the scourge of the media to a military Mephistopheles, compared to a 'shark' and a 'gloomy demon'. Even Stalin called him a 'fanatic', found him hard to restrain, and enjoyed telling stories of his 'ludicrous zeal'.

With a nimbus-like plumage of black hair and a pointed, bird-like face, Mekhlis played a part as large in his way as Molotov or Beria. Born in Odessa in 1889 of Jewish parents, leaving school at fourteen, he only joined the Bolsheviks in 1918 after working with the Jewish Social Democratic Party but he served as a ruthless commissar in the Crimea during the Civil War, executing thousands. He first met Stalin during the Polish campaign, becoming one of his assistants, learning all the secrets. Devoted to 'my dear Comrade Stalin', for whom he worked in a neurotic, blood-curdling frenzy, he was too energetic and talented to remain hidden in the back rooms like Poskrebyshev. Married to a Jewish doctor, he placed Lenin's portrait with a red ribbon in his baby's cot and recorded the reactions of this New Man in a special diary. In 1930, Stalin appointed him *Pravda* editor where his management of writers was impressively brutal.*

---

* Just after the announcement of the shooting of the generals, Mekhlis discovered that the 'Proletarian Poet' Demian Bedny was resisting orders and secretly writing Dantean verses under the pseudonym Conrad Rotkehempfer. But Mekhlis immediately wrote to Stalin: 'What should I do? He explained it was his own literary method.' Stalin replied with dripping sarcasm: 'I'm answering with a letter you can read to Demian. To the new apparent Dante, alias Conrad, oh actually to Demian Bedny, the fable or poem 'Fight or Die' is mediocre. As a criticism of Fascism, it's unoriginal and faded. As a criticism of Soviet construction (not joking) it's silly but transparent. It's junk but since we [Soviet people] have a lot of junk around, we must increase the supply of other kinds of literature with another fable ... I understand that I must say sorry to Demian-Dante for my frankness.' Mekhlis locked Stalin's letters in his safe whence he extracted them to impress journalists whom he asked if they recognized the handwriting. 'In the middle of the night of 21 July,' he reported urgently to Stalin, 'I invited Bedny to criticize his poem' and to hear Stalin's damning letter. Bedny just said, 'I'm crazy ... maybe I'm too old. Maybe I should go to the country and grow cabbages.' Even this comment struck Mekhlis as suspicious and he floated the idea of arresting Bedny: 'Maybe he's implicated.' Stalin did not rise. Bedny was cut from Stalin's circle but remained free, dying in 1945.

Mekhlis, who left the Tsarist army as a bombardier, was now promoted to Deputy Defence Commissar, Head of its Political Department, descending on the army like a galloping horse of the Apocalypse. Stalin and his Five now devised an astonishing lottery of slaughter designed to kill a whole generation.

20

Blood Bath by Numbers

They did not even specify the names but simply assigned quotas of deaths by the thousands. On 2 July 1937, the Politburo ordered local Secretaries to arrest and shoot 'the most hostile anti-Soviet elements' who were to be sentenced by *troikas*, three-man tribunals that usually included the local Party Secretary, Procurator and NKVD chief.

The aim was 'to finish off once and for all' all Enemies and those impossible to educate in socialism, so as to accelerate the erasing of class barriers and therefore the bringing of paradise for the masses. This final solution was a slaughter that made sense in terms of the faith and idealism of Bolshevism which was a religion based on the systematic destruction of classes. The principle of ordering murder like industrial quotas in the Five-Year Plan was therefore natural. The details did not matter: if Hitler's destruction of the Jews was genocide, then this was democide, the class struggle spinning into cannibalism. On 30 July, Yezhov and his deputy Mikhail Frinovsky proposed Order No. 00447 to the Politburo: that between 5 and 15 August, the regions were to receive quotas for two categories: Category One – to be shot. Category Two – to be deported. They suggested that 72,950 should be shot and 259,450 arrested, though they missed some regions. The regions could submit further lists. The families of these people should be deported too. The Politburo confirmed this order the next day.

Soon this 'meat-grinder' achieved such a momentum, as the witch hunt approached its peak and as the local jealousies and ambitions spurred it on, that more and more were fed into the machine. The quotas were soon fulfilled by the regions who therefore asked for bigger numbers, so between 28 August and 15 December, the Politburo agreed to the shooting of another 22,500 and then another 48,000. In this, the Terror differed most from Hitler's crimes which systematically destroyed a limited target:

Jews and Gypsies. Here, on the contrary, death was sometimes
random: the long-forgotten comment, the flirtation with an
opposition, envy of another man's job, wife or house, vengeance
or just plain coincidence brought the death and torture of entire
families. This did not matter: 'Better too far than not far enough,'
Yezhov told his men as the original arrest quota ballooned to
767,397 arrests and 386,798 executions, families destroyed,
children orphaned, under Order No. 00447.*

Simultaneously, Yezhov attacked 'national contingents' – this
was murder by nationality, against Poles and ethnic Germans
among others. On 11 August, Yezhov signed Order No. 00485 to
liquidate 'Polish diversionists and espionage groups' which was to
consume most of the Polish Communist Party, most Poles within
the Bolshevik leadership, anyone with social or 'consular
contacts' – and of course their wives and children. A total of
350,000 (144,000 of them Poles) were arrested in this operation,
with 247,157 shot (110,000 Poles) – a mini-genocide. As we will
see, this hit Stalin's own circle with especial force.† Altogether, the
latest estimates, combining the quotas and national contingents,
are that 1.5 million were arrested in these operations and about
700,000 shot.

'Beat, destroy without sorting out,' Yezhov ordered his henchmen. Those who showed 'operational inertness' in the arrests of
'counter-revolutionary formations within and outside the Party ...
Poles, Germans and kulaks' would themselves be destroyed, but
most now 'tried to surpass each other with reports about gigantic
numbers of people arrested'. Yezhov, clearly taking his cue from
the 'Five', actually specified that 'if during this operation, an extra

* There has been a debate between those such as Robert Conquest who insisted that
Stalin himself initiated and ran the Terror, and the so-called Revisionists who argued
that the Terror was created by pressure from ambitious young bureaucrats and by the
tensions between centre and regions. The archives have now proved Conquest right,
though it is true that the regions outperformed their quotas, showing that the
Revisionists were right, too, though missing the complete picture. The two views
therefore are completely complementary.
† 170,000 Koreans were also deported. Bulgarians and Macedonians were soon
added. Stalin was delighted by the Polish operation, writing on Yezhov's report: 'Very
good! Dig up and purge this Polish espionage mud in the future as well. Destroy it
in the interest of the USSR!' If Poles and Germans took the brunt of this operation,
other nations deported included Kurds, Greeks, Finns, Estonians, Iranians, Latvians,
Chinese, returnees from the Harbin railway and Romanians. Most exotically, the
NKVD shot 6,311 priests, lords and Communist officials, about 4 per cent of the
population in the satellite state of Mongolia where the Mongoloid parody of Stalin,
Marshal Choibalsang, also arrested and shot his own Tukhachevsky, Marshal Demid.

thousand people will be shot, that is not such a big deal.' Since Stalin and Yezhov constantly pushed up the quotas, an extra thousand here and there was inevitable but the point was that they deliberately destroyed an entire 'caste'. And, like Hitler's Holocaust, this was a colossal feat of management. Yezhov even specified what bushes should be planted to cover mass graves.

Once this massacre had started, Stalin almost disappeared from public view, appearing only to greet children and delegations. The rumour spread that he did not know what Yezhov was doing. Stalin spoke in public only twice in 1937 and once in 1938, cancelling all his holidays (he did not go southwards again until 1945). Molotov gave the 6 November addresses in both years. The writer Ilya Ehrenburg met Pasternak in the street: 'he waved his arms around as he stood between the snowdrifts: "If only someone would tell Stalin about it."' The theatrical director Meyerhold told Ehrenburg, 'They conceal it from Stalin'. But their friend, Isaac Babel, lover of Yezhov's wife, learned the 'key to the puzzle': 'Of course Yezhov plays his part but he's not at the bottom of it.'

Stalin was the mastermind but he was far from alone. Indeed, it is neither accurate nor helpful to blame the Terror on one man because systematic murder started soon after Lenin took power in 1917 and never stopped until Stalin's death. This 'social system based on blood-letting', justified murder now with the prospect of happiness later. The Terror was not just a consequence of Stalin's monstrosity but it was certainly formed, expanded and accelerated by his uniquely overpowering character, reflecting his malice and vindictiveness. 'The greatest delight,' he told Kamenev, 'is to mark one's enemy, prepare everything, avenge oneself thoroughly and then go to sleep.' It would not have happened without Stalin. Yet it also reflected the village hatreds of the incestuous Bolshevik sect where jealousies had seethed from the years of exile and war. Stalin and his faction regarded the Civil War as their finest hour: 1937 was a Tsaritsyn reunion, as Stalin even reminisced to a group of officers:

'We were in Tsaritsyn with Voroshilov,' he began. 'We exposed [Enemies] within a week, even though we didn't know military affairs. We exposed them because we judged them by their work and if today's political workers judge men by their actual work, we would soon expose the Enemies in our army.' The anti-Bolshevik resurgence in Germany was real enough, the Spanish war setting new standards for betrayal and brutality. Economic disasters were glaring: Molotov's papers reveal there was still famine and cannibalism,* even in 1937.

The corruption of grandees was notorious: Yagoda seemed to be running palaces and diamond deals out of official funds, Yakir renting out dachas like a landlord. The wives of marshals, such as Olga Budyonny and her friend Galina Yegorova, Stalin's fancy at Nadya's last supper, blossomed at embassies and 'salons, reminiscent of glittering receptions ... in aristocratic Russia' with 'dazzling company, stylish clothes'.

'Why have the prices flown upwards 100% while nothing is in the shops,' Maria Svanidze asked her diary. 'Where is the cotton, flax and wool when medals were won for beating the Plan? And the construction of private dachas ... crazy money spent on magnificent houses and resthomes?'

The responsibility lies with the hundreds of thousands of officials who ordered, or perpetrated, the murders. Stalin and the magnates enthusiastically, recklessly, almost joyfully, killed, and they usually killed many more than they were asked to kill. None was ever tried for these crimes.

Stalin was surprisingly open with his circle about the aim to 'finish off' all their Enemies. He could tell his cronies this quite openly at Voroshilov's May Day party, as reported by Budyonny. He seems to have constantly compared his Terror to Ivan the Terrible's massacre of the *boyars*. 'Who's going to remember all this riffraff in ten or twenty years time? No one. Who remembers the names now of the *boyars* Ivan the Terrible got rid of?† No one ... The people had to know he was getting rid of all of his enemies. In the end, they all got what they deserved.'

'The people understand, Joseph Vissarionovich, they understand and they support you,' replied Molotov. Similarly, he told Mikoyan, 'Ivan killed too few *boyars*. He should have killed them all, to create a strong state.' The magnates were not as oblivious of Stalin's nature as they later claimed.

---

* On 14 April 1937, Procurator-General Vyshinsky wrote to the Premier to inform him of a cluster of cases of cannibalism in Cheliabinsk in the Urals in which one woman ate a four-month-old child, another ate an eight-year-old with her thirteen-year-old, while yet another consumed her three-month-old baby.

† This is eerily like Hitler's comment on the genocide of the Jews, referring to the Turkish slaughter of the Armenians in 1915: 'After all, who today speaks of the massacre of the Armenians?'

While the regions fulfilled their nameless quotas, Stalin was also killing thousands whom he knew well. Yezhov visited Stalin virtually every day. Within a year and a half, 5 of the 15 Politburo members, 98 of the 139 Central Committee members and 1,108 of the 1,966 delegates from the Seventeenth Congress had been arrested. Yezhov delivered 383 lists of names – which were known as 'albums' since they often contained photographs and potted biographies of the suggested victims – and proposed: 'I request sanction to condemn them all under the First Category.'

Most of the death-lists were signed by Stalin, Molotov, Kaganovich and Voroshilov but many were also signed by Zhdanov and Mikoyan. On some days, for example 12 November 1938, Stalin and Molotov signed 3,167 executions. Usually they simply wrote: 'For', VMN or *Viskha*. Molotov admitted: 'I signed most – in fact almost all – the arrest lists. We debated and made a decision. Haste ruled the day. Could one go into all the details? ... Innocent people were sometimes caught. Obviously one or two out of ten were wrongly caught, but the rest rightly.' As Stalin had put it, 'Better an innocent head less, than hesitations in the war.' They ordered the deaths of 39,000 on these lists of names. Stalin marked lists with notes to Yezhov: 'Comrade Yezhov, those whose names I've marked "arr" should be arrested if not already.' Sometimes Stalin simply wrote: 'Shoot all 138 of them.' When Molotov received regional death-lists, he simply underlined the numbers, never the names. Kaganovich remembered the frenzy of that time: 'What emotions.' They were 'all responsible' and perhaps 'guilty of going too far'.

Stalin declared that the son should not suffer for the sins of the father but then carefully targeted the families of Enemies: this may have reflected his Caucasian mentality or merely the incestuous labyrinth of Bolshevik connections. 'They had to be isolated,' explained Molotov, 'otherwise they'd have spread all kinds of complaints.' On 5 July 1937, the Politburo ordered the NKVD to 'confine all wives of condemned traitors ... in camps for 5–8 years' and to take under State protection children under fifteen: 18,000 wives and 25,000 children were taken away. But this was not enough: on 15 August, Yezhov decreed that children between one and three were to be confined in orphanages but 'socially dangerous' children between three and fifteen could be imprisoned 'depending on the degree of danger'. Almost a million of these children were raised in orphanages and often did not see their mothers for twenty years.*

Stalin was the engine of this murderous machine. 'Now everything will be fine,' he wrote on 7 May 1937 to one of his killers who complained that he had not 'lost his teeth' but had become somewhat dazed: 'The sharper the teeth the better. J.St.' This is just one of the many notes in the newly opened archives that show not merely Stalin's bureaucratic orders but his personal involvement in encouraging even junior officials to slaughter their comrades. The teeth were never sharp enough.

While all the leaders could save some of their friends – and not others – Stalin himself could protect whoever he wished: his whims only added to his mystique. When his old friend from Georgia, Sergo Kavtaradze, was arrested, Stalin did not approve his death but put a dash next to Kavtaradze's name. This tiny crayon line saved his life. Another old friend, Ambassador Troyanovsky, appeared on a list: 'Do not touch,' wrote Stalin.† However much someone was denounced, Stalin's favour could be well nigh impregnable but once his trust was shattered, damnation was final though it might take years to come. The best way to survive was to be invisible because sometimes ghastly coincidences brought people into fatal contact with Stalin: Polish Communist Kostyrzewa was tending her roses near Kuntsevo when she found Stalin looking over her fence: 'What beautiful roses,' he said. She was arrested that night – though this was at the time of the anti-Polish spy mania and perhaps she was on the lists anyway.

Stalin often forgot – or pretended to forget – what had happened to certain comrades and years later assumed an air of disappointment when he heard they had been shot. 'You used to have such nice people,' he later remarked to Polish comrades. 'Vera Kostyrzewa for example, do you know what's become of her?' Even his remarkable Rolodex of a memory could not remember all his victims.

* This reached its climax when sixty children aged between ten and twelve were accused of forming 'a terrorist counter-revolutionary group' in Leninsk-Kuznetsk and were imprisoned for eight months, until the NKVD themselves were arrested and the children released.

† Stalin's papers contain fascinating glimpses of his interventions: a father denounced his son to the police for having too many outrageous parties but the boy was arrested and embroiled in a case against Tomsky. The father appealed to Stalin who wrote on his note: 'It's necessary to change the punishment!' The father wrote to thank Stalin.

Stalin enjoyed rattling his colleagues: one such was Stetsky, formerly in Bukharin's kindergarten of young protégés who had successfully joined Stalin's CC Cultural Department. Now Bukharin, at one of his 'confrontations' with his accusers, gave Stalin an old letter Stetsky had written criticizing him: 'Comrade Bukharin,' Stalin wrote to Stetsky, 'gave me your letter to him [from 1926–7] with the hint that everything about Stetsky is not always clean. I have not read the letter. I'm giving it back to you. With Communist greetings, Stalin.' Imagine Stetsky's terror on receiving this handwritten note. He wrote back immediately:

'Comrade Stalin, I've received your letter and thank you for your trust. On my letter ... written when I was not clean ... I belonged to the Bukharin group. Now I'm ashamed to remember it ...' He was arrested and shot.

Stalin played games even with his closest comrades: Budyonny, for example, had performed well at the trial but when the arrests reached his own staff, he went to Voroshilov to complain with a list of innocent men under investigation. Voroshilov was terrified: 'Speak to Stalin yourself.' Budyonny confronted Stalin:

'If these are the Enemy, who made the Revolution? It means we must be jailed too!'

'What are you saying, Semyon Mikhailovich?' Stalin laughed. 'Are you crazy?' He called in Yezhov: 'Budyonny here claims it's time to arrest us.' Budyonny claimed that he gave his list to Yezhov who released some of the officers.

Stalin himself specialized in reassuring his victims and then arresting them. Early in the year, the wife of one of Ordzhonikidze's deputies at Heavy Industry was called by Stalin himself: 'I hear you're going about on foot. That's no good ... I'll send you a car.' Next morning the limousine was there. Two days later, her husband was arrested.

The generals, diplomats, spies and writers, who had served in the Spanish War, sunk in a quagmire of betrayals, assassinations, defeats, Trotskyite intrigues and denunciations, were decimated even when they had apparently done little wrong. Stalin's Ambassador to Madrid, Antonov-Ovseenko, an ex-Trotskyite, entangled himself by trying to prove his loyalty; he was recalled, affably promoted by Stalin, and arrested the next day. When Stalin received the journalist Mikhail Koltsov, he teased him about his adventures in the Spanish Civil War, calling him 'Don Miguel', but then asked: 'You don't intend to shoot yourself? So long, Don Miguel.' But Koltsov had played a deadly game in Spain, denouncing others to Stalin and Voroshilov. The 'Don' was arrested.

Stalin's office was bombarded with notes of execution from the regions: a typical one on 21 October 1937, listed eleven shot in Saratov, eight in Leningrad then another twelve, then six in Minsk then another five … a total of 82. There are hundreds of such lists, addressed to Stalin and Molotov. On the other hand, Stalin received a stream of miserable cries for help. Bonch-Bruevich whose daughter was married into Yagoda's circle, insisted:

'Believe me, dear Joseph Vissarionovich, I'd bring a son or daughter to the NKVD myself if they were against the Party …' Stalin's own secretary from the twenties, Kanner, who had been in charge of his dirty tricks against Trotsky and others, was arrested. 'Kanner cannot be a villain,' wrote a certain Makarova, perhaps his wife. 'He was friends with Yagoda but who could think the Narkom of Security could be such scum? Believe, Comrade Stalin, that Kanner deserved your trust!' Kanner was shot.

Often the appeals were from Old Bolsheviks who had been close friends, such as Vano Djaparidze whose tragic letter read: 'My daughter's been arrested. I cannot imagine what she could have done. I ask you dear Joseph Vissarionovich to ease the terrible destiny of my daughter …'

Then he received letters from doomed leaders desperate to save themselves: 'I am unable to work, it's not a question of Partymindedness, but it's impossible for me not to act on the situation around me and to clear the air and understand the reason for it … Please give me a moment of your time to receive me …' wrote Nikolai Krylenko, the People's Commissar of Justice no less and signer of many a death sentence. He too was shot.

Yezhov was the chief organizer of the Terror, with Molotov, Kaganovich and Voroshilov as enthusiastic accomplices. But all the magnates had the power over life and death: years later Khrushchev remembered his power over a junior agronomist who crossed him:

'Well of course I could have done anything I wanted with him, I could have destroyed him, I could have arranged it so that, you know, he would disappear from the face of the earth.'

21

'The Blackberry' at Work and Play

Stalin received Yezhov 1,100 times during the Terror, second only to Molotov in frequency – and this only counted formal appointments in the Little Corner. There must have been many meetings at the dacha. The archives show how Stalin noted down those to be arrested in little lists to discuss with the 'Blackberry': on 2 April 1937, for example, he writes in his blue and red pencils to Yezhov a list of six points, many ominous, such as 'Purge State Bank'.* Sometimes Stalin gave him a lift home to his dacha.

Yezhov followed a punishing schedule of work, intensified by the terrible deeds he supervised and the pressure, from both above and below, to arrest and kill more: he lived the Stalinist nocturnal existence and was constantly exhausted, becoming paler and nervier. We now know how he worked: he tended to sleep in the morning, dine at home with his wife, meet his deputy Frinovsky for a drink at their dachas – and then drive to Butyrki or Lubianka to supervise the interrogations and tortures. Since Yezhov had been in the top echelons of the Party for about seven years, he often knew his victims personally. In June 1937, he signed off on the arrest of his 'godfather' Moskvin and his wife, whose house he had often visited. Both were shot. He could be brutal. When Bulatov, who had run a CC Department alongside Yezhov and had visited his home, was being interrogated for the fifth time, the Commissar-General appeared through a door in the wall:

'Well, is Bulatov testifying?'

'Not at all, Comrade Commissar-General!' replied the interrogator.

'Then lay it on him good!' he snapped and departed. But sometimes he clearly found his job difficult: when he had to witness the execution of a friend, he looked distressed. 'I see in

* Yezhov replied in black: 'In addition to the copy of Uzakovsky's report sent to you, I sent another one of 7th Division of GUGB [State Security] about the activities of Chinese-Trotskyites. Yezhov.'

your eyes that you feel sorry for me!' said the friend. Yezhov was flustered but ordered the executioners to fire. When another old buddy was arrested, Yezhov seemed moved but drunkenly ordered his men 'to cut off his ears and nose, put out his eyes, cut him to pieces', yet this was for show: he then chatted to his friend late into the night but he too was shot. The Politburo greatly admired Yezhov who, thought Molotov, 'wasn't spotless but he was a good Party worker'.

Sometimes, amidst all the murder and thuggery, Yezhov showed his old side. When he received Stalin's doctor, Vinogradov, who had to testify in the upcoming Bukharin trial against his own teacher, Yezhov tipsily advised him: 'You're a good person but you talk too much. Bear in mind that every third person is my person and informs me of everything. I recommend you talk less.'

The Commissar-General was at his peak. On holidays, Yezhov was filmed strolling through the Kremlin, laughing with Stalin while absurdly smoking what appears to be a very big cigarette. During the long November 6th speeches at the Bolshoi Theatre, US Ambassador Davies watched 'Stalin, Voroshilov and Yezhov obviously whispering and joking among themselves'. *Pravda* hailed him as 'an unyielding Bolshevik who without getting up from his desk, night and day, is unravelling and cutting the threads of the Fascist conspiracy'. Towns and stadiums were named after him.* For the Kazakh 'bard' Dzhambul Dzhabaev, he was 'a flame, burning the serpents' nests'.

He and Yevgenia now lived luxuriously in a dacha, with the usual cinema, tennis court and staff, at Meshcherino near Leninskie Gorki where many leaders had their homes. They had adopted a daughter, Natasha, an orphan from a children's home. Yezhov was tender, teaching her to play tennis, skate and bicycle. In the photographs, he stands next to his friends, hugging Natasha like any other father. He spoiled her with presents and played with her on his return from work.

When Yezhov began to feed foreign Communists and returned émigrés into the meat-grinder, he received an appeal from an anxious, pretty and very pregnant Russian émigré named Vera

---

* His huge portraits were borne past the Mausoleum on all the State holidays. The pun on the resemblance of his name to the 'steel gauntlet' had now spawned vast posters showing his iron grip 'strangling the snakes' with the heads of Trotsky, Rykov and Bukharin. The other Yezhovite slogan read: '*Yezhovy rukavitsy* – rule with an iron rod!'

Trail, who was the daughter of Alexander Guchkov, the pre-revolutionary liberal. She received a call after midnight:

'Kremlin speaking. The Comrade Commissar will see you now.' A limousine took her into the Kremlin where she was led in to his long, dimly lit study with a green lampshade. The aphrodisiac of power working its wonders, she immediately admired his 'finely chiselled face', his 'brown wavy hair and blue eyes – the deepest blue I'd ever seen' and his 'small graceful slender hands'. She mentioned a list of friends, mainly writers, who had been arrested. He was acutely perceptive, 'a marvellous listener'. Blackberry dismissed his guards to receive her: 'I certainly don't make the habit of receiving total strangers unprotected.'

'I'm not even carrying a handbag,' she flirted back at him.

'No, only Belomor cigarettes. But you said you were pregnant.'

'Said? Can't you see?' Her belly was enormous.

'I see a bulge,' joked Yezhov, 'but how am I to know it's not a time-bomb cleverly wrapped in a pillow? You weren't searched ... were you?' Yezhov stood up and walked around the desk as if he was about to feel her belly but halfway he stopped and sat down, laughing:

'Of course you're pregnant. I was only joking.' Here was an authentic Yezhovian moment in which the Commissar displayed his clunkingly puerile humour (though thankfully, an improvement on the farting contests), the swagger of menace – and his paranoia. He promised to review her case and receive her again, kindly suggesting that she must go straight to bed. The next night, Yezhov's office called again:

'Leave for Paris at once.' She left on the train the next morning and was convinced that he had, for whatever reason, gone out of his way to save her life. Every one of the friends on her list were destroyed – but he saved her.

Yet personal attraction was rarely a reason to save the life of an Enemy: Blackberry had enjoyed a love affair with another Yevgenia, the wife of the Ambassador to Poland, throughout the thirties, offering to maintain her in Moscow. However Yevgenia Podoskaya refused, was arrested in November 1936 and shot on 10 March 1937.

Yezhov bombarded Molotov with reports of the conspiracies he had discovered. He and Kaganovich were enthusiasts: 'I've always considered that those chiefly responsible were Stalin and we who encouraged it, who were active. I was always active, I'd always supported the measures taken,' said Molotov. 'Stalin was right – "better an innocent head less ..." ' Kaganovich agreed: 'Otherwise we'd never have won the war!' Molotov notoriously reviewed one list of arrests and personally wrote VMN next to a woman's name. It was Molotov who signed and apparently added names to the list of wives of Enemies such as Kosior and Postyshev, who were all shot. Of the twenty-eight Commissars under Premier Molotov in early 1938, twenty were killed. When he found the name of a Bolshevik named G. I. Lomov on a list Stalin asked: 'What about this?'

'In favour of immediate arrest of that bastard Lomov,' wrote Molotov. In the case of some unfortunate professor, Molotov asked Yezhov: 'Why is this professor still in the Foreign Ministry and not in the NKVD?' When some books by Stalin and Lenin were burned by mistake, Molotov ordered Yezhov to accelerate the case. When Molotov heard that a regional Procurator had grumbled about the Purge and joked, quite understandably, that it was amazing Stalin and Molotov were still alive when there were so many terrorists trying to kill them, he ordered the NKVD: 'Investigate, having agreed with Vyshinsky [the official's boss in Moscow]. Molotov.' Kaganovich boasted there was not one railway 'without Trotskyite/Japanese wreckers', writing at least thirty-two letters to the NKVD demanding eighty-three arrests – and signing death lists for 36,000. So many railwaymen were shot that an official telephoned Poskrebyshev to warn that one line was entirely unmanned.

Yet all the leaders also knew that they themselves were constantly being tested: both Molotov's secretaries were arrested. 'I sensed danger gathering around me,' he said as they collected testimony against him. 'My first assistant threw himself down the liftshaft at the NKVD.' No one was safe: they had their families to consider. Stalin had made it amply clear that the Enemies had to be destroyed 'without looking at their faces'. If they had hoped that their rank would protect them, the arrests of Politburo members like Rudzutak had corrected that impression. Testimonies were prepared against all, including Molotov, Voroshilov and Kaganovich. Their chauffeurs were arrested so frequently that Khrushchev grumbled to Stalin, who said: 'They're gathering evidence against me too.' All of them must have thought like Khrushchev who asked: 'Do you think I'm confident ... that tomorrow won't transfer me from this office to a prison cell?'

* * *

The case of Marshal Budyonny surely concentrated their minds: on 20 June 1937, soon after the execution of Tukhachevsky, Stalin told the cavalryman: 'Yezhov says your wife's conducting herself dishonourably and bear in mind we won't let anyone, even a wife, compromise you in the Party and the State. Talk to Yezhov about it and decide what to do if it's necessary. You missed an Enemy near you. Why do you feel sorry for her?'

'A bad wife is family, not political business, Comrade Stalin,' replied Budyonny. 'I'll look into it myself.'

'You must be brave,' said Stalin. 'Do you think I don't feel sorry when my closest circle turn out to be Enemies of the People?' Budyonny's wife, Olga, was a Bolshoi singer, who was best friends with the actress wife of Marshal Yegorov. It seems Olga was cuckolding Budyonny with a Bolshoi tenor and flirting with Polish diplomats. Budyonny went to Yezhov who told him that his wife 'along with Yegorova, visits foreign embassies ...' When he was inspecting the troops, his wife was arrested in the street, interrogated and sentenced to eight years and then another three. Budyonny sobbed, 'the tears pouring down his cheeks'. Olga went mad in solitary confinement. There used to be a legend that Stalin was more merciful to women: certainly female CC members were more likely to survive.* But Galina Yegorova, forty, was shot even before her Marshal husband. No chivalry there. Her flirtation with Stalin on the night of Nadya's suicide cannot have helped her case but he was always more pitiless if there was a hint of sexual debauchery.

The Terror was, among many more important things, the triumph of prissy Bolshevik morality over the sexual freedom of the twenties. The destruction of Yenukidze, Tukhachevsky and Rudzutak involved what Molotov called that 'weak spot ... women!' The scent of actresses, the whirl of diplomatic balls, and

* Alexandra Kollontai, now sixty-five and Ambassador to Sweden, was a beautiful Bolshevik noblewoman who wrote the manifesto of feminism and free love, her novel *Love of Worker Bees*. Her scandalous sex-life shocked and amused Stalin and Molotov. Several of her famous Bolshevik lovers were shot in the Great Terror. Yet she herself survived. Perhaps her letters to Stalin, always addressed to 'highly respected Joseph Vissarionovich' with 'friendly greetings from an open heart' with the flirtatious romanticism of a once beautiful woman, appealed to his chivalry. Similarly Stalin muttered to Dmitrov about the veteran Bolshevik Yelena Stasova that 'we shall probably arrest Stasova. Turned out she's scum.' Yet she was allowed to survive and continued to write Stalin warm letters of gratitude into honourable old age.

the glow of foreign decadence were sometimes enough to convince the lonely Stalin and the priggish Molotov, both reeking of Puritanical envy, that treason and duplicity lurked. But debauchery was never the real reason their victims were destroyed. That was always political. The accusations of sexual deviance were deployed to dehumanize them among their former colleagues. Yenukidze and Rudzutak were both said to seduce what Kaganovich called 'little girls'. Since it is unlikely that the Central Committee contained a cell of paedophiles, as well as a web of terrorists and spies, it seems more likely these hedonistic grandees just 'protected' ballerinas like millionaires past and present. None the less Stalin had tolerated (and probably enjoyed) Yenukidze's parties for years. Womanizers, such as Bulganin and Beria, continued to prosper, providing they were loyal and competent politically but no one could say this was mere tittle-tattle at Stalin's court.* People died of gossip.

Stalin was an awkward man of the nineteenth century: flirtatious with, and appreciative of, the well-dressed women of his circle, strictly prudish about his own daughter, shocked at the feminism and free love of the early twenties, yet crudely macho among his male friends. His prudishness was thoroughly 'Victorian': the appearance of Svetlana's knees, even her bold stare in a photograph, provoked absurd crises. Stalin disapproved of the 'first kiss' in Alexandrov's *Volga, Volga*, which was too passionate, with the result that not only was the kiss cut, but *all kissing* was almost banned from all Soviet films by over-zealous officials. In Eisenstein's *Ivan the Terrible, Part Two*, Stalin, who identified so closely with the Tsar, was embarrassed by Ivan's kiss which he said went on much too long and had to be cut. When Tatiana appeared in the opera *Onegin* wearing a sheer gown, Stalin exclaimed: 'How can a woman appear before a man dressed like that?' The director immediately restored 'Bolshevik modesty' to

---

* In their generation, the proud exception to this narrow-minded hypocrisy were those rare Bolsheviks who combined Party discipline with European Bohemianism, the Foreign Commissar Maxim Litvinov and his English wife Ivy. She sneered openly at humbugs like Molotov and flaunted her promiscuity with a parade of Germanic lovers: 'I don't care a pin what anyone says ... for I feel head and shoulders taller than anyone who can gloat on such outworn topics of scandal as who sleeps with whom.' Meanwhile Commissar Litvinov, the plump, rumpled and tough Jewish intellectual who had known Stalin a long time but was never close to him, started an affair with a 'very pretty, decidedly vulgar and very sexy indeed' girl who lodged with them. She even accompanied him to diplomatic receptions and arrived at the office in tight riding breeches.

Pushkin's worldliness. In old age, seeing a Georgian cigarette packet illustrated with a racy girl, Stalin furiously ordered the entire brand to be redesigned: 'Where would she learn to sit like that? Paris?'

He encouraged bourgeois morality among his magnates: Zhdanov's wife wanted to leave him for his alcoholism but just as Hitler insisted Goebbels return to his wife, so Stalin ordered, 'You must stay together.' It was the same with Pavel Alliluyev. When Stalin heard that Kuibyshev mistreated his wife, he exclaimed: 'If I'd known about it, I'd have put an end to such beastliness.'

However if an old friend needed help in an embarrassing situation, Stalin was amused to oblige, as a fascinating letter from his archives shows. Alexander Troyanovsky, probably the diplomat, asked for his help with a mistress (one F. M. Gratsanova) who worked for the NKVD and had been given a job by Yagoda. Now if they both left their jobs simultaneously, 'there'll be gossip. So can I leave earlier than her … Please solve this for me as an old comrade,' he wrote to Stalin who helped with a snigger, writing:

'Comrade Yagoda, Arrange this business of Troyanovsky. He's entangled, the devil, and we are responsible [for helping him out]. Oh to God, or to the Devil, with him! Arrange this business and make him a calm bloke [*muzhik*]. Stalin.' In 1938, Troyanovsky again wrote to ask Stalin to get Yezhov to let the lady keep her apartment. Stalin helped again.

* * *

One of the mysteries of the Terror was Stalin's obsession with forcing his victims to sign elaborate confessions of unlikely crimes before they died. It was only with the slaughter of the NKVD and military brass between March and July 1937 that Stalin emerged as the absolute dictator. Even then, he still had to convince his magnates to do his bidding. How did he do it?

There was the character of Stalin himself: the cult of personality was so pervasive in the country that 'Stalin's word was law', said Khrushchev. 'He could do no wrong. Stalin could see it all clearly.' Mikoyan thought that the cult was the reason no one could challenge Stalin. But the Terror was not merely Stalin's will: he may have inspired much of it, and it may have reflected his own hatreds and complexes, but his magnates were constantly urging him to purge more Enemies. None the less when they knew the victim, they required proof. That was the reason Stalin paid such attention to the written words of confession, signed by the victims.

As soon as he received testimonies from Yezhov, Stalin distributed them to the Politburo who found this deluge of self-incrimination and denunciation hard to refute: in March 1937, Stalin typically sent a cover note to Molotov, Voroshilov, Kaganovich and Mikoyan:

'I ask you to recognize the testimony of Polish-German spies Alexandra (mother) and Tamara (daughter) Litzinskaya and Minervina, former secretary of A. Yenukidze.' All the magnates knew Yenukidze well so Stalin made sure they saw all the evidence. When Mikoyan doubted the confessions, Stalin accused him of weakness but then called him back and showed him the signed testimonies: 'He writes it himself … signs every page.' These preposterous confessions were enough to convince Kaganovich: 'How could you not sign it [the death sentence] if according to the investigation … this man was an Enemy?' Zhdanov, according to his son, 'did trust the denunciations from Yezhov … For some time, my father did believe there were Tsarist agents among the Leningrad leadership.' But when his parents knew the victims personally as friends, then his mother would say, 'If he's an Enemy of the People, I am one too!' Again and again, in whispered conversations, the leaders and their wives used these same words to express their doubts about one or two of the arrests although they believed in the guilt of most of the victims.

The magnates were being disingenuous in their shock. When they knew the person, they naturally took a special interest in the proof, but all of them understood and accepted that the details of the accusations and confessions did not matter. So why were they all killed? Nadezhda Mandelstam wrote that they were killed 'for nothing' while Maya Kavtaradze, whose parents were arrested, simply says: 'Don't ask why!' They were killed not because of what they *had* done but because of what they *might* do. As Molotov explained, 'The main thing was, that at the decisive moment, they could not be depended on.' Indeed, some, such as Rudzutak, were not even 'consciously' disloyal. It was the *potential* nature of this betrayal which meant that Stalin could still admire the work or even personality of his victims: after Tukhachevsky and Uborevich's shootings, he could still lecture the Politburo about the talent of the former and encourage soldiers to 'Train your troops as Uborevich did.' But there was also a peculiarly religious aspect.

When Stalin briefed Vyshinsky on the January 1937 trial, he addressed the accused thus: 'You lost faith' – and they must die for losing it. He told Beria: 'An Enemy of the People is not only one who does sabotage but one who doubts the rightness of the Party line. And there are a lot of them and we must liquidate them.' Stalin himself implied this when he told a desperate comrade, who asked if he was still trusted, 'I trust you politically, but I'm not so positive in the sphere of the future perspectives of Party activities,' which seems to mean that he trusted him now but not necessarily in the coming war.

'There is something great and bold about the political idea of a general purge,' Bukharin, who understood Stalin so well, wrote to him from prison, because it would 'arouse an everlasting distrust ... In this way, the leadership is bringing about a full guarantee for itself.' The stronger the enemies of the State, the stronger the State (and Stalin) had to be. This circle of 'everlasting distrust' was his natural habitat. Did he believe every case? Not forensically, but this flint-hearted politician believed only in the sanctity of his own political necessity, sometimes fused with personal vengeance.

At the lunch after the 7 November parade, held as usual at Voroshilov's flat and attended by the magnates including Yezhov, Khrushchev and Redens, Mikoyan played the toastmaster proposing 'witty toasts for everyone in turn'. Then 'once more (a toast) to the great Stalin' who then stood up to explain and encourage the Terror: anyone who dared to weaken the power of the Soviet State 'in their thoughts, yes even their thoughts' would be considered an Enemy and 'we will destroy them as a clan'. Then he actually toasted this massacre: 'To the complete destruction of all Enemies, them and their kin!' at which the magnates gave 'approving exclamations: To the great Stalin!' This might have been a medieval Caucasian chieftain talking, 'a brilliant politician of the Italian Renaissance' – or Ivan. He explained that he, no great orator and an unimpressive fellow, had succeeded the 'eagle' Lenin because that was what the Party wanted. He and his men were driven by 'holy fear' of not justifying the trust of the masses. Thus, Stalin went on to explain, this was truly a holy terror that stemmed from Bolshevism's Messianic nature. No wonder Yezhov called the NKVD his 'secret sect'.

The squalidity of this sacred thuggery beggars belief: the distance from the torture chambers of the Lubianka to Stalin's Little Corner is about a mile, but it was much closer then.

22

Bloody Shirtsleeves:
the Intimate Circle of Murder

In the mornings, Blackberry visited the Politburo and attended meetings, coming straight from the torture chambers. Khrushchev one day noticed spots of clotted blood on the hem and cuffs of Yezhov's peasant blouse. Khrushchev, who himself was no angel, asked Yezhov what the spots were. Yezhov replied, with a flash of his blue eyes, that one should take pride in such specks because they were the blood of the Enemies of the revolution.

Stalin often wrote instructions beside the names. In December 1937, he added the order 'Beat, beat!' next to a name. 'Isn't it time to squeeze this gentleman and force him to report on his dirty little business,' Stalin wrote beside another. 'Where is he – in a prison or a hotel?' The Politburo specified that torture should be used officially in 1937. As Stalin later asserted, 'The NKVD practice of the use of physical pressure ... permitted by the Central Committee' was a 'totally correct and expedient method'.

Yezhov supervised his torturers who had their own jargon for their work: they called the process of destroying an innocent human 'French wrestling' – '*frantsuskaya borba*'. When some of them were interrogated themselves years later, they revealed how they used the *zhguti*, the special club, and the *dubinka*, the truncheon, as well as the more traditional prevention of sleep and constant interrogation that they called the 'conveyor belt'. The Cheka had long had a cult of torture: indeed Leonid Zakovsky, one of Yagoda's men, had written a guide to torture.

Frequently, the Politburo, such as Molotov and Mikoyan, would go over to interrogate their comrades in Yezhov's grand office at the Lubianka: 'Rudzutak had been badly beaten and tortured,' said Molotov about one such session. 'It was necessary to act mercilessly.' Kaganovich thought 'it was very difficult *not* to be cruel' but 'one must take into consideration that they were experienced Old Bolsheviks; how could they give testimonies voluntarily?' This may make it sound as if 'the Politburo was filled with gangsters', in Molotov's words. They may not have been Mafia hitmen – few except Yezhov and later Beria personally tortured or killed their victims, and no Mafia hitman would be foolish enough to spend so much time on tedious cod-ideology – but it is sometimes hard to tell the difference.

Stalin and his magnates often laughed about the NKVD's ability to get people to confess. Stalin told this joke to someone who had actually been tortured: 'They arrested a boy and accused him of writing *Eugene Onegin*,' Stalin joked. 'The boy tried to deny it ... A few days later, the NKVD interrogator bumped into the boy's parents: "Congratulations!" he said. "Your son wrote *Eugene Onegin*." '* Many of the prisoners were beaten so hard that their eyes were literally popped out of their heads. They were routinely beaten to death, which was registered as a heart attack.

Yezhov himself devised the system of execution. Instead of using the cellars of the Lubianka or the other prisons, as his predecessors had done, he created a special abbatoir. Slightly behind and to the left of Lubianka, he used another NKVD building on Varsonofyevsky Lane. The prisoners were driven in Black Crows across the road from the Lubianka (there was no tunnel) and into the courtyard where a low squarish building had been specially constructed with a concrete floor sloping towards a far wall built of logs, to absorb the bullets, and hosing facilities to wash away the fluids. After a shot to the back of the head, the victims were placed in metal boxes and driven to one of the crematoria. in Moscow. The ashes were usually dumped into a mass grave such as the one at the Donskoi Cemetery.

The road that ended in the Donskoi often began in a note on Stalin's desk. Stalin received not only pleas for life but denunciations demanding death. Once the Terror was unleashed, denunciations worked like kerosene on a fire, keeping it flaring up. These denunciations were already a vital part of the Stalinist system: everyone was expected to denounce everyone else. In the Bolshevik universe, there were only two ways for mistakes to come to the notice of the leaders: accidents – and denunciations. Denunciations poured into Stalin's office: some were valid. 'If we lived in a capitalist state, they'd be

* The primitive interrogators tried to suit the crime to the criminal with often absurd results: on his arrest, the First Secretary of the Jewish Autonomous Oblast in Birobizhan was appropriately accused of poisoning Kaganovich's gefilte fish during his visit there. Presumably, throughout the many republics of the USSR, the poison was secreted in the national dishes – from the sausages of the Baltics to the spicy soups of the Buriats and the lamb stews of the Tajiks.

talking about us in the Parliament and newspapers,' said Voroshilov. Some denunciations were the Stalinist equivalent of awkward Parliamentary questions and investigative reporters:

'You probably find it unpleasant that such letters are written, but I'm glad,' Stalin explained. 'It would be a bad thing if no one complained. Don't be afraid of quarrelling … This is better than friendship at the Government's expense.' But usually these poison letters were the result of witch-hunting mania, cannibalistic malice and amoral ambition.

Stalin relished the decision on how to treat the denunciations. If he did not like the person, the letters went to the NKVD with a note 'Check!' and death probably followed. If he wished to 'preserve' the person, he would file it and he might reactivate it years later. Hence his papers overflow with denunciations, some from ordinary people, others from top officials: a typical one, from a Comintern official, denounced Enemies in the Foreign Commissariat. One can only guess at the atmosphere of fear and intrigue within the Kremlin: Ordzhonikidze's ex-secretary, surely trying to save his skin, wrote to Stalin to denounce Sergo's widow, Zinaida, who had 'said several times she can't live without Sergo and I'm worried she'll do something silly … She's often telephoned by the wives of traitors to our Party. These wives turn to her with requests (to give to Comrade Yezhov). It's not right and she must be told not to do it … I ask for your instructions. Every order will be fulfilled to the last drop of blood. Devoted to you, Semyushkin.' Sometimes farce turned swiftly to tragedy, like the story of how Stalin's voice* was sabotaged by wreckers.

---

* At the end of 1936, when Stalin inaugurated the new Constitution, Shumiatsky, the film boss, asked Molotov if he could record Stalin's speech. On 20 November, Molotov gave permission. Maltsev, the chief of the All-Union Committee of Radiofication and Radiosound, reported joyfully to Stalin that the speech had been successfully recorded and approved. Now he wanted permission to make it into a gramophone record 'for you to hear it personally'. Stalin agreed. But on 29 April 1937, when the terrified officials of the Gramophone Plant Trust factory listened to the gramophone, something was wrong with Stalin's voice. They immediately reported to Poskrebyshev that there were: '1. Big noises. 2. Big intervals. 3. The absence of whole phrases. 4. Closed grooves. And 5. Jumps and lack of clarity.' The file also contained a nervous analysis of the sibilance of Stalin's voice and how hard it was to render on gramophone. Worse, a thousand of these gramophones had been manufactured. Some officials wanted to recall the discs but, typically for the period, the chief attacked this suggestion for its disrespect to Comrade Stalin's voice. He thought it more respectful to distribute them regardless of the gaps, noises, jumps. The file ends with a report from *Komsomolskaya Pravda* that suggested that something very sinister had happened to Comrade Stalin's voice at the Gramophone Factory where the insistence of Comrade Straik to 'distribute the discs more speedily' was a 'strange position'. He was obviously a wrecker and all the guilty wreckers at the factory 'must be harshly punished'. No doubt the NKVD came to listen to Comrade Straik's record collection.

A typical denunciation which Stalin read and marked, came from a certain Krylov in distant Saratov, who told his leader that 'Enemies have friends inside the NKVD and the Procuracy and are hiding enemies.' The military were as avid as anyone else: 'I ask you to dismiss Commander ... Osipov,' wrote an officer from Tiflis, 'who is a very suspicious person.' Stalin underlined 'suspicious' with his blue pen.

The lightning of this Muscovite Zeus struck the regions in different ways: in July 1937, Liushkov, a ruthless Chekist who had already ravaged Rostov, was summoned to the Kremlin and ordered to the Far East. Stalin talked about the lives of men as if they were old clothes – some we keep, some we throw away: the Far Eastern First Secretary Vareikis was 'not completely reliable', having his own clique, but 'it was necessary to keep' Marshal Blyukher. Liushkov obediently arrested Vareikis.

A less reliable way was to harness a local tool such as Polia Nikolaenko, the 'heroic denunciatrix of Kiev', championed by Stalin. The speciality of this terrifying crone, responsible for the deaths of as many as 8,000 people, was to stand up at meetings and shriek accusations: Khrushchev saw how she 'pointed her finger and said, "I don't know that man over there but I can tell by the look in his eyes that he's an Enemy of the People."' This talk of the 'look in the eyes' was another sign of the Terror's religious frenzy. The only way to rebut this was to answer quickly: 'I don't know this woman who's just denounced me but I can tell from the look in her eyes, she's a prostitute.' Now Polia Nikolaenko appealed to Stalin. Her cover note catches her simplicity:

'To the anteroom of Comrade Stalin. I ask you to give this declaration personally to Comrade Stalin. Comrade Stalin talked about me at the February Plenum.' Her letter did reach Stalin, with devastating consequences for her enemies: 'Dear Leader, Comrade Stalin,' she wrote on 17 September 1937, cunningly exposing how the local bosses were ignoring Stalin's orders. 'I ask for your intervention in Kiev matters ... Enemies here again gather unbeatable power ... sitting in their *apparat* doing bad deeds. Starting from the Plenum when you spoke about Kiev and my case as a "little person", they have actively organized my discrediting to destroy me politically.' Senior officials treated her as an 'Enemy' and once again used the language of witchcraft against the witch herself: 'One connected to Enemies of the People cried, "It's in her eyes, she's two-faced!"' Kosior, Ukrainian leader, and others ridiculed her 'amidst noisy laughter'. 'I was, am and will be devoted to the Party and the Great Leader. You helped me to find Truth. STALIN'S TRUTH IS STRONG! This time I again ask you to do all you can to the Kiev organization ...' Ten days later, Stalin swooped to her aid, telling the Ukrainian bosses:

'Pay attention to Comrade Nikolaenko (look at her letter). Can you protect her from this audience of hooligans! According to my information, Glaz and Timofeev really are not especially trustworthy. Stalin.' Those two men were presumably arrested while Kosior survived for the moment.

The regions were soon killing too many, too quickly: Khrushchev,* Moscow leader, effectively ordered the shooting of 55,741 officials which more than fulfilled the original Politburo quota of 50,000. On 10 July 1937, Khrushchev wrote to Stalin to request shooting 2,000 ex-kulaks to fulfil the quota. The NKVD archives show him initialling many documents proposing arrests. By spring 1938, he had overseen the arrest of thirty-five of the thirty-eight provincial and city Secretaries, which gives some idea of this fever. Since he was based in Moscow, he brought death-lists directly to Stalin and Molotov.

'There can't be so many!' exclaimed Stalin.

'There are in fact more,' replied Khrushchev, according to Molotov. 'You can't imagine how many there are.' The city of Stalinabad (Askabad) was given a quota of 6,277 to shoot but actually executed 13,259.

But mostly, they were killing the wrong people. The regional bosses selected the victims, finding it irresistible to destroy their opponents and preserve their friends. Yet it was precisely these 'princes' with their entourages that Stalin wished to destroy. Thus the First Secretaries' initial blood-letting not only did not save them: it provided an excuse for their own eradication. It was only a matter of time before the centre unleashed a second wave of terror to eradicate the 'princes' themselves.

Only Stalin's personal viceroys, Zhdanov in Leningrad and Beria in Transcaucasia, did not require this 'help'. Zhdanov was another enthusiastic believer that Trotskyites had infiltrated Leningrad,

---

* Khrushchev was as fanatical a Stalinist terrorist as it was possible to be during the thirties yet his ability to destroy incriminating documents, and his memoirs, have shrouded his real conduct in mystery. A. N. Shelepin, ex-KGB boss, testified in 1988 that Khrushchev's death-lists had been removed by the secret policeman I. V. Serov. 261 pages of Khrushchev's papers were burned between 2 and 9 July 1954.

though he sometimes mused on cases: 'You know I never thought Viktorov would turn out to be an Enemy of the People,' said Zhdanov to Admiral Kuznetsov, who 'heard no doubt in his voice, only surprise ... We spoke ... as of men who had passed beyond the grave.' He oversaw the arrest of 68,000 in Leningrad. As for Beria, this professional Chekist oversaw his initial quota of 268,950 arrests and 75,950 executions. The quota was later raised. Ten per cent of the Georgian Party, which was particularly well-known to Stalin, were killed. Beria distinguished himself by personally performing the torture of Lakoba's family, driving his widow mad by placing a snake in her cell and beating his teenage children to death.

The solution was the despatch of Stalin's favourites to destroy the 'princes'; also a useful test of a magnate's loyalty. There was no better blooding than a trip to the regions. Like the warlords of the Civil War they set off riding shotgun with NKVD thugs in their own armoured trains. Mikoyan, Foreign Trade and Food Supply Commissar, enjoys the reputation of one of the more decent leaders: he certainly helped the victims later and worked hard to undo Stalin's rule after his death. In 1936, however, Mikoyan praised the executions of Zinoviev and Kamenev – 'how just the verdict!' he enthused to Kaganovich. In 1937, he too signed death-lists and proposed the arrest of hundreds of his officials. Throughout Stalin's reign, Mikoyan was shrewd enough to avoid intrigues, eschew ambition for the highest offices, and with his sharp intelligence and prodigious capacity for work, concentrate on his responsibilities: he knew how to play the game and do just enough.

The magnates saved friends but they mainly saved them in 1939 in a different environment. Andreyev's anteroom, his daughter claimed, 'was full of those he helped' but Kaganovich honestly admitted that 'it was impossible to save friends and relatives' because of 'the public mood'. They had to kill a lot to save a few. Mikoyan probably did more than most, appealing to Stalin that his friend Andreasian had been accused of being a French agent by the moronic investigators because his first name was 'Napoleon'.

'He's as French as you!' joked Mikoyan. Stalin burst out laughing.* Voroshilov, who was responsible for so many deaths, passed on the appeal of a friend's arrested daughter to Stalin himself who wrote on

* Such absurdities abounded: in her terrible labour camp, Bukharin's widow encountered this spirit when another prisoner informed on her because she owned a book named *Dangerous Liaisons* that was presumed to be a deadly espionage guide.

it as usual: 'To Comrade Yezhov, check this out!' Her father was released and called to thank Voroshilov, who asked:

'Was it terrible?'

'Yes, very terrible.' The two friends never discussed it again.

Stalin was so besieged with requests that he passed a Politburo decree banning appeals. If a leader intervened to save a friend, the vital thing was to avoid him falling into the hands of another leader. Mikoyan managed to save one comrade and begged him to leave Moscow immediately but the Old Bolshevik, with all the punctiliousness of a knight who must have his sword returned, insisted on getting his Party card back. He called Andreyev who had him rearrested.

Perhaps Mikoyan's kindnesses reached Stalin's ears for he suddenly cooled towards him. In late 1937, he tested Mikoyan's commitment by despatching him to Armenia with a list of three hundred victims to be arrested. Mikoyan signed it but he crossed off one friend. The man was arrested anyway. Just as he was speaking to the Yerevan Party meeting, Beria arrived in the room, to watch him as much as to terrorize the locals. A thousand people were arrested, including seven out of nine Armenian Politburo members. When Mikoyan returned to Moscow, Stalin warmed to him again.

All the magnates set off on bloody tours of the country. Zhdanov purged the Urals and Middle Volga. Ukraine was unfortunate enough to welcome Kaganovich, Molotov and Yezhov. Kaganovich visited Kazakhstan, Cheliabinsk, Ivanovo and other places, spreading terror: 'First study ... shows the Obkom Secretary Epanchikev must be arrested at once ...' began his first telegram from Ivanovo in August 1937, which continued: 'Right-Trotskyite wrecking has assumed broad dimensions here, in industry, agriculture, supply, healthcare, trade, education and political work ... exceptionally infested.' But this was nothing compared to the killing frenzy of the two most prolific monsters on tour.

Andrei Andreyev, now forty-two, small, moustachioed and hangdog of countenance, had failed to rise to the challenge of the Soviet railways but he came into his own running the CC Secretariat with Yezhov. One of the rare proletarians among the leadership, this quiet Tchaikovsky addict, mountaineer and nature photographer, married to Dora Khazan, to whom he wrote loving postcards about their children, became the unchallengeable master of these murderous roadshows.

On 20 July, he arrived in Saratov to ravage the Volga German Republic:* 'All means are necessary to purge Saratov,' he told Stalin in the first of a stream of excited, fanatical telegrams. 'The Saratov organization meets all decisions of CC with great pleasure.' This was hard to believe. Everywhere he discovered how the local bosses 'did not want to discover the terrorist group' and had 'pardoned exposed Enemies'. By the next day, Andreyev was frantically arresting suspects: 'we had to arrest the Second Secretary ... On Freshier, we have evidence he was member of Rightist-Trotskyite organization. We ask permission to arrest.' One group consisted of 'twenty very obstructively working in the Machine Tractor Station. We decided to arrest and prosecute two of the directors' who turned out to be part of a '"Right-kulak organization" that had "wrecked tractors" or rather they had worked slowly since "only 14 out of 74 were ready".' At 11.38 that night, Stalin replied in his blue pencil: 'Central Committee agrees with your proposals about prosecution and shooting of former MTS workers.' Twenty were shot. Three days later, Andreyev boasted to Stalin that he had found 'a Fascist organization – we plan to arrest at once the first group of 50–60 people ... We had to arrest the Premier of the Republic, Luf, for proven membership of Right-Trotskyites.' He proceeded to Kuibyshev and then to Central Asia where he removed all the leaderships since Stalin had told him: 'Generally, you can act as you consider.' The result was that in Stalinabad, 'I have arrested 7 Narkoms, 55 CC chiefs, 3 CC Secretaries' and returning to Voronezh, he declared cheerfully: 'There is no Buro here. All arrested as Enemies. Off to Rostov now!'

Andreyev was accompanied on these manic trips by a plump young man of thirty-five, Georgi Malenkov, the killer bureaucrat whose career benefited the most from the Purges but who hailed from the provincial intelligentsia, a scion of Tsarist civil servants, and a nobleman.† He travelled with Mikoyan to Armenia and

* After interviewing Andreyev and Dora Khazan's daughter Natasha and hearing of his innocence of all crimes, the author came upon this damning file. Andreyev's notes and letters have survived because unlike his fellow criminals, such as Kaganovich, Malenkov and Khrushchev, he was out of power after Stalin's death when the others managed to destroy so many incriminating documents.

† Lenin, the founder of the Cheka Felix Dzerzhinsky, and the Foreign Commissar until 1930, Chicherin, were hereditary noblemen, as were Molotov, Zhdanov, Sergo and Tukhachevsky, according to Peter the Great's Table of Ranks which decreed rank until 1917. None were titled nobility.

Yezhov to Belorussia. One historian estimates that Malenkov was responsible for 150,000 deaths.

Small, flabby, pale and moon-faced with a hairless chin, freckles across his nose and dark, slightly Mongol eyes, his black hair hanging across his forehead, Malenkov had broad, female hips, a pear shape and a high voice. It is no wonder that Zhdanov nicknamed him 'Malanya' or Melanie. 'It seemed that under the layers and rolls of fat', a lean and hungry man was trying to get out. His great-great-grandfather had come from Macedonia during the reign of Nicholas I but as Beria joked, he was hardly Alexander the Great. Malenkov's ancestors had governed Orenburg for the Tsars. Descended from generals and admirals, he saw himself in the tradition of a *posadnik*, an elected administrator of old Novgorod, or a *chinovnik* like his forefathers. Unlike Stalinist bullies such as Kaganovich, who shouted and punched officials, Malenkov stood when subordinates entered his room and spoke quietly in fine Russian without swearing, though what he said was often chilling.

Malenkov's father had shocked the family by marrying a formidable blacksmith's daughter who had three sons. Georgi, who loved his dominant mother, was the youngest. He studied at the local classical *Gymnasium*, learning Latin and French. Malenkov, like Zhdanov, passed among cobblers and joiners for an educated man, qualifying as an electrical engineer. Like many other ambitious youngsters, he joined the Party during the Civil War: his family unconvincingly claim that he rode in the cavalry but he was soon on safer ground on the propaganda trains where he met his domineering wife, Valeria Golubtseva, who came from a similar background.

Happily married, Malenkov was known as a wonderful father to his highly educated children, teaching them himself and reading them poetry even when he was exhausted at the height of the war. His wife helped get him a job in the Central Committee where he was noticed by Molotov, joined Stalin's Secretariat and became Secretary of the Politburo during the early thirties, one of those keen young men like Yezhov who won first Kaganovich's, then Stalin's notice for their devotion and efficiency. Yet in company, he had a light sense of humour.

This cunning but 'eunuch-like' magnate never spoke unless necessary and always listened to Stalin, scribbling in a notebook headed 'Comrade Stalin's Instructions'. He succeeded Yezhov as head of the CC Personnel Registration department that selected cadres for jobs. In 1937, Mikoyan said, he played a 'special role'. He was the bureaucratic maestro of the Terror. One note in Stalin's papers laconically illustrates their relationship:

'Comrade Malenkov – Moskvin must be arrested. J.St.' The young stars Malenkov, Khrushchev and Yezhov were such close friends, they were called 'the Inseparables'. Yet in this paranoic lottery, even a Malenkov could be destroyed. In 1937, he was accused at a Moscow Party Conference of being an Enemy himself. He was talking about joining the Red Army in Orenburg during the Civil War when a voice cried out:

'Were there Whites in Orenburg at the time?'

'Yes –'

'That means you were with them.' Khrushchev intervened:

'The Whites may have been in Orenburg at the time but Comrade Malenkov was not one of them.' It was a time when hesitation could lead to arrest. Simultaneously, Khrushchev saved his own skin by going to Stalin personally and confessing a spell of Trotskyism during the early twenties.

The entourage rabidly encouraged the Terror. Even decades later, these 'fanatics' still defended their mass murder: 'I bear responsibility for the repression and consider it correct,' said Molotov. 'All Politburo members bear responsibility ... But 1937 was necessary.' Mikoyan agreed that 'everyone who worked with Stalin ... bears a share of responsibility'. It was bad enough to kill so many but their complete awareness that many were innocent even by their own arcane standards is the hardest to take: 'We're guilty of going too far,' said Kaganovich. 'We all made mistakes ... But we won WW2.' Those who knew these mass murderers later reflected that Malenkov or Khrushchev were 'not wicked by nature', not 'what they eventually became'. They were men of their time.

In October, another Plenum approved the arrest of yet more members of the Central Committee. 'It happened gradually,' said Molotov. 'Seventy expelled 1–15 people then sixty expelled another 15.' When the terrified local leaders appealed to Stalin 'to receive me for just ten minutes on personal matters – I'm accused in a terrible lie,' he scribbled in green to Poskrebyshev:

'Say I'm on holiday.'

23

Social Life in the Terror: the Wives
and Children of the Magnates

Yet all of this tragedy took place in a public atmosphere of jubilation, a never-ending fiesta of triumphs and anniversaries. Here is a scene from the years of the Terror that might have taken place anywhere and any time between a daughter, her best friend and her embarrassing papa. Stalin met his daughter Svetlana in his apartment for dinner daily. At the height of the Terror, Stalin dined with Svetlana, then eleven, and her best friend, Martha Peshkova, whose grandfather, Gorky, and father had both supposedly been murdered by Yagoda, her mother's lover. Stalin wanted Svetlana to be friends with Martha, introducing them especially. Now the girls were playing in Svetlana's room when the housekeeper came and told them Stalin was home and at table. Stalin was alone but in a very cheerful mood – he clearly adored coming home to see Svetlana for he would often appear shouting, 'Where's my *khozyaika*!' and then sit down and help her do her homework. Outsiders were amazed at how this harsh creature 'was so gentle with his daughter'. He sat her on his knee and told one visitor:

'Since her mother died, I always tell her she's the *khozyaika* but she so believed it herself that she tried to give orders in the kitchen but was made to leave immediately. She was in tears but I managed to calm her down.'

That night, he teased Martha, who was very pretty but with a tendency to blush like a beetroot:

'So Marfochka, I hear you are being chased by all the boys?' Martha was so embarrassed she could not swallow her soup or answer. 'So many boys are chasing you!' Stalin persisted. Svetlana came to her rescue:

'Come on, papa, leave her alone.' Stalin laughed and agreed, saying he always obeyed his darling *khozyaika*. Dinner, recalled Martha, 'was miserable for me', but she was not afraid of Stalin because she had known him since childhood. Yet nothing was quite what it seemed for these children: so many of Svetlana's parents' friends had disappeared. Martha had just seen* her mother's new lover arrested.

For the children of the leaders who were not arrested, there had never been a time of greater joy and energy. The jazz craze was still sweeping the country: Alexandrov's latest musical, *Volga, Volga,* came out in 1938 and its tunes were played over and over again in the dancehalls. At parties for the diplomatic corps, the killers danced to the jazz: Kaganovich hailed jazz as 'above all the friend of the jolly, the musical organizer of our high-spirited youth'. Kaganovich wrote a jazz guide leaflet with his friend Leonid Utesov, the jazz millionaire, entitled *How to Organize Railway Ensembles of Song and Dance and Jazz Orchestras* in which 'the Locomotive' commanded that there should be a '*dzhaz*' band at every Soviet station. They certainly needed cheering up.

'It was truly a time of huge hope and joy for the future,' remembers Stepan Mikoyan. 'We were perpetually excited and happy – the new Metro opened with its chandeliers, the giant Moskva Hotel, the new city of Magnitogorsk, and all sorts of other triumphs.' The propaganda machine sung of heroes of labour like the super-miner Stakhanov, of aviation, of exploration. Voroshilov and Yezhov were hailed as 'knights' in ballads. The movies had names like *Tales of Aviation Heroes.* 'Yes, it was an age of heroes!' reminisces Andreyev's daughter Natasha. 'We were not afraid then. Life was full – I remember smiling faces and climbing mountains, heroic pilots. Not everyone was living under oppression. We knew as children the first thing to be done was to make people strong, to make a New Man, and educate the people. At school, we learned how to use different tools, we went into the countryside to help with the harvest. No one paid us – it was our duty.'

The NKVD were heroes too: on 21 December, the 'Organs' celebrated their twentieth anniversary at a Bolshoi gala. Beneath flowers and banners of Stalin and Yezhov, Mikoyan in a Party tunic declared:

---

* Martha and her mother had been invited to Tiflis for the celebration of the poet Rustaveli's 750th anniversary by Timosha's new lover, Academician Lupel. There, through a slit in the door, she had seen him arrested at the dead of night: 'I saw five men take him away,' she remembered. Timosha's later affair with Stalin's court architect, Merzhanov, also ended in his arrest. 'I'm cursed,' Timosha Peshkova exclaimed. 'Everyone I touch is ruined.'

'Learn the Stalinist style of work from Comrade Yezhov just as he learned it from Comrade Stalin.' But the crux of his speech was: 'Every citizen of the USSR should be an NKVD agent.'

The country celebrated the anniversary of Pushkin's death as well as the anniversary of the Georgian poet Rustaveli which was organized by Beria and attended by Voroshilov and Mikoyan. Stalin was deliberately fusing traditional Russian culture with Bolshevism as Europe lurched closer to war. The Soviets were now fighting the Fascists by proxy in the Spanish Civil War, sparking a craze for Spanish songs and Spanish caps, 'blue with red edging on the visor', and big berets, 'tilted at a rakish angle'. Women wore Spanish blouses. 'If Tomorrow Brings War' was one of the most popular tunes. All the children of the leaders wanted to be pilots or soldiers:

'Even we children knew that war was coming,' recalls Stalin's adopted son Artyom, 'and we had to be strong not to be destroyed. One day, Uncle Stalin called we boys and said, "What would you like to do with your life?" Artyom wanted to be an engineer. 'No, we need men who understand the artillery.' Artyom and Yakov, already an engineer, both joined the artillery. 'This was the only privilege I ever received from my Uncle Stalin,' says Artyom. But aviators were the élite: more magnates' children joined 'Stalin's falcons' than any other service: Vasily trained as a pilot, alongside Stepan Mikoyan and Leonid Khrushchev.

Yet the families of the leaders endured a special experience during that time. For the parents, it was a daily torment of depression, uncertainty, exhilaration, anxiety as friends, colleagues and relatives were arrested. Yet to read Western histories and Soviet memoirs, one might believe that this new Bolshevik élite were convinced that all those arrested were innocent. This reflects the postdated guilt of those whose fathers took part in the slaughter. The truth was different: Zhdanov told his son Yury that Yezhov was right even in the most unlikely cases:

'The devil knows! I've known him many years but then there was Malinovsky!' he said, referring to the notorious Tsarist spy. Andreyev knew there were Enemies but thought they had to be 'thoroughly checked' before they were arrested. Mikoyan had his reservations on many arrests but his son Sergo knew his father was, in his words, a 'Communist fanatic'. The wives were if anything more fanatical than the husbands: Mikoyan recalled how his wife utterly believed in Stalin and was least likely to question his actions. 'My father,' says Natasha Andreyeva, 'believed wreckers and Fifth Columnists were destroying our State and had to be destroyed. My mother was utterly convinced. We prepared for war.'

The magnates never discussed the Terror before the children who lived in a world of lies and murder. The 'reluctance to reveal one's thoughts even to one's son was the most haunting sign of these times', remembered Andrei Sakharov the physicist. Yet the children naturally noticed when their uncles and family friends disappeared, leaving unspeakable and unaskable voids in their lives. The Mikoyan children heard their parents and uncles whispering about the arrests in Armenia, but their father sometimes could not stop himself exclaiming, 'I don't believe it!' Andreyev 'never mentioned it to us – it was our parents' business', recalls Natasha Andreyeva. 'But if someone important was arrested, my father would call to mama, "Dorochka, can you speak with me for a minute."' Indeed, Dora told her family she could identify Enemies by looking into their eyes. They whispered behind the kitchen door. Whenever his wife asked him something dangerous, Mikoyan replied: 'Shut up.' Before his death, Ordzhonikidze quietened his wife with a firm 'Not now!' Parents were constantly going for walks in the woods or round the Kremlin.

The inhabitants of the House on the Embankment, the hideous luxury building for younger leaders including the Khrushchevs, most of the People's Commissars and Stalin's cousinhood, like the Svanidzes and Redens, waited each night for the groan of the elevators, the knock on the doors, as the NKVD arrived to arrest their suspects.* As Trifonov relates in his novel *House on the Embankment*, every morning the uniformed doorman told the other inhabitants who had been arrested during the night. Soon the building was filled with empty apartments, doors ominously sealed by the NKVD. Khrushchev worried about the gossiping women in his family, furious when his peasant mother-in-law spent her time chattering downstairs, knowing well how loose talk cost lives.

Parents kept bags packed for prison and Mauser and Chagan

---

* Nadezhda Mandelstam wrote beautifully of how she and her husband had lain awake in the Writers' Union building until the lift had passed their floor.

pistols under their pillows, ready to commit suicide. The cleverer ones arranged a schedule for their children in case they were arrested: the mother of Zoya Zarubina, the stepdaughter of a Chekist, showed her how to gather warm clothes and take her little sister, aged eight, to a distant relative in the countryside.

The children noticed frequent house-moving because every execution created a vacant apartment and dacha which were eagerly occupied by survivors and their aspirational Party housewives, ambitious for grander accommodation. Stalin exploited this way of binding the leaders to the slaughter. Yezhov's family moved into Yagoda's apartments. Zhdanov received Rudzutak's dacha, Molotov acquired Yagoda's and later Rykov's. Vyshinsky was the most morbidly avaricious of all: he had always coveted the dacha of Leonid Serebryakov: 'I can't take my eyes off it ... You're a lucky man, Leonid,' he used to say. Days after Serebryakov's arrest on 17 August 1936, the Procurator demanded the dacha for himself, even managing to get reimbursed for his old house and then to receive 600,000 roubles to rebuild the new one. This vast sum was approved on 24 January 1937, the very day Vyshinsky cross-examined Serebryakov in the Radek trial.* Woe betide anyone who refused these ill-starred gifts: Marshal Yegorov unwisely rejected the dacha of a shot comrade. 'The souls of former owners,' wrote Svetlana Stalin, 'seemed to linger within those walls.'

'We were never afraid in 1937,' explains Natasha Andreyeva because she believed absolutely that the NKVD only arrested Enemies. Therefore she and their parents would never be arrested. Stepan Mikoyan 'wasn't worried but only later did I realize my parents lived in constant apprehension'. Furthermore, Politburo members were sent all the interrogation records. Stepan used to creep in and peep at the extraordinary revelations of their own family friends who turned out to be Enemies. Every household had its 'expunger': in the Mikoyan household, Sergei Shaumian, adopted son of a late Old Bolshevik, went through all the family photograph albums erasing the faces of Enemies as they were arrested and shot, a horrible distortion of the colouring-in books that most children so enjoy.

---

* After Stalin's death, the Serebryakovs managed to get half the property returned to them but the Vyshinskys kept the other half. Thus in 2002, sixty years after their father was shot by their neighbour, the Serebryakovs spend each weekend next to the Vyshinskys.

Even if they did not grasp the randomness of death, they were aware that it was ever present and they accepted that the coming of war meant Enemies had to be killed. The children talked about it among themselves: Vasily Stalin gleefully told Artyom Sergeev and his Redens cousins about arrests. Protected by whispers and mysteries at home, it was at school that the children learned more. Most of the leaders' children were at Schools No. 175 (or 110), driven there by their fathers' chauffeurs in their Packards and Buicks which could be as embarrassing as a Rolls-Royce at the school gates in the West. The Mikoyans insisted on the car dropping them off so they could walk the last half kilometre. At this élite school, the teachers (who included the English-teaching wife of Nikolai Bulganin, a rising leader) pretended nothing was happening, while the danger was just dawning on the children, who saw their friends being repressed: Stepan Mikoyan's best friend was Serezha Metalikov, son of the senior Kremlevka doctor and nephew of Poskrebyshev, who saw both of his parents arrested during 1937.

Svetlana was treated like a Tsarevna at school by the cringing teachers. A schoolgirl there recalled how her desk gleamed like a mirror, the only one to be polished. Whenever a parent was arrested, their children were removed mysteriously from Svetlana's class so this Tsarevna did not have to rub shoulders with the kin of Enemies.

Sometimes friends were actually arrested at teenage parties in front of all the others. Vasily Stalin and Stepan Mikoyan were carousing at a party given by one of their friends at the Military Academy when the doorbell rang. A man in plain clothes asked to speak to Vasily Stalin who came to the door where he was told, as a sign of almost feudal respect, that the NKVD had arrived to arrest a boy at the party. Vasily returned and told his friend to go to the door while whispering to Stepan that he was being arrested. They watched from the window as the Chekists put the boy into a black car as a 'member of a teenage anti-Soviet group'. He was never seen again.

Parents carefully vetted their children's friends: 'My stepfather was very cautious about my boyfriends,' remembered Zoya Zarubina. 'He always wanted to know who their parents were ...' and would check them out at the Lubianka. The Voroshilovs were stricter than the Mikoyans who were stricter than the Zhdanovs: when one of the Voroshilov children was phoned by a boy whose father had just been arrested, Ekaterina Voroshilova ordered him to break off relations. Zhdanov's son Yury claims that his parents let him bring the children of Enemies home. 'My parents made no objections.' But it was all a matter of timing: in the frenzy of 1937–8, this is hard to believe. After Stepan Mikoyan started going out with a girl called Katya, he found an NKVD report that mentioned her friendship with the son of an Enemy. 'I was waiting for my father to say something to me ... but he never did.' However, when some families close to Mikoyan fell under suspicion, he cut off all contact with them.

* * *

During early 1937, the arrival of Poskrebyshev and Yezhov's glamorous young wives meant that the entourage had never been more colourful and cosmopolitan. Out at Zubalovo, Stalin still took the family out for picnics, bringing chocolates for his daughter and Martha Peshkova. As the country shivered from the depredations of the NKVD, Stalin was solicitous to the children: once Leonid Redens, who was nine, got lost at Kuntsevo and finally galloped up to some adults who all laughed except Stalin. 'Have you got lost?' he asked. 'Come with me, I'll show you the way.' However, the old familiarity with Stalin was gradually freezing into fear.

Part Five

Slaughter: Beria Arrives,
1938–1939

24

Stalin's Jewesses and the Family in Danger

Once, when Stalin was resting at Zubalovo, Pavel and Zhenya Alliluyev's middle child Sergei kept crying and the parents worried that he would be disturbed. Pavel, who had a hysterical temper like his sister Nadya, slapped his daughter Kira for not keeping him quiet. Kira, now a teenager, was irrepressible and, having grown up around Stalin, could not understand the danger. When she refused to eat something Stalin offered her, Pavel kicked her under the table. Yet the children played around Stalin and his killers as obliviously as birds fluttering in and out of a crocodile's open mouth.

Stalin still visited his comrades' houses, often calling at Poskrebyshev's for dinner where there was dancing and he played charades. Poskrebyshev had recently married a sparky girl who had joined Stalin's circle. In 1934, this unlikely romantic hero went to a party at the house of the Kremlin doctor Mikhail Metalikov, whose wife Asya was indirectly related to Trotsky, her sister being married to his son, Sedov. Metalikov's real name was Masenkis, a family of Jewish Lithuanian sugar barons, a dangerous combination.

Metalikov's sister was Bronislava, dark and lithe, full of the energy and playfulness that was so often missing from Old Bolshevik women. The 24-year-old Bronka was married to a lawyer with whom she already had a daughter, while qualifying as an endocrinologist. Photographs show her slim, mischievous elegance in a polkadot dress. That day at the party, she was playing some sort of game, running round the table from which Poskrebyshev, Stalin's simian *chef de cabinet* of forty-three, watched her. When she started a food fight, she threw a cake that missed its target and landed right on Poskrebyshev's Party tunic: he fell in love with Bronka and married her soon afterwards. Family photographs show the worshipful devotion of Poskrebyshev, who appears in history as a Quasimodo but is seen here as the loving husband resting his head on his wife's lustrous shoulder, nuzzling her brown hair.

Beauty and the Beast caused much merriment in Stalin's entourage: Kira Alliluyeva heard 'Poskrebyshev's beautiful Polish wife joke that he was so ugly that she only went to bed with him in the dark'. But Poskrebyshev was proud of his ugliness: Stalin chose him for his hideous countenance. He cheerfully played court jester: Stalin dared Poskrebyshev to drink a glass of vodka in one gulp without a sip of water or to see how long he could hold up his hands with burning paper under each nail.

'Look!' Stalin would laugh. 'Sasha can drink a glass of vodka and not even wrinkle his nose!' Stalin liked Bronka, one of a new generation of lighthearted girls, secure in the heart of the élite, where she was accustomed to meet the magnates. She called Stalin the familiar *ty* and if she travelled abroad, she, like the Alliluyev women, always brought a present for Svetlana, calling Stalin to ask if she could give it. 'Will it suit her?' he asked about a Western pullover.

'Oh yes!'

'Then give it to her!'

Bronka's best friend was Yevgenia Yezhova, editor and irrepressible literary groupie. These two giggly and flighty glamour pusses of Jewish Polish or Lithuanian origins were so similar that Kira Alliluyeva thought they were sisters. They even shared the same patronymic Solomonova though they were no relation. Yezhov and Poskrebyshev were close friends too – they would go fishing together while their wives gossiped.

While Blackberry, now promoted to candidate Politburo member, massacred his victims, his wife was friends with all the artistic stars and slept with most of them. The enchanting Isaac Babel was Yezhova's chief lion: 'If you invited people "for Babel", they all came,' wrote Babel's wife, Pirozhkova. Solomon Mikhoels, the Yiddish actor who performed *King Lear* for Stalin, jazz-band leader Leonid Utesov, film director Eisenstein, novelist Mikhail Sholokhov and journalist Mikhail Koltsov attended the salon of this fascinating flibbertigibbet. At the Kremlin parties, Yezhova foxtrotted the most, not missing a dance. Her best friend, Zinaida Glikina, had also created a literary salon. When her marriage broke up, Yezhov invited her to live with them and seduced her. She was far from being his only mistress, while Yevgenia enthusiastically pursued literary affairs with Babel, Koltsov and

Sholokhov. Few refused an invitation from Yezhov's wife: 'Just think,' Babel said, 'our girl from Odessa has become the first lady of the kingdom!'

After Nadya's death, there was a rumour that Stalin fell in love with and married Lazar Kaganovich's sister, Rosa, his niece (also named Rosa) or his daughter Maya. This was repeated and widely believed: there were even photographs showing Rosa Kaganovich as a dark pretty woman. The Kaganoviches were a good-looking family – Lazar himself was handsome as a young man and his daughter Maya grew up to be compared to Elizabeth Taylor. The significance of the story was that Stalin had a Jewish wife, useful propaganda for the Nazis who had an interest in merging the Jewish and Bolshevik devils into Mr and Mrs Stalin. The Kaganoviches, father and daughter, were so emphatic in their denials that they perhaps protested too much but it seems this particular story is a myth.*

The story is doubly ironic since the Nazis had no need to invent such a character: Stalin was surrounded by Jewesses – from Polina Molotova and Maria Svanidze to Poskrebysheva and Yezhova. Beria's son, reliable on gossip, dubious on politics, recalled that his father gleefully listed Stalin's affairs with Jewesses.

These pretty young Jewesses fluttered around Stalin but they were all of 'dubious origins'. They were more interested in clothes, jokes and affairs than dialectical materialism. Along with Zhenya Alliluyeva and Maria Svanidze, they were surely the life and soul of this fatally interwoven society of Stalin's family and comrades. Stanislas Redens, chief of the Moscow NKVD, often took his family and the other Alliluyevs over to the Yezhovs. The children were fascinated by the NKVD boss: 'Yezhov pranced down the steps in the full dress uniform of Commissar-General in a rather scary way as if he was very full of himself,' recalls Leonid Redens. 'He was so sullen while my father was so open.' Kira Alliluyeva enjoyed the frothy banter of Yevgenia Yezhova and Bronka Poskrebysheva. Yezhov, who worked all night, was usually too tired to socialize so Kira and the other teenagers hid behind a curtain. When the minuscule Blackberry strode past in his boots, they started giggling. But their fathers, Pavel Alliluyev and

---

* There were two Rosa Kaganoviches: Lazar's sister Rosa died young in 1924 while his niece Rosa lived in Rostov and then moved to Moscow where she still lives. It is possible that they met Stalin but they did not marry him.

Stanislas Redens, who understood what was at stake, were furious with them – but how could they explain how dangerous a game it was? Now, the promiscuous horseplay of the women around Stalin made them suddenly vulnerable.

In the spring, Stalin began to distance himself from the family, whose gossipy arrogance suddenly seemed suspicious. When they gathered at his apartment for Svetlana's eleventh birthday on 28 February 1937, Yakov, Stalin's gentle Georgian son, brought Julia, his Jewish wife, for the first time. She had been married to a Chekist bodyguard when she met Yakov through the Redens, whom Stalin immediately blamed for making a match with 'that Jewish woman'. Maria Svanidze, always intriguing, called Julia 'an adventuress' and tried to persuade Stalin:

'Joseph, it's impossible. You must interfere!' This was enough to win Stalin's sympathy for his son.

'A man loves the woman he loves!' he retorted, whether she was a 'princess or a seamstress'. After they married and had their daughter Gulia, Stalin noticed how well Julia kept Yakov's clothes. She was a *baba* after all. 'Now I see your wife's a good thing,' Stalin finally told Yasha who lived with his little family in the grand apartment building on Granovsky Street. When Stalin finally met Julia, he liked her, made a fuss of her and even fed her with a fork like a loving Georgian father-in-law.

Stalin, losing patience with the family, did not attend the party. Maria Svanidze thought she could understand why: the Alliluyevs were useless: 'crazy Olga, idiot Fyodor, imbecilic Pavel and Niura [Anna Redens], narrow-minded Stan [Redens], lazy Vasya [Vasily Stalin], soppy Yasha [Djugashvili]. The only normal people are Alyosha, Zhenya and me and … Svetlana.' This was ironic since it was the Svanidzes who were the first to fall. Maria herself was ebulliently egotistical, tormenting her own husband with letters that boasted, 'I'm better looking than 70% of Bolshevik wives … Anyone who meets me remembers forever.' This was true but far from helpful at Stalin's court. One pities these haughty, decent women who found themselves in the quagmire of this place and time which they so little understood.

That spring, Stalin and Pavel played Svanidze and Redens at billiards. The losers traditionally had to crawl under the table as their penalty. When Stalin's side lost, Pavel diplomatically suggested that the children, Kira and Sergei, should crawl under the table for them. Sergei did not mind – he was only nine – but

Kira, who was eighteen, refused defiantly. As outspoken as her mother and fearless with it, she insisted that Stalin and her father had lost and under the table they should go. Pavel became hysterical and clipped her with the billiard cue.

Soon afterwards, Stalin and the blue-eyed, dandyish Svanidze suddenly ceased to be 'like brothers'. 'Alyosha was quite a liberal, a European,' explained Molotov. 'Stalin sensed this …' Svanidze was Deputy Chairman of the State Bank, an institution filled with urbane cosmopolitans now under grave suspicion. On 2 April 1937, Stalin wrote an ominous note to Yezhov: 'Purge the staff of the State Bank.' Svanidze had also done secret and sensitive work for Stalin over the years. Maria Svanidze's diary stopped in the middle of the year: her access to Stalin had suddenly ended. By 21 December, they were under investigation and not invited for Stalin's birthday which must have been agony for Maria. Days later, the Svanidzes visited Zhenya and Pavel Alliluyev in the House on the Embankment (where they all lived). Maria showed off her low-cut velvet dress. After they left at midnight, Zhenya and Kira were doing the dishes when the bell rang. It was Maria's son from her first marriage: 'Mama and Alyosha have been arrested. She was taken away in her beautiful clothes.' A few months later, Zhenya received a letter from Maria who begged her to pass it on to Stalin: 'If I don't leave this camp, I'll die.' She took the letter to Stalin who warned her:

'Don't ever do this again!' Maria was moved to a harsher prison. Zhenya sensed the danger for her and her children of being so close to Stalin, although she adored him until the end of her days, despite her terrible misfortunes. She drew back from Stalin while nagging Pavel to speak to him about their arrested friends. Apparently he did so: 'They're my friends – so put me in jail too!' Some were released.

The other Alliluyevs also did their bit: grandmother Olga, living a *grande dame*'s life in the Kremlin, said little. While the others believed that Stalin did not know the details and was being tricked by the NKVD, she alone of this ship of fools understood: 'nothing happens that he does not know about.' But her estranged husband, the respected Sergei, appealed repeatedly to Stalin, waiting for him on the sofa in his apartment. Oftentimes he fell asleep there and awoke in the early hours to find Stalin arriving from dinner. There and then he begged for someone's life. Stalin teased his father-in-law by repeating his favourite expression: 'Exactly exactly':

'So you came to see me, "Exactly Exactly",' Stalin joked.

Just after Svanidze's arrest, Mikoyan arrived as normal at Kuntsevo for dinner with Stalin who, knowing how close he was to Alyosha, walked straight up to him and said:

'Did you hear we've arrested Svanidze?'

'Yes ... but how could it happen?'

'He's a German spy,' replied Stalin.

'How can it be?' replied Mikoyan. 'There's no evidence of his sabotage. What's the benefit of a spy who does nothing?'

Stalin explained that Svanidze was a 'special sort of spy', recruited when he was a German prisoner during the Great War, whose job was simply to provide information. Presumably, after this revelation, dinner at Stalin's continued as usual.

* * *

Once a leader was under attack, the Terror followed its own momentum. Just demoted, Postyshev, the tough, sallow-faced and arrogant 'prince' of the Ukraine, who had so entertained Stalin by slow-dancing with Molotov, frantically proved his ferocity by eliminating virtually the entire bureaucracy in the Volga town of Kuibyshev.* Now, at the Plenum in January 1938, he was to be destroyed for killing the wrong people.

'The Soviet and Party leaderships were in enemy hands,' claimed Postyshev.

'All of it? From top to bottom?' interrupted Mikoyan.

'Weren't there any honest people?' asked Bulganin.

'Aren't you exaggerating, Comrade Postyshev?' added Molotov.

'But there were errors,' Kaganovich declared, a cue to Postyshev to say:

'I shall talk about my personal errors.'

'I want you to tell the truth,' said Beria.

'Please permit me to finish and explain the whole business to the best of my ability,' Postyshev pleaded at which Kaganovich boomed: 'You're not very good at explaining it – that's the whole point.' Postyshev got up to defend himself but Andreyev snapped:

'Comrade Postyshev, take your seat. This is no place for strolling around.' Postyshev's strolling days were over: Malenkov attacked him. Stalin proposed his demotion from the Politburo: Khrushchev, who was soon appointed to run the Ukraine, replaced him as candidate member, stepping into the front rank. But the attacks

---

* The ancient city of Samara had been renamed after Kuibyshev on his death in 1935.

on Postyshev contained a warning for Yezhov whose arrests were increasingly frenzied. Meanwhile Stalin seemed undecided about Postyshev:* his high-handedness attracted enemies who perhaps persuaded Stalin to destroy him. His last hope was a personal appeal to Stalin, probably written after a confrontation with his accusers:

'Comrade Stalin, I ask you to receive me after the meeting.'

'I cannot receive you today,' Stalin wrote back. 'Talk to Comrade Molotov.' Within days, he had been arrested. Stalin signed another order for 48,000 executions by quota while Marshal Yegorov followed his 'beautiful' wife into the 'meat-grinder'. But Yezhov was already so exhausted that on 1 December 1937, Stalin was commissioned to supervise his week-long holiday.

In early February, a drunken Blackberry led an expedition to purge Kiev where, aided by the new Ukrainian viceroy Khrushchev,† another 30,000 were arrested. Arriving to find that virtually the whole Ukrainian Politburo had been purged under his predecessor Kosior, Khrushchev went on to arrest several commissars and their deputies. The Politburo approved 2,140 victims on Khrushchev's lists for shooting. Here again, he over-fulfilled his quota. In 1938, 106,119 people were arrested in Khrushchev's Ukrainian Terror. Yezhov's visit accelerated the bloodbath: 'After Nikolai Ivanovich Yezhov's trip to Ukraine … the real destruction of hidden Enemies began,' announced Khrushchev, hailed as an 'unswerving Stalinist' for his 'merciless uprooting of Enemies'. The NKVD unveiled a conspiracy to poison horses and arrested two professors as Nazi agents. Khrushchev tested the so-called poison and discovered that it did not kill horses. Only after three different commissions had been appointed did he prove this particular conspiracy to be false – but one suspects that Khrushchev only questioned the NKVD's work when Stalin had signalled his displeasure.

In his cups in Kiev, Yezhov displayed alarming recklessness, boasting that the Politburo was 'in his hands'. He could arrest

---

* Did Stalin recall Postyshev's slight cheekiness in 1931? When Stalin wrote to him to complain about the list of those to receive the Order of Lenin: 'We give the Order of Lenin to any old shitters'. Postyshev replied cheerfully that the 'shitters' were all approved by Stalin himself.

† Khrushchev, like other regional bosses such as Beria and Zhdanov, became the object of an extravagant local cult: a 'Song of Khrushchev' soon joined the 'Song for Beria' and odes to Yezhov in the Soviet songbook.

anyone he wanted, even the leaders. One night he was literally carried home from a banquet. It could not be long before Stalin heard of his excesses, if not his dangerous boasting.

Yezhov returned in time for the third and last show trial of the 'Anti-Soviet Bloc of Rightists and Trotskyites' which opened on 2 March, starring Bukharin, Rykov and Yagoda, who admitted killing Kirov and Gorky among others. Bukharin scored his own private triumph in a confession of guilt, laced with oblique Aesopian mockery of Stalin and Yezhov's infantile plots. But this changed nothing. Yezhov attended the executions. He is said to have ordered Yagoda to be beaten:

'Come on, hit him for all of us.' But there was a hint of humanity when it came to the death of his old drinking companion, Yagoda's ex-secretary Bulanov: he had him given some brandy.

When it was over, Yezhov proposed a fourth super-trial against the Polish spies in the Comintern, which he had been preparing for months. But Stalin cancelled the trial. He rarely pursued one policy to the exclusion of all others: Stalin's antennae sensed that the massacre was exhausting his own lieutenants, especially the louche Blackberry himself.

25

Beria and the Weariness of Hangmen

On 4 April, Yezhov was appointed Commissar of Water Transport which made some sense since the building of canals was the task of the NKVD's slave labour. But there was a worrying symmetry because Yagoda had been appointed to a similar Commissariat on his dismissal. Meanwhile Yezhov ravaged even the Politburo: Postyshev was being interrogated; Eikhe of West Siberia was arrested. Stalin promoted Kosior from Kiev to Moscow as Soviet Deputy Premier. However, in April 1938, Kosior's brother was arrested. His one hope was to denounce his kin:

'I'm living under suspicion and distrust,' he wrote to Stalin. 'You can't imagine how that feels to an innocent man. The arrest of my brother casts a shadow over me too ... I swear on my life I've not only never suspected the real nature of Casimir Kosior, he was never close to me ... Why has he invented all this? I can't understand it but Comrade Stalin, it was all invented from start to finish ... I ask you Comrade Stalin and all the Politburo to let me explain myself. I am a victim of an enemy's lies. Sometimes I think this is a silly dream...' How often these victims compared their plight to a 'dream'. On 3 May he was arrested, followed by Chubar. Kaganovich claimed, 'I protected Kosior and Chubar' but faced with their handwritten confessions, 'I gave up.'

Yezhov, living a vampiric nocturnal existence of drinking and torture sessions, was being crushed under the weight of his work. Stalin noticed Blackberry's degeneration. 'You call the ministry,' Stalin complained, 'he's left for the Central Committee. You call the Central Committee, he's left for the ministry. You send a messenger to his apartment and there he's dead drunk.' The pressure on these slaughtermen was immense: just as Himmler later lectured his SS butchers on their special work, so now Stalin worked hard to reassure and encourage his men. But not all of them were strong enough to stand the pace.

The executioners survived by drinking. Even the sober purgers were dizzy with death. The official investigating the Belorussian Military District admitted to Stalin that 'I didn't lose my teeth but I must confess ... I became disorientated for a while.' Stalin reassured him. Even dread Mekhlis almost had a breakdown at the beginning of the Terror when he still ran *Pravda*, writing an extraordinary letter to Stalin that gives a fascinating window on to the pressures of being a Stalinist potentate in the whirlwind of terror:

> *Dear Comrade Stalin,*
>
> *My nerves did not stand up. I did not comport myself as a Bolshevik; especially I feel the pain of my words in our 'personal talk' when I personally owed my whole life and my* Partiinost *to you. I feel absolutely crushed. These years take away from us a lot of people ... I must run* Pravda *in a situation when there is no secretary and no editor, when we have not approved a theme, when I found myself finally in the role of 'persecuted editor'. This is organized bedlam which can eat up everybody. And it has eaten up people! In the last days, I've felt ill without sleep and only able to get to sleep at eleven or twelve in the morning ... I'm all the more frantic in my apartment after sleepless nights at the newspaper. It's time to relieve me [of this job]. I can't be chief of* Pravda *when I'm sick and sleepless, incapable of following what is happening in the country, economics, art and literature, never getting the chance to go to the theatre. I had to tell you this personally but it was silly, lying. Forgive me my dear Comrade Stalin for that unpleasant minute I gave you. For me it's very hard to experience such a trauma!*

The Procurator-General Vyshinsky also felt the pressure, finding this on his desk: 'Everyone knows you're a Menshevik. After using you, Stalin will sentence you to *Vishka* ... Run away ... Remember Yagoda. That's your destiny. The Moor has done his duty. The Moor can go.'

Constantly drunk, Yezhov sensed Stalin was, as he later wrote to his master, 'dissatisfied with the NKVD work which deteriorated my mood still further'. He made frantic attempts to prove his worth: he was said to have suggested renaming Moscow as 'Stalinodar'. This was laughed off. Instead Yezhov was called upon to kill his own NKVD appointees whom he had protected. In early 1938, Stalin and Yezhov decided to liquidate the veteran Chekist, Abram Slutsky, but since he headed the Foreign Department, they devised a plan so as not to scare their foreign agents. On 17 February, Frinovsky invited Slutsky to his office where another of Yezhov's deputies came up behind him and drew a mask of chloroform over his face. He was then injected with poison and died right there in the office. It was officially announced that he had died of a heart attack.* Soon the purge began to threaten those closer to Yezhov. When his protégé Liushkov was recalled from the Far East, Yezhov tipped him off. Liushkov defected to the Japanese. Yezhov was so rattled by this fiasco that he asked Frinovsky to go with him to tell Stalin: 'On my own I did not have the strength.' Yezhov 'literally went mad'. Stalin rightly suspected Yezhov of warning Liushkov.

Sensing his rising doubts, Stalin's magnates, who had proved their readiness to kill, began to denounce Yezhov's degeneracy and lies. Zhdanov in particular was said to oppose Yezhov's terror. His son Yury claims his father had wanted to talk to Stalin alone but Yezhov was always present: 'Father finally managed to see Stalin tête-à-tête and said, "Political provocation is going on ..."' This is convincing because Zhdanov was closest to Stalin personally but Malenkov's children tell a similar story. Molotov and Yezhov had a row in the Politburo in mid-1938. Stalin ordered the latter to apologize. When another NKVD agent, Alexander Orlov, the resident agent in Spain, defected, Yezhov was so scared of Stalin, that he tried to withhold this information.

On 29 July, Stalin signed another death-list that included more of Yezhov's protégés. Yezhov was so distraught with fear and foreboding that he started shooting prisoners who might incriminate him. Uspensky, the Ukrainian NKVD chief, was in Moscow and discovered that a thousand people were going to be shot in the next five days. 'The tracks should be covered,' Yezhov warned him. 'All investigation cases should be finished in an accelerated procedure so it'll be impossible to make sense of it.'

Stalin gently told Yezhov that he needed some help in running the NKVD and asked him to choose someone. Yezhov requested Malenkov but Stalin wanted to keep him in the Central Committee so someone, probably Kaganovich, proposed Beria. Stalin may have wanted a Caucasian, perhaps convinced that the cut-throat traditions of the mountains – blood feuds, vendettas and secret murders – suited the position. Beria was a natural, the only First Secretary who personally tortured his victims. The

---

* His splendid gravestone in the Novodevichy Cemetery not far from Nadya Stalin's grave gives no hint of his sinister end.

blackjack – the *zhguti* – and the truncheon – the *dubenka* – were his favourite toys. He was hated by many of the Old Bolsheviks and family members around the leader. With the whispering, plotting and vengeful Beria at his side, Stalin felt able to destroy his own polluted, intimate world.

Yezhov probably tried to arrest Beria, but it was too late. Stalin had already seen Beria during the Supreme Soviet on 10 August. Beria was coming to Moscow.

He had come a long way since 1931. Beria, now thirty-six, was complex and talented with a first-class brain. He was witty, a font of irreverent jokes, mischievous anecdotes and withering put-downs. He managed to be a sadistic torturer as well as a loving husband and warm father but he was already a Priapic womanizer whom power would distort into a sexual predator. A skilled manager, he was the only Soviet leader whom 'one could imagine becoming Chairman of General Motors', as his daughter-in-law put it later. He could run vast enterprises with a mixture of villainous threats – 'I'll grind you to powder' – and meticulous precision. 'Everything that depended on Beria had to function with the precision ... of a clock' while 'the two things he could not bear were wordiness and vagueness of expression.'* He was 'a good organizer, businesslike and capable', Stalin had told Kaganovich as early as 1932, possessing the 'bull nerves' and indefatigability that were necessary for survival at Stalin's court. He was a 'most clever man', admitted Molotov, 'inhumanly energetic – he could work a week without sleep'.

Beria had the 'singular ability to inspire both fear and enthusiasm'. 'Idolized' by his own henchmen even though he was often harsh and rude, he would shout: 'We'll arrest you and let you rot in the camps ... we'll turn you into camp dust.' A young man like Alyosha Mirtskhulava, whom Beria promoted in the Georgian Party, was still praising Beria for his 'humanity, strength, efficiency and patriotism' when he was interviewed for this book in 2002.† Yet he liked to boast about his victims: 'Let me have one night with him and I'll have him confessing he's the King of England.' His favourite movies were Westerns but he identified with the Mexican bandits. Well-educated for a Bolshevik

---

* He usually signed documents in tiny neat writing in a distinctive turquoise ink or on a turquoise typewriter that did not clash with Stalin's blue or red crayons.
† The author is grateful to Alyosha Mirtskhulava, Beria's Georgian Komsomol boss, and later Georgian First Secretary, for his interview in Tbilisi.

magnate, Stalin teased this architect *manqué* that his pince-nez were made of clear glass, worn to give an impression of intellectual gravitas.

This deft intriguer, coarse psychopath and sexual adventurer would also have cut throats, seduced ladies-in-waiting and poisoned goblets of wine at the courts of Genghis Khan, Suleiman the Magnificent or Lucrezia Borgia. But this 'zealot', as Svetlana called him, worshipped Stalin in these earlier years – theirs was the relationship of monarch and liege – treating him like a Tsar instead of the first comrade. The older magnates treated Stalin respectfully but familiarly, but even Kaganovich praised him in the Bolshevik lexicon. Beria however said, 'Oh yes, you are so right, absolutely true, how true' in an obsequious way, recalled Svetlana. 'He was always emphasizing that he was devoted to my father and it got through to Stalin that whatever he said, this man supported him.' Bearing a flavour of his steamy Abkhazia to Stalin's court, Beria was to become even more complex, powerful and depraved, yet less devoted to Marxism as time went on but in 1938, this 'colossal figure', as Artyom puts it, changed everything.

Beria, like many before him, tried to refuse his promotion. There is no reason to doubt his sincerity – Yagoda had just been shot and the writing was on the wall for Yezhov. His wife Nina did not want to move – but Beria was rapaciously ambitious. When Stalin proposed Beria as NKVD First Deputy, Yezhov pathetically suggested that the Georgian might be a good commissar in his own right. 'No, a good deputy,' Stalin reassured him.

Stalin sent Vlasik down to arrange the move. In August, after hurrying back to Georgia to anoint a successor to run Tiflis, Beria arrived in Moscow where, on 22 August 1938, he was appointed First Deputy Narkom of the NKVD. The family were assigned an apartment in the doom-laden House on the Embankment. Stalin arrived to inspect the flat and was not impressed. The bosses lived much better in the warm fertile Caucasus, with its traditions of luxury, wine and plentiful fruit, than elsewhere: Beria had resided in an elegant villa in Tiflis. Stalin suggested they move into the Kremlin but Beria's wife was unenthusiastic. So finally Stalin chose the Georgian new boy an aristocratic villa on Malaya Nikitskaya in the centre of the city, once the home of a Tsarist General Kuropatkin, where he lived splendidly by Politburo standards. Only Beria had his own mansion.

Stalin treated the newly arrived Berias like a long-lost family. He adored the statuesque blonde Nina Beria whom he always treated 'like a daughter': when the new Georgian leader Candide Charkviani was invited to dinner *chez* Beria, there was a phone call and a sudden flurry of activity.

'Stalin's coming!' Nina said, frantically preparing Georgian food. Moments later, Stalin swept in. At the Georgian *supra*, Stalin and Beria sang together. Even after the Terror, Stalin had not lost a certain spontaneity.

Beria and Yezhov ostensibly became friends: Beria called his boss 'dear Yozhik', even staying at his dacha. But it could not last in the jungle of Stalin's court. Beria attended most meetings with Yezhov and took over the intelligence departments. Beria waged a quiet campaign to destroy Blackberry: he invited Khrushchev for dinner where he warned him about Malenkov's closeness to Yezhov. Khrushchev realized that Beria was really warning him about his own friendship with Yezhov. No doubt Beria had the same chat with Malenkov. But the most telling evidence is the archives: Beria finagled Vyshinsky into complaining to Stalin about Yezhov's slowness.* Stalin did not react but Molotov ordered Yezhov:

'It is necessary to pay special attention to Comrade Beria and hurry up. Molotov.' That weather vane of Stalin's favour, Poskrebyshev, stopped calling Yezhov by the familiar *ty* and started visiting Beria instead.

Beria brought a new spirit to the NKVD: Yezhov's frenzy was replaced with a tight system of terror administration that became the Stalinist method of ruling Russia. But this new efficiency was no consolation to the victims. Beria worked with Yezhov on the interrogations of the fallen magnates, Kosior, Chubar and Eikhe, who were cruelly tortured. Chubar appealed to Stalin and Molotov, revealing his agonies.

Stalin, Blackberry and Beria now turned to the Far East where the army, under the gifted Marshal Blyukher, had largely escaped the Terror. In late June, the 'gloomy demon' Mekhlis descended on Blyukher's command with rabid blood-lust. Setting up his headquarters in his railway carriage like a Civil War chieftain, he was soon sending Stalin and Voroshilov telegrams like this:

---

* The case in question concerned an investigation to find the person who had mistakenly burned the books of Lenin, Stalin and Gorky in a furnace: another example of the absurdity and deadliness of the Terror.

'The Special Railway Corps leaves bits and pieces of dubious people all over the place ... There are 46 German Polish Lithuanian Latvian Galician commanders ... I have to go to Vladivostok to purge the corps.' Once there, he boasted to Stalin, 'I dismissed 215 political workers, most of them arrested. But the purge ... is not finished. I think it's impossible to leave Khabarovsk without even more harsh investigations ...' When Voroshilov and Budyonny tried to protect officers, Mekhlis sneaked on Voroshilov (they hated each other) to Stalin: 'I reported to CC and Narkom (Voroshilov) about the situation in the secret service department. There are a lot of dubious people and spies there ... Now C. Voroshilov orders the cancellation of the trial ... I can't agree with the situation.' Even Kaganovich thought Mekhlis 'was cruel, he sometimes overdid it!'

As Mekhlis headed east, the Japanese Kwangtung Army probed Soviet defences west of Lake Khasan, leading to a full-scale battle. Blyukher attacked the Japanese between 6 and 11 August and drove them back with heavy losses. Encouraged by Mekhlis, and alarmed by the losses and Blyukher's hesitations, Stalin berated the Marshal down the telephone:

'Tell me honestly, Comrade Blyukher, do you really want to fight the Japanese? If you don't, then tell me straight, like a good Communist.'

'The sharks have arrived,' Blyukher told his wife. 'They want to eat me. Either they eat me or I eat them, but the latter is unlikely.' The killer-shark sealed Blyukher's fate. Mekhlis arrested four of Blyukher's staff, requesting Stalin and Voroshilov to let him 'shoot all four without prosecution by my special order'. Blyukher was sacked, recalled and arrested on 22 October 1938.

'Now I am done for!' sobbed Yezhov in his office, as he went on executing any prisoners who 'may turn against us'. On 29 September, he lost much of his power when Beria was appointed to run the heart of the NKVD: State Security (GUGB). He now co-signed Yezhov's orders. Blackberry tried to strike back: he proposed to Stalin that Stanislas Redens, Beria's enemy married to Anna Alliluyeva, become his other deputy. There was no hope of this.

Yezhov sat boozing at his dacha with his depressed cronies, warning that they would soon be destroyed, and fantasizing about killing his enemies: 'Immediately remove all people posted in the Kremlin by Beria,' he loudly ordered the head of Kremlin security during one such bout, 'and replace them with reliable people.' Soon he said, in a slurred voice, that Stalin should be killed.

26

The Tragedy and Depravity of the Yezhovs

News of the lion-hunting literary sex-life of Yevgenia Yezhova suddenly reached Stalin. Sholokhov, one of his favourite novelists, had started an affair with her. Yezhov bugged his room at the National Hotel and was furious to read the blow-by-blow account of how 'they kissed each other' then 'lay down'. Yezhov was so intoxicated and jealous that he slapped Yevgenia in the presence of their lissom house-guest, Zinaida Glikina (with whom he was sleeping) but later forgave her. Sholokhov realized he was being followed and complained to Stalin and Beria. Stalin summoned Blackberry to the Politburo where he apologized to the novelist.

The magnates steered cautiously between Yezhov and Beria. When Yezhov arrested one commissar, Stalin sent Molotov and Mikoyan to investigate. Back at the Kremlin, Mikoyan acclaimed the man's innocence and Beria attacked Yezhov's case. 'Yezhov displayed an ambiguous smile,' wrote Mikoyan, 'Beria looked pleased' but 'Molotov's face was like a mask.' The Commissar* became what Mikoyan called a 'lucky stiff', back from the dead. Stalin released him.

When one NKVD officer needed the chief's signature, Yezhov was nowhere to be found. Beria told him to drive out to Yezhov's dacha and get his signature. There he found a man who was either 'fatally ill or had spent the night drinking heavily'. Regional NKVD bosses started to denounce Yezhov.

The darkness began to descend on Yezhov's family where his silly, sensual wife was unwittingly to play the terrible role of black widow spider: most of her lovers were to die. She herself was too

---

* Stalin backed Beria's dismissal of the case against Shipping Commissar Tevosian but told Mikoyan: 'Tell him the CC knows he was recruited by Krupp as a German agent. Everyone understands a person gets trapped ... If he confesses it honestly ... the CC will forgive him.' Mikoyan called Tevosian into his office to offer him Stalin's trick but the Commisssar refused to confess, which Stalin accepted. Tevosian was to be one of the major industrial managers of WW2.

sensitive a flower for Yezhov's world. Both she and Yezhov were promiscuous but then they lived in a world of high tension, dizzy power over life and death, and dynamic turmoil where men rose and fell around them. If there was justice in Yezhov's fall, it was a tragedy for Yevgenia and little Natasha, to whom he was a kind father. A pall fell on Yevgenia's literary salon. When a friend walked her home to the Kremlin after a party, she herself reflected that Babel was in danger because he had been friends with arrested Trotskyite generals: 'Only his European fame could save him ...' She herself was in greater peril.

Yezhov learned that Beria was going to use Yevgenia, an 'English spy' from her time in London, against him so he asked for a divorce in September. The divorce was sensible: in other cases, it actually saved the life of the divorcee. But the tension almost broke the nervy Yevgenia, who went on holiday to the Crimea with Zinaida to recover. It seems that Yezhov was trying to protect his wife from arrest, hence her loving and grateful letter to him.

'Kolyushenka!' she wrote to her beleaguered husband. 'I really ask you – I insist that I remain in control of my life. Kolya darling! I earnestly beg you to check up on my whole life, everything about me ... I cannot reconcile myself to the thought that I am under suspicion of committing crimes I never committed ...'

Their world was shrinking daily: Yezhov had managed to have her ex-husband Gladun shot before Beria took control of the NKVD, but another ex-lover, the publisher Uritsky, was being interrogated. He revealed her affair with Babel. Yezhov's secretary and friends were arrested too. Yezhov summoned Yevgenia back to Moscow.

Yevgenia waited at the dacha with her daughter Natasha and her friend Zinaida. She was desperately worried about the family – and who can blame her? Her nerves cracked. In hospital, they diagnosed an 'asthenic-depressive condition perhaps cyclothymia', sending her to a sanatorium near Moscow.

When Zinaida was arrested, Yevgenia wrote to Stalin: 'I beg you Comrade Stalin to read this letter ... I am treated by professors but what sense does it make if I am burned by the thought that you distrust me? ... You are dear and beloved to me.' Swearing on her daughter's life that she was honest, she admitted that 'in my personal life, there have been mistakes about which I could tell you, and all of it because of jealousy.' Stalin doubtless already knew all her Messalinian exploits. She made the sacrificial offer:

'Let them take away my freedom, my life ... but I will not give up the right to love you as everybody does, who loves the country and the Party.' She signed off: 'I feel like a living corpse. What am I to do? Forgive my letter written in bed.' Stalin did not reply.

The trap was swinging shut on Yevgenia and her Kolyushenka. On 8 October, Kaganovich drafted a Politburo resolution on the NKVD. On 17 November, a Politburo commission denounced 'very serious faults in the work of the Organs of NKVD'. The deadly *troikas* were dissolved. Stalin and Molotov signed a report, disassociating themselves from the Terror.

At the 7 November parade, Yezhov appeared on the Mausoleum but lingered behind Stalin. Then he disappeared and was replaced by Beria in the blue cap and uniform of a Commissar First Class of State Security. When Stalin ordered the arrest of Yezhov's friend, Uspensky, Ukrainian NKVD chief, the dwarf forewarned him. Uspensky faked suicide and went on the run. Stalin (probably rightly) suspected that Yezhov was bugging his phones.

In her own way, Yevgenia loved Yezhov, despite all their infidelities, and adored their daughter Natasha, because she was willing to sacrifice herself to save them. Her friend Zinaida Ordzhonikidze, Sergo's widow, visited her in hospital, a heroic act of loyalty. Yevgenia gave her a letter for Yezhov in which she offered to commit suicide and asked for a sleeping draught. She suggested that he send a little statuette of a gnome when the time came. He sent Luminal, then, a little later, he ordered the maid to take his wife the statuette. Given Yezhov's dwarfish stature, this deadly gnome seems farcical: perhaps the statuette was an old keepsake representing 'darling Kolya' himself from the early days of their romance. When Glikina's arrest made her own inevitable, Yevgenia sent a note bidding Yezhov goodbye. On 19 November, she took the Luminal.

At 11 p.m., as she sank into unconsciousness, Yezhov arrived at the Little Corner, where he found the Politburo with Beria and Malenkov, who attacked him for five hours. Yevgenia died two days later. Yezhov himself reflected that he had been 'compelled to sacrifice her to save himself'. She had married a monster but died young to save their daughter which, in its way, was a maternal end to a life devoted to innocent fun. Babel heard that 'Stalin can't understand her death. His own nerves are made of steel so he just can't understand how, in other people, they give out.' The Yezhovs' adopted daughter* Natasha, nine, was taken in by his ex-wife's sister and then sent to one of those grim orphanages for the children of Enemies.

Two days after Yevgenia's death, on 23 November, Yezhov returned for another four hours of criticism from Stalin, Molotov and Voroshilov, after which he resigned from the NKVD. Stalin accepted it but he remained in limbo as CC Secretary, Commissar of Water Transport, and a candidate Politburo member, living in the Kremlin like a tiny ghost for a little longer, experiencing what his victims had known before him. His friends 'turned their back upon me as if I was plague-ridden ... I never realized the depth of meanness of all these people.' He blamed the Terror on the *Vozhd*, using a Russian idiom: 'God's will – the Tsar's trial' with himself as the Tsar and Stalin as God.

Yezhov consoled himself with a series of drunken bisexual orgies in his Kremlin apartment. Inviting two drinking buddies and homosexual lovers from his youth to stay, he enjoyed 'the most perverted forms of debauchery'. His nephews brought him girls but he also returned to homosexuality. When one crony, Konstantinov, brought his wife to the party, Yezhov danced the foxtrot with her, pulled out his member, and then slept with her. On the next night, when the long-suffering Konstantinov arrived, they drank and danced to the gramophone until the guest fell asleep only to be awoken: 'I felt something in my mouth. When I opened my eyes, I saw that Yezhov had shoved his member into my mouth.' Unzipped and undone, Yezhov awaited his fate.

Beria, whom Stalin nicknamed 'the Prosecutor', was triumphantly appointed Commissar on 25 November,† and summoned his Georgian henchmen to Moscow. Having destroyed the entourages of the Old Bolshevik 'princes', Stalin now had to import Beria's whole gang to destroy Yezhov's.

---

* Her name was changed to that of Yevgenia's first husband, Khayutin – but she remained loyal to her adoptive father into the next millennium. Natasha Yezhova survived after enduring terrible sufferings on her stepfather's behalf. Vasily Grossman, the author of the classic novel *Life and Fate*, who knew the family, attending the salons with Babel and others, wrote a short story about Natasha's tragic childhood. She became a musician in Penza and Magadan. In May 1998 she applied for Yezhov's rehabilitation. Ironically she had a case since he was certainly not guilty of the espionage for which he was executed. Her appeal was denied. At the time of writing, she is alive.

† The switch between the two secret police chiefs was seamless: on the 24th, Dmitrov, the Comintern leader, was still discussing arrests with Yezhov at his dacha but by nighttime on the 25th, he was working on the same cases with Beria at *his* house.

Ironically, Beria's courtiers were much more educated than Kaganovich or Voroshilov but education is no bar to barbarism. The grey-haired, charming and refined Merkulov, a Russified Armenian, who was to write plays under the pseudonym Vsevolod Rok that were performed on Moscow stages, had known Beria since they studied together at the Baku Polytechnic and had joined the Cheka in 1920. Beria, who, like Stalin, coined nicknames for everyone, called him 'the Theoretician'. Then there was the renegade Georgian prince (though aristocrats are as plentiful in Georgia as vines) Shalva Tsereteli, once a Tsarist officer and member of the anti-Bolshevik Georgian Legion, who had the air of an old-fashioned gentleman but was Beria's private assassin, among his other duties in the NKVD's Special Department. Then there was the bejewelled 300-pound giant – 'the worst man God put on the face of the Earth' – Bogdan Kobulov. 'A burly oversized Caucasian with muddy brown bullish eyes', the 'fat face of a man [who] likes good living ...hairy hands, short bow legs', and a dapper moustache, he was one of those hearty torturers who would have been as at home in the Gestapo as in the NKVD. He was so squat that Beria called him 'the Samovar'.

When Kobulov beat his victims, he used his fists, his elephantine weight and his favourite blackjack clubs. He arranged wiretaps of the magnates for Stalin but he also became a court jester, replacing the late Pauker, with his funny accents. He soon proved his usefulness: Beria was interrogating a victim in his office when the prisoner attacked him. Kobulov boasted about what happened next: 'I saw the boss [he used the Georgian slang – *khozeni*] on the floor and I jumped on the fellow and crushed his neck with my own bare hands.' Yet even this brute sensed that his work was not right for he used to visit his mother and sob to her like an overgrown Georgian child: 'Mama, mama, what are we doing? One day, I'll pay for this.'

The arrival of these exotic, strutting Georgians, some even convicted murderers, must have been like Pancho Villa and his *banditos* riding into a northern town in one of Beria's favourite movies. Stalin later made a great play of sending some of them home, replacing them with Russians, but he remained very much a Georgian himself. Beria's men gave Stalin's entourage a distinctly Caucasian flavour. On the official date of Beria's appointment, Stalin and Molotov signed off on the shooting of 3,176 people so they were busy.

Beria appeared nightly in Lefortovo prison to torture Marshal Blyukher, assisted by 'the Theoretician' Merkukov, 'the Samovar' Kobulov, and his top interrogator, Rodos, who worked on the Marshal with such relish that he called out: 'Stalin, can you hear what they're doing to me?' They tortured him so hard that they managed to knock out one of his eyes and he later died of his wounds. Beria drove over to tell Stalin who ordered the body's incineration. Meanwhile, Beria settled scores, personally arresting Alexander Kosarev, the Komsomol chief, who had once insulted him. Stalin later learned this was a personal vendetta: 'They told me Beria was very vindictive but there was no evidence of it,' he reflected years later. 'In Kosarev's case, Zhdanov and Andreyev checked the evidence.'

Beria revelled in the sport of power: Bukharin's lovely widow, Anna Larina, still only twenty-four, was shown into his Lubianka office by Kobulov who then brought in sandwiches like an infernal Jeeves.

'I should tell you that you look more beautiful than when I last saw you,' Beria told her. 'Execution is for one time only. And Yezhov would certainly have executed you.' When she would not betray anyone, Beria and Kobulov stopped flirting. 'Whom are you trying to save? After all, Nikolai Ivanovich [Bukharin] is no longer with us ... You want to live? ... If you don't shut up, here's what you'll get!' He put a finger to his temple. 'So will you promise me to shut up?' She saw that Beria wanted to save her and she promised. But she would not eat Kobulov's sandwiches.*

* * *

Stalin was careful not to place himself completely in the hands of Beria: the chief of State Security (First Branch), his personal security, was in a sensitive but dangerous position. Two had been shot since Pauker but now Stalin appointed his personal bodyguard, Vlasik, to the job, in charge of the leader's security as well as the dachas, food for the kitchens, the car pool and millions of roubles. Henceforth, explains Artyom, Stalin 'ruled through Poskrebyshev in political matters and Vlasik in personal ones'. Both were indefatigably industrious – and sleazy.

The two men lived similar lives: their daughters recall how they

---

* Anna Larina spent twenty years in the camps. Her son Yury was eleven months old when she was arrested in 1937 and she did not see him again until 1956, just one of many heart-breaking stories.

spent only Sunday at home. Otherwise they were always with Stalin, returning exhausted to sleep. No one knew Stalin better. At home they never discussed politics but chatted about their fishing expeditions. Vlasik, who lived in the elegant villa on Gogolevsky Boulevard, was doggedly loyal, uneducated and drunkenly dissolute: he was already an insatiable womanizer who held parties with Poskrebyshev. He had so many 'concubines', he kept lists of them, forgot their names, and sometimes managed to have a different one in each room at his orgies. He called Stalin *Khozyain*, but 'Comrade Stalin' to his face, rarely joining him at table.

Poskrebyshev's social status was higher, often joining the magnates at dinner and calling Stalin 'Joseph Vissarionovich'. He was the butt and perpetrator of jokes. He sat doggedly at his desk outside Stalin's office: the Little Corner was his domain. The magnates cultivated him, playing to his dog's vanity so that he would warn them if Stalin was in a bad mood. Poskrebyshev always called Vyshinsky to say that Stalin was on his way to Kuntsevo so the Procurator could go to bed, and he once protected Khrushchev. He was so powerful that he could even insult the Politburo. The 'faithful shield-bearer', in Khrushchev's words, played his role in Stalin's most mundane deeds and the most terrible, boasting later about their use of poison. He was a loving husband to Bronka, and an indulgent father to the two children, Galya by her first husband and his own Natalya. But when the *vertushka* rang on Sundays, no one else was allowed to answer it. He was proud of his position: when his daughter had an operation, he lectured her that she had to behave in a way that befitted their station. Poskrebyshev worked closely with Beria: they often visited each other's families but if there was business to conduct, they walked in the garden. But ultimately both Vlasik and Poskrebyshev were obstacles to Beria's power. The same could no longer be said of the Alliluyev family.

27

Death of the Stalin Family: a Strange
Proposal and the Housekeeper

Letting Beria into the family was like locking a fox in a chicken coop but Stalin shares responsibility for their fates. 'All our family,' wrote Svetlana, 'was completely baffled as to why Stalin made Beria – a provincial secret policeman – so close to himself and the Government in Moscow.' This was precisely why Stalin had promoted him: no one was sacred to Beria.

The magnates and retainers all grumbled constantly about the self-importance of the 'aunties'. Impertinent with the greatness of his new power and burning with the inferiority complex of a scorned provincial, Beria was determined to prove himself by destroying these glamorous but snobbish members of the new nobility. In the early thirties, Beria had tried to flirt with Zhenya while her husband and Stalin were sitting near by. Zhenya strode up to Stalin:

'If this bastard doesn't leave me alone, I'll smash his pince-nez.' Everyone laughed. Beria was embarrassed. But when Beria began to appear more regularly at Kuntsevo, he still flirted with Zhenya who appealed to Stalin: 'Joseph! He's trying to squeeze my knee!' Stalin probably regarded Beria as something of a card. The family were typical of the élite he was trying to destroy. When Beria turned up in a turtleneck pullover for dinner, Zhenya, who was always dressed to the nines without a hint of Bolshevik modesty, said loudly, 'How dare you come to dinner like this?' Grandfather Alliluyev regularly described Beria as an 'Enemy'.

In November 1938, Stalin's family life really ended. Beria expanded the Terror to include anyone connected to Yezhov, who had not only appointed Stalin's brother-in-law, Stanislas Redens, to run the NKVD in Kazakhstan but had even requested him as his deputy: this was the kiss of death. Relations had certainly been warm when Stalin received the Redens family before they set off for Alma-Ata. We know little about Redens' role in the Terror but Moscow and Kazakhstan had been slaughtered on his watch. The arrival of Beria, his nemesis in Tiflis in 1931, was bad news but even without it, Stanislas would probably have been doomed.

Meanwhile Pavel Alliluyev's job, as a tank forces commissar, placed him in harm's way: close to the executed generals, he was also involved in spying on German tank production. When he saw the Soviet spy Orlov before his defection, Alliluyev warned him: 'Don't ever inquire about the Tukhachevsky affair. Knowing about it is like inhaling poison gas.' Then Pavel had been out in the Far East where the generals appealed to him and he had flown back, according to his daughter Kira, with evidence that proved their innocence. He clearly did not understand that evidence only existed to persuade others, not to prove guilt. Pavel is said to have put together a letter to Stalin, co-signed by three generals, suggesting the Terror be brought to a close. The generals' timing seemed fortuitous; the Terror was ebbing. Stalin did not openly punish them but he had clearly tired of Pavel's interference.*

After holidaying in Sochi, Pavel returned on 1 November. The next morning, Pavel ate breakfast and went to the office where he found that most of his department had been arrested, according to Svetlana: 'He attempted to save certain people, trying to get hold of my father, but it was no use.' At two in the afternoon, Zhenya was called: 'What did you give your husband to eat? He's feeling sick.' Zhenya wanted to rush over but they stopped her. He was sent to the Kremlevka clinic. In the words of the official medical report, 'When he was admitted, he was unconscious, cyanotic and apparently dying. The patient did not recover consciousness.' This was strange since the doctor who telephoned Zhenya to tell her this news said: 'Why did it take you so long? He had something to tell you. He kept asking why Zhenya didn't come. He's already dead.' So died the brother who had given Nadya her pistol. The inconsistencies in an already suspicious death, at a time when medical murder was almost routine, makes foul play possible. Stalin kept the death certificate. Zhenya was later accused of murdering Pavel. Stalin sometimes accused others of his own crimes. We will never know the truth.

'The next time I saw him,' Kira says, 'was lying in state at the Hall of Columns. He was only 44, and he was lying there all

---

* The three generals who signed the letter were said to be Stalin's Tsaritsyn crony, Grigory Kulik, commanders Meretskov and Pavlov plus commissar Savchenko. Savchenko was executed in October 1941; the fate of the others are told later in this book. All suffered grievously at Stalin's hands. Only Meretskov outlived him.

sunburnt, very handsome with his long eyelashes.' Looking into the casket, Sergei Alliluyev mused that there was no more tragic thing than to bury your own children.

Redens himself headed back to Moscow where he arrived on 18 November. At Kuntsevo, Vasily heard Beria demand that Stalin let him arrest Redens. 'But I trust Redens,' replied Stalin 'very decisively.' To Vasily's surprise, Malenkov supported Beria. This was the beginning of the alliance between these two who would not have pressed the arrest without knowing Stalin's instincts: these scenes of pretend argument resemble the mooting exercises practised by trainee lawyers. Yet Stalin was highly suggestible. Redens had the misfortune, like Pavel Alliluyev, to be in two or three overlapping circles of suspicion. Beria is always blamed for turning Stalin against his other brother-in-law but there was more to it than that. Stalin had removed Redens from the Ukraine in 1932. He was close to Yezhov. And he was a Pole. Stalin listened to Beria and Malenkov and then said: 'In that case, sort it out at the Central Committee.' As Svetlana put it, 'My father would not protect him.' On the 22nd, Redens was arrested on his way to work and was never seen again.

Anna Redens started phoning Stalin. She was no longer welcome at Zubalovo. She could not get through to Stalin. 'Then I'll call Voroshilov, Kaganovich and Molotov,' she sobbed. When the children arrived, they found their mother, hysterical at the disappearance of her beloved Stan, lying in bed reading Alexandre Dumas. She appealed to everyone until finally Stalin took her call. Stalin summoned her to the Little Corner. Redens 'would be brought and we shall make an inquiry about all this' but he made one condition: 'And bring Grandfather Sergei Yakovlevich with you.' Sergei, who had now lost two children, no longer waited for Stalin on the sofa every night but he agreed to come. At the last moment, he backed out. Beria either threatened him, or perhaps Sergei thought Redens was guilty of something in his unsavoury work at the Lubianka: Redens' son Leonid stressed that there were tensions between Old Bolsheviks like Sergei and the brash élite like Redens. Grandmother Olga went instead, a brave but foolish move since Stalin loathed interfering women:

'Why have you come? No one called you!' he snarled at her. Anna shouted at Stalin, who had her removed. Redens and the Svanidzes were in jail; Pavel Alliluyev dead. Stalin had allowed the Terror to ravage his own circle. When the Bulgarian Communist, Georgi Dmitrov, appealed for some arrested comrades, Stalin shrugged: 'What can I do for them, Georgi? All my own relatives are in prison too.' This is a revealing excuse. Certainly, with Pavel, Nadya's pistol must have always been on his mind but so were his military connections and intercession for 'Enemies'. Perhaps Stalin was settling private scores against his over-familiar, interfering family who reminded him of Nadya's rejection. But he did not regard the Terror as a private spree: he was cleansing his encircled country of spies to safeguard his vast achievements before war broke out. His family were among the casualties. He regarded them as *his own sacrifice* as the supreme pontiff of Bolshevism. But he was also asserting his own separation from private ties and, perhaps refreshingly, shaking off old obligations of family and friendship:* his vendettas were those of the Party because, as he told Vasily, 'I'm not Stalin … Stalin IS Soviet power!' But they also provided a living excuse for demanding that his comrades sacrifice *their* own families. None the less, he could have saved anyone he wanted and he did not. The familial world of Stalin and his children was still shrinking.

Svetlana lost another part of her support system: Carolina Til, the dependable housekeeper, that cosy link to her mother, was sacked in the purge of Germans. Beria found her replacement in a niece of his wife Nina from Georgia – though as ever, his true motives are unclear. Svetlana's new governess was Alexandra Nakashidze, tall, slim, long-legged, with perfect pale skin and long thick blue-black hair. A naïve and poorly educated girl from a Georgian village, this NKVD lieutenant entered this increasingly monocoloured world like a purple-feathered peacock. The Alliluyevs and Mikoyan boys are still struck by her today.

Svetlana resented her so-called governess. Nakashidze's arrival shows Beria's special role in the family: could she be his spy in Stalin's household that was otherwise controlled by Vlasik? We know that the court encouraged Stalin to remarry: was she there for Stalin?† However, there was a more obvious candidate almost within the family.

* His old lover of 1913, 'my darling' Tatiana Slavotinskaya, is an example: Stalin had protected her well into the Thirties, promoting her in the Central Committee apparatus but now the protection stopped abruptly. Her family was repressed and she was expelled from the House on the Embankment. Slavotinskaya was the grandmother of Yury Trifonov, author of the novel, *House on the Embankment*.

† She remained a presence in the household until after the end of the war when she married an NKVD general and returned to Georgia where she had children. Her daughter still lives in Georgia.

Zhenya Alliluyeva was a widow but she was convinced her husband had been murdered by Beria. Was she guilty about her relationship with Stalin? There is no evidence of this. Her husband had surely known (or chosen not to know) what was going on, but the relationship with Stalin, such as it was, had already cooled by 1938. But now Stalin missed her and made a strange, indirect proposal to her. Beria came to see Zhenya and said: 'You're such a nice person, and you're so fine looking, do you want to move in and be housekeeper at Stalin's house?' Usually this is interpreted as a mysterious threat from Beria but it is surely unlikely that he would have made such a proposal without Stalin's permission, especially since she could have phoned him to discuss it. In Stalin's mind, a 'housekeeper' was his ideal *baba*, the *khozyaika*. This was surely a semi-marriage proposal, an awkward attempt to salvage the warmth of the old days from the destruction that he himself had unleashed. It was unforgivably clumsy to send Beria, whom Zhenya loathed, on this sensitive mission but that is typical of Stalin. If one has any doubt about this analysis, Stalin's reaction to Zhenya's next move may confirm it.

Zhenya was alarmed, fearing that Beria would frame her for trying to poison Stalin. She swiftly married an old friend, named N. V. Molochnikov, a Jewish engineer whom she had met in Germany, perhaps the lover who had almost broken up her marriage. Stalin was appalled, claiming that it was indecent so soon after Pavel's death. Beria's proposal puts Stalin's hurt in a slightly different light. Beria fanned the flames by suggesting that perhaps Zhenya had poisoned her husband, an idea with resonance in this poisoners' coven. Some say the body was dug up twice for tests. In spite of the poisoning allegations, Stalin retained his fascination with Zhenya, going out of his way just before the war to quiz her daughter Kira: 'How's your mother?' Zhenya and Anna Redens were banned from the Kremlin and Stalin looked elsewhere for his 'housekeeper'.

* * *

A young maid named Valentina Vasilevna Istomina had worked at Zubalovo since her late teens in the early thirties. In 1938, she came to work at Kuntsevo. Stalin was attracted to a specific ideal: the busty, blue-eyed, big-haired and retroussé-nosed Russian peasant woman, submissive and practical, a *baba* who could make a home without in any way becoming involved in his other life.

Zhenya had the looks but there was nothing submissive about her. He also found the same looks coupled with haughtiness in the top artistes of the time. Stalin was an avid attender of the theatre, opera and ballet, regularly visiting the Politburo (formerly imperial) *loge* in the Bolshoi or the Moscow Arts Theatre. His favourite singers were the soprano Natalya Schpiller, who was a blue-eyed Valkyrie, and the mezzo Vera Davydova. He liked to instruct them 'in a fatherly way' but he also played one off against the other. He acted being in love with Davydova who later boasted that he proposed marriage: if so, it was only a joke. He teased her by suggesting that she improve her singing by copying Schpiller. When Davydova appeared in a glittery belt, he told her, 'Look, Schpiller's a beguiling woman too but she dresses modestly for official receptions.'

These *divas* were much too glamorous for Stalin but there was no shortage of available admirers, as Vlasik told his daughter. There are many stories of women invited to Kuntsevo: Mirtskhulava, a young Georgian official, remembers Stalin at a Kremlin dinner in 1938 sending him to ask a girl in his Komsomol delegation if she was the daughter of some Old Bolshevik, then inviting her to the dacha. Stalin insisted Mirtskhulava asked her secretly, without either the knowledge of the magnates at his table or of the Georgians. The same happened with a beautiful Georgian pilot whom he met at the Tushino air show in 1938 and who regularly visited Stalin.

This was probably the pattern of his trivial dalliances but what happened at Kuntsevo is beyond our knowledge. Everyone who knew Stalin insists that he was no womanizer and he was famously inhibited about his body. We know nothing about his sexual tastes but Nadya's letters suggest they had a passionate relationship. A fascinating glimpse into his relations with women – perhaps connected to his views on sex – is provided by his attitude to dancing. He liked making Russian dance steps and kicks on his own but dancing *à deux* made him nervous. He told the tenor Kozlovsky at a party that he would not dance because he had damaged his arm in exile and so 'could not hold a woman by the waist'.

Stalin warned his son Vasily against 'women with ideas', whom he found uncomfortable: 'we've known that kind, herrings with ideas, skin and bones.' He was most at home with the women of the service staff. The maids, cooks and guards at his houses were all employed by Vlasik's department and all signed confidentiality contracts though these were hardly necessary in this kingdom of fear. Even when the USSR collapsed, very few of them ever spoke.* The Kremlin hairdresser, who so upset Nadya, was one of these and so was his maid Valentina Istomina, known as Valechka, who gradually became the mainstay of Stalin's home life.

'She laughed all the time and we really liked her,' said Svetlana, 'she was very young, with pink cheeks and she was liked by everyone. She was a pleasant figure, typically Russian.' She was Stalin's 'ideal' woman, buxom and neat, 'round-faced and pug-nosed', primitive, simple and unlettered; she 'served at table deftly, never joined in the conversation', yet she was always there when she was needed. 'She had light brown mousy hair – I remember her well from about 1936, nothing special, not fat not thin but very friendly and smiling,' says Artyom Sergeev. Out of Stalin's presence, she was fun in an unthreatening way, even shrewd: 'She was a clever one, talkative, a chatterbox,' recalled one of Stalin's bodyguards.

Valechka was promoted to housekeeper, taking care of Stalin's 'clothes, the food, the house and so on and she travelled with him wherever he went. She was a comfortable soul to be quiet with, yet he trusted her and she was devoted to him.' Stalin was farcically proud of the way she prepared his underwear: after the war, one Georgian official was amazed when he showed off the piles of gleaming white smalls in his wardrobe, surely a unique moment in the history of dictators.

At the Kremlin apartment, Valechka often served Svetlana and her friend Martha who recalls her 'in her white apron, like a kind woman from the villages, with her fair hair and shapeless figure, not fat though. Always smiling. Svetlana loved her too.' Artyom was one of the few who heard how Stalin spoke to her: 'he'd say about her birthday or something, "Of course I must give you a present."

'"I don't need anything, Comrade Stalin," she replied.

'"Well, if I forget, remind me."' At the end of the thirties, Valechka became Stalin's trusted companion and effectively his

---

* President Vladimir Putin's grandfather was a chef at one of Stalin's houses and revealed nothing to his grandson: 'My grandfather kept pretty quiet about his past life.' As a boy, he recalled bringing food to Rasputin. He then cooked for Lenin. He was clearly Russia's most world-historical chef since he served Lenin, Stalin and the Mad Monk.

secret wife, in a culture when most Bolshevik couples were not formally married. 'Valya looked after Father's creature comforts,' Svetlana said. The court understood that she was his companion and no more was said about it. 'Whether or not Istomina was Stalin's wife is nobody's business,' said the ageing Molotov. 'Engels lived with his housekeeper.' Budyonny and Kalinin 'married' their housekeepers.

'My father said she was very close to him,' asserts Nadezhda Vlasika. Kaganovich's daughter-in-law heard from 'Iron Lazar': 'I only know that Stalin had one common-law wife. Valechka, his waitress. She loved him.'*

Valechka appeared like a jolly, quiet and buxom hospital sister, always wearing a white apron at Stalin's dinners. No one noticed when she attended Yalta and Potsdam: this was as Stalin wished it. Henceforth Stalin's private life was frozen in about 1939: the dramas of Nadya and Zhenya that had caused him pain and anger were over. 'These matters,' recalled the Polish Communist Jakob Berman, who was often at Kuntsevo during the forties, 'were arranged with extreme discretion and never filtered out beyond his closest circle. Stalin was always very careful there shouldn't be any gossip about him ... Stalin understood the danger of gossip.' If other men could be betrayed by their wives, there at least he was safe. He sometimes asked Valechka's political opinions as an ordinary person. None the less, for this political man, she was no companion. He remained lonely.

* * *

Between 24 February and 16 March 1939, Beria presided over the executions of 413 important prisoners, including Marshal Yegorov and ex-Politburo members, Kosior, Postyshev and Chubar: he was already living in the dacha of the last of these. Now he suggested to Stalin that they call a halt, or there would be no one left to arrest. Poskrebyshev marked up the old Central Committee with VN – Enemy of the People – and the date of execution. The next day, Stalin reflected to Malenkov: 'I think

---

* Stalin's bodyguards, whose inaccurate but revealing memoirs were collected long after his death, were not sure about the Valechka relationship. When she became older, she married and, during Stalin's later years, she complained of her husband's jealous reproaches. After Stalin's death, Valechka never spoke of their relationship but when she was asked if the opera singer Davydova ever visited Kuntsevo, her answer perhaps displayed a proprietorial sting: 'I never saw her at the dacha ... She'd have been thrown out!' Valechka was not a Party member.

we're well and truly rid of the opposition millstone. We need new forces, new people ...' The message was sent down the *vertikal* of power: when Mekhlis demanded more arrests in the army for 'lack of revolutionary loyalty', Stalin replied:

'I propose to limit ourselves to an official reprimand ... (I don't see any ill-will in their actions – these aren't mistakes but misunderstandings).'* Blaming all excesses on Yezhov, Stalin protected his other grotesques. The 'denunciatrix' of Kiev, Nikolaenko, was discredited. But she once again appealed to Stalin and Khrushchev: 'I ask you to check everything, where I was mistaken, where I was lied to and where I was provoked, I'm ready to be punished,' she wrote to Khrushchev. But then, still playing high politics, she warned Stalin: 'I'm sure there are too many remnants of Enemies in Kiev ... Dear Joseph Vissarionovich, I've no words to tell you how to understand me but you understand us, your people, without words. I write to you with bitter tears.' Stalin protected her: 'Comrade Khrushchev, I ask you to take measures to let Nikolaenko find calm and fruitful work, J.St.'

The victims of his creatures could now appeal to Stalin. Khrulev, who was to be the outstanding Red Army quartermaster during the Second World War, complained to Stalin about the peripatetic, pompous Mekhlis. 'The lion is the king of the jungle,' Stalin laughed.

'Yes but Mekhlis's a dangerous animal,' said Khrulev, 'who told me he'd do all he could ... [to destroy me].' Stalin smiled genially:

'Well if me and you ... fight Mekhlis together, do you think we'll manage?' retorted the 'lion-king'.

Stalin had not forgotten his greatest enemy: Beria and one of the talented dirty tricks specialists in quiet and quick death, Pavel Sudoplatov, were received in the Little Corner where, pacing silently in soft Georgian boots, Stalin laconically ordered: 'Trotsky should be eliminated within a year.'

* * *

* Vyshinsky reported that the arrest of hundreds of teenagers in Novosibirsk had been faked by the NKVD: 'the children were innocent and have been released but three senior officials including the head of the NKVD and the town Procurator were guilty of "betraying revolutionary loyalty" and expelled from the Party'. What should be done with them? On 2 January 1939, Stalin scribbled: 'It's necessary to have a public trial of the guilty.'

On 10 March 1939, the 1,900 delegates of the Eighteenth Congress gathered* to declare the end of a slaughter that had been a success, if slightly marred by Yezhov's manic excesses. The survivors, from Molotov to Zhdanov, remained at the top but were challenged by the younger generation: Khrushchev joined the Politburo while Beria was elected candidate and 'Melanie' Malenkov became a CC Secretary. This leadership ruled the country for the next decade without a single casualty: contrary to his myth, Stalin, a master of divide and rule, could be surprisingly loyal to his protégés. But not to the Blackberry.

Yezhov was on ice yet he still attended the Politburo, sat next to Stalin at the Bolshoi and turned up for work at Water Transport, where he sat through meetings throwing paper darts. He caroused by day but appeared at Congress evening sessions, trying to get permission to speak. 'I strongly ask you to talk with me for only one minute,' he wrote to Stalin. 'Give me the opportunity.' Still a CC member, he attended the meeting of Party elders where the names for the new body were selected. No one objected to his name until Stalin called Yezhov forward:

'Well what do you think of yourself? Are you capable of being a member of the Central Committee?' Yezhov protested his devotion to the Party and Stalin – he could not imagine what he had done wrong. Since all the other murderers were being promoted, the dwarf's bafflement is understandable.

'Is that so?' Stalin started mentioning Enemies close to Yezhov.

'Joseph Vissarionovich!' Yezhov cried out. 'You know it was I – I myself – who disclosed their conspiracy! I came to you and reported it ...'

'Yes yes yes. When you felt you were about to be caught, then you came in a hurry. But what about before that? Were you organizing a conspiracy? Did you want to kill Stalin? Top officials of the NKVD are plotting but you are supposedly not involved. You think I don't see anything? Do you remember who you sent on a certain date for duty with Stalin? Who? With revolvers? Why revolvers near Stalin? Why? To kill Stalin? Well? Go on, get out of here! I don't know, comrades, is it possible to keep him as a member of the Central Committee? I doubt it. Of course think about it ... As you wish ... But I doubt it.'

---

* In the ugly wooden chamber that had been created by vandalizing the sumptuous Alexandrovsky Hall in the Great Kremlin Palace.

Yezhov was determined to spread the guilt and avenge his betrayal by destroying Malenkov, whom he now denounced. On 10 April, Stalin ordered Yezhov to attend a meeting to hear these accusations. Yezhov reported to Malenkov who ritualistically removed Yezhov's photograph from the array of leadership icons on his office wall like an angel removed from the heavens. Beria and his Georgian prince-executioner, Tsereteli, opened the door and arrested Blackberry, conveying 'Patient Number One' to the infirmary inside Sukhanov prison.

The search of Yezhov's apartment revealed bottles of vodka, empty, half-empty and full, lying around, 115 counter-revolutionary books, guns and those macabre relics: the flattened bullets, wrapped in paper, labelled Zinoviev and Kamenev. More importantly, the search revealed that Yezhov had collected materials about Stalin's pre-1917 police record: was this evidence that he was an Okhrana spy? There was also evidence against Malenkov.* The papers disappeared into Beria's safe.

Stalin was now so omnipotent that when he mispronounced a word from the podium, every subsequent speaker repeated the mistake. 'If I'd said it right,' Molotov reminisced, 'Stalin would have felt I was correcting him.' He was very 'touchy and proud'.† Europe was on the verge of war and Stalin turned his attention to the tightrope walk between Nazi Germany and the Western democracies. Meanwhile, Zhdanov heralded the end of Yezhov's slaughter, joking (in execrable taste) about 'big Enemies', 'little Enemies' and 'wee Enemies' while Stalin and Beria planned some of their most wanton acts of depravity.

* This blackmail against Malenkov, accusing him of noble connections, may have formed part of the basis of his alliance with Beria though Stalin knew of the evidence. 'Think yourself lucky these documents are in my hands,' Beria told him. When the latter was arrested in June 1953, after Stalin's death, these papers were given to Malenkov who destroyed them.
† On 5 February 1939, that shrewd observer of power, Svetlana Stalin, aged 13, listed the survivors of the Terror in a note: '1. To Stalin. 2. Voroshilov. 3. Zhdanov. 4. Molotov. 5. Kaganovich. 6. Khrushchev. Daily Order No. 8. I'm travelling to Zubalovo ... leaving you on your own. Hold onto your bellies with an iron hand! Setanka, mistress of the house.' The grandees each replied revealingly: 'I obey. Stalin, the poor peasant. L. Kaganovich. The obedient Voroshilov. The diligent escapee Ukrainian N. Khrushchev. V. Molotov.'

Index

'This grim masterpiece, shot through with lashes of black humour ... The personal details are riveting'

Antonia Fraser, *Mail on Sunday*

'This fascinating book ... [Montefiore] concentrates, as any good historian should, on pushing forward the boundaries of our knowledge of the subject ... [He] provides rich detail of daily life and family relationships in a world of human values turned inside out ... scrupulously fair in the way he describes Stalin's qualities – including his ability to charm, his uncanny grasp of geopolitical issues, his brilliant handling of foreign statesmen and his genuine passion for literature' Antony Beevor, *Sunday Times*

'His masterful and terrifying account of Stalin ... seldom has the picture been put in finer focus than by Sebag Montefiore. It is partly through his diligent interviews with the children of survivors and his admirable combination of history and gossip that one sees the awful banality, the brutal crudity of the men who carelessly sent so many millions to their senseless deaths' Alistair Horne, *The Times*

'This magnificent portrait ... Simon Sebag Montefiore has mined the rich veins of recent Russian writing on the Stalin age and of newly opened archives to give us an intimate history ... The stifling, contiguous life of the Soviet elite in and around the Kremlin is wonderfully conveyed, in some of the most striking and literary passages in the book ... Striking the balance between political narrative and personal biography is a difficult one ... Montefiore keeps both in perspective ... a wonderfully rich and vibrant portrait of the Stalinist elite who lived in the shadow of a remarkable and dangerous colossus'

Richard Overy, *Literary Review*

'Everyone in Westminster has been reading [*Stalin*] during these turbulent leadership times. I've met Labour ministers and Tory backbenchers reeling from stories ... reading this book for tips on how to become an efficient fighting machine ... Everyone is mugging up on Stalin' Alice Thomson, *Daily Telegraph*

'Read it or face social Siberia ... a cross-over success. Academically and intellectually rigorous, it's also a riveting read ... it takes a

great writer to make it seem fresh. And Sebag Montefiore certainly does that … Sebag Montefiore's greatest achievement has been to "humanise" Stalin. Uncle Joe was a mass murderer and a paranoid sociopath. But he was also charming, friendly and flirtatious'
100 Best Things in the World Right Now, GQ magazine

'Grimly brilliant' Andrew Marr, *Daily Telegraph*

'Excellent … This book is like a vast Russian novel full of characters, colour, terror, passion and treachery … love affairs, marriages, divorces, imprisonments and killings'
Susannah Tarbush, *Al-Hayat*

'Montefiore's masterful study of Stalin and his entourage provides the best personal portrait to date of the man and his group' Daniel Beer, *Jewish Chronicle*

'Montefiore has managed to get inside the mind of the 20th century's worst mass murderer. What he has found there will affect your view of human nature … a thoughtful book of first-class scholarship as well as a transfixing narrative … all … vividly recreated by Montefiore's caustically witty prose'
Andrew Roberts, *Daily Telegraph*

'Its extraordinary revelation of the evil – the complete amorality – at the heart of the dictator's court will change the way historians approach the great historical questions about the Stalinist regime'
Orlando Figes, *Sunday Telegraph*

'An astonishingly good and important book … he provides a remarkably fresh and exciting account of one of history's darkest periods' Simon Heffer, *Country Life*

'This is no ordinary scholarly life, it's ultra reader-friendly, lively, gossipy, and packed with revelations about the intimacies and intrigues of Stalin the man and his courtiers. Brilliant'
Evening Standard, Metro Life magazine

'For anyone with the slightest interest in 20th-century history, this is essential, utterly compelling, page-turning reading. The book is a masterpiece of horror' Robert Harvey, *The Tablet*